BLACK WOMEN AND INTERNATIONAL LAW

Deliberate Interactions, Movements, and Actions

From Compton to Cairo and Bahia to Brixton, Black women have been disproportionally affected by poverty, illiteracy, unemployment, discrimination, and violence. Despite being one of the largest and most geographically dispersed groups in the world, they are rarely referenced or considered as a subject of analysis in international law literature. Thus, it is vital that scholars refashion global discourse by reconceptualizing international law and relations from their unique experiences and perspectives.

This unique and eclectic collection covers a broad range of topics and issues that examine the complex interactions – as subjects and objects – between Black women and international law. The book critically explores the manifold relationships between them with a view toward highlighting the historic and contemporary ways in which they have influenced and been influenced by transnational law, doctrine, norms, jurisprudence, public policy, public discourse, and global governance. It purports to unearth old law and fashion new paradigms born out of the experiences of Black women.

Jeremy I. Levitt is Dean and Vice Chancellor's Chair at University of New Brunswick Faculty of Law and Distinguished Professor of International Law at Florida A&M University College of Law. Professor Levitt is a leading scholar on the international law of the use of force, human rights law, peace studies, and the international law and politics of Africa. In 2012–13, he was the Fulbright Research Chair in Human Rights and Social Justice at the University of Ottawa. He has authored two books, edited four, and written more than thirty academic articles. He recently completed a groundbreaking study titled *Illegal Peace in Africa: An Inquiry into the Legality of Power Sharing with Warlords, Rebels, and Junta* (2012).

Black Women and International Law

DELIBERATE INTERACTIONS, MOVEMENTS, AND ACTIONS

Edited by

JEREMY I. LEVITT

University of New Brunswick Law School

CAMBRIDGE
UNIVERSITY PRESS

CAMBRIDGE
UNIVERSITY PRESS

32 Avenue of the Americas, New York, NY 10013-2473, USA

Cambridge University Press is part of the University of Cambridge.

It furthers the University's mission by disseminating knowledge in the pursuit of education, learning, and research at the highest international levels of excellence.

www.cambridge.org
Information on this title: www.cambridge.org/9781107021303

First published 2015

A catalog record for this publication is available from the British Library.

Library of Congress Cataloging in Publication Data
Black women and international law : deliberate interactions, movements, and actions /
Jeremy I. Levitt, University of New Brunswick Law School.
pages cm
1. Law. 2. Women, Black – Legal status, laws, etc.
I. Levitt, Jeremy I., 1970– editor. II. McDonald, Gabrielle Kirk, honouree.
K561.B57 2015
342.08′78–dc23 2014043734

ISBN 978-1-107-02130-3 Hardback

Judge Gabrielle Kirk McDonald

Contents

Contributors

Adjoa A. Aiyetoro
Associate Professor
University of Arkansas at Little Rock
William H. Bowen School of Law

Carol Boyce-Davies
Professor of English and African Studies
Cornell University
Ithaca, New York

Karen E. Bravo
Associate Professor of Law
Indiana University School of Law
Bloomington, Indiana

Eleanor Marie Lawrence Brown
Associate Professor of Law
George Washington University School of Law
Washington, DC

Fatou Kiné Camara
Associate Professor of Law
Faculty of Judicial and Political Science
Cheikh Anta Diop University
Dakar, Senegal

Erika George
Professor of Law
University of Utah S. J. Quinney College of Law
Salt Lake City, Utah

Linda Sheryl Greene
Evjue-Bascom Professor of Law
University of Wisconsin–Madison School of Law
Madison, Wisconsin

Gabrielle Kirk McDonald
Judge
Iran–United States Claims Tribunal
The Hague, The Netherlands

Judith A. M. Scully
Professor of Law
Stetson University School of Law
Gulfport, Florida

Anna Spain
Associate Professor of Law
University of Colorado Law School
Boulder, Colorado

Adrien Katherine Wing
Bessie Dutton Murray Professor of Law
University of Iowa College of Law
Iowa City, Iowa

Foreword

Against all odds, Black women have carved themselves a remarkable niche in history. Our contributions to humanity are significant and undeniable. Since antiquity, we have built nations, fashioned law, led armies, ruled empires, and forged peace agreements and global alliances. Queen Hatshepsut of Egypt was one of the ancient world's most prominent Black woman leaders; after decades of war with the Hyksos and other nations, "Her Majesty the King," as she was known, brought prosperity to the vast Egyptian Empire. From the ancient Candace women leaders of Meroë, in what is now Sudan, to the seventeenth-century Queen Nzinga of Angola, powerful Black women have contributed much to African history.

But centuries of the slave trade, enslavement, colonialism, apartheid, racial oppression, and wars took a heavy toll on people of African descent, in Africa and elsewhere. The toll on women was, perhaps, particularly heavy.

After generations of oppression and inequality, we have begun to see tremendous progress in women's rights around the world. Black women, too, are advancing. They participate or hold high office in national governments and legislatures. Black women's groups and organizations in Africa and across the Diaspora are more organized and effective, both locally and transnationally, than they have ever been. Black women are playing key roles in global governance – from national governments to international organizations such as the UN, international courts and tribunals, and nongovernmental organizations – as well as in national and multinational corporations.

Yet this tide of progress is still not strong enough to ensure that women – and Black women in particular – can benefit from conditions of equality. Women remain sorely underrepresented in decision making at the local, national, regional, and international levels. They experience gender-based violence or sexual assault disproportionately. Women, globally, do not receive equal pay for equal work. They do not have equal access to resources. And particularly – but not exclusively – in developing countries, they struggle against constraints on their sexual and reproductive health and rights. So far, the human rights of women have not been given their rightful, central place in the agenda for human development. This must change.

Black women have been at the forefront of protecting the principles of equity, equality, and nondiscrimination. Black women lawyers – pioneers like my dear friend Judge Gabrielle Kirk McDonald – have committed their lives to serving the public good through their affirmative efforts and model performance. Professor Levitt's commendable study of the interactions and interplay between Black women and international law provides vital insights into the various ways in which they are portrayed as objects rather than subjects of international law. It documents an often tense and unacknowledged relationship, and it highlights the various ways in which Black women have contributed to the normative development of international law.

The life, career, and persona of Judge Gabrielle Kirk McDonald embody Zora Neal Hurston's wry saying, "I do not weep at the world – I am too busy sharpening my oyster knife." As a fellow international judge, I admire her record as one of the most prominent international jurists of the late twentieth and early twenty-first centuries. She was one of the eleven judges appointed to the International Criminal Tribunal for the former Yugoslavia (ICTY) in 1993, and became its president from 1997 to 1999 – a crucial period as the newly created international criminal court, mandated to effectuate international criminal justice, became operational. Judge McDonald was the first (and only) female president of the court. As presiding judge in Trial Chamber II, she issued the court's verdict against Duško Tadić – the first person to be prosecuted in an international war crimes court since the days of the Nuremberg Trials and the International Military Tribunal for the Far East. Her efforts, in no small part, set the ICTY on course to prosecute gender-related crimes, such as rape as a war crime and a crime against humanity, forever changing the course of international criminal justice.

In 2001, Judge McDonald was appointed to the Iran–United States Claims Tribunal in The Hague, which had been established by agreement between the United States and Iran to adjudge state-to-state claims and claims for compensation by U.S. citizens regarding assets nationalized by the Iranian government. One of three American arbitrators, Judge McDonald was the only woman and the only person of African descent on the nine-person panel. She served on the Claims Tribunal for thirteen years and distinguished herself as a leading arbitrator, unafraid to be objective and impartial.

This volume of essays is a timely and apt tribute to Judge McDonald for her tireless work for the international public good and her service as a role model, particularly for women of African descent. Over the course of twenty years, she played an important role in international criminal law and international arbitration, in both instances advancing the greater cause of human rights and justice. Her life is a vivid example of intellectual ingenuity, fortitude, and excellence in pursuit of freedom and justice.

Navi Pillay
UN High Commissioner for Human Rights

Preface

It is a great privilege to edit and contribute to this volume in honor of my mentor and friend, Judge Gabrielle Kirk McDonald, a preeminent African-American international jurist, scholar, and advocate who served as one of three American arbitrators on the Iran–United States Claims Tribunal and as former president of the International Criminal Tribunal for the former Yugoslavia. This short book of assorted essays on Black women and international law is a tribute to her remarkable career and legacy as a pioneering African-American internationalist. Judge McDonald's renowned career as an advocate for the disadvantaged and oppressed has spanned fifty years, giving meaning to the imitable words of Shirley Chisolm, "Service is the rent that you pay for room on this earth." Judge McDonald's life is brilliant testimony that one courageous and righteous soul, steadfast in her conviction for justice, can chart the course of history.

This unique and eclectic collection of contributions addresses a narrow theme that is reflected in the title, *Black Women and International Law*. The chapters cover a broad range of topics and issues that examine the complex interactions – as subjects and objects – between Black women and international law. In addition to honoring Judge McDonald, the book critically explores the manifold relationship between Black women and international law with a view to highlighting the historic and contemporary ways in which they have influenced international law, doctrine, norms, jurisprudence, public policy, public discourse, and global governance. The term "Black women" is broadly construed in the Pan-African context to include all women of African descent, irrespective of their place of birth or national origin.

I began thinking about a *Black Women and International Law* project in 2002. My work and research in Africa signaled a shift in the perception of Black women from mere objects to formidable subjects of international law and development. And, while this transference is ongoing, I was compelled to provide preliminary context to it. Consequently, on March 4, 2010, I organized a thought-provoking roundtable discussion entitled "Towards an International Law of Black Women: New Theory, Old Praxis" at Florida A&M University College of Law in Orlando, Florida. Six months later, on September 10, 2010, I chaired another provocative panel discussion with the same panelists at the Third National People of Color Conference at Seton Hall School of Law. Amended versions of some of the papers that originated from these panels, as well as offerings made by other scholars, comprise the essays in this book. What emanated from these discussions is a preliminary understanding that Black women have participated in authoring protective regimes on human rights, women's rights, children's rights, armed conflict, racial discrimination and reparations, humanitarian law, international criminal law, environmental law, democracy, self-determination, microfinance, and intellectual property norms, among other areas. It is my sincere hope that this limited collection of essays will spur a new field of inquiry on Black women and international law and address the multifarious ways in which they interact and contribute to its development.

The book seeks to reinterpret and determine – through global lenses – the extent to which Black women have impacted and been impacted by transnational law, norms, doctrine, jurisprudence, policy, processes, and thinking. It purports to unearth old law and fashion new paradigms born out the experiences of Black women. To this end, the book falls within the intellectual rubric of what the eminent international law scholar Henry J. Richardson III refers to as the Black International Tradition (BIT), which sits squarely within Pan-African philosophy. The BIT provides a malleable chronological corridor to Black claims and demands to "outside" or international law that offers "liberation-promising normative authority" "outside" of law and policy shaped by the internal vocation of racial and sexual domination and oppression.[1]

Traditional international law discourse, as well as, for example, the newly formed regimes on women and racial discrimination and women and peace-building, are generally conceived in gender-bias and/or gender- or race-neutral terms. Black women are rarely specifically referenced or considered a subject of analysis in international law literature. Consequently, as one of the largest and geographically dispersed groups in the world, it is vital that Black scholars refashion global discourse by reconceptualizing international

[1] Henry J. Richardson III, "Two Treaties, and Global Influences of the American Civil Rights Movement, through the Black International Tradition," VA J. Soc. Pol'y & Law, Vol. 18, No. 1 (2010), p. 61.

law and relations from their unique experiences and perspectives. From Compton to Cairo and Bahia to Brixton, Black women have been disproportionally affected by poverty, illiteracy, unemployment, discrimination, and violence; notwithstanding, they have also been among the most intuitive, inventive, and ingenious actors in developing normative responses to local, national, regional, and international crises. Whereas international law and policy too often ignore the role that race and gender play in shaping it, this book will explore their intersectional ties with a view toward observing Black women as distinct subjects of international law.

The volume examines a myriad of topics, beginning with a biographical note on Judge Gabrielle Kirk McDonald and a short reflective essay written by her. Part I, entitled *Leadership, Human Rights, and Peace-building*, examines the contributions of African women to the development of human rights and peace-building norms. Part II, entitled *Black Women's Movements*, builds on the previous theme and contemplates the impact that transnational Black women's movements have had on the women's rights, reparations, and environmental protection regimes. Part III, titled *Feminine Sovereignty*, assesses the global complexities of female sovereignty, choice, and health in Africa and the Diaspora. Chapter 3 follows the biographical note and reflective essay and provides a short reflective essay on the complexities, challenges, and triumphs of Black women in governance, with a focus on how they have written themselves into political leadership. In Chapter 4, Adrien Wing surveys various international human rights documents and cases to determine the extent to which these sources specifically concern Black women and/or treat them as distinct subjects of international law, with a specific emphasis on the African Union Protocol on Women's Rights. Chapter 5, by Fatou Kiné Camara, analyzes the role African women have played as activists and technicians in conceptualizing and fashioning the gender parity provisions in the African Union Protocol to the African Charter of the Human and People's Rights of Women. In Chapter 6, the editor comparatively references peace deals birthed in the post–Cold War era in Africa and evaluates the extent to which African women's movements have influenced the gendered dimensions of what the author refers to as "peace construction." In this context, the chapter contemplates the role that law indicates for itself to play in informing, shaping, and regulating gender equality in transnational political power-sharing deals. Chapter 7, by Anna Spain, explores the instrumental role that Black women have played in advancing peace-building norms, rules, and practices under international law and how these normative contributions advance peace-building capacity.

Part II of the volume begins with Chapter 8, in which Linda Greene surveys the unique and substantive role Black women played in the Fourth World Conference on Women in Beijing, China in 1995 and considers the role that the African-American Women's Caucus had in formally and successfully integrating race, gender, and poverty considerations into the Beijing Declaration and Platform for Action. Chapter 9, by Adjoa Aiyetero, reflects on the contributions that women's leadership has made to the development of national reparative programs in the Diaspora and Africa and the impact they have had on the international discourse on reparations and the accompanying international rules. In Chapter 10, Erika George considers the impact that environmental activism and the "bottom-up" approaches of Black women have had on the development of international law and global discourse on climate change.

Part III begins with Chapter 11 by Judith Scully, who examines the activism of Black women (in Africa and the Diaspora) around issues of population control, sterilization abuse, contraceptives, and coercive and intrusive family planning programs and policies and their impact on the development of the international human rights conception of reproductive health. In Chapter 13, Karen Bravo explores the contrasts between the status of Black females as chattel ("things") and their choices and actions in pursuit of the "things" of importance to them, as well as the normative impact of those choices on international law and policy, including the connection between Black African (female) enslavement and the status of the Black indigenous people of Tasmania. Chapter 12, by Eleanor Brown, contemplates whether a normative regime on sex workers is developing and examines the extent to which Black women are functionaries in its development. The study challenges predominate thinking about the utility of a normative asset/development-based framework that seeks to empower women to manage "sex resources."

Acknowledgments

I dedicate this book to the enduring power, strength, and spirit of Black women to whom the world owes an eternal debt of gratitude. I graciously thank my beloved wife, Latrice, and enlightening daughters, Makayla and Zara, for teaching me how to unconditionally love and courageously advocate for the public good.

For nearly thirteen years, I have desired to edit a collection of essays on *Black Women and International Law*. From Bahia to Brixton and from Compton to Cairo, I have admired the brilliant works of Black women. From sheepherders and nation-builders to priestesses and advocates, Black women have shaped and influenced the world in extraordinary ways. On March 4, 2010, I organized and hosted a provocative roundtable discussion entitled "Towards an International Law of Black Women: New Theory, Old Praxis" at Florida A&M University College of Law in Orlando, Florida. Six months later on September 10, 2010, I chaired another provocative panel discussion with the same panelists at the Third National People of Color Conference at Seton Hall School of Law. I thank all of the presenters and contributors to these events. I especially thank my friend and mentor Dean LeRoy Pernell for embracing and supporting the Black women and international law project. I am also indebted to John Berger of Cambridge University Press for his unqualified support of my work on international law and the Black world. Without him, this project would not see the light of day.

The examination of the crossings between Black women and international law or global norm making is new, and it is my sincere hope that this volume will serve as a catalyst for more nuanced inquiry. I am the beneficiary of the intellectual gifts of several friends and scholars; however, no one has guided my intellectual path more than Henry J. Richardson III, the dean of Black international lawyers. I thank the following scholars for their enduring support and encouragement: Makau Mutua, Adrien Wing, Linda Greene, Mamphela Ramphele, Matthew Whitaker, Craig Jackson, Muna Ndulo, Colin Bruce, David Wippman, Ruth Wedgwood, Evelyn Ankumah, Edward Kwakwa, Abigail Noko, Leslye Obiora, Roderick Zak, Peniel Joseph, Ricky Jones, Yohuru Williams, Jelani Cobb, Lucie Lamarche, and all of the scholars who wrote chapters for this volume.

Finally, I am forever indebted to the hundreds of students that I have trained over the past decade and a half. Their various curiosities and queries heartened my desire for the project. I specifically thank Sabrina Collins, my former research assistant, for her affable assistance.

1

Judge Gabrielle Kirk McDonald: A Biographical Note

Jeremy I. Levitt

Distinguished Professor of Law
Florida A&M University College of Law

> I love the law and like solving problems. And certainly for a racial minority, I think the rule of law is the way we bring about justice, equality and inclusion in the U.S. and throughout the world.
>
> – Gabrielle Kirk McDonald

Judge Gabrielle (Gaby) Kirk McDonald is an African-American woman and legal pioneer who progressively shaped the development of civil rights law in the United States, international criminal law, and international arbitration law. Whether defending civil rights statutes in the United States as a litigator or federal judge in Texas or adjudicating war crimes or arbitration awards in The Hague, Judge McDonald has dedicated her life to the rule of law and justice for all. In September 2013, she retired from the Iran-United States Claims Tribunal where she had served as one of three American Arbitrators since 2001. In November 1993, Judge McDonald was one of the first eleven judges elected by the United Nations General Assembly to serve on the International Criminal Tribunal for the former Yugoslavia (ICTY), the first international war crimes tribunal since the end of World War II, in The Hague, Netherlands, becoming its president in 1997. Whether advocating for the enforcement of civil rights as an NAACP Legal Defense and Educational Fund lawyer or as a judge with the ICTY and the International Criminal Tribunal for Rwanda (ICTR), she has blazed a dynamic trail in the defense of justice that has elevated civil rights, human rights, and women's rights norms. Judge McDonald is the mother of a son, Michael, who is an attorney, and a daughter, Stacy, who is a screenwriter and former attorney.

Judge McDonald was born on April 12, 1942, in St. Paul, Minnesota. As a young child, she moved with her mother, Frances English Kirk, and brother, James Kirk III, to Manhattan, then Riverdale, New York, at the age of eight, and finally to Teaneck, New Jersey, following her parents' divorce. She graduated from Teaneck High School. Gaby McDonald was tall, athletic, and widely popular among students. She was one of only two African-American students at the school, where she played field hockey and was elected president of the girls' leadership club. Frances Kirk worked as a secretary for several newspapers, magazines, and publishers, such as Prentice Hall. James Kirk II was a World War II veteran, and, like his father, he worked as a porter or dining car waiter for the Northern Pacific Railway. Both parents and grandparents played critical roles in nurturing a strong sense of self-esteem, motivation, pride, equality, and justice in Gaby and James. Her mother, who was a formidable influence on her, was a very light-skinned biracial woman of Swedish (mother) and African-American (father) ancestry during a time when interracial marriage was considered taboo in the United States. Judge McDonald inherited her disdain for injustice and the courage to combat it from her mother. (Frances once famously challenged a racist taxi driver who, thinking Frances Kirk was white, apologized for the scent in his car because the previous passenger was an African American.) In an article in the *MPLS St. Paul Magazine*, Kitty Felde noted that "[w]hen beauticians balked at working on Gaby's hair, Frances calmly but firmly insisted. In New York, Gaby encountered the word 'nigger' for the first time. That led to fistfights that the mild-mannered Gaby didn't like and didn't win." Her personal and family experiences and her mother's example of hard work and audacity, combined with a solid secondary school education, inspired her to attend law school and become a civil rights lawyer.

After attending Boston University (1959–1961) and Hunter College in New York (1961–1963), Judge McDonald enrolled at Howard University Law School and earned an LL.B. in 1966. She served as research assistant to Professor Jeanus Parks in her first year, and, by her second year, she earned a tuition scholarship from the Ford Foundation. Judge McDonald served as secretary to the student bar association and Notes Editor for the *Howard Law Journal* before graduating cum laude and first in her class in 1966, at a time when there were only 142 Black women lawyers in the country. This ranking would be only one of the many firsts achieved during her impressive legal career. Howard University Law School was a vital think tank of national and international civil and human rights movements. She was taught and mentored by Patricia Roberts Harris, former professor (beginning in 1961) and Dean of the Howard Law School (1969–1972), former U.S. Secretary of Housing and Urban Development (1977–1979), and U.S. Secretary of Health, Education, and Welfare (1979–1980) during the Carter Administration. In 1965, Harris was appointed U.S. Ambassador to Luxembourg under President Lyndon B. Johnson, making her the first African-American woman to represent the United States as an ambassador. Under Harris's tutelage, Judge McDonald's intellectual development and passions were cultivated by one of the preeminent woman lawyers and public servants of the twentieth century. She dedicated herself to fulfilling these expectations.

After graduating from Howard, Gaby accepted a position as staff attorney with the NAACP Legal Defense and Educational Fund Inc. in New York. For three years, McDonald canvassed Alabama, Mississippi, and Georgia to assist local residents and lawyers with issues involving school desegregation, equal employment, housing, and voting rights. Moreover, she worked on some of the first plaintiff employment discrimination cases asserting violations of Title VII of the Civil Rights Act of 1964. In 1967, for example, she was the lead Legal Defense Fund (LDF) staff attorney in the suit against Philip Morris Companies Inc. for its discriminatory seniority system. It was the first significant plaintiff victory under Title VII.

In 1969, Judge McDonald established a private practice with her husband, Mark T. McDonald, in Houston, Texas. For nearly a decade, she secured numerous victories against firms such as the Monsanto Company and the Union Carbide Corporation. Her largest negotiated settlement of $1.2 billion from the Lone Star Steel Company provided salary arrears to 400 African-American steel workers. During this time, Judge McDonald had two children and taught labor law at the University of Texas. In the 1970s, she also taught several courses at the Texas Southern University Thurgood Marshall School of Law. Two years later, at the age of 37, President Jimmy Carter named her to the U.S. District Court in Houston, thus making her the first African-American woman on the federal bench in Texas history and the third African American to be appointed to the federal judiciary in the United States.

During her tenure on the bench, Judge McDonald ruled, often quite controversially, on a wide variety of constitutional cases. In *SDJ Inc. v. City of Houston*, she ruled that a local ordinance regulating the location of strip clubs did not abrogate the Freedom of Expression clause of the Constitution. In another case, Judge McDonald dismissed a plea agreement for a three-year sentence between the U.S. Attorney and a sheriff who plead guilty to violating the civil rights of prisoners. In 1984, in the *Le Roy v. City of Houston* case, she refused to recuse herself on racial grounds after the Houston City Council asserted that, as a Black woman, she was a member of the class that would benefit from the suit (her decision was upheld by the Fifth Circuit Court). Judge McDonald stated that "if my race is enough to disqualify me hearing this case, then I must disqualify myself as well from a substantial portion of cases on my docket . . . an action that would cripple my efforts to fulfill my oath as a federal judge." There were also instances when discrimination cases appeared on her docket, and she entertained various motions to recuse herself. For example, in *Vietnamese Fishermens Association v. The Knights of the Klu Klux Klan*, the movant in that case, the Grand Dragon, argued that her race would prevent her from being impartial. In this case, the Klan was interfering with and harassing Vietnamese fisherman. Even with the Grand Dragon's claims and death threats to her and family, she refused to back down. She not only ruled in favor of the fishermen and determined that the Klan had interfered with their right to free competition, but she also ordered the Klan to close its paramilitary training camps. Concurrently, the former U.S. attorney in Houston, Daniel Hedges, praised her for "not permitting her civil rights background to cloud her judgment as a federal judge. She was always evenhanded."

In 1988, she decided to retire from the bench. While maintaining a practice in Austin, Texas, she taught at Texas Southern University Thurgood Marshall School of Law and at St. Mary's University School of Law. She taught courses in federal jurisdiction and procedure and various civil rights law seminars. In 1993, immediately after accepting a distinguished professorship at the Thurgood Marshall School of Law, the U.S. Department of State nominated her to serve as a judge for an international war crimes tribunal that was being formed by the United Nation's Security Council. After she agreed, the UN General Assembly elected Judge McDonald by the largest number of votes of all judges of the newly formed ICTY. She would be the sole American on the court and one of only two women. In a few months, she was off to The Hague to help create the fledgling court. Not only did the ICTY have the barest of facilities and a budget of only $250,000, but its entire legal framework also needed drafting. As the only American judge on the world's first truly international criminal court, Judge McDonald and ten other colleagues drafted the Tribunal's rules of procedure and evidence. By 1997, the Tribunal's budget had grown to $48 million, a legal framework was in place, and more than 70 indictments had been handed down.

Judge McDonald first served as presiding judge in the tribunal's Trial Chamber II. In the role of presiding judge, she not only conducted evidence and deferral hearings in a number of cases, but she also heard the historic case of one of Bosnia's most notorious criminals, Dušsko Tadić (pronounced Doosko TadiCH), the first trial of the ICTY (May 1997 verdict) and the first war crimes trial since Nuremberg.[1] The rulings she made there as presiding judge helped establish the precedents and thus the policy, procedure, and

[1] The Nuremberg Trials were a series of military tribunals held by the victorious Allied forces of World War II that prosecuted, in 1945–46, members of the political, military, and economic leadership of defeated Nazi Germany.

practice of the ICTY, ICTR, and future international criminal courts, including the International Criminal Court (ICC). Judge McDonald's experience as a civil rights lawyer and her emergence as an advocate during legal segregation in the United States prepared her to substantively confront the political and legal complexities inherent in establishing an international court charged with adjudicating terrible crimes birthed in the ethnopolitical conflict and carnage in the former Yugoslavia.

As presiding judge over Trial Chamber II, Judge McDonald directed proceedings over several high-profile cases including the *Rajić* case (September 1996),[2] the *Lasva Valley* case (May 1995), and *Erdemović* case (May 1996), as well as preliminary motions in the *Blaskic* (July 1997), *Dokmanović* (July 1997), and *Celebići* cases.[3] She is most famous for being the presiding judge in the *Tadić* case, which she ruled on after a year of reviewing thousands of documents and hearing hundreds of witnesses. In 1992, Tadić was found guilty of crimes against humanity, grave breaches of the Geneva Conventions, and violations of the laws and customs of war for the systematic beating and killing of Muslims in a Serb-run prison camp, among other places. He was sentenced to twenty years in prison. International commentators noted that, as presiding judge, Judge McDonald skillfully balanced her concern for the victims of the war crimes, especially rape victims, with scrupulous fairness and respect for the rights of the defendants. The ICTY's findings in the *Tadić* case were significant in that they proved under international law the Serb policy of "ethnic cleansing" and set a precedent for further war crimes prosecutions and courts, including the ICTR and ICC. On May 20, 1997, Judge McDonald was re-elected for a second term on the tribunal and, on November 19, 1997, was nominated and elected by the judges on the court as the President. As President, she also presided over the Appeals Chamber, which also served as the Appeals Chamber for the ICTR in Arusha, Tanzania. The ICTR was modeled after the Yugoslav Tribunal to bring to justice those responsible for the Rwandan Genocide and other serious violations of international law in Rwanda.

As presiding judge of the Appeals Chamber, Judge McDonald ruled on several interlocutory appeals from the Yugoslavia and Rwanda Tribunals. Most notably, the *Bagasora* case highlighted the very different roles of the

[2] The *Rajić* case represented the first Rule 61 hearing that considered the agency concept for a finding that an armed conflict is international in character.

[3] In the *Blaskic* case, a series of hearings on the subpoena issue led to a groundbreaking Decision by the Appeals Chamber regarding the authority of the Tribunal to issue binding orders to States. During preliminary hearings, the first challenge to the arrest of an indictee was made in the *Dokmanović* case. Preliminary hearings in the *Celebići* cases interpreted and applied major rules of procedure and evidence of the Tribunal.

Office of the Prosecutor and the Chambers, and, in the *Barayagwiza* case, the Trial Chamber was directed to release one of the accused because he was held in illegal provisional detention by the ICTR for eleven months without being formally charged and an additional three months awaiting his arraignment. During her term as president, Judge McDonald consolidated the operation of the Tribunal, making it more effective and efficient. She led efforts to add two new courtrooms to handle the increased number of ongoing trials, and additional trial and appeal chamber judges were added to the ICTY by the UN Security Council. She also launched a public outreach campaign to educate the global public, especially Yugoslavians, about the ICTY. She established a vibrant Outreach Program aimed at informing the peoples of the former Yugoslavia of the work of the Tribunal and to contest propaganda and misunderstandings about its mission and activities.

In 1999, at the end of her tenure as president of the ICTY and ICTR, Judge McDonald argued that a permanent court with stronger backing from the UN would have brought war criminals to trial more quickly than had been the case in Serbia and in the similar tribunal dealing with atrocities in Rwanda. Such insights informed her role as presiding judge of the Women's International War Crimes Tribunal for the Trial of Japanese Military Sexual Slavery, established by a group of non-Western, regionally based nongovernmental organizations to account for the abhorrent treatment of Korean women and girls (aka "Comfort Women") held as sexual slaves by the government of Japan during World War II. The Women's International War Crimes Tribunal for the Trial of Japanese Military Sexual Slavery seemingly influenced the ICC drafters of the Rome Statute to include sexual slavery (although its definition is unnecessarily narrow) as a war crime and a crime against humanity, as well as shaped the international law principle of continuing harm. Judge McDonald was greatly moved by the courage of all of these women and civil society organizations that advocated for an ad hoc quasi-judicial process to address monumental historic injuries to themselves and their families and friends. The establishment of the ICC in 2002 crystalized Judge McDonald's ideals about criminal justice.

Two years after she left the ICTY, she was called to serve on another historic tribunal, the Iran-United States Claims Tribunal, as one of three American Arbitrators and the only woman. She served as a judge on the Claims Tribunal until September 2013. The international tribunal, also based in The Hague, was established by agreement between Iran and the United States in 1981, and it has, since then, adjudicated claims by American and Iranian nationals for compensation for confiscated assets and claims by the governments against each other.

Judge McDonald resides in New York and remains steadfast in her support of international justice. In November 2011, at the ICTY annual Global Legacy Conference, she emphasized the importance of ensuring fairness in international prosecutions. Throughout her tenure on the ICTY and Iran-United States Claims Tribunal, Judge McDonald was committed to protecting the rule of law. As Matt Stearns of *The Netherlander* stated, "the law never let her down. It's her talisman and her companion." As Judge McDonald herself further reiterated, "I believe in the rule of law not just intellectually. It's visceral for me, it's in my heart and soul. ... It's what protects people from anarchy." As far as her accomplishments in The Hague, the late Antonio Cassese, her colleague and the first president of the ICTY, wrote in the War Report, that she "is the best that America can offer: she is straightforward, direct, intelligent and hard-working; ... she is firm in her conviction; she is principled but she is not jingoistic." Secretary of State Madeleine Albright echoed Cassese at a dinner honoring Judge McDonald, stating that she was "one of the pioneering civil rights litigators in our country. And she has since become a pioneering justice for international war crimes law. ... I am confident that she will continue to be a voice for justice wherever she goes."

Judge McDonald has raised the consciousness of the American public about the workings of international tribunals, and her civil rights experience always comes into play, neatly joining her various professional accomplishments. "One of my major goals as an American," Judge McDonald explained, "is to point out the obvious: these are groups of people, whose differences are based on ethnicity and religion, engaging in atrocities because of those differences. ... We [Americans] have such seeds of divisiveness present in our society. ... It calls to my mind, as a racial minority, things that have happened in the United States, including a failure to account for past events."

Judge McDonald's experience as a Black American woman has provided her with the insights, fortitude, intelligence, wisdom, and determination to be an international pioneer. She has received numerous awards and honors. The National Bar Association presented her with its first Equal Justice and Ronald Brown International Law Awards. The American Society of International Law honored her with the Goler Teal Butcher Award for Human Rights, and she received the 2001 Human Rights Award from the Minnesota Advocates for Human Rights. She was also presented with the American Bar Association Commission on Women in the Profession Margaret Brent Women Lawyers of Achievement Award. In 2007, she was a recipient of the first Women Groundbreakers in International Justice Award from the Open Society Institute. In 2008, Judge McDonald received the Dorothy I. Height Lifetime Achievement Award. She has received the Doctor of Law Honoris

Causa from various institutions, including the Georgetown University Law Center, the University of Notre Dame, Howard University, the Stetson College of Law, and Amherst College. She was a member of the board of trustees of Howard University, her alma mater, for 23 years and continues to be a trustee emerita. She was on the board of the American Bar Association Human Rights Center and the Genocide Prevention Task Force. She is a member of the board of directors of the American Arbitration Association and honorary president of the American Society of International Law. She is admitted to practice law in the states of New York and Texas.

Judge McDonald is also the author of several published works, including *Substantive and Procedural Aspects of International Criminal Law, The Experience of International and National Courts*, edited with Olivia Swaak-Goldman, KLUWER LAW INT. (2000); *The International Criminal Tribunals: Crime and Punishment in the International Arena*, 7 ILSA J. INT'L & COMP. L. 667 (2001); *Reflections on the Contributions of the International Criminal Tribunal for the Former Yugoslavia*, 24 HASTINGS INT'L & COMP. L. REV. 155 (2001); *Problems, Obstacles and Achievements of the ICTY*, 2 J. INT'L CRIM. JUST. 558 (2004); (Published Address) *In Memoriam, Justice Thurgood Marshall*, 24 ST. MARY'S L.J. 959 (1993); (Published Address) *War Crimes Tribunals: The Record and the Prospects*, 13 AM. U. INT'L L. REV. 1441 (1998); (Published Address) *International Support for International Criminal Tribunals and an International Criminal Court*, 13 AM. U. INT'L L. REV. 1413 (1998); and the published addresses, *The Eleventh Annual Waldemar A. Solf Lecture: The Changing Nature of the Laws of War*, 156 MIL. L. REV. 30 (1998); and *Friedmann Award Address – Crimes of Sexual Violence: The Experience of the International Criminal Tribunal*, 39 COLUMBIA. J. TRANSNAT'L L. 1 (2000).

> She has never held political office. She is not the head of a multimedia entertainment empire. Yet, Gabrielle Kirk McDonald may be the most powerful African American women in the world.
>
> – Kitty Felde, *Los Angeles Times*, Sunday, February 7, 1999

2

Reflections on My Journey for Justice

Gabrielle Kirk McDonald

Black History means different things to Americans. Black Americans look to this occasion as a time to remind us of the rich heritage we have inherited. And, all Americans benefit from learning that African Americans have made so many contributions to this country and that our very diversity is a treasure. That is what the Black scholar and professor, Carter G. Woodson, intended when he established Black History Month.

Yet, annual events are not sufficient to bridge racial barriers that still exist. As U.S. Attorney General Eric Holder said in a Black History speech at the Department of Justice, if we are to get past the racial divide, we must make a conscious effort to discuss and understand it and, when needed, to confront it. And, we will not accomplish this unless we stop being cowards, as he put it, about discussing racial matters.

Black women have been trailblazers in the country since America's founding. Our history dictates that from the sweltering heat of cotton plantations to the air-conditioned corridors of the White House, Black women have anchored their families while simultaneously surpassing racial and gender stereotypes to assume leadership positions throughout our society. We have done so even when it seems we are ignored; too often, it is to Black men that we turn for the story of Black America, and it is White women who are listened to on issues of gender equality.

African Americans have a tradition of telling stories from one generation to the next. It began at a time when it was a crime to teach a Black slave to read or write. It was the way we kept our history. I want to do that today. I want to speak to the life and work of two African-American women judges – first,

This short reflection is a modified version of a keynote address I delivered on February 23, 2012, on the occasion of the Twenty-Fourth Annual Black History Month Program sponsored by the U.S. Attorney's Office of the South District of Texas.

Judge Constance Baker Motley, the first Black American woman to serve as an Article III federal judge; and, then I want to offer my story, as I have heard Judge Motley tell hers. For some, these stories may offer testimony that we can overcome prejudice and make a difference in the world. For others, perhaps our experiences as Black woman judges can serve as a new bridge of sorts to begin the conversations Eric Holder spoke about.

CONSTANCE BAKER MOTLEY (SEPTEMBER 14, 1921–SEPTEMBER 28, 2005)

Constance Baker Motley played a pivotal role in this nation's quest for justice and equality for African Americans. She was a generous friend and role model. After graduating from Columbia University School of Law, she joined the NAACP Legal and Educational Fund Inc. (LDF). She became the associate director-counsel under Thurgood Marshall and helped successfully wage a campaign to end officially mandated racial segregation in schools, buses, and lunch counters. She drafted the original complaint in *Brown v. Board of Education*, and gained the admission of James Meredith to the University of Mississippi – with the support, I should add, of 5,000 federal troops sent by President Kennedy. She argued a total of ten cases before the Supreme Court, winning nine of them. She visited the Reverend Dr. Martin Luther King in jail in Americus, Georgia. In her autobiography, *Equal Justice Under Law*, she wrote that she then realized, "that we did indeed have a new civil rights leader – a man willing to die for our freedom."

President Johnson appointed her to the Southern District of New York in 1966; she was the first African-American woman to become an Article III judge. Judge Motely became Chief Judge in 1982. She passed away in 2005 at the age of 84.

Even after Judge Motley assumed the bench, however, she found that some doors were still closed to Blacks and women and that, for her, the position did not guarantee respect. I had similar experiences some thirteen years later. For example, in her autobiography, Judge Motley recounts that, in 1966, the U.S. Attorney's office in the Southern District of New York had never assigned a woman to handle criminal cases. The only woman employed was limited to handling civil matters. When I joined the bench in 1979, there were no women Assistant U.S. Attorneys in our District. Times have certainly changed. Women have been appointed U.S. Attorneys throughout the Nation. Black women sit at the forefront of the American judiciary as judges and litigators, but more must be done to ensure African-American leadership in the justice system.

As a Texas transplant, I remember when the doors to the federal Clerk's Office in Houston were closed to African Americans. I recall inviting the new Clerk of the Court, Jesse Clark, to visit me in Chambers to discuss – how shall I put it – the "complexion" of the Clerk's Office. I showed him race statistics from the Southern District of Mississippi and said "They're doing better than us," which, of course, didn't take much doing! It's a different day, now. Sometimes small and thoughtful interventions can be as effective as mass movements.

Judge Motley has also explained how she came to be admitted to a private club, notorious for excluding women, where a judges' dinner meeting was being held. It turns out that the chief judge, as she said, "told a little white lie" to gain her admission, saying that she was the secretary and she was needed to take notes. I, too, was painfully made aware of "my place," so to speak, at the reception for newly appointed judges hosted by one of the incumbent judges. During the gaiety, the host directed me to the kitchen to meet his Black maid. She had her hands deep in water, and, as she wiped them and shook my hand, her overwhelming pride in meeting me made the shameful feeling I had, as a guest nevertheless being escorted to the kitchen, almost bearable. My father, however, was furious. By the time I resigned from the bench, though, my skin was thicker – thick enough to stifle a gasp when I opened my departing gift from one of my White male colleagues to reveal a pink nightgown to a room full of guests. This occurrence reminded me that the world is not a meritocracy and that, despite our individual and collective achievement, the color line can be bold and unforgiving. The great promise of the law has perhaps been my greatest solace.

GABRIELLE KIRK MCDONALD (APRIL 12, 1942–PRESENT)

On long transatlantic flights, I was invariably asked this the very question: "How did *you* get that position with the United Nations War Crimes Tribunal?" I would suppress a chuckle because their puzzled inflection – telegraphed in their eyes, as well as their voice – silently screamed "How does this woman . . . no, a woman of *her hue*, hold such a position?" The answer is complex, but it begins with the Civil Rights Movement. I have been blessed and had a lot of support along the way; yet, at a basic level, it begins with the African-American yearning for equality.

My story, as does anyone's, begins in childhood, when you realize that others believe that your God-given skin color is a liability, a reason to hold you down. It begins with talks, some more subtle than others, with your Black parents who break the news to you: like a story my light-skinned mother told me of how a New York City taxicab driver apologized for the foul smell in the car because a "nigger" passenger had just exited, or when I saw for myself, when I was only eight years old, the reaction of the landlord to my black skin after my mother rented an apartment from him. It begins with all the experiences of African Americans in this country that you carry in your soul and genes, that hatch a wish that things were different, and then, sometimes, a determination to make them different.

HOWARD UNIVERSITY SCHOOL OF LAW

I never wanted to be just a lawyer. I wanted to be a *civil rights* lawyer. I wanted to be like Constance Baker Motley. Students of the Civil Rights Movement understand that the struggle was both on the streets and in our nation's courts. It was local, national, and international in scope and influence. Lawyers at Howard had been the architects of the campaign to end racial discrimination in America, and that is exactly where I wanted to be; I applied only to that law school, and that before I even received my undergraduate degree from Hunter College. I was in a hurry to get involved.

When I entered Howard University School of Law in 1963, the Civil Rights Movement was in full swing – the Rev. Dr. Martin Luther King, Jr. was arrested and jailed and wrote his seminal *Letter from a Birmingham Jail*. A few months later, he gave his "I Have a Dream" speech at the March on Washington. That same year, Medgar Evers, the Mississippi NAACP Field Secretary, was gunned down outside his home; Bull Connor used fire hoses and police dogs on Black demonstrators; and, on Sunday September 15, 1963, four little girls attending Sunday School were killed by a bomb planted by white supremacists at the Sixteenth Street Baptist Church, in Birmingham, Alabama. The murder of these innocent girls signaled a critical shift in the American conscious because it depicted to the world the degree to which racial hatred can spawn horrific, unprovoked violence and unleash the power of nonviolent protest.

In 1964, three civil rights workers, two White and one Black, were murdered while trying to register Black voters in Mississippi. These events convinced President Johnson to sign the Civil Rights Act of 1964. In my second year, in 1965, one month after Malcolm X was gunned down in New York, Black and White marchers in support of the right to vote were brutally beaten and stampeded on what has been called "Bloody Sunday." This horrific incident was considered to be the catalyst for the Voting Rights Act of 1965, which Congress shortly adopted.

NAACP LEGAL DEFENSE AND EDUCATIONAL FUND, INC., AND TEXAS CIVIL RIGHTS PRACTICE

Upon graduating from Howard Law, I was fortunate to get what for me was my "plum job" at the LDF in New York City. The LDF was, and remains, the premier civil rights organization and has argued more cases before the Supreme Court than any other.

So, in 1966, after I graduated from law school, I traveled the South with the LDF, handling discrimination cases. I visited Texas to handle one with my future husband, Mark T. McDonald, and to work on another with Barbara Jordan. After we married, the law firm of McDonald & McDonald was soon handling civil rights cases against major employers and unions throughout Texas. In handling these cases, we faced the same fear victims of discrimination often experience. One of the cases we brought was against the Houston Police Department for racially discriminatory hiring and promotional practices.

Mark and I were both harassed by members of the police department, which was then led by the notorious Herman Short. Once, I was followed by a police car into my driveway when I had my five-year-old son in the car. I was also subjected to so-called routine traffic stops. Mark and another Black lawyer were physically abused by the police. In other cases, we toured steel mills and petrochemical plants as part of our discovery procedures and met in churches in East Texas, often feeling the back of my neck prickle as we were leaving late into the night. But all of this was slight compared to what our clients repeatedly endured. More than anything else, it is their determination and faith in the legal process that has stuck with me.

UNITED STATES DISTRICT COURT FOR THE SOUTHERN DISTRICT OF TEXAS

In 1979, I received a call from Senator Lloyd Bentsen's office. At the time, I was a 35-year-old mother of two and surprised he contacted me; I had not been active in political matters, and, frankly, I thought my race, gender, and age made me an unlikely candidate for the federal bench. I later had two meetings with him. The senator said he was impressed with my civil rights career and believed I would make a good federal judge. I am profoundly indebted to Senator Bentsen for the faith he showed in me. In life, you may be denied ninety-nine out of one hundred opportunities, but it only takes one opportunity or idea to transform your life.

One of the most notorious cases I heard involved the Ku Klux Klan. In April 1981, a lawsuit was filed by the Southern Poverty Law Center on behalf of Vietnamese fishermen in Galveston [Texas] Bay under various civil rights acts and also alleged a violation of Section 1 of the 1890 Sherman Antitrust Act to prevent interference, through intimidation and violence, with the rights of the Vietnamese to pursue their fishing trade during the shrimping season. The Klan had become involved in a dispute in the area between the Vietnamese and American fisherman over shrimping rights and were holding rallies where crosses were burned. Boats owned by Vietnamese were burned, and shots were fired against them. Indeed, the *New York Times* carried a front-page story, showing a flotilla of shrimp boats moving down the channel in Seabrook with robed and armed Klansmen aboard and an effigy of a Vietnamese fisherman hanged on the deck. The case was randomly assigned to me, one of eight judges in the Southern District of Texas, all of whom were White. The Klan filed a motion asking that I recuse myself from the case for bias, and the Grand Dragon Louis Beam, testified that "my people" – referring to me as "partly Negro" – were prejudiced against the Klan. I denied the motion, finding that no extrajudicial bias had been shown, and I advised Mr. Beam that he "is not entitled to a judge of his choice, but only a fair and impartial one, as I would be." They did not appeal that ruling. I entered a preliminary injunction the day before the shrimping season was to open prohibiting the defendants from threatening, intimidating, or harassing the Vietnamese fishermen or inciting others to do likewise. I subsequently entered a permanent injunction and ordered the Texas Emergency Reserve (the Klan's private "army" of some 2,500 members) to disband as being in violation of the Texas statute prohibiting individuals from associating as a military organization.

I was later, again, asked to recuse myself because of my race in the City (Houston) Council redistricting case. I also denied that request by the City of Houston. In a rare showing of unanimity, leaders of minority groups (NAACP, ACLU, Anti-Defamation League of B'nai B'rith, and American Jewish Committee) criticized the City Attorney's request. An appeal was taken in this instance, and my decision was upheld. In what was reported to have been the first case of its kind nationwide, the Fifth Circuit found that a contrary decision would be an offensive precedent against judges who are members of minority groups. A contrary ruling would have crippled my ability to handle my docket and truly rendered me a second-class judge.

Serving as a federal judge is an unparalleled opportunity for any lawyer. It was a rewarding time for me, as well. I gained invaluable insights into human behavior by participating in the trial process, and I was exposed to a wide variety of legal issues, some more challenging and exciting than others, but all contributing to the volume of experience I gained. And, my daughter, Stacy, formerly a lawyer and now a screenwriter, but who was six at the time, had a good time singing into the microphone on the judge's bench when we were not in trial. My son, Michael, now a lawyer, was content to play football in chambers with some of my law clerks. So, we all had some fun times when there was a lull in the justice business.

THE INTERNATIONAL CRIMINAL TRIBUNAL FOR THE FORMER YUGOSLAVIA

The world undoubtedly saw media images of the violence that took place in the former Yugoslavia in the early 1990s. Serbian, Croatian, and Muslim military and paramilitary forces were embroiled in an armed conflict in Bosnia and Croatia of horrendous dimensions. Civilians were targeted because of their religious-ethnic background, resurrecting old, unresolved grievances dating back centuries. Unspeakable atrocities were committed in concentration camps reminiscent of Nazi Germany. People were expelled from their regions, and the rape of women was widespread. The international community could not agree on whether it should, or would, take military action.

Instead, the United States took the lead in proposing the establishment of an international tribunal to halt the violence. On May 25, 1993, the International Criminal Tribunal for the former Yugoslavia was established by the UN Security Council. While I was still teaching at Texas Southern University, Thurgood Marshall School of Law, a historic Black university, I was nominated by the United States and elected by the General Assembly to serve as one of the eleven judges in that Tribunal. As an African-American women raised during Jim Crow segregation and a civil rights lawyer bent on fighting injustice, inequality, and oppression, I felt morally compelled to contribute to justice in the Balkans.

The international legal arena was new to me. Other than receiving the grand prize of $50 for achieving the highest grade in a basic course in international law while at Howard University School of Law decades previously and some limited exposure as a federal judge to international law, my focus had been on domestic law. Yet, it was Goler Teal Butcher, a Black woman, in whose name the American Society of International Law's Medal for Distinguished Service in Human Rights is given, who saw the interrelatedness between civil rights and human rights. In an article in *Howard Law Journal*, she wrote that human rights are civil rights "writ large on the international screen." And she noted that "the sensitivity derived from our unique background" makes Howard lawyers especially suited for this field. She knew this first hand, for she was a 1957 summa cum laude graduate of that law school, the first woman to be elected editor-in-chief of its law journal, and is said to have been the first Black person to serve in the State Department's Legal Adviser's Office. She joined the faculty of the law school in 1966 as a professor of international law in the fall of the year I graduated and died in 1993, the year I was elected to the International Criminal Tribunal for the former Yugoslavia (ICTY). Sometimes I felt that her spirit was somehow within my soul, moving me as my careers as a civil rights lawyer and professor of law coalesced with my experience in criminal law as a federal judge when I joined that Tribunal. It was, therefore, a singular honor for me to receive the Goler Teal Butcher Award in 1998.

The early challenge, however, once the judges arrived in The Hague, was to create this institution, and it proved enormous. We had no premises, no staff, no budget – and when we met in The Hague to draft the rules of procedure and evidence to guide our trials, we were informed that the Prosecutor had resigned. Many thought we were doomed for failure. Yet, we moved forward, another Prosecutor was appointed, and eventually the institutional framework was established. Slowly, very slowly, states and international enforcement agencies began to co-operate and, most importantly, to arrest persons charged by the Tribunal.

The Trial Chamber that I presided over conducted the first trial and found Dušsko Tadić guilty of killings and other brutal acts as crimes against humanity, grave breaches of the Geneva Conventions, and violations of laws and customs of war. This was the first international war crimes trial since the Nuremberg and Tokyo trials by victorious Allies in the 1940s. Just as Professor Butcher did, I, too, saw parallels between the ethnic conflicts in the Balkans and the struggle for civil rights in America. During this trial, I heard horrific testimony of the atrocities the people of the region brought to bear upon each other, spurred on by propaganda that dehumanized groups who, in some areas of the region, for decades had lived in harmony, intermarrying and putting their historical conflicts behind them. I was haunted by the fact that, on a basic level, the root causes of the conflict – intolerance, fear, and ignorance – were not that dissimilar from what I saw in the turbulent 1960s in the United States.

And, when I traveled by helicopter over the lush rolling hills of Rwanda to a genocide site when I was President of the International Criminal Tribunal for Yugoslavia, I saw the effects of colonial imperialism characterized by racist dominance that had defined slavery in America – colonial imperialism that had created artificial geographic boundaries and new hierarchies within the indigenous population. I was shown row after row of skeletons in what was formerly a school, grim reminders of the mayhem that took the lives of 800,000 Tutsis and moderate Hutus at the hands of Hutus still infected with the colonial past. And when I left, I wondered how we could explain to our children what we had done to each other in a four-month period in 1994.

I was elected Tribunal President by my fellow judges, and presided over the Appeals Chamber for both the Yugoslav and Rwanda Tribunals. I was the first woman and person of color to assume the office of president of an international tribunal. I did not seek this office; I would have preferred to remain a trial judge. I was drafted by my fellow judges. The Tribunal was growing at a rapid pace because, at long last, states began to cooperate and detainees were being arrested and transferred to the Tribunal for trial. We built two additional courtrooms, and, as President, I requested the Security Council to amend the statute establishing the Tribunal to add a fourth Trial Chamber. We addressed two other priorities – tightening the relationship with our sister Tribunal, the International Criminal Tribunal for Rwanda, which suffered from the lack of a technologically sound infrastructure that its counterpart in Europe was guaranteed, and amending our rules to provide speedier trials to the detainees who now filled our detention center in The Hague. But, most importantly, we created an Outreach Program to explain the procedures of our Tribunal located hundreds of miles from the Yugoslav region and that was charged with helping to bring peace and security to that region through the judgments we rendered. It was a tall order, but it has proved to be an essential component of the Tribunal's mandate. At its height, the Tribunal had a staff of approximately 1,800 and a budget of $342 million. The Tribunal has a broad legacy but, most importantly, it demonstrated that international criminal justice is possible, and that such justice can end the cycle of impunity enjoyed by perpetrators of mass international crimes. Its experiences also spawned the establishment of a permanent international court: the International Criminal Court (ICC) also located in The Hague.

TOKYO WOMEN'S TRIBUNAL

After I left the Yugoslav Tribunal, I had the opportunity to serve as the presiding judge of the Women's International War Crimes Tribunal for the Trial of Japanese Military Sexual Slavery. This Tribunal was established by a group of non-Western, regionally based nongovernmental organizations primarily headed by women to develop a historical record of the abhorrent treatment of women and girls, ironically called the "Comfort Women," who were held as sexual slaves by the government of Japan at "Comfort Stations," an organized sexual slavery system in areas where its military operated during World War II. A hearing was held in Tokyo in December 2000, where testimony was received from survivors, expert witnesses, and former Japanese soldiers. The judgment, finding Japanese officials during World War II guilty of sexual slavery as crimes against humanity, was delivered in The Hague in December 2001. The judgment, while not enforceable as findings of guilt, made significant contributions to international law. First, it has been said that it convinced the drafters of the Rome Statute creating the ICC to include sexual slavery (although its definition is unnecessarily narrow) as both a war crime and a crime against humanity. And its analysis of the concept of continuing harm should help the ICC to better understand that reparations for victims are not static and should include damages for the continuing effects of their injuries. Unfortunately, the judgment, documenting the horrors brought to bear on the Comfort Women, has yet to result in a full acknowledgment, apology, and reparations to them by the government of Japan. For me, once again, I was inspired by the courage and determination of those women who so believed in the rule of law that they turned to civil society to create a quasi-judicial system to address their injury when the state refused to do so. It was an emboldening sight to see these women, then the age of my grandmother, sometimes wiping their tears, as they resolutely challenged the impunity of the Japanese officials gained decades before because of the failure of the Tokyo Tribunal to address their wrongs shortly after World War II.

IRAN–UNITED STATES CLAIMS TRIBUNAL

A few months before the delivery of the Comfort Women Judgment, I received a call from the State Department asking if I would be willing to serve with the Iran–United States Claims Tribunal, also located in The Hague. It was born out of the November 1979 hostage crisis and the negotiated settlement between Iran and the United States to resolve commercial disputes between the two nations before a panel of nine arbitrators. Iran and the United States each appoint three arbitrators, and we have three others from third party countries: currently, two arbitrators from Germany and the president of the Tribunal from Belgium. I was the only woman and person of color on the Tribunal. And I have been the only woman to have ever served. I enjoyed my work on this historic Tribunal from 2001 until September 2013, and I also liked maintaining contact with my former colleagues at the Yugoslav Tribunal. And who would complain about living in The Hague?

CONCLUDING THOUGHTS

In closing, let me come back to yet another transatlantic flight, this time when I was returning to The Netherlands from UN headquarters in June 1998. Before I boarded, I heard about the savage killing of James Byrd, Jr., in Jasper, Texas, which revived America's nightmarish legacy of lynching and racially motivated violence. You all know what happened: three White men dragged Mr. Byrd behind a pick-up truck, pulling him along for about three miles, then dismembering him and dumping his body in an African-American cemetery in Jasper.

I will never forget that flight and the feelings that ran through me – sadness and anger. But I also felt a sense of displacement and helplessness. Here I was, traveling to The Hague, adjudicating some of the worst acts of inhumanity committed in the last century, yet, in my own country, in my own state, an equally brutal act was committed on an American whose only infraction was to have been born Black. I was once again seeing brutal parallels between the quest for civil rights and that for human rights and how hatred can push humans to descend into violence. These appear to be patterns that are increasing in brutality and frequency: witness Trayvon Martin and Jordan Davis – two Black male Florida teens who were senselessly killed in 2012 by angry and fearful White men for daring to live in their autonomy as Black youth. Need I mention the heartless killings of Mike Brown & Eric Garner by police officers in Ferguson, MI & NewYork respectively. Whether in the Balkans, in Africa, or in America, this violence has, at its root, hatred, which cannot be permitted to trump the rule of law.

Let me leave you with two thoughts: first, let me return to the theme with which I opened. The reason why we need dialogue, as Eric Holder urged in his 2009 speech, is not to ensure that our society will not descend into the widespread violence that occurred in the former Yugoslavia and Rwanda – I have faith that we, as a nation, will not. However, the reason why we must continue our conversation is to nurture our desire to remain a diverse nation, with all of us, Black, White, Native American, Asian, Hispanic, Middle Eastern, rising – but also falling – together. Let us not be reluctant, not just today, but at other times, as well, to talk about race matters or the gendered dimensions of race. President Obama reminded us that "this union may never be perfect, but generation after generation has shown that it can always be perfected." It is through such conversations that we begin the process of dismantling rigid positions based on fear and misinformation and move toward understanding and respect.

Second, when I left the Yugoslav Tribunal, I felt a sense of relief and gratitude. I arrived in The Hague carrying on my shoulders an overwhelming sense of responsibility, not just to the victims in the Balkans and the world community, but also to my own country that chose me as the sole American on this new global venture into criminal justice. I also, though, carried with me the responsibility I felt as an African American. Most African Americans know what that means. You represent the entire race. Yet, this load is lightened if we allow our history to remind us that if we carry within ourselves the memory of the stalwart journey of our people, we will come to understand that we are evidence of the success of that journey. I have faced every challenge by summoning the courage and persistence I learned especially from my mother and grandmother and from Black women role models in the law (as few as they were in my early days) that empowered me as a civil rights lawyer in Texas. They, as well as the many Black males who have engaged in the struggle for equal justice under the law, are proof positive of our collective success.

PART I

LEADERSHIP, HUMAN RIGHTS, AND PEACEBUILDING

3

Writing Black Women into Political Leadership: Reflections, Trends, and Contradictions

Carol Boyce-Davies

In a short but incisive essay entitled "Bringing More Women into Leadership,"[1] Dessima Williams, who had served briefly in the leadership of Grenada's short-lived New Jewel Movement, described the abysmally low representation of women in government as a manifestation of "global gendered apartheid." For her, the fact that, at the turn of the twenty-first century, women, who made up 50 percent of the world's population, held only 6 percent of seats in national cabinets and 13 percent of seats in world parliaments deserved the challenging language that she used. Removing this imbalance necessitated, in her view, the deliberate advancement of women's leadership, which often has a direct effect on policies related to youth, education, opposition to militarization, and protection of the natural environment. Today, although it is important to note that 165 countries, including the entire Caribbean region, have ratified the United Nation's 1980 Convention on the Elimination of All Forms of Discrimination against Women (CEDAW), the United States is one of the few countries in the world (along with states such as Saudi Arabia) that has not ratified it.[2] Activist-intellectuals like Williams often

Carole Boyce Davies is Professor of Africana Studies and English at Cornell University. She is author of LEFT OF KARL MARX: THE POLITICAL LIFE OF BLACK COMMUNIST CLAUDIA JONES (2008) and BLACK WOMEN, WRITING AND IDENTITY: MIGRATIONS OF THE SUBJECT (1994). The author of more than 100 academic articles, she is also the editor of a number of path-breaking critical anthologies and essay collections, the most recent of which is BEYOND CONTAINMENT: CLAUDIA JONES: AUTOBIOGRAPHICAL REFLECTIONS, POETRY, ESSAYS (2011). Her forthcoming work is CARIBBEAN SPACES: ESCAPE ROUTES FROM TWILIGHT ZONES (University of Illinois Press 2013).

[1] BOSTON GLOBE, March 8, 2000. Dessima Williams was arrested while on a diplomatic posting for her country in 1983 when the United States invaded Grenada. She subsequently became a professor in sociology and gender studies at Brandeis University and was appointed as Grenada's ambassador to the United Nations in 2008.

[2] The recent failure to pass the Violence against Women Act in the United States has been identified by Tara Culp-Ressler, *Violence against Women Act debacle: Why congress should be more diverse*, ATLANTIC, January 2013, as directly related to the White male dominance of the

argue that there is a direct relationship between the advancement of women into leadership and the world's continued well-being. Minimally, CEDAW calls for a basic fairness or balance in political representation.

Political activist Claudia Jones,[3] who was the only Black woman elected to the central committee of the Communist Party USA (CPUSA) in 1945 and who championed the idea of tripled rights for Black women – as workers, as women, and as Black people – in her essay, "An End to the Neglect of the Problems of Black Women" (1949),[4] had already described the ways in which a number of institutions, including progressive ones, tended not to account for Black women either as participants or as leaders and thereby reproduced the dominant patterns of the society that they dismissed, patterns in which Black women are not seen as thinking and acting subjects. For this reason, in her 1953 speech to the court before being sentenced for holding communist ideas, she asserted that Black women were thinking political actors: "You dare not, gentlemen of the prosecution, assert that Negro women can think, and speak and write!"[5] Up until her deportation to London in 1955, Claudia Jones entitled her column in *The Daily Worker* "Half the World," using a framework that is now commonplace post-Beijing UN language to describe the disproportionate representation of women in leadership when viewed against their actual numbers as citizens of the various countries of the world.

Whereas Dessima Williams's "global gendered apartheid" seemed then to be an extreme phrasing of the actual conditions of women at the turn of the twenty-first century, her polemic referring to the situation as "apartheid," a word used to describe the extreme racial segregation that existed in South Africa during the twentieth century, asserted an extreme imbalance in terms of political representation and signaled the need to correct the inequality that still exists. By 2012, however, we have witnessed the gradual rise of a few Black women to political leadership in Africa, the Caribbean, and the United States. It is thus useful to examine some of the gains and struggles of women in political leadership within the context of Williams's assessment. I am cautious, nonetheless, lest we repeat the same mistakes of postcolonial states, which saw the rise of men to political leadership but continue to suffer the effects of

House of Representatives, *available at* http://www.theatlantic.com/sexes/archive/2013/01/violence-against-women-act-debacle-why-congress-should-be-more-diverse/266784/

3 See my Left of Karl Marx: The Political Life of Black Communist Claudia Jones (2008). Sometimes referred to as the "triple jeopardy" or "triple oppression" thesis, this reappears in the works of Angela Davis, including Women, Race and Class (1981).

4 *In* Beyond Containment: Claudia Jones: Autobiographical Reflections, Poetry, Essays (Carole Boyce Davies ed., 2011), at 75–85. This article was first published in June 1949.

5 *Black women can think and speak and write* (Statement before being sentenced) in Claudia Jones: Beyond Containment, at 8.

sometimes oppressive, corrupt, or incompetent leadership. For this reason, in my view, one has to keep open a series of generating questions, with the hope that they can serve as cautionary pauses as one assesses the choices that come with political power. I raised some of these questions in a prior discussion of women and leadership, and I repeat them here as follows:[6] What happens when members of a subordinated group rise to power within an oppressive system? Whom do these people end up representing? How does a Black woman manage political demands while understanding her location in history? How does the larger African or diasporic context impact domestic decisions? How do class, status, and political affiliation affect the nature of one's participation in the political and intellectual process? How do we begin to subject the rise of Black women to leadership positions to the kind of internal critique that is fair and necessary? How does sexuality inform the construction of women in political leadership?

In many ways, the rise of Black women to political leadership reflects decades of feminist, decolonialist, and civil rights activism, all of which challenged the logic that leadership is always and only White and/or male. Whereas in the United States there were Black male senators in the immediate post-Emancipation period, it was not until after the Civil Rights Movement that we saw the steady rise of Black male, and then female, leadership to political positions, although not without contestation.[7] Not surprisingly, the rise of a Black president in the United States in 2009, which is seen as the culmination of at least a century of activist work, has been met with mixed responses along a continuum ranging from extreme racism to amazing joy.

HISTORICAL ERASURES OF BLACK WOMEN'S LEADERSHIP

The fact is that Black women have continuously exercised leadership in many different ways. This leadership has tended to be subject to historical erasure, given the ways that histories have been written to privilege White/male power. An illustrative example is that although Marcus Garvey has become synonymous with the leadership of the Universal Negro Improvement Association (UNIA), is credited with having formed the largest pan-African organization in history, and is mythologized in ceremonial form from photography to the lyrics and iconography of Rastafari, both of his wives were significant to the

6 *"Con-di-fi-cation": Black women, leadership and political power.* 7 FEMINIST AFRICA 67–84 (2007).

7 *See, i.e.*, Christian Grose, CONGRESS IN BLACK AND WHITE: RACE AND REPRESENTATION IN WASHINGTON AND AT HOME. (2011) and Clarence Lusane, THE BLACK HISTORY OF THE WHITE HOUSE (2011).

advancement of this mission. Amy Ashwood Garvey, his first wife, on record as a cofounder of the organization, was erased from consideration in this capacity for at least half a century. In July 1914, she had been identified already, at seventeen, as a brilliant orator, and this organizational skill was sought after by Marcus Garvey to help him move the dream of an organization to reality. After an acrimonious separation and throughout her post-Marcus life, Amy Ashwood's continuous claim for cofounder status, seen for a long time as the claims of a bitter ex-wife, is now backed up by the historical record.[8] She was tasked with generating membership and with laying out and documenting the initial objectives of the UNIA: the evidence indicates that those objectives were published in October 1914 under the hand of Amy Ashwood. Throughout her life, Amy Ashwood is reported to have activated some of the intent of the organization, minus the extreme romanticization of Africa that she thought characterized the Garvey Movement and that was one of the sources of their disagreement. One example of her activism was her direct organizational work in "forty-two states of the U.S.A." Internationally, in "all the islands of the Caribbean, South and Central America; Europe as far north as Turkey and the British Isles, and now in the West of Africa, she has made a detailed tour of Sierra Leone, Liberia, Nigeria, the Gold Coast (now Ghana) French West Africa, French Equatorial Africa, British and French Cameroons, Spanish Guinea and the Belgian Congo."[9] Amy Ashwood would also lay out an elaborate project for studying the African woman, with a section on African women's leadership in traditional structures.[10] Additionally, one of her later roles was to prepare the ground for what would become the Caribbean feminist movement.[11] Making connections with African communities of women worldwide, she travelled by ship throughout the Caribbean, meeting and charging women activists and creating alliances. What is now defined as Caribbean Feminism, Reddock argues, relocates Ashwood-Garvey solidly in the role of early articulator. Marcus Garvey's second wife, Amy Jacques Garvey, wrote and published *The Philosophy and Opinions of Marcus*

[8] Tony Martin, AMY ASHWOOD GARVEY: PAN-AFRICANIST, FEMINIST AND MRS. MARCUS GARVEY NO. 1 OR A TALE OF TWO AMIES (2007) and Carole Boyce Davies, *Enduring legacies of the First Mrs. Garvey*. 6 PROUDFLESH: NEW AFRIKAN JOURNAL OF CULTURE, POLITICS, AND CONSCIOUSNESS (2007), *available at* http://www.africaknowledgeproject.org/index.php/proudflesh/article/viewArticle/164

[9] Nadji Hillal H., *A Garvey comes home to Africa*, CHICAGO DEFENDER, August 6, 1949, 230.

[10] The outline of this project is available as an appendix to Martin, *supra* note 8.

[11] Rhoda Reddock, THE FIRST MRS. GARVEY AND OTHERS: PAN-AFRICANISM AND FEMINISM IN THE EARLY 20TH CENTURY BRITISH COLONIAL CARIBBEAN, Center for Gender and Development, University of the West Indies, St. Augustine, Trinidad (unpublished manuscript).

Garvey[12] and is said to have crafted many of his speeches herself. During Marcus's struggles with a concocted mail fraud charge and his subsequent incarceration, Amy Jacques assumed leadership of the UNIA and became at times the face of the movement. Still, in the end, she returned to Jamaica with her two sons, leaving the relationship at a time when Marcus Garvey, during an economically difficult period in his life in London before his death in 1940, was unable to take care of his family's financial needs. Because she lived some thirty years longer than he, she was also able to define in many ways what the movement sought to achieve. We observe in these women's lives two distinct approaches to women's leadership: Amy Ashwood was characterized by an independent feminist approach, and Amy Jacques is described by Ula Taylor as a "community feminist."[13] In the end, both did the organizational work that is often needed to maintain a credible public presentation, work that few would dispute is the embodiment of leadership.

Men who were leaders of major nationalist movements throughout the twentieth century often had wives or women co-workers who were ideologically in tune with or able to help advance their various projects.[14] Because women's contributions in that period were often taken for granted by the dominant culture, they were too often written out of history. Additionally, sexuality has always figured in the construction of these women, either in relation to the men in their lives or to their demise, as the stories of Amy Ashwood, Amy Jacques Garvey, or Shirley Graham DuBois[15] indicate. The more recent and similar experience of Winnie Mandela demonstrates well how the assumptions are that women should remain unpartnered for decades and faithful while their men are away, as Mandela did during the incarceration of her husband Nelson, and that, if they do not, the punishments and public censure can be harsh. On the other hand, if they exercised leadership, as Winnie Mandela did for the twenty-seven years of her husband's incarceration, their work can be discounted or trivialized based on sexuality.[16] Women are still defined more by their sexuality than by their political contributions

[12] THE PHILOSOPHY AND OPINIONS OF MARCUS GARVEY (Amy Jaques Garvey ed.). The book was first published in two volumes in 1923 and 1925 and then combined and published by Routledge in 1978 and the Majority Press in 1986.

[13] Ula Taylor, THE VEILED GARVEY: THE LIFE AND TIMES OF AMY JACQUES GARVEY (2001).

[14] Examples include Aime Cesaire, C. L. R. James, George Padmore, W. E. B. DuBois, Paul Robeson, and Martin Luther King Jr. For further discussion *see* Carole Boyce Davies, *Sisters Outside: Tracing the Caribbean/Black Radical Intellectual tradition*, 28 SMALL AXE 193–202 (March 2009).

[15] Gerald Horne, RACE WOMAN: THE LIVES OF SHIRLEY GRAHAM DUBOIS (2002). According to Horne, Shirley Graham DuBois was instrumental in DuBois's alignment with the CPUSA.

[16] See Winnie Mandela's PART OF MY SOUL WENT WITH HIM (1985) and her more recent book, Winnie Madikizela-Mandela, 491 DAYS. PRISONER NUMBER 1323/69 (2013).

unless those contributions are recovered and made meaningful by other thinking individuals.

Looking specifically at the United States, we can identify another pattern of historical erasure if we bring back for attention the presence of Congresswoman Shirley Chisholm who became, in 1968, the first Black woman elected to Congress, representing New York's 12th Congressional District for seven terms, from 1969 to 1983. In 1972, she also made history by becoming the first African American and the first woman to run for the U.S. presidency on a Democratic ticket. Although she may be forgotten or unknown by a new generation, her example is worth recalling here because she represents a possible model for understanding how some Black women have navigated mainstream political systems.

Congresswoman Chisholm, who straddled the Brooklyn Caribbean Diaspora community and the African-American community, campaigned with the slogan "unbought and unbossed,"[17] offering a political position of integrity and claiming to navigate power on her terms. Chisholm, in her autobiography, repeatedly indicates that she had the right to run. Even though she failed, she provided the example of writing future women into leadership. This tendency of calling for future leadership seems to define the activism and articulations of a variety of women throughout the twentieth century.

Congresswoman Barbara Jordan from Texas became a popular political figure during the 1974 Watergate Hearings. Known for her deep and sonorous voice, she was a Texas state senator from 1966 to 1972, the first Black woman to hold such an office in the South. In 1972, she was elected to the U.S. House of Representatives; she retired from office in 1979 because of ill health. At her zenith, Jordan was even mentioned as a possible running mate to Jimmy Carter, and, at the Democratic National Convention that year, she became the first African-American woman to deliver the keynote address. Current generations remain unaware of her existence, even as they are surprised by the knowledge of Ida B. Wells Barnett,[18] who was a pioneering activist and journalist in the decades prior to the Civil Rights Movement of the 1950s.

[17] Teaching her autobiography, UNBOUGHT AND UNBOSSED (1972, expanded edition, Take Root Media, 2010), to this current generation of students often elicits incredulity that she existed before Obama. Many are surprised that they did not know about her presence until our discussion.

[18] *See* the work of Paula Giddings on Ida Wells Barnett. Her *Missing in action: Ida B. Wells, the NAACP, and the historical record*, 1:2 MERIDIANS 1–17 (Spring, 2001) and her biography of Barnett, IDA: A SWORD AMONG LIONS: IDA B. WELLS AND THE CAMPAIGN AGAINST LYNCHING (2009) indicate that Wells was a cofounder of the NAACP and was also the instrumental force for the first national Black women's movement in the United States.

Since the rise of Black feminist assessments in the mid–twentieth century, many have recognized that it was Black women's particular experience of the combination of racism and sexism that kept Barbara Jordan and Shirley Chisholm from the presidency, as it certainly was not ability, competence, preparation, or political skill. Since then, there have been several women elected as local, state, and federal representatives in the United States. Condoleezza Rice was National Security Advisor from 2001 to 2005 and served as Secretary of State from 2005 to 2008 under George W. Bush. In the Obama administration, Susan Rice has served as Ambassador to the UN (2009–2013) and as National Security Advisor (2013–present). Barbara Lee of California (who was the only congresswoman to vote against the war on Iraq and who sponsored the bill making June Caribbean-American Heritage Month) provides a different model of leadership. Barbara Lee indicates in interviews given at the founding of Caribbean Heritage Month that it was the example of Shirley Chisholm and her challenge to her as a young student that inspired her to seek leadership.

TRENDS IN BLACK WOMEN'S INTERNATIONAL LEADERSHIP

The rise of Black women to various positions of international leadership between 2005 and 2012 allows us to see the beginning of a new trend in international leadership. In 2005, Liberia's Ellen Johnson Sirleaf became the first democratically elected female president in Africa and won a hotly contested election; she began her second term in 2012. Her autobiography, *This Child Will Be Great: Memoir of a Remarkable Life by Africa's First Woman President*, documents an abusive marriage and her subsequent determination to make Liberia livable for current and future generations.[19] Leymah Gbowee,[20] head of the Women's Peace and Security Network, shared the 2011 Nobel Peace Prize with Sirleaf and charts the activism generated to secure the rights of women as fundamental to national rebuilding following the ravages of corrupt and violent male leadership.

In Jamaica, Portia Simpson-Miller was able to win her first independently managed election, defeating the compromised Bruce Golding to reclaim her place as the first woman to serve as prime minister; she had served from 2006 to 2007, after P. J. Patterson, then prime minister, relinquished his position. After serving as leader of the opposition from 2007 to 2012, she again became

[19] Ellen Johnson-Sirleaf, This Child Will Be Great: A Memoir of a Remarkable Life by Africa's First Woman President (Harper Perennial, 2010).

[20] Leymah Gbowee, Mighty Be Our Powers: How Sisterhood, Prayer, and Sex Changed a Nation at War (2011).

prime minister in 2012 and, importantly, won the battle over attempts to paint her as out of control. Cultural critic Carolyn Cooper places Portia Simpson-Miller in the tradition of strong Jamaican women, creating a legacy for her that extends back to her African roots: "Sister P effectively uses her organ of speech to show her supporters (and detractors) that she's a militant woman in the tradition of Nanny of the Maroons and a whole host of African warrior women like Queen Nzinga of Angola and Nana Yaa Asentewaa of Ghana."[21] At her inauguration, which I attended, rap artist Shaggy turned his "Strength of a Woman" into an ode to the prime minister, although with its lyrics, which include the phrase "scent of a woman," he also offered a clever double entendre that captured well the constantly recurring issue of sexuality and Black women's leadership.

Although there have been a few ceremonial appointments like Michaëlle Jean, the twenty-seventh Governor General of Canada from 2006 to 2010, one needs still to mark the fact that a Black woman nonetheless occupied such a position. Similarly, Valerie Amos, who became Baroness Amos in 1997, was appointed by the Blair government to a ceremonial position as leader of the House of Lords from 2003 to 2007 and subsequently became the UN Under-Secretary-General for Humanitarian Affairs.

There has been a consistent pattern of women contesting their exclusions, rejecting the attempts to dispossess them of power, and asserting their right to occupy leadership positions, particularly when they have the credentials, experience, and ability to lead. Joyce Banda became another example when she became Malawi's first female president and only the second woman to serve as President of an African country. Having fought consistently for women's rights and having suffered domestic violence (as had Ellen Sirleaf Johnson and Wangari Maathai), she took power following the death of seventy-eight-year-old President Bingu wa Mutharika. Ironically, Mr. Mutharika's decision to appoint her as his running mate for the 2009 elections seemed largely ceremonial in a Malawi that had never before had a female vice president. But even more courageous was her decision to publicly stand up to him by refusing to endorse postcolonial male nepotistic leadership strategies by appointing his brother, Foreign Affairs Minister Peter Mutharika, to succeed him as president in 2014, when he was due to retire. Instead, she took power as the constitution demanded in the wake of the president's untimely passing. African woman also gained representation through the election of Nkosazana Dlamini-Zuma as the first female head of the African Union (AU) Commission. Michelle

[21] Carolyn Cooper, *Drawing Sister P's tongue*, Jamaica Gleaner (December 25, 2011).

Bachelet, then Executive Director of UN Women, described the Union as taking a "step forward to advance women's leadership and representation."[22] As these developments unfold, it can be assumed that global society has entered a new period in Black women's political leadership, one that has to be marked, studied, and analyzed in various ways as the years progress. As in the case of the accession of President Obama in the United States, we move from cautious optimism or happiness at these victories to an assumption that this is a demographic right, not a gift of any sort. Clearly, this phenomenon of women in leadership positions has also been on the rise in Latin America with the presence of women as political leaders of Brazil and Argentina. Dilma Rousseff won the presidency of Brazil, her first elective office, in October 2011. In her inaugural address, Rousseff said her goal would be to "consolidate the transformational work" of former president Luiz Inácio Lula da Silva Lula, adding that she would also strive to "open doors so that many other women also can, in the future, be president." Representing the leftist Workers' Party, Rouseff indicated, "I don't come here to extol my biography, but to glorify the life of each Brazilian woman. ... My supreme commitment is to honor women, protect the weakest, and govern for all."[23] So far she has overseen the introduction of an affirmative action policy in Brazil that allows Afro-Brazilians access to university education from which they had been barred for numbers of years by an educational structure that kept them located in poverty. Her handling of mass strikes in 2013 and her political stance against U.S. surveillance of Latin American heads of state, including herself, reveals a certain self-assurance in the leadership position.

Black women who assume leadership roles, our experience tells us, have to suffer through a range of "misrecognitions" along with entrenched notions about Black women – often from their own constituencies. Not only must they work twice as hard, receive twice the blame, and garner half the praise, but one learns the hard way that one can only have an impact on what is achieved at the time of leadership and that, just as easily as one builds, there are those waiting to destroy or reverse those gains. Additionally, certain forms of male recalcitrance or subversion must sometimes be seen as part of the

[22] *UN Women welcomes first woman head of African Union Commission*. Statement July 18, 2012, *available at* http://www.unwomen.org/en/news/stories/2012/7/un-women-welcomes-first-woman-head-of-african-union-commission, accessed October 17, 2013. Importantly, as well for the UN, an African woman, Phumzile Mlambo-Ngcuka, was sworn in as Executive Director on August 19, 2013. *See UN Women executive director Phumzile Mlambo-Ngcuka sworn in today*, *available at* http://www.unwomen.org/ru/news/stories/2013/8/new-executive-director-takes-oath-of-office#sthash.WnOnXS4J.GE68s1Pb.dpuf

[23] Global Post (September 18, 2011).

political landscape.[24] Still we continue to strive, recognizing that history is always a better judge.

Finally, it is important also to delineate a Black bourgeois feminist leadership model that is sometimes desired or courted by oppressive or dominant institutional structures. Although correctly identifying the American birth defect of slavery and the scourge of segregation, Condoleezza Rice uses the civil rights struggle as her own personal victory. Thus, in her speech to the Republican National Convention in 2012, she said, "On a personal note, a little girl grows up in Jim Crow Birmingham. The segregated city of the south where her parents cannot take her to a movie theater or to restaurants, but they have convinced her that even if she cannot have a hamburger at Woolworths, she can be the president of the United States if she wanted to be, and she becomes the secretary of state."[25] So, basically, in this construction, it is largely the parents' lessons (and not decades of speeches, sit-ins, marches, freedom rides, assassinations, legislation, and institutional challenges of all sorts advanced by progressive forces) that led African Americans to high political office – even if this same little girl was cautioned by those same parents not to participate in those activities and even though she ultimately became their beneficiary anyway. This also explains why, at the 2012 Republican Convention, Rice remained the only Black woman on the convention's list of major speakers and gave a talk that attempted to obliterate group advancement, as we have shown. Still of significance, however, is that she remained a single Black woman, making her way up the various institutional power ladders without the necessary partnering access that is often expected, although she was not without White male patronage over the years.

The Contradictions of Leadership in Black First Lady Status

Scholars in the future will have to study the leadership of the only Black first lady of the United States as of this writing, Michelle Robinson Obama, who represents an interesting blend of political power and wife-as-helpmate status and who has manifested an amazing dignity as the first Black woman to occupy this highly visible position. With Michelle Obama, we see the beginnings of a different model, one that is being crafted as we watch. Although

[24] Self-possessed Black women who became presidents in academic institutions in which there were traditional and sometimes religious male boards of trustees, as at Shaw University or Bennett College, have sometimes had to relinquish those positions in the face of demands for more amenable or conservative leadership.

[25] *Available at* http://www.foxnews.com/politics/2012/08/29/transcript-condoleezza-rice-speech-at-rnc/#ixzz28GFK94K2, accessed October 18, 2013.

located by the nature of the position of "wife," she exemplifies an assertive and independent professional presence, leveraged by her confidence in a history of community service. It is already known that the constructed American "first lady" is an economically privileged and racialized White female subject who operates largely in support of her husband's execution of the presidency and in the national imaginary as the ideal model of the supportive wife. This mythology has been substantially confronted by the presence of a Black woman, historically the antithesis of that construction and indeed one historically aligned with service to that idealized White female identity. Michelle Obama presents images of strength in her physicality, in an unabashed sense of personal style, and, above all, in an amazing love for family and community and people in general. This has not come easily because the construction of what is considered beautiful in the various cultural imaginaries is being substantially challenged on a day-to-day basis by her very presence and self-presentation. Her self-constructed "Mom-in-chief" is a giveaway to that American imaginary of what a first lady should be, a subtle recognition of American cultural values (like mom and apple pie).

But there is another trajectory through which one can identify an intellectual Michelle Obama. This begins with her work as an African-American Studies minor at Princeton University, where she produced a thesis that examined the nature of Princeton-educated Blacks and their relationship with community and argued for the responsibility of educated African Americans to give service to community.[26] In this well-developed albeit preliminary research project, she brought together for analysis themes that continue to inform the nature of her work with Black communities at the intellectual and experiential level and that continue, even in this day and time, to have salience for minority students and faculty on predominately White campuses, including those who work in fields such as Black/Africana Studies. Additionally, she has maintained in her various speeches that getting an education was necessary to her empowered self-definition. She has also challenged the elitism of academic institutions (especially the "Ivy League"), choosing for her first presentation a working-class university community and pointing out, for example, in a commencement speech to the University of California, Merced, on May 15, 2009, that when she was growing up, the University of Chicago failed to be accessible to neighborhood children, including the young Michelle who lived in the surrounding community, although she had the intelligence to get into Princeton. "I grew up just a

[26] Michelle La Vaughn Robinson. PRINCETON-EDUCATED BLACKS AND THE BLACK COMMUNITY (Unpublished B.A. thesis, Princeton University, 1985).

few miles from the University of Chicago in my hometown. The university, like most institutions, was a major cultural, economic institution in my neighborhood. . . . Yet that university never played a meaningful role in my academic development. The institution made no effort to reach out to me – a bright and promising student in their midst."[27] And, even at Princeton, the struggle continued for full recognition in light of her documented encounters with racism.

Her recent (2011) charge to Spelman graduates at an institution organized to make Black women into leaders in their professions reiterated that history and described her own experience as a professional who chose community work instead of the corporate life. It is worth quoting, as she describes some of her own professional pathways: "So, much to the surprise of my family and friends, I left that secure, high-paying job and eventually became the Executive Director of a nonprofit, working to help young people get involved in public service. I was making a lot less money – a lot – and my office was a lot smaller. But I woke up every morning with a sense of purpose and possibility. I went to work every day feeling excited – because with every young person I inspired, I felt myself becoming inspired. With every community I engaged, I felt more engaged and alive than I'd felt in years."[28] The intellectual Michelle Obama risks being obscured by all the other popular constructions available in the popular media, especially as magazine images and covers proliferate.[29]

It is easy, in the midst of all these representations, to forget that she herself is a Black woman who is a major political force in the African Diaspora world, even though within the United States the first lady is meant to subordinate herself to state power, not say much, smile a lot, and look endearingly at her husband. Michelle Obama is not quite that. Her critical thought, which began to develop during her undergraduate years, and the already substantial archive of ideas that she herself has been generating in the contemporary public sphere through speeches and interviews, merits serious study. Even with training as a lawyer from one of the nation's leading institutions, an executive/administrative career before coming to the White House, and her emergence as a major orator on the campaign trail, her presence became a disorienting factor in the larger media world, a world that has few tools of

[27] *Available at* http://www.graduationtalk.com/michelle-obama-commencement-speech-at-university-of-california-merced/, accessed October 17, 2013.

[28] *Available at* http://www.whitehouse.gov/the-press-office/2011/05/15/remarks-first-lady-spelman-college-commencement, accessed October 17, 2013.

[29] Ryann Alexander. Beyond Michelle Obama's Arms. Media Representations of a Black First Lady (M.A. thesis, Africana Studies, Cornell University, 2010).

analysis to engage this new phenomenon of a Black woman as a leadership partner at the highest political office in the world.

A commitment to service continues to characterize her presence, as seen in her speech at the Democratic National Convention, which contrasted sharply with the logic of individualism that Rice had offered. Instead, Michelle Obama offered an analysis that countered the American ethic of working one's way up to the top singly. Instead, one got an additional sense of someone who is trying to make a way for others now that she has succeeded: "You see, Barack and I were both raised by families who didn't have much in the way of money or material possessions but who had given us something far more valuable – their unconditional love, their unflinching sacrifice, and the chance to go places they had never imagined for themselves. … So when it comes to rebuilding our economy, Barack is thinking about folks like my dad and like his grandmother. He's thinking about the pride that comes from a hard day's work. That's why he signed the Lilly Ledbetter Fair Pay Act to help women get equal pay for equal work. … If farmers and blacksmiths could win independence from an empire … if immigrants could leave behind everything they knew for a better life on our shores … if women could be dragged to jail for seeking the vote … if a generation could defeat a depression, and define greatness for all time … if a young preacher could lift us to the mountaintop with his righteous dream … and if proud Americans can be who they are and boldly stand at the altar with who they love then surely, surely we can give everyone in this country a fair chance at that great American Dream … our collection of struggles and hopes and dreams."[30]

CONCLUSION: THE LIMITS AND GAINS OF LEADERSHIP

As writers like Toni Morrison demonstrate at the highest level, the presence of Black women as creative, thinking individuals whose work we read and as scholars whose work we study has accompanied the rise of women to positions of leadership in a range of organizations (churches, political parties, companies, traditional religious institutions, and academic institutions). This persistent movement is now seen in the presence of women of color as presidents and prime ministers of countries – Jamaica, Malawi, Liberia, Haiti, Trinidad and Tobago and, Brazil. It is clear that we are seeing the results of women's movement activity that challenged continued subordination of women in various fields legally and internationally through various political initiatives.

[30] *Available at* http://www.npr.org/2012/09/04/160578836/transcript-michelle-obamas-convention-speech, accessed October 17, 2013.

The well-known "invisibility" thesis, as put forward by Ralph Ellison in *Invisible Man* (1954), had already demonstrated that invisibility existed because dominant culture was not able to really "see" the Black man.[31] But although there is a recognized Black intellectual tradition, Black women have not been identified as belonging solidly to this intellectual tradition or to any other.[32]

I want to move then beyond the visual, from seeing Black women in leadership, to the intellectual – hearing, reading, and understanding the ideas of Black women as creative and political subjects. The intent is to think through and come to an understanding of the ideas of Black women who exist in a variety of political, ideological, geographical, and identitarian intersections. This discussion has paid attention to the ways in which Black women have written leadership into existence and therefore have contributed to an ongoing understanding of some of the world's current social problems as they pursue a range of cultural and intellectual advances. So, while the UN Convention on the Political Rights of Women went into force in 1954, enshrining women's equal rights to vote, hold office, and access public services at the start of the rise of the postcolonial state, it would take another fifty years to get to the 6 percent average that Dessima Williams laments. Still, in many ways, Williams's challenge effects a calling of Black women into leadership, a calling to which we are only now seeing the responses. In fourteen years, we have moved a tiny bit more rapidly from those abysmally low numbers to a still low average of approximately 20 percent worldwide in state assemblies in 2014. All indicators, though, point to a steady but slow increase as we continue to write women into political leadership.

[31] Clint Eastwood's dramatization was able to capture the invisible man trope in a televised presentation to an empty chair, which he addressed as the president at the Republican National Convention in Florida in 2012.

[32] Boyce, *Sisters Outside*, *supra* note 14.

4

International Human Rights and Black Women: Justice or Just Us?

Adrien Katherine Wing

INTRODUCTION

Women's issues and perspectives have become more salient in international law over the past few decades. When I joined the American Society of International Law (ASIL) in 1982, there were a few tables of female international lawyers; we met over lunch and made note of our small numbers and our exclusion from the subjects featured and the people found worthy of being panelists at the annual meeting. Since that time, the Convention on the Elimination of all Forms of Discrimination against Women (CEDAW) came into effect and now has 187 state parties.[1] Women became more prominent as international law scholars; many wrote about traditional subjects, while a few wrote on gender. A feminist article even debuted in the *American Journal of International Law*.[2] Eventually, the very active ASIL Women's Interest Group grew large enough to have year-round programs and needed an entire ballroom for the luncheon at the annual meeting.

Although some relative strides have been made for women overall in various aspects of international law, little attention has been paid to women of color. Even at the ASIL annual meetings, we would still fill only one or two tables. It is notable that two of us, the late Professor Goler Butcher, and myself, stayed around long enough and were active enough to be elected to serve as ASIL vice presidents, albeit two decades apart.

Women of color remain marginalized in a normative and physical sense, as they have been historically within U.S. domestic law. The issues and perspectives of women of color are commonly thought to be appropriately subsumed

[1] Convention on the Elimination of All Forms of Discrimination against Women, G.A. Res. 34/180, U.N. GAOR, 34th Sess. Supp. No. 107, U.N. Doc. A/Res/34/180 (Dec. 18, 1979) [hereinafter CEDAW].

[2] Hilary Charlesworth, Christine Chinkin, & Shelley Wright, *Feminist approaches to international law*, 85 AMER. J. INT'L L. 613 (1991).

under the rubric of all people, all women, or all people of color. When a group like women of color is not mentioned specifically and salient issues about that group are not discussed within a discipline, then a subtle or overt message may be sent out that this group does not count or that it has no distinct issues worthy of mention. Moreover, the bulk of the information that does get into the media is negative, often portraying women of color as poor, silent, brutalized victims in need of rescue by others.

Dean Jeremy Levitt of the University of New Brunswick Faculty of Law and former Associate Dean and Distinguished Professor of International Law at Florida A&M University, helped to address the marginalization of one group of women of color – Black women – when he hosted a historic roundtable entitled "Towards an International Law of Black Women: New Theory, New Praxis" in March 2010. The distinguished panel included Penelope Andrews, former Dean of Albany Law School; Indiana University law professor Karen Bravo; Linda Greene, Wisconsin-Madison law professor Villanova law professor Ruth Gordon; Northeastern law professor Hope Lewis; Arizona law professor and former Nigerian Minister of Mines Leslye Obiora; Loyola-New Orleans law professor Jeanne Woods; and myself. This event was followed-up with a panel on the same theme at the Third National People of Color Legal Scholarship Conference in September 2010.

This chapter contributes to the demarginalization of Black women in one area of international law – international human rights. The work surveys various international human rights documents and cases to determine the extent to which these sources specifically concern Black women and/or treat them as distinct subjects of international law. The chapter also looks at Black women as contributors to human rights law themselves. The result will illustrate that Black women's issues have been and are contributing to the field and that Black women are active participants, not just passive or silent victims of human rights violations.

I leave to others to address the particularities of issues that may be relevant outside of human rights. For instance, Black women are making contributions in fields like international business transactions and international arbitration. I also leave for further development issues that apply to other women of color, including Asians, Latinas, indigenous peoples, and Arabs, for instance.

The perspective utilized in this chapter is that of *critical race feminism* (CRF), a jurisprudential theme that emphasizes the legal status of women of color both domestically and internationally. Therefore, the next section first describes CRF in more detail, illustrating its links to other progressive jurisprudential trends such as critical legal studies (CLS), critical race theory (CRT), and feminist jurisprudence.

The third section, "Problems Facing Black Women," highlights some of the challenges Black women face around the world. Although, obviously, there are Black women in North and South America, as well as in the Caribbean and Europe, this chapter emphasizes Black women on the African continent in particular.

The fourth section, "Women's Protocol and CERD General Recommendation No. 25," looks at two documents involving Black women that attempt to provide solutions to some of the problems confronting them. Africa made an important contribution to the international human rights of women by enacting the Women's Protocol[3] of the African Charter on Human and Peoples' Rights.[4] The Women's Protocol, which came into effect in November 2005,[5] makes significant contributions to African women's rights, at least on paper. The second document is somewhat different. In 2000, the Committee on Elimination of Race Discrimination (CERD Committee), the United Nations treaty body that provides oversight for the Convention for the Elimination of Race Discrimination (CERD), issued General Recommendation No. 25, which concerns gender.[6]

The section "Legal Entities: ICTR, Sierra Leone TRC, Liberia TRC" explores how three particular legal entities have redressed injustices involving Black women within their jurisdiction. The International Criminal Tribunal for Rwanda (ICTR) defined rape for the purposes of the international law in the *Akayesu* decision. The Truth and Reconciliation Commissions (TRCs) for Sierra Leone and Liberia paid particular attention to the harms faced by Black women, a feature missing from most TRCs.

The sixth section, "Legal Actors," details the various positive roles Black women are playing as legal actors in international human rights: presidents, prime ministers, and Nobel Prize winners; judges; prosecutors and special advisers; members of human rights treaty bodies; nongovernmental organization (NGO) activists; and professors. Far from being silent, these women are speaking out, even though their numbers are small. The final section concludes with the issue of whether Black women can ever achieve justice under

3 *See* Protocol to the African Charter on Human and Peoples' Rights on the Rights of Women in Africa (July 11, 2003), http://wgd.au.int/en/content/protocol-african-charter-human-and-peoples-rights-rights-women-africa (last visited September 24, 2013) [hereinafter Women's Protocol].

4 *See* African Charter on Human and Peoples' Rights, June 27, 1981, OAU Doc. CAB/LEG/67/3/rev. 5, 21 I.L.M. 58 (1982) (entered into force October 21, 1986) [hereinafter Banjul Charter].

5 The Women's Protocol came into force on November 27, 2005.

6 CERD Committee. General Recommendation No. 25: Gender Related Dimensions of Racial Discrimination: 03/20/2000, *available at* http://www2.ohchr.org/english/bodies/cerd/comments.htm (last visited August 1, 2013).

international human rights frameworks or if they are destined to remain "just us," alone – de facto outside the protections theoretically offered.

CRITICAL RACE FEMINISM

CRF[7] examines the legal status of women of color, whether they are minorities within the United States or Europe or part of majority cultures elsewhere. These women are disproportionately stalled at the bottom of every society – economically, socially, and politically. CRF seeks to identify their problems and to formulate relevant solutions.

CRF originated out of a much broader set of legal and social movements – most notably CLS, CRT, and feminist jurisprudence. CRF agrees with the progressive postmodern tenets of CLS,[8] which challenge conceptions of law as objective and neutral, and uses this framework to expose how the law has served as a tool in perpetuating not only class distinctions, but also unjust race and gender hierarchies. CRF, as part of CRT, challenges conventional strategies of providing social and economic justice by using an antisubordination approach that brings race discourse into progressive class analysis.[9] CRF uses some tenets of feminism,[10] yet distinguishes the unique and varied experiences of women of color[11] as distinct from those of White women. Similarly, CRF has drawn from the energy and ideas of Black feminism and "womanist" feminism to address the concerns for equality and fair treatment of women of color. CRF is a gender intervention in CRT that illustrates that women of color may have perspectives on race and ethnicity issues that differ from those of their male peers.

CRF also introduces its own distinct analytical contributions. Most notable is the concept of *antiessentialism*. CRF contradicts the traditional feminist ideology of the "essential female voice" and instead relies on the theory of intersectionality, in which CRF demarginalizes the antiessentialist plight of

[7] *See* Adrien K. Wing, *Introduction: Global critical race feminism for the twenty-first century in* GLOBAL CRITICAL RACE FEMINISM: AN INTERNATIONAL READER (Adrien K. Wing ed., 2000).

[8] For sample publications on CLS, *see, e.g.*, CRITICAL LEGAL STUDIES (James Boyle ed., 1992); CRITICAL LEGAL STUDIES (Peter Fitzpatrick and Alan Hunt eds., 1987); CRITICAL LEGAL STUDIES (Alan Hutchinson ed., 1989).

[9] For anthologies on CRT, *see, e.g.*, *Introduction* to CRITICAL RACE THEORY: THE KEY WRITINGS THAT FORMED THE MOVEMENT *xix* (Kimberlé Crenshaw et al. eds., 1996); and CRITICAL RACE THEORY: THE CUTTING EDGE (Richard Delgado ed., 1995).

[10] For collections on feminism, *see, e.g.*, FEMINIST LEGAL THEORY (Frances E. Olsen ed., 1995); FEMINIST LEGAL THEORY: FOUNDATIONS (D. Kelly Weisberg ed., 1993); Lisa R. Pruitt, *A survey of feminist jurisprudence*, 16 U. ARK. LITTLE ROCK L. REV. 183 (1994).

[11] *See* Angela P. Harris, *Race and essentialism in feminist legal theory*, 42 STAN. L. REV. 581 (1990).

women of color by analyzing the intersection of their race and gender identities.[12] A related term is "multiple consciousness," which Mari Matsuda used to describe the intersectional identities of women of color.[13] Matsuda also has called for scholars to "look to the bottom," to the lives of women themselves.[14] In earlier scholarship, I have chosen to use the word "multiplicative" to configure identity that can also include class, age, disability, religion, sexual orientation, parental status, marital status, or nationality.[15]

Global CRF extends some of the concepts just described into the realms of international and comparative law.[16] CRF has embarked on international legal journeys, interrogating issues in public international law, international business transactions, and human rights. CRF has contributed to global feminism and postcolonial theory by moving women of color away from the margins, in both a theoretical and a practical sense. In this regard, women of color are nonessentialized subjects of international law.

Thus, this chapter uses a demarginalizing and intersectional approach to illustrate how Black women's issues and Black women themselves are not only not silent, but are instead at the forefront in human rights efforts. By looking to the bottom, we will reveal the problems faced by Black women, but we will also illustrate solutions made for and by them.

PROBLEMS FACING BLACK WOMEN

Although Black women face problems wherever they are around the world,[17] this part of the chapter focuses on Africa, where the largest number of Black women live.[18] The worldwide media has frequently focused on the bleak

[12] Kimberlé Crenshaw, *Demarginalizing the intersection of race & sex: A black feminist critique of antidiscrimination doctrine, feminist theory and antiracist politics*, 1989 U. CHI. LEGAL F. 139.

[13] Mari Matsuda, *When the first quail calls: Multiple consciousness as jurisprudential method*, 11 WOMEN'S RTS. L. REP. 7 (1989).

[14] Mari Matsuda, *Looking to the bottom: Critical legal studies and reparations*, 22 HARV. C.R.-C.L. L. REV. 323 (1987).

[15] Adrien K. Wing, *Brief reflections on a theory and praxis of being*, 6 BERKELEY J. GENDER L. & JUST. 181 (1990–91).

[16] *See* Adrien K. Wing, *Introduction: Global critical race feminism for the twenty-first century in* GLOBAL CRITICAL RACE FEMINISM: AN INTERNATIONAL READER (Adrien K. Wing ed., 2000); Penelope E. Andrews, *Globalization, human rights and critical race feminism: Voices from the margins*, 3 J. GENDER RACE & JUST. 373 (2000).

[17] This section draws in part from Adrien K. Wing & Tyler Murray Smith, *The new African Union and women's rights*, 13 TRANSNAT'L L. & CONTEMP. PROBS. 33 (2003).

[18] For Black women in the Americas, *see, e.g.*, Hope Lewis, *Universal mother: Transnational migration and the human rights of Black Women in the Americas*, 5 J. GENDER RACE & JUST. 197 (2001). For more on women in Africa, *see* VOICES OF AFRICAN WOMEN: WOMEN'S RIGHTS IN GHANA, UGANDA, AND TANZANIA (Johanna Bond ed., 2005); ENGENDERING HUMAN RIGHTS:

plight of African women. They do suffer from a myriad of intersecting civil, political, economic, social, and cultural problems. Yet, rarely is positive emphasis given to the vital roles they play in their communities and how they shape law, doctrine, and norms. Although this section highlights challenges, those that follow will explore the more positive aspects of Black women's lives and contributions.

Family, inheritance, and property laws in many countries are still based on customary practices.[19] Under customary law, women do not own property.[20] Polygamy, specifically polygyny – a man having more than one

CULTURAL AND SOCIOECONOMIC REALITIES IN AFRICA (Obioma Nnaemeka & Joy Ezeilo eds., 2005); Otiocha E. Eleazar, INTERNATIONAL HUMAN RIGHTS: THE PROTECTION OF THE RIGHTS OF WOMEN AND THE FEMALE CHILD IN AFRICA: THEORY AND PRACTICE (2011); Tamar Ezer et al., *Human rights clinic report: Divorce reform: Rights protection in the New Swaziland*, 8 GEO. J. GENDER & L. 883 (2007); Uche Ewelukwa, *Centuries of globalization; centuries of exclusion: African Women, human rights, and the "new" international trade regime*, 20 BERKELEY J. GENDERV L. & JUST. 75 (2005); Esther Kisaakye, *Reflections on the contribution of Georgetown's International Women's Human Rights Clinic to advancing the protection of women's rights in Uganda and Tanzania*, 7 GEO. J. GENDER & L. 343 (2006); Julie R. Hess, *United States and Africa on FGM: Cultural comparativists, resolutions, and rights*, 10 ILSA J. INT'L & COMP. L. 581 (2003–2004); Ben K. Twinomugisha, *Do the rights of poor women really matter? Globalization and the protection of reproductive health rights in Uganda*, 13 EAST AFRICAN J. PEACE HUMAN RTS. 81 (2007); Penelope E. Andrews, *Who's afraid of polygamy? Exploring the boundaries of family, equality and custom in South Africa*, 11 J. L. & FAM. STUD. 303 (2009); Llezlie L. Green, *Gender hate propaganda and sexual violence in the Rwandan Genocide: An argument for intersectionality in international law*, 33 COLUM. HUM. RTS. L. REV. 733 (2002); Flynn Coleman, *Pan-African strategies for environmental preservation: Why women's rights are the missing link*, 23 BERKELEY J. GENDER L. & JUST. 181 (2008); Lisa Vetten, *The imprisonment of women in Africa*, *in* HUMAN RIGHTS IN AFRICAN PRISONS 134 (Jeremy Sarkin ed., 2008); Melanie R. Wallace, *Voiceless victims: Sex slavery and trafficking of African women in Western Europe*, 30 GA. J. INT'L & COMP. L. 569 (2002); Tamar Ezer, *Inheritance law in Tanzania: The impoverishment of widows and daughters*, 7 GEO. J. GENDER & L. 599 (2006); Association of the Bar of the City of New York, *Gender-based violence laws in sub-Saharan Africa*, 63 THE RECORD 200 (2008); Fareda Banda, *Understanding women's economic and social human rights*, 12 EAST AFRICAN J. PEACE HUMAN RTS. 232 (2006); Esther Kisaakye, *Global rights, local harms: The case of the human rights of women in sub-Saharan Africa*, *in* WOMEN, CRIME AND SOCIAL HARM: TOWARDS A CRIMINOLOGY FOR THE GLOBAL AGE 123 (Maureen Cain & Adrian Howe eds., 2008); Fareda Banda, *Building on a global movement: Violence against women in the African context*, 8 AFRICAN HUMAN RTS. L. J. 1 (2008); Florence Shu-Acquaye et al., WOMEN, THE LAW, AND HIV/AIDS IN AFRICA: A CONUNDRUM FOR THE LEGISLATURE (2008); Rachel Slate, *Gender violence or violence against women? The treatment of forced marriage in the special court for Sierra Leone*, 13 MELBOURNE J. INT'L L. 732 (2012).

19 *See generally* Leon Shaskolsky Sheleff, THE FUTURE OF TRADITION: CUSTOMARY LAW, COMMON LAW AND LEGAL PLURALISM (2000).

20 *See, e.g.*, Celestine I. Nyamu, *How should human rights and development respond to cultural legitimization of gender hierarchy in developing countries?*, 41 HARV. INT'L. L. J. 381 (2000).

wife – is a declining practice but is still prevalent in many communities on the African continent.[21]

Religious practices around the world, including in Africa, are deeply patriarchal. Due to space constraints, I discuss here only Islam. Pursuant to Islamic *sharia* law, a Muslim woman must marry a Muslim man, but a Muslim man can marry up to four women, whether they are Muslim, Christian, or Jewish.[22] A Muslim woman inherits only a half share compared to a man of the same level, and she needs a male guardian.[23] Islam requires people accused of adultery to be confronted by four male witnesses, whereas a woman who gives birth outside of marriage is presumed guilty of adultery in places like Nigeria.[24]

African women face many kinds of violence, whether in wartime, as in Rwanda or the Congo,[25] or through the much more prevalent avenue of domestic violence. They are overrepresented as refugees.[26] They can suffer severe short- and long-term effects from female genital surgery (FGS), also known as female circumcision or female genital mutilation.[27] They lack the ability to make decisions with respect to all issues involving reproductive autonomy,[28] and they are disproportionately affected by HIV.[29]

Women face considerable discrimination in other areas as well. Customs often favor male children in education, with fewer females attending or completing schooling.[30] The labor market favors men to the exclusion of women, making women dependent on men for financial support for themselves and their children.[31] There are even places where women are literally

[21] Adrien Katherine Wing, *Polygamy from southern Africa to Black Britannia to Black America: Global critical race feminism as legal reform for the twenty-first century*, 11 J. CONTEMP. LEGAL ISSUES 811, 844 (2001) [hereinafter *Polygamy*].

[22] *Id.* at 841.

[23] *Id.*

[24] *Id.*

[25] *See* Stefan Kirchner, *Wartime rape in the Congo*, *in* CRIMES AGAINST WOMEN 81 (David Wingeate Pike ed., 2011).

[26] J. Oloka-Onyango, *The plight of the larger half: Human rights, gender violence and the legal status of refugee and internally displaced women in Africa*, 24 DENV. J. INT'L L. & POL'Y 349, 393–94 (1996).

[27] Fitnat Naa-Adjeley Adjetey, *Religious and cultural rights: Reclaiming the African woman's individuality: The struggle between women's reproductive autonomy and African society and culture*, 44 AM. U. L. REV. 1351, 1362 (1995).

[28] *Id.* at 1351.

[29] *See* Alexandra Arriaga, *HIV/AIDs and violence against women*, 29 (3) HUM. RTS. Q. Summer 2002, at 18.

[30] Joy K. Asiema, *Gender equity, gender equality, and the legal process: The Kenyan experience*, 10 TRANSNAT'L L. & CONTEMP. PROBS. 561, 571–72 (2000).

[31] Michelo Hansungule, *The African Charter on Human and Peoples' Rights: A critical review*, AFRICAN YEARBOOK OF INTERNATIONAL LAW 265, 325 (2001).

enslaved in unique ways, ways that are different from the slavery that may still exist in places like Mauritania and Sudan.[32] For example, the practice of *trokosi* in Ghana keeps girls and women as slaves to atone for sins of the family.[33]

These human rights problems have contributed to the vast underrepresentation of African women in the political arena. On the positive side, Rwanda now has the highest percentage of women – 56 percent – in any parliament in the world.[34] Through affirmative action, the African National Congress of South Africa reserves one-quarter of its parliamentary seats for women.[35] Finally, in 2005, Africa elected its first female president, Liberian Ellen Johnson Sirleaf, who will be mentioned again later, in the section "Legal Actors."[36]

When African states adopt and ratify international conventions that promise to protect women's rights, protections that are sometimes even mirrored in the states' own constitutions and national laws, these documents often fail to penetrate deeply because implementing mechanisms or laws are not passed.[37] Women may not be aware of the international or national protections available.[38]

The culmination of the denial of women's rights in the domestic and public spheres result in "spirit injuries" – a critical race-feminist term that contemplates the psychological, spiritual, and cultural effects of multiple assaults upon women.[39] Nonetheless, the spirit injuries inflicted on African women as a result of decades of repression should not be taken as a sign of hopelessness. Instead, they should serve as a reminder and an inspiration for the urgency of addressing all violations against Black women. The remaining parts of the chapter illustrate ways in which international human rights law and Black women themselves are assisting in the solutions to human rights problems, including those specifically affecting Black women.

[32] A. Yasmine Rassam, *Contemporary forms of slavery and the evolution of the prohibition of slavery and the slave trade under customary international law*, 39 Va. J. Int'l. L. 303, 321 (1999).

[33] Sam Kiley, *Child slaves "used by West Africans to appease spirits," Times* (London), September 17, 1996, at 11.

[34] *See Quota Project: Global database of quotas for women, available at* http://www.quotaproject.org/country.cfm?SortOrder=Percentage (last visited May 26, 2013).

[35] Adrien Katherine Wing & Mark Richard Johnson, *The promise of a post-genocide constitution: Healing Rwandan spirit injuries*, 7 Mich. J. Race & L. 247, 302 (2002).

[36] *See Liberia; celebrate in joy and gladness*, Africa News, December 12, 2005.

[37] Juliette Ayisi Agyei, *African women: Championing their own development and empowerment – case study, Ghana*, 21 Women's Rts. L. Rep. 117, 120 (2000).

[38] Takyiwaa Manuh, Africa Recovery Briefing Paper, *Women in Africa's development: Overcoming obstacles, pushing for progress*, U.N. Dep't of Pub. Info., No. 11, 12 (1998).

[39] Global Critical Race Feminism, *supra* note 16, at 14.

WOMEN'S PROTOCOL AND CERD GENERAL RECOMMENDATION NO. 25

This part of the chapter discusses two international rules that address the above-mentioned problems facing Black women: the Women's Protocol of the Banjul Charter and the CERD General Recommendation No. 25.[40]

Women's Protocol

The Banjul Charter of the Organization of African Unity (OAU) was adopted in 1981 and entered into force in 1986.[41] Although the Charter does make direct reference to gender issues, including an antidiscrimination clause that includes "sex,"[42] "tradition," and "culture," other provisions that aspire to preserve African tradition and culture proved to be open floodgates for human rights violations. These sections institutionalized myriad practices of gender discrimination that were already inherent in African culture.

The African Union (AU), which came into being in 2000 as the successor to the OAU, has among its objectives the protection of human rights, including gender equality.[43] The Women's Protocol[44] is perhaps the most promising

[40] This subsection draws from Adrien K. Wing, *Women's rights and Africa's evolving landscape: Can the Women's Protocol of the Banjul Charter make a contribution? in* AFRICA: MAPPING NEW BOUNDARIES IN INTERNATIONAL LAW 13 (Jeremy I. Levitt ed., 2008).

[41] *See* Banjul Charter, *supra* note 4, art. 30.

[42] *Id.* at art. 2.

[43] Preamble to Constitutive Act of the African Union, July 11, 2000, OAU Doc. CAB/LEG/23.15 (entered into force May 26, 2001), *available at* http://www.africa-union.org/About_AU/Constitutive_Act.htm.

[44] For more on the Women's Protocol, see Rachel Mayanja, *The Protocol on the Rights of Women in Africa, in* THE AFRICAN UNION: LEGAL AND INSTITUTIONAL FRAMEWORK. A MANUAL ON THE PAN-AFRICAN ORGANIZATION 455 (A.A. Yusef & F. Ouguergouz eds., 2012); Danwood Mzikenge Chirwa, *African regional human rights system: The promise of recent jurisprudence on social rights, in* SOCIAL RIGHTS JURISPRUDENCE: EMERGING TRENDS IN INTERNATIONAL AND COMPARATIVE LAW 323 (Malcolm Langford ed., 2008); BREATHING LIFE INTO THE AFRICAN UNION PROTOCOL ON WOMEN'S RIGHTS IN AFRICA (Roselynn Musa et al. eds., 2006); Ebenezer Durojaye, *Addressing human rights concerns raised by the mandatory HIV testing of pregnant women through the Protocol to the African Charter on the Rights of Women*, 52 J. AFRICAN L. 43 (2008); Rachel Rebouche, *Labor, land, and women's rights in Africa: Challenges for the New Protocol on the Rights of Women*, 19 HARV. HUM. RTS. J. 235 (2006); Ntombizozuko Dyani, *Protocol on the Rights of Women in Africa: Protection of women from sexual violence during armed conflict*, 6 AFRICAN HUM. RTS. L. J. 166 (2006); Kaniye S. A. Ebeku, *Considering the Protocol on the Rights of Women in Africa*, RECHT IN AFRIKA 171 (2006); Rachel Murray, *Women's rights and the Organization of African Unity and African Union: The Protocol on the Rights of Women in Africa, in* INTERNATIONAL LAW: MODERN FEMINIST APPROACHES 253 (Doris Buss & Ambreena Manji eds., 2005). For more on African Union, see Karen Stefiszyn, *The African Union: Challenges and opportunities for*

vehicle theoretically at the AU's disposal for promoting and protecting African women's rights. It is the first international treaty to specifically protect Black women. It addresses domestic violence, forbids FGS, favors monogamy, and calls for the right to abortion in certain circumstances – all of which are unprecedented in international law. As of 2014, thirty-six countries had ratified it.[45]

The Women's Protocol, the first international treaty to contemplate Black women's rights, requires that states use education and communication "to modify the social and cultural patterns of conduct" that perpetuate sexual discrimination.[46] It encourages education for more women as well.[47] Women have a right to dignity, which precludes exploitation or degradation.[48] Similar to the South African Constitution, the Protocol prohibits violence from both public and private sources.[49] Female refugees have an equal status to male refugees.[50] Women must be protected in armed conflict.[51] FGS is listed as a harmful practice that must be prohibited.[52] The Women's Protocol does not ban polygamy, but declares a preference for monogamy as a form of marriage.[53] Women are entitled to keep their own names and nationalities[54] and to acquire property.[55] They have the same ability to separate or terminate marriages and to obtain marital property as do their husbands.[56] Widows can get custody of their children; it is not presumed that the fathers own the children.[57] Moreover, widows have a right to inheritance and to live in the matrimonial house because it is not presumed that the husband's family owns his possessions after death.[58] Finally, widows can remarry the person of their choice, thus undercutting forced marriage practices. The Women's

women, 5 AFRICAN HUM. RTS. L. J. 358 (2005); Tiffany M. McKinney Gardner, *The commodification of women's work: Theorizing the advancement of African Women*, 13 BUFF. HUM. RTS. L. REV. 33 (2007); Fareda Banda, *Blazing a trail: The African Protocol on Women's Rights comes into force*, 50 J. AFRICAN L. 72 (2006).

45 *See* Solidarity for African Women's Rights, *SOAWR congratulates the Republic of Cameroon on its ratification of the AU Protocol*, April 13, 2013, *available at* www.soawr.org/en/news

46 Women's Protocol, *supra* note 3, at art. 2(2).

47 *Id.* at art. 12.

48 *Id.* at art. 3.

49 *Id.* at art. 4(2)(a); South Afr. Const. Art. 12.

50 Women's Protocol, *supra* note 3, at art. 2(k).

51 *Id.* at art. 11.

52 *Id.* at art. 5.

53 *Id.* at art. 6.

54 *Id.*

55 *Id.*

56 *Id.* at art. 7.

57 Women's Protocol, *supra* note 3, at art. 20.

58 *Id.* at art. 21.

Protocol encourages female political participation through affirmative action and encourages equal pay and benefits.[59] It calls for a minimum age for work,[60] as well as paid pre- and postnatal maternity leave.[61] Women should be provided with adequate food, water, and housing,[62] as well as a healthy and sustainable environment along with sustainable development.[63]

Most notable is the provision in the reproductive rights article that authorizes abortion in cases of rape or incest or to preserve the health of the mother.[64] Significantly, this is the first explicit mention of abortion in international law.[65] Even though the Women's Protocol does not promote the right to abortion on demand, it does go further than many national laws in Africa on the subject, and it elevates the issue in the global sphere.

Success in interpretation and implementation of the Women's Protocol, however, depends in large part on the new African Human Rights Court.[66] NGOs or individuals can apply to the Court if the Court permits.[67] As of 2014, the Court has not taken up women's issues.[68] The African Commission for Human and Peoples' Rights has not discussed these issues either.[69]

The potential theoretical contribution of the Women's Protocol to international law and the achievement of women's rights is great. The main challenges facing its implementation include gaps and ambiguities; general lack of awareness of the document; weakening of the women's movement in the region; lack of political will on the part of governments; strength of patriarchy, tradition, culture, and religion; public/private dichotomies; and lack of resources.[70]

59 *Id.* at art. 13.

60 *Id.*

61 *Id.*

62 Women's Protocol, *supra* note 3, at arts. 15, 16.

63 *Id.* at arts. 18, 19.

64 *Id.* at art. 14(2).

65 *See* Chad Gerson, *Toward an International standard of abortion rights: Two obstacles*, 5 CHI. J. INT'L. L. 753, 753 (2005).

66 Women's Protocol, *supra* note 3, at art. 27.

67 *See* art. 5 Protocol to the African Charter on Human and Peoples' Rights on the Establishment of the African Court on Human and Peoples' Rights, *available at* http://www.achpr.org/english/_info/court_en.html.

68 Rashida Manjoo, *Women's human rights in Africa, in* THE AFRICAN REGIONAL HUMAN RIGHTS SYSTEM 137, 143 (Manisula Ssenyonjo ed., 2012).

69 *Id. See generally* Udeme Essien, *The African Commission on Human and Peoples' Rights: Eleven years after*, 6 BUFF. HUM. RTS. L. REV. 93 (2000). For more on the African system, see Obiora Chinedu Okafor, THE AFRICAN HUMAN RIGHTS SYSTEM, ACTIVIST FORCES, AND INTERNATIONAL INSTITUTIONS (2007); Melinda Adams, *Regional women's activism: African women's networks and the African Union, in* GLOBAL FEMINISM: TRANSNATIONAL WOMEN'S ACTIVISM, ORGANIZING, AND HUMAN RIGHTS 187 (Myra Marx Ferree and Aili Mari Tripp eds., 2006).

70 Rosemary Semafumu Mukasa, THE AFRICAN WOMEN'S PROTOCOL: HARNESSING A POTENTIAL FORCE FOR POSITIVE CHANGE 72 (2009).

African women and men must be involved in confronting these challenges in the future if they are to enable the Women's Protocol to live up to its potential.

Committee on the Elimination of Racial Discrimination (CERD) General Recommendation No. 25

In the CERD General Recommendation No. 25 on the gender-related dimensions of racial discrimination, the CERD Committee arguably adopts a critical race feminist approach on race issues. It embraces the intersectionality approach and the idea that, on the grounds of race, color, descent, or national or ethnic origin, women of color face different realities than do other women or men of color.[71] African women played a critical role in the adoption of the recommendation. It notes that women of color face specific harms on the basis of gender, such as sexual violence, forced sterilization, abuse in informal sectors or as domestic workers abroad, and inability to access complaint mechanisms due to the gender-biased nature of those systems.[72] The recommendation contains a four-point intersectionality questionnaire that asks about the form the violation takes, the circumstances in which the violation occurs, the consequences of a violation, and the availability and accessibility of remedies and complaint mechanisms.[73] The CERD Committee requested that states disaggregate the data so that the situation of women facing racial discrimination will be clear, after which the CERD Committee and the states will be able to take steps to provide remedies to women specifically.[74] Many of the CERD Committee reports do mention General Recommendation No. 25 to encourage states not to forget the plight of women of color or other minority-group females. Unfortunately, like all treaty bodies, the CERD Committee has no police power to follow up on states violating CERD or any of the General Recommendations. Notwithstanding, the theoretical and normative value of the recommendation is significant. It provides a useful and needed tool to combat the exclusion of Black women and their concerns under the CERD treaty and other instruments that may have an impact on the gender-related dimensions of racial discrimination.

[71] *See* Lisa A. Crooms, *To establish my legitimate name inside the consciousness of strangers: Critical race praxis, progressive women-of-color theorizing, and human rights*, 46 How. L. J. 229, 247 (2003); CERD, *supra* note 6, para. 1.

[72] *Id.* para. 2.

[73] *Id.* para. 5.

[74] *Id.* para. 6.

LEGAL ENTITIES: ICTR, SIERRA LEONE TRC, LIBERIA TRC

This part of the chapter discusses how the ICTR and the Sierra Leone and Liberia TRCs have intentionally carved out a normative framework on the protection of women based on the horrific experiences of Black women as objects and subjects of international law. The TRCs have thus contributed to the development of gender-based international criminal law, humanitarian law, and human rights law. The ICTR defined rape under international law in the 1998 *Akayesu* case, and the TRCs of Sierra Leone and Liberia emphasized harms to Black women, more so than other truth commissions.

Gender strategies were used at the ICTR and the International Criminal Tribunal for the Former Yugoslavia (ICTY) that led to solid gains for women under international law.[75] Historically, most leaders have dismissed crimes against women, either considering them not to be crimes or to be private crimes that did not warrant public attention. Cases heard at both tribunals helped end these crude presumptions, which had been common even though rape and sexual violence were designated violations under the 1949 Geneva Conventions, the 1948 Genocide Convention, and the 1984 Torture Convention and are considered a crime against humanity under customary international law. The ICTR's decision in the *Akayesu* case was historic because it was the first to punish sexual violence in a civil war and determine that systematic rape could amount to genocide, as well as being an act of torture.[76] Former Taba commune mayor Jean-Paul Akayesu was originally charged in the ICTR in 1996; none of the initial twelve counts included sexual violence. Ultimately, he was sentenced to three life sentences for genocide and crimes against humanity and to eighty years for other violations, including rape and encouraging widespread sexual violence.[77] Presiding Judge Navanethem Pillay, a South African, stated: "From time immemorial, rape has been regarded as spoils of war. Now it will be considered a war crime. We want to send out a strong message that rape is no longer a trophy of war."[78] In the *Muhimana* case, sexual violence was a component of the crime of genocide.[79] In the *Nahimana, Barayagwiza & Ngeze* case, the court found the defendants committed the crime of direct and public incitement to

[75] Patricia Viseur Sellers, *Gender strategy is not a luxury for international courts*, 17 AM. U. J. GENDER & SOC. POL'Y. & L. 301 (2009).

[76] *Id.*

[77] *See* Prosecutor v. Akayesu, Case No. ICTR-96–4-T, Judgment (September 2, 1998).

[78] *Id.*

[79] *See* Prosecutor v. Muhimana, Case No. ICTR-95–1B-T, Judgment (Apr. 25, 2005); Prosecutor v. Gacumbitsi, Case No. ICTR-2001–64-T, Judgment (June 17, 2004).

commit genocide.[80] These cases, which included Black women victims, judges, and prosecutors as the key actors, have chiseled out a new jurisprudential framework on the prohibition of sexual violence during war.

The Sierra Leone and Liberia TRCs presented rare examples in which the concerns of Black women shaped their legal frameworks and operations.[81] Unlike the South African TRC, violence in the private sphere was analyzed.[82] Both TRCs included women commissioners (50 percent in the case of the Liberian TRC), provided gender training for commissioners, hired senior women staff, held women's-only hearings, and had a large number of women testify.[83] Both TRC acts also required their respective governments to implement TRC recommendations, including taking legislative action. In Sierra Leone, a number of laws have been passed: the Domestic Violence Act, which broadened the definition of domestic violence and allowed for criminal and civil sanctions; the Devolution of Estates Act, which entitled a widow to inherit her husband's property; and the Registration of Customary Marriages and Divorce Act.[84] The Liberian TRC formally incorporated sexual crimes into its legal framework, including the jurisprudence of the ICTR and ICTY. More than any other TRC, it targeted perpetrators of sexual violence within its mandate. Unfortunately, the government of Liberia has been unable to implement TRC recommendations that could provide justice and reparation to women victims of Liberia's various episodes of armed conflict.[85]

The ICTR and the Sierra Leone and Liberia TRCs laid a foundation that other tribunals and TRCs will undoubtedly follow in the future. Women and

80 *See* Prosecutor v. Nahimana, Barayagwiza & Ngeze, Case No. ICTR-99–52-T, Judgment (December 3, 2003).

81 *See, e.g*, Paul James-Allen et al., *Liberia: Beyond the Truth and Reconciliation Commission: Transitional justice options in Liberia* 5, ICTJ, May 2010, *available at* http://www.ictj.org/sites/default/files/ICTJ-Liberia-Beyond-TRC-2010-English.pdf; Sierra Leone Truth & Reconciliation Commission, The Mandate of the Truth and Reconciliation, Vol. 1, Ch. 1, para. 55 in Final Report, *available at* http://www.sierraleonetrc.org/index.php/view-report-text-vol-1/item/vol-one-chapter-one?category_id=19; An Act to Establish the Truth and Reconciliation Commission (TRC) of Liberia art. IV, § 4, May 12, 2005 (Liber.), *available at* http://trcofliberia.org/reports/final-report; Truth and Reconciliation Commission Act 2000, Schedule (a)(v), § 10.(2), *available at* http://www.sierra-leone.org/Laws/2000–4.pdf; Truth and Reconciliation Commission Act 2000, Schedule (a)(v), § 10.(2), *available at* http://www.sierra-leone.org/Laws/2000–4.pdf (requiring gender to be taken into account when forming the commission).

82 Margaret (Peggy) Maisel, *Have truth and reconciliation commissions helped remediate human rights violations against women? A feminist analysis of the past and formula for the future*, 20 Cardozo J. Int'l & Comp. L. 143, 167 (2011–12).

83 *Id.* at 168. South Africa held all-female hearings. *Id.* at 152.

84 *Id.* at 169–70.

85 *See Liberia truth and reconciliation final report*, available at http://trcofliberia.org/ (December 3, 2009).

men of all backgrounds will ultimately benefit from the normative development of protective principles originally made for and in part fashioned by Black women.

LEGAL ACTORS

Going beyond any notions of victimhood, this part of the chapter details selected roles that Black women are playing in international law and relations as transnational legal actors: presidents, prime ministers, and Nobel Prize winners; judges; prosecutors and advisers; members of human rights treaty bodies; NGO activists; and professors. Although most of these women are not widely known, they have been in the forefront of global governance in their respective fields. Some of the women may be the first Black person or the first Black woman to hold their respective positions. In that capacity, their mere existence can be an overt or subtle message that Black women can obtain and succeed in positions of power. The women are role models not only for other Blacks or Black women, but also for everyone. In some cases, these women may hold a post specifically related to race or gender issues, such as being members of the CERD or CEDAW committees. In those posts, their day-to-day work is on the forefront of achieving global justice for Blacks, women, or Black women.

Africa has produced two female presidents. Both Liberian President Ellen Johnson Sirleaf, who was the first democratically elected female president in the continent, and Malawian President Joyce Banda are committed to enhancing the status of women in Africa. They have also pledged to support the AU's Women's Decade as principal actors. Unfortunately, Liberia and Malawi rank very low in areas such as empowerment, education, and maternal health, according to the UN Millennium Development Goals.[86] Sirleaf won the 2011 Nobel Peace Prize for her efforts that led to the end of the Liberian civil war, and she has pledged that in her second term she will make women's rights a top national priority.[87] Liberian women eagerly await action.

Africa is not the only place where Black women have held leadership roles. Portia Lucretia Simpson-Miller became the seventh prime minister of Jamaica in 2012. She was previously PM in 2006–07. She has headed the People's National Party since 2006 and has been a member of Parliament since 1976. Simpson-Miller held a number of cabinet positions over the years and has been very active in the Caribbean region and at international levels.

[86] Travis Lupick, *Africa: Continent's two female presidents join forces for women*, Africa.com, *available at* http://allafrica.com/stories/201205091149.html (May 9, 2012).

[87] *Id.*

She serves on the Council of Women World Leaders, which is an international group of current and former women presidents and prime ministers who focus on women's issues.[88]

Black female Nobel Peace Prize winners include Liberian Leymah Gbowee, whose efforts helped to end the civil war in Liberia, and Kenyan environmental rights activist Wangari Mathai, who started a green movement. Both women are mentioned in the section "Legal Entities: ICTR, Sierra Leone TRC, Liberia TRC."

Black women are now represented at the highest levels in international judicial bodies. Judge Gabrielle Kirk McDonald, to whom this book is dedicated, was the third African-American female to be a U.S. federal judge, serving as a federal district judge in Texas. She was named one of the first eleven judges to serve on the ICTY in 1993. As presiding judge of Chamber II, she issued the decision against Duško Tadić, which was the first international war crimes case involving sexual violence charges. She was the president of the ICTY between 1997 and 1999, and she remains the only woman to have held that position. And until August 2014 served as one of three American arbitrators on the Iran–U.S. Claims Tribunal at The Hague.[89]

Other women of grand stature have followed in her footsteps. Ugandan Judge Julia Sebutinde joined the International Court of Justice in 2012. Before that, she had served on the Special Court for Sierra Leone since 2005. In Uganda, she had previously served as a judge on the High Court. She has written on the topic of violence against women in Uganda and Sierra Leone.[90]

Several Black women serve as judges on the International Criminal Court (ICC). Fatoumata Dembele Diarra, a Malian, has served since 2003 and also served a term as first vice president. Prior to that, she was also a member of the ICTY.[91] Akua Kuenyehia, a Ghanaian, was the first vice president of the ICC and has also served since 2003. Prior to that, she spent most of her career as a law professor, and she was the dean of the University of Ghana.[92] Joyce

88 *Jamaica, nation on a mission, available at* http://www.jis.gov.jm/ja50/v2/pm-profiles/portia-simpson-miller/ (last visited May 26, 2013).

89 *About the ICTY, former presidents, available at* http://www.icty.org/sid/155 (last visited May 28, 2013).

90 *International Court of Justice current members, available at* http://www.icj-cij.org/court/?p1=1&p2=2&p3=1&judge=194 (last visited May 28, 2013).

91 *About the ICC, available at* http://www.icc-cpi.int/en_menus/icc/structure%20of%20the%20court/presidency/the%20first%20vice%20president/Pages/judge%20fatoumata%20dembele%20diarra%20_mali__%20first%20vice_president.aspx (last visited May 28, 2013).

92 *About the ICC, available at* http://www.icc-cpi.int/en_menus/icc/structure%20of%20the%20court/chambers/the%20judges/Pages/first%20vice%20president%20%20judge%20akua%20kuenyehia.aspx (last visited May 28, 2013).

Aluoch, a Kenyan, has also served on the ICC since 2009. She had been a member of the Kenyan Court of Appeal prior to that appointment.[93]

Among the other Black women serving on the ICTY is Andresia Vaz. She had a career as a judge in Senegal, rising to the Supreme Court. She was appointed to the ICTR in 2001 and was named vice president of this tribunal before joining the ICTY in 2005.[94] Judge Elizabeth Gwaunza is an ad litem judge of the ICTY and also serves as a judge of appeal on the Supreme Court of Zimbabwe. She has written a number of publications on family and inheritance law.[95]

Black women judges are affiliated with the ICTR as well. Judge Florence Rita Arrey served on the Cameroonian Supreme Court prior to joining the ICTR. She has been president of the Cameroon chapter of the International Association of Women Judges.[96] Solomy Balunga Bossa has worked as an ad litem judge for the tribunal since 2003. She has also served as a judge for the East African Court of Justice.[97]

Justice Sophia A. B. Akuffo, a Ghanaian, was elected president of the African Court on Human and Peoples' Rights in 2012 for a two-year term. She was first elected as a Judge in 2006 for a two-year term, then re-elected in 2008 for a six-year term. She was elected vice president of the African Court in September 2008 for a two-year term, and re-elected in September 2010 for a final two-year term. She is also a judge of the Supreme Court of Ghana.[98]

Elsie Nwanwuri Thompson, a Nigerian, was elected to the African Court for a term of six years in 2010. She is also a judge of the High Court of Rivers State, Nigeria. Prior to her appointment as a High Court Judge, she was in active private legal practice for twenty years and worked on human rights cases. She has served in several associations, notably the International Federation of Women Lawyers (FIDA).[99]

93 *About the ICC*, *available at* http://www.icc-cpi.int/en_menus/icc/structure%20of%20the%20 court/chambers/the%20judges/Pages/judge%20joyce%20aluoch%20_kenya_.aspx (last visited May 28, 2013).

94 ICTY, Chambers judges, Andresia Vaz, *available at* http://ictr-archive09.library.cornell.edu/ENGLISH/factsheets/vaz.html (last visited September 25, 2013).

95 ICTY, Chambers Judges, Elizabeth Gwaunza, *available at* http://www.icty.org/x/file/About/Chambers/judges_bios_en/ALJ_Gwaunza_Bio_en.pdf (last visited May 28, 2013).

96 ICTR, About the Court, *available at* http://ictr-archive09.library.cornell.edu/ENGLISH/fact sheets/arrey.html (last visited May 28, 2013).

97 ICTR, About the Court, *available at* http://www.unictr.org/AboutICTR/ICTRStructure/The Chambers/JudgeSolomyBalungiBossa/tabid/144/Default.aspx (last visited May 28, 2013).

98 African Court on Human and Peoples' Rights, *available at* http://www.african-court.org/en/index.php/about-the-court/jurisdiction-3/office-of-the-president (last visited August 1, 2013).

99 *Id.*

Former Justice Kelello Justina Mafoso-Guni is from the Kingdom of Lesotho. She served as a magistrate in Zimbabwe for twelve years, becoming the first woman to be appointed to the bench. Returning to Lesotho, Justice Kelello took up a position at the High Court Bench, another post to which she was the first female appointee. She was elected a judge of the African Court in 2006 for a four-year term.[100]

Black women have extended their service to the newest Hague tribunal. Judge Janet Nosworthy, a Jamaican, has served as an alternate trial judge and a judge for the Special Tribunal for Lebanon. Before joining that court, she was an ad litem judge at the ICTY.[101]

Fatou Bensouda was named Prosecutor of the ICC in 2012. She had previously been Deputy Prosecutor since 2004. Prior to joining the ICC, she was senior legal advisor and head of the Legal Advisory Unit for the ICTR. She is from Gambia.[102]

Patricia Viseur Sellers was named a special adviser to the ICC in 2012, focusing on international criminal law prosecution strategies.[103] She was previously acting senior trial lawyer and legal adviser for gender at the ICTY. She has written extensively on gender violence and is a recipient of the ASIL Prominent Women in International Law Award.

The African Commission on Human Rights has a post known as the Special Rapporteur on Women's Rights in Africa; this person promotes and protects women in Africa. She assists governments and takes fact-finding missions. She prepares reports, drafts resolutions on women, and proposes recommendations to be adopted by the African Commission. She conducts studies, defines guidelines for state reports to the African Commission, and collaborates with relevant parties to promote and protect women's rights.[104] The current Rapporteur is attorney Soyata Maiga from

[100] *Id.*

[101] Special Tribunal for Lebanon, *available at* http://www.stl-tsl.org/en/about-the-stl/biographies/judges-of-the-special-tribunal-for-lebanon/trial-chamber-judge-janet-nosworthy (last visited September 25, 2013).

[102] ICC, Structure of the Court, *available at* http://www.icc-cpi.int/en_menus/icc/structure%20of%20the%20court/office%20of%20the%20prosecutor/Pages/theprosecutor2012.aspx (last visited May 28, 2013).

[103] *ICC Prosecutor Fatou Bensouda appoints Patricia Sellers, Leila Sadat and Diane Marie Amann as Special Advisers*, Press release December 12, 2012, *available at* http://www.icc-cpi.int/en_menus/icc/press%20and%20media/press%20releases/news%20and%20highlights/Pages/pr861.aspx (last visited May 28, 2013).

[104] Solidarity for African Women's Rights, A GUIDE TO USING THE PROTOCOL ON THE RIGHTS OF WOMEN IN AFRICA FOR LEGAL ACTION 5 (2011).

Mali.[105] Unfortunately, some believe that the Special Rapporteur position has been ineffective in practice.[106] This lack of success may represent the general weakness of special rapporteur positions more broadly, rather than a problem with this particular post. Alternatively, this job may also suffer simultaneously from weaknesses found in employment related to gender issues in the international arena.

A number of Black women have served on the various human rights treaty bodies that supervise the implementation of international human rights treaties. The chosen experts serve for several years and are supposed to be independent of any government influence. At the time of writing this chapter CERD committee members include Patricia Nozipho January-Bardill (South Africa) and Fatimata-Binta Victoire Dah/Diallo (Burkina Faso).[107] Gaby McDougall was the first American to serve on CERD. As an African-American female, she was a strong proponent of understanding how gender and race intertwined in her work. Now Chair of the International Council of the Minority Rights Group International, she has served on the board of the Global Fund for Women.[108] The Human Rights Committee, which is affiliated with the International Covenant for Civil and Political Rights (ICCPR), has Dr. Zonke Zanele Majodina (South Africa), whose many affiliations include serving on the board of directors of the Human Rights Institute of South Africa.[109] The UN Committee on the Rights of Persons with Disabilities (UNCRPD) includes Wangechi Maine Edah (Kenya), who was the inaugural vice president and Rapporteur for 2010.[110] The Committee on Migrant Workers (CMW) included Vice Chairperson Myriam Poussi (Burkina Faso), Andrea Miller-Stennett (Jamaica), and still includes Fatoumata Abdourhamana Dicko (Mali).[111] The Committee on the Rights

[105] *See* resume of Soyata Maiga, *available at* http://www.achpr.org/files/members/12/bio_soyata_maiga.pdf (last visited August 1, 2013).

[106] Manjoo, *supra* note 67.

[107] Office of United Nations High Commissioner for Human Rights, members of the CERD Committee, *available at* http://www2.ohchr.org/english/bodies/cerd/members.htm (last visited August 1, 2013).

[108] *See* International Human Rights Law Group, *available at* http://www.hrlawgroup.org/about_ihrlg/bios/gay_mcdougall.asp (last visited September 10, 2013).

[109] Office of the United Nations High Commissioner for Human Rights, members of the Human Rights Committee, *available at* http://www2.ohchr.org/english/bodies/hrc/membersCVs/majodina.htm (last visited August 1, 2013).

[110] Office of the United Nations High Commissioner for Human Rights, members of the CRPD Committee, *available at* http://www.ohchr.org/EN/HRBodies/CRPD/Pages/Membership.aspx (last visited August 1, 2013).

[111] Office of the United Nations High Commissioner for Human Rights, members of the CMW Committee, *available at* http://www2.ohchr.org/english/bodies/cmw/members.htm (last visited August 1, 2013).

of the Child (CRC) has Dr. Agnes Akosua Aidoo (Ghana).[112] The CEDAW Committee includes Barbara Evelyn Bailey (Jamaica), Hilary Gbedemah (Ghana), and Theodora Oby Nwankwo (Nigeria).[113]

African women have been human rights activists in many countries. For example, the Niger Delta Women for Justice waged a successful campaign to get oil companies to provide concessions to the community. It gained worldwide attention because these poor women also threatened to disrobe and afflict the company with "the curse of nakedness."[114] This group started in 1998 and was committed to improving the status of women and to ensure their environmental and other human rights.[115] Similarly, Wangari Mathai's Green Belt activism to restore green spaces for the environment in Kenya led to a Nobel Prize. It helped raise consciousness and also encouraged more women to participate in government.[116] Leymah Gbowee, who won the Nobel Prize in 2011 with President Sirleaf, is a mother of six who was instrumental in building a women's peacebuilding movement in Liberia. Her efforts helped lead to an end to the civil war and made it possible for Liberia to elect its first woman president.[117]

Black women have become professors of international human rights, and this subpart features some who live in the United States. Although the field of international law is still mainly populated by White men, there are some extraordinary Black women who have broken in and excelled. They have made wonderful contributions to teaching, scholarship, and service, albeit mainly unknown to the general public. Some of these women have emphasized Black issues, women's issues, or Black women's issues in their work.

The "mother" of all Black women in the international human rights field was Professor Goler Teal Butcher, who passed away in 1993. She heavily emphasized Africa throughout her life. Her career included stints at the Office of the Legal Advisor at the State Department and work as a consultant to the House Foreign Affairs Committee's Subcommittee on Africa. She worked for the Africa unit in the U.S. Agency for International Development (USAID), as well as for the Clinton transition team for USAID. She spent many years as a

[112] Office of the United Nations High Commissioner for Human Rights, members of the CRC Committee, *available at* http://www2.ohchr.org/english/bodies/crc/members.htm (last visited August 1, 2013).

[113] Office of the United Nations High Commissioner for Human Rights, members of the CEDAW Committee, *available at* http://www.ohchr.org/EN/HRBodies/CEDAW/Pages/Membership.aspx (last visited August 1, 2013).

[114] Deseriee A. Kennedy, *Transversal feminism and transcendence*, 15 S. Cal. Rev. L. & Women's Stud. 65 (2005–06).

[115] *Id.* at 83.

[116] *Id.* at 91.

[117] Leymah Gbowee, Mighty Be Our Powers: How Sisterhood, Prayer, and Sex Changed a Nation at War (2011).

law professor at Howard, her law school alma mater. She was at the forefront in the struggle to end apartheid and was also the first Black woman to become vice president of ASIL, which later created the Butcher medal for human rights in her honor. Howard sponsors the Butcher International Moot Court Team.[118]

Another Black woman who has also emphasized Africa in her work recently served as the first female Dean and President of Albany Law School. Penelope Andrews is a native of South Africa and spent most of her teaching career at CUNY Law School at Queens College in New York, where she served as Associate Dean for Academic Affairs. In her honor, there is an Andrews Human Rights Award at the University of KwaZulu-Natal in South Africa. In 2006, she was a finalist for a position on the South African Constitutional Court. Andrews has also emphasized women's rights from a CRF perspective and has published on race and gender issues, including in South Africa and Australia. Her latest book is *From Cape Town to Kabul: Rethinking Strategies for Pursuing Women's Human Rights.*[119]

Leslye Obiora is a notable Nigerian jurist who has also emphasized Africa and gender issues. She is a law professor at the University of Arizona. She is unique among this group of professors in that she also served in her government as the Nigerian Minister of Mines and Steel Development. Her teaching includes courses on gender and the law, as well as on human rights. Her scholarship has tackled controversial issues such as African Feminism and FGS.[120]

[118] *See* Clay Smith, *Tribute: United States foreign policy and Goler Teal Butcher*, 37 How. L. J. 139, 160 (1994).

[119] *See Penelope Andrews to be 17th president and dean, available at* http://www.albanylaw.edu/faculty/infocus/Pages/Penelope%20Andrews%20to%20be%2017th%20President%20Dean.aspx. Her biography can be found at http://www.albanylaw.edu/faculty/pages/faculty-listing.aspx?ind=Andrews,%20Penelope%20(Penny). Her publications include: From Cape Town to Kabul: Rethinking Strategies for Pursuing Women's Human Rights (2013); *Sixty years on: The human rights movement today*, 24 Md. J. Int'l L. 47 (2009); *Who's afraid of polygamy, supra* note 18; *"Democracy stops at my front door": Obstacles to gender equality in South Africa*, 5 Loy. U. Chi. Int'l L. Rev. 15 [(2007); *Big love? The recognition of customary marriages in South Africa*, 64 Wash. Lee L. Rev. 211 (2007); *Learning to love after learning to harm: Post-conflict reconstruction, gender equality and cultural values*, 15 Mich. St. J. Int'l L. 41 (2007); *Some middle-aged spread, a few mood swings and growing exhaustion: The human rights movement at middle age*, 41 Tulsa L. Rev. 693 (2005); *Women's human rights and the conversation across cultures*, 67 Alb. L. Rev. 609 (2003); *From gender apartheid to non-sexism: The pursuit of women's rights in South Africa*, 26 N.C. J. Int'l L. & Com. Reg. 693 (2001).

[120] Leslye Obiora's biography can be found at https://www.law.arizona.edu/faculty/, click on Obioral. Her publications include: *"Supri, supri, supri, Oyibo?": An interrogation of gender*

Hope Lewis has used a CRF perspective to focus on Black women in the African Diaspora, especially in the economic rights field. She has overcome blindness to become a leading scholar. Teaching at Northeastern Law School, she cofounded the Program on Human Rights and the Global Economy. Her areas of specialty include international disability rights and critical approaches to identity and the law (i.e., race, gender, culture, and transnational migration). She co-authored *Human Rights and the Global Marketplace: Economic, Social, and Cultural Dimensions*, a winner of the 2008 U.S. Human Rights Network Notable Contribution to Human Rights Scholarship Award. Lewis also co-edits the online abstracts journal *Human Rights and the Global Economy*, and she regularly contributes to *IntLawGrrls.com*, the international law professors' blog. The American Bar Association Section on International Law named her the 2012 recipient of the Mayre Rasmussen Award for supporting the advancement of women in international law.[121]

In addition to a CRF perspective, there are Black women using a CRT perspective in their scholarship. Villanova law professor Ruth Gordon has written in the field of CRT and international law,[122] and her courses have included international environmental law. She co-authored a UN Council for Namibia study addressing Namibia's violations of UN decrees and

mainstreaming deficits, 29 SIGNS: JOURNAL OF WOMEN IN CULTURE AND SOCIETY 649 (2004); *Bridges and barricades: Rethinking polemics and intransigence in the campaign against female circumcision*, 47 CASE W. RES. L. REV. 275 (1997); *Reconsidering African customary law*, 17 LEGAL STUD. F. 217 (1993).

[121] Hope Lewis's biography can be found at http://www.northeastern.edu/law/faculty/directory/lewis.html. Her publications include: Stephanie Ortoleva & Hope Lewis, *Forgotten sisters – A report on violence against women with disabilities: An overview of its nature, scope, causes and consequences* (Northeastern University School of Law Research Paper 104–2012 (2012); Hope Lewis & Rachel E. Rosenbloom, *The Boston Principles – An introduction*, 1 NOTRE DAME J. INT'L. COMP. HUM. RTS. L. 145 (2011); *Transnational dimensions of racial identity: Reflections on race, the global economy, and the human rights movement at 60*, 24 MD. J. INT'L. L. 296 (2009); *Female genital mutilation and female genital cutting, in* ENCYCLOPEDIA OF HUMAN RIGHTS (David P. Forsythe et. al. eds., 2009); *Human rights and the global economy: The promises and failures of globalization, in* PROGRESSIVE LAWYERING, GLOBALIZATION AND MARKETS: RETHINKING IDEOLOGY AND STRATEGY (Clare Dalton ed., 2007); HUMAN RIGHTS AND THE GLOBAL MARKETPLACE: ECONOMIC, SOCIAL AND CULTURAL DIMENSIONS (Jeanne M. Woods & Hope Lewis eds., 2005); *Embracing complexity: Human rights in critical race feminist perspective*, 12 COLUM. J. GENDER & L. 510 (2003); *Lionheart gals facing the dragon: The human rights of inter/national Black women in the United States*, 76 OR. L. REV. 567 (1997); *Between Irua and "female genital mutilation": Feminist human rights and the cultural divide*, 8 HARV. HUM. RTS. J. 1 (1995).

[122] *See* Ruth Gordon, *Critical race theory and international law: Convergence and divergence*, 45 VILL. L. REV. 827 (2000). For other publications, *see* http://www1.villanova.edu/villanova/law/academics/faculty/Facultyprofiles/RuthGordon.html.

resolutions, and she has written on the impact of Hurricane Katrina.[123] Her work has also focused on failed states and constitutionalism.[124]

My own work has used a CRT and CRF perspective to address the human rights of Black people generally, Black women, and other people of color, as well as other women as well. I am unique among the group in that I advised the founding fathers and mothers of three constitutions: South Africa, Palestine, and Rwanda. I was particularly concerned with the human rights provisions of these documents, including the rights of women. I have maintained a central focus on human rights for thirty years and am now the director of the University of Iowa Center for Human Rights. In addition to teaching the human rights course, I teach other courses that all involve human rights such as Law in the Muslim World, Critical Race Theory, and Sex Discrimination Law.[125] I am the author of more than one hundred publications, and my international scholarship has emphasized two regions: Africa, especially South Africa, and the Middle East, in particular the Palestinian legal system. Constitutionalism, women's rights, rape in Bosnia, Muslim headscarves in France, Tunisian secularism, Turkish democracy, and the Arab Spring are among the topics of my articles. I currently serve on the ABA Middle East/North Africa Law Initiative, which is concerned with human rights issues in both regions.

The major contributions that all the Black women featured in this part of the chapter have made to international human rights need to be better publicized. They should not just be inspirational to other Black women, but also to everyone interested in this field. If more people knew of their accomplishments, it would make a critical contribution to defeating the notion that Black women are and have only been victims.

CONCLUSION

This chapter has used a CRF approach to illuminate the contributions of Black women in the human rights protective regime and has demarginalized rather than essentialized them as transnational actors. Whereas Black

[123] *See* Ruth Gordon, *Afro America and the third world in the wake of Hurricane Katrina*, 21 (3) NAT'L. BLACK L. J. 1(2009).

[124] *See* Ruth Gordon, *Saving failed states: Sometimes a neocolonialist notion*, 12 AM. U. INT'L L. REV. 903 (1997); *Intervention by the United Nations: Iraq, Somalia, and Haiti*, 31 TEX. INT'L. L. J. 43 (1996); *Some legal problems with trusteeship*, 28 CORNELL INT'L. L. J. 301, 306 (1995); *United Nations Intervention in internal conflicts: Iraq, Somalia, and Beyond*, 15 MICH. J. INT'L. L. 519 (1994); *Growing constitutions*, 1 U. PA. J. CONST. L. 528 (1999).

[125] My biography can be found at http://www.law.uiowa.edu/faculty/adrien-wing.php with links to my publications.

women's issues may be invisible to many and unimportant to others, this chapter has shown that these issues have begun to be addressed by Black women, especially in the area of international human rights. The Women's Protocol and the CERD General Recommendation No. 25 are two examples where "looking to the bottom," in the words of Matsuda, and placing Black women at the center of the analysis makes important contributions to the ways in which we think about and rationalize international law. Exploring the decisions of the ICTR and the Sierra Leone and Liberia TRCs shows how the law can aid Black women specifically, at least on a theoretical and normative basis. The chapter shows that Black women are not only victims of human rights violations, but also vibrant contributors to the making and implementing of international law.

It is thus clear that Black women are entitled to, and are beginning to get, international recognition and justice in theory and practice. Despite these gains, hundreds of millions of Black women still feel that it is "just us" and are overwhelmed with the efforts of day-to-day survival for themselves and their families. On the other hand, it is also true that some Black women are on the front lines of authoring and shaping, or attempting to author and shape, international law and justice. Some of us are committed to aiding other Black women in particular and others to helping humanity more generally as well. We stand on the shoulders of our ancestors, sung and unsung, sheroes and heroes, and acknowledge the contributions of men dedicated to achieving global justice.

In the future, it is clear that a multidimensional approach is required for improving Black women's status – incorporating legal and nonlegal remedies and utilizing individuals, civil society, NGOs, and corporate and governmental sectors. Black women must be at the center of the process, not only at the margins. Because Black women remain disproportionally disempowered, there is the need for coalitional praxis working with all types of dedicated people, male and female. Dr. Levitt's role in bringing together the conference upon which this chapter is based is a perfect example of the commitment and cooperation needed to move Black women forward in the twenty-first century.

5

African Women and the Gender Equality Regime in Africa: From Patriarchy to Parity

Fatou Kiné Camara

> The wisest of the philosophers asked: "We admit that our predecessors were wiser than we. At the same time we criticize their comments, often rejecting them and claiming that the truth rests with us. How is this possible?" The wise philosopher responded: "Who sees further, a dwarf or a giant? Surely a giant, for his eyes are situated at a higher level than those of the dwarf. But if the dwarf is placed on the shoulders of the giant, who sees further? ... So, too, we are dwarfs astride the shoulders of giants. We master their wisdom and move beyond it. Due to their wisdom, we grow wise and are able to say all that we say, but not because we are greater than they."
>
> – Isaiah di Trani (c. 1180–c. 1250)

> These ancient legacies have more than poetic value. They serve to inspire contemporary intellectual work and political mobilizations, pointing to modes of agency and activism that lie outside the narrow frames of modern political analysis and liberal democratic assumptions.
>
> – Amina Mama[1]

INTRODUCTION

The African Charter on Human and Peoples' Rights (the African Charter)[2] was adopted on June 27, 1981, in Nairobi by the Conference of Heads of State and

Fatou Kiné Camara, Ph.D. is Associate Professor of Law, Faculté des Sciences Juridiques et politiques, Université Cheikh Anta Diop de Dakar, Senegal.

[1] *Editorial*, 4 Feminist Africa – Women Mobilised (2005), *available at* http://www.feministafrica.org/index.php/regional-networking (accessed December 16, 2011).

[2] ACHPR, *available at* http://www1.umn.edu/humanrts/instree/z1afchar.htm (accessed October 22, 2012). Rose M. D'Sa, *Human and peoples' rights: Distinctive features of the African Charter*, 29 J. AFRICAN L. 72–81 (Spring, 1985); U. O. Umozurike, *The African Charter on Human and Peoples' Rights*, 77 AM. J. INT'L. L. 902–12 (October 1983).

Government of the Organization of African Unity (OAU).[3] It came into force on October 21, 1986, after ratification by twenty-five states. The African Charter has been considered relatively evolutionary because it enshrines the three "generations" of human rights: civil and political rights; economic, social, and cultural rights; and collective rights or the rights of peoples. In spite of that innovative aspect, the African Charter does not adequately and explicitly address the human rights of African women who suffer grievous abuse of their fundamental rights.[4] Despite the widespread pattern of violence against women around the world, the following statement is still worth considering: "In contemporary sub-Saharan Africa (SSA), women are facing human rights abuses unparalleled elsewhere in the world."[5]

Hence, in its Thirty-First Ordinary Session in Addis Ababa, Ethiopia, in June 1995, the Assembly of Heads of State and Government of the OAU endorsed, by resolution AHG/Res. 240 (XXXI), the recommendation of the African Commission on Human and Peoples' Rights to elaborate a Protocol on the Rights of Women in Africa.[6]

Consequently, African women rights organizations, the Special Rapporteur on the Rights of African Women of the African Commission on Human and Peoples' Rights, the Inter-African Committee on Harmful Traditional Practices Affecting the Health of Women and Children (IAC), and the Women's Unit of the OAU came together to draft a protocol to the African

[3] OAU Charter, *available at* http://www.au.int/en/sites/default/files/OAU_Charter_1963_0.pdf (accessed October 22, 2012). It was adopted on May 25, 1963, in Addis Ababa, Ethiopia, by the Heads of State and Governments of Africa. The OAU was created during the decolonization process in Africa. Its main objective was to unify the independent states and to facilitate the end of colonialism on the continent. Immanuel Wallerstein, *The early years of the OAU: The search for organizational preeminence* 20 INTERNATIONAL ORGANIZATION 774–87 (Autumn, 1966).

[4] Claude E. Welch Jr., *Human rights and African women: A comparison of protection under two major treaties*, 15 HUM. RTS. Q. 549, 555–56 (1993); Makau Mutua, *The African human rights system, a critical evaluation, available at* http://hdr.undp.org/en/reports/global/hdr2000/papers/MUTUA.pdf (accessed October 10, 2011).

[5] Kathryn Birdwell-Wester, *Violated: Women's human rights in sub-Saharan Africa*, Topical Review Digest: Human Rights in Sub-Saharan Africa, *available at* http://www.du.edu/korbel/hrhw/researchdigest/africa/WomensRights.pdf (accessed March 6, 2012). According to Birdwell-Wester, 42 percent of African girls are married before the age of 18. Almost 80,000 women worldwide die each year from unsafe abortions; approximately 40 percent of those deaths occur on the African continent. "In sub-Saharan Africa, already 57 percent of all HIV-positive adults are women, and 75 *percent of young people living with HIV are women and girls* [emphasis added]," ILO Report, December 2004, *Women, Girls, HIV/AIDS and the World of Work, available at* http://www.ilo.org/aids/Publications/WCMS_115049/lang–en/index.htm (accessed November 6, 2012).

[6] See, Preamble, Protocol to the African Charter on Human and Peoples' Rights on the Rights of Women in Africa (July 11, 2003), *available at* http://www.africa-union.org/home/Welcome.htm (last visited August 1, 2012).

Charter dealing specifically with the rights of women in Africa.[7] Their efforts came to fruition on July 11, 2003, in Maputo, Mozambique, where the heads of states and governments of the newly created African Union (AU)[8] adopted a groundbreaking women's rights instrument,[9] the Protocol to the African Charter on Human and Peoples' Rights on the Rights of Women in Africa, otherwise known as "The African Women's Protocol."[10]

This chapter's first purpose is to highlight how the African Women's Protocol was born within an African context and from a process led by African women's movements. That process can be traced to a matriarchal African tradition existing prior to European colonial conquest, when women, through their own organizations, shaped their own lives and participated fully in the social and political structures of the communities in which they lived. Second, this chapter shows that the provisions contained within the African Women's Protocol requiring "positive action to promote participative governance and the equal participation of women in the political life of their countries through affirmative action"[11] and equal representation of men and

[7] Fareda Banda, *Blazing a trail: The African Protocol on Women's Rights comes into force*, 50 J. AFRICAN L. 72–74 (2006); Mutoy Mubiala, *The draft protocol to the African Charter on Human and Peoples' Rights on the Rights of Women in Africa* (text in French), *available at* www.uneca.org/acgd/gender/frachr_protocol.doc (accessed October 28, 2012).

[8] In 2002, the OAU transformed into the African Union (AU). The full text of the Constitutive Act of the African Union is available on the African Union official website: http://www.africa-union.org/root/au/aboutau/constitutive_act_en.htm (accessed August 13, 2012). *See* Corinne A. A. Packer & Donald Rukare, *The new African Union and its constitutive act*, 96 AM. J. INT'L. L. 365–79 (April 2002); Tiyanjana Maluwa, *The OAU/African Union and international law: Mapping new boundaries or revising old terrain?*, 98 PROCEEDINGS OF THE ANNUAL MEETING (American Society of International Law) 232 (March 31–April 3, 2004); Kofi Oteng Kufuor, *The collapse of the Organization of African Unity: Lessons from economics and history*, 49 J. AFRICAN L. 132–44 (2005).

[9] It guarantees rights in a more explicit and comprehensive manner than the Convention on the Elimination of All Forms of Discrimination against Women (CEDAW) and other preexisting international human rights instruments, such as the right to safe abortion and protection from HIV (art. 14). *See* Banda, *supra* note 7, at 72–84; *Contra* Kristin Davis, *The emperor is still naked: Why the Protocol on the Rights of Women in Africa leaves women exposed to more discrimination*, 42 VAND. J. TRANSNAT'L. L. 949–60.

[10] African Women's Protocol, *available at* http://www.africa-union.org/root/au/Documents/Treaties/Text/Protocol%20on%20the%20Rights%20of%20Women.pdf (accessed October 22, 2012).

[11] Article 9 of the African Women's Protocol – Right to Participation in the Political and Decision-Making Process.

1. States Parties shall take specific positive action to promote participative governance and the equal participation of women in the political life of their countries through affirmative action, enabling national legislation and other measures to ensure that
   (a) women participate without any discrimination in all elections;
   (b) women are represented equally at all levels with men in all electoral processes;
   (c) women are equal partners with men at all levels of development and implementation of State policies and development programs.

women in the judiciary and law enforcement organs[12] are based on an African tradition of women's empowerment. The underlying tradition of women's social entrepreneurship helps explain why African women's organizations remain at the forefront of the struggle for gender parity in continental political institutions at the local, national, and international levels.

This culture-based approach to women's rights is in keeping with the African Charter and with the African Women's Protocol, both of which elevate positive African cultural values.[13] It also stems from the need to make the historical fact that there is a matriarchal African tradition that can be opposed to the existing patriarchal one more widely known.[14] Tamale rightfully points out "the potential that culture holds for emancipating women in Africa."[15] Therefore, African feminists can and should appeal to African culture in their advocacy for respect for women's rights in the continent. If they do not bring to light the empowering norms and institutions that existed on the African continent before colonization, who will? Culture is nowhere static. Regarding Africa in particular, it is important not to let the cultural discourse be hijacked by those players who want to keep patriarchal control over African women, bearing in mind that, as Tamale writes, "most of what is understood as 'Culture' in contemporary Africa is largely a product of constructions and (re)interpretations by former colonial authorities in collaboration with African male patriarchs."[16]

2. States Parties shall ensure increased and effective representation and participation of women at all levels of decision-making.

[12] Art. 8 – Access to Justice and Equal Protection before the Law: "Women and men are equal before the law and shall have the right to equal protection and benefit of the law. States Parties shall take all appropriate measures to ensure: (. . .) c) that women are represented equally in the judiciary and law enforcement organs."

[13] According to the African Charter, art. 29, "The individual shall also have the duty: . . . 7. To preserve and strengthen positive African cultural values in his relations with other members of the society, in the spirit of tolerance, dialogue and consultation and, in general, to contribute to the promotion of the moral well being of society." Art. 61 refers to "African practices consistent with international norms on Human and Peoples' Rights," The African Women's Protocol recognizes "the crucial role of women in the preservation of African values based on the principles of equality, peace, freedom, dignity, justice, solidarity and democracy" (Preamble). Art. 17 is a provision on the "Right to Positive Cultural Context."

[14] "The opposition of 'culture' and 'rights' is not uncommon in feminist legal discourse. This paper argues that such an approach is fraught with danger, as it creates an extremely restrictive framework within which African women can challenge domination; it limits our strategic interventions for transforming society and essentially plays into the hands of those seeking to perpetuate and solidify the existing structures of patriarchy." Sylvia Tamale, *The right to culture and the culture of rights: A critical perspective on women's sexual rights in Africa, available at* http://fahamu.org/mbbc/wp-content/uploads/2011/09/Tamale-2007-Right-to-Culture.pdf (accessed November 5, 2012).

[15] *Id.* at 152.

[16] *Id.* at 153.

This chapter's central contention is that much of Africa's crippling legacy of patriarchal authoritarianism is foreign-born. In some areas, it is due to the spread of Islam, a religion very much marked by the patriarchal culture that surrounded and permeated the faith in its Middle Eastern birthplace. In other areas, the systemic victimization of women was either introduced or strengthened during European colonization and is hence one of several unfortunate offspring of the era of slavery and colonialism.[17] Ifi Amadiume accurately identifies a structure of violence and appropriation established in present-day Africa by a colonial order characterized by a monolithic, White male-gendered power structure[18] that is profoundly different from the many traditions that included strong female-generated social and moral values.[19] So, for example, Jeremy Levitt refers to the overly paternalistic and authoritarian regime established by the U.S. government in Liberia as "paternaltarianism."[20]

[17] Arlette Gautier, *Femmes et colonialisme*, LE LIVRE NOIR DU COLONIALISME, XVIE-XXE SIÈCLE: DE L'EXTERMINATION À LA REPENTANCE, 569–607 (M. Ferro ed., 2003); Cheikh Anta Diop, THE CULTURAL UNITY OF BLACK AFRICA: THE DOMAINS OF PATRIARCHY AND OF MATRIARCHY IN CLASSICAL ANTIQUITY (1989); Siga Sow, *The matriarchal system as a proof of the social role played by the woman in African traditional society*, THE CIVILIZATION OF THE WOMAN IN AFRICAN TRADITION 337–54 (1975); Milandré van Wyk, *Take a seat: Women's political representation in sub-Saharan Africa*, June 1, 2010, *available at* http://www.consultancyafrica.com/index.php?option=com_content&view=article&id=419:take-a-seat-womens-political-representation-in-sub-saharan-africa&catid=59:gender-issues-discussion-papers&Itemid=267 (accessed December 16, 2011).

[18] Amadiume very rightly emphasizes the following facts: "It was not the colonialists who dealt the final blow to the traditional autonomy and power of African women, however, but the elites who inherited the colonial machinery of oppression and exploitation, which they have turned against their own people." Ifi Amadiume, REINVENTING AFRICA, MATRIARCHY, RELIGION, CULTURE 177 (1997, second impression 2001); Fatou K. Camara, *Women and the law: A critique of the Senegalese family law*, 13 SOCIAL IDENTITIES JOURNAL FOR THE STUDY OF RACE, NATION AND CULTURE 787–800; Cheikh Anta Diop, "Africa's Cultural Unity" *in* TOWARDS THE AFRICAN RENAISSANCE, ESSAYS IN AFRICAN CULTURE & DEVELOPMENT: 1946–1960 130 (1996).

[19] Amadiume, *supra* note 18, at 15. Amadiume's analysis is based on the following definition of matriarchy: "Patriarchy and matriarchy are social and political ideologies which directly decide the role and status of women in society; how society is to be organized; and how social subjects are to relate to one another. They are also ideologies which decide the degree of violence and abuse of human rights that is permissible in society. Matriarchy as was constructed by African women, had a very clear message about social and economic justice. It was couched in a very powerful goddess-based religion, a strong ideology of motherhood, and a general moral principle of love." *Id.* at 101. In *The Queen Mother, matriarchy, and the question of female political authority in precolonial West African monarchy*, 27 (5) J. BLACK STUD. 579 (May 1997), Tarikhu Farrar defines the Eurocentric view of matriarchy as follows: "It is the world turned upside down; a world in which women become ruthless, petty dictators in a family form and a society under their domination. ... When scholars began to search for actual examples of this type of society, historically and ethnographically, they could not find any."

[20] Jeremy L. Levitt, THE EVOLUTION OF DEADLY CONFLICT IN LIBERIA: FROM "PATERNALTARIANISM" TO STATE COLLAPSE (2005).

Considering those facts, this chapter aims to show how modern feminism can be informed by African gender-sensitive laws and institutions. Parity in decision-making bodies is the most striking example. The quality of this example reflects the fact that this is a right closely related to the much longer history (characterized by feminism and/or female militancy) of social entrepreneurship of women in Africa.

THE AFRICAN WOMEN'S PROTOCOL: THE VOICE OF AFRICAN WOMEN

It is especially important to emphasize the African character of the African Women's Protocol precisely because opponents of equality and gender equity on the continent often base their arguments on the spurious claim that Western imperialism is at work, trying to impose foreign constructions on Africans. Consequently, showing that the African Women's Protocol does indeed carry the voice of African women is the focus of the first paragraph. Another label used to stigmatize African feminist activists is that they are "alienated" or "elite" women who operate outside their own culture and tradition and should therefore be considered and treated as outcasts. The second paragraph of this first section will put such claims to rest by firmly anchoring the advocacy movement for women's rights on the historical continuum of an African tradition of female social entrepreneurship.

A Process Led by African Women's Movements

In 2002, the transformation of the OAU into the AU[21] brought new developments and initiatives, especially with regard to the protection of human rights on the continent.[22] For example, Article 4(L) of the Constitutive Act of the AU specifically provides that the AU "shall function in accordance with the

[21] The Constitutive Act of the AU expressly states that its main objectives are to promote and protect human and peoples' rights in accordance with the African Charter and other relevant human rights instruments, to promote gender equality and social justice, to ensure balanced economic development, and to condemn and reject impunity and unconstitutional changes of government. On the transformation of the OAU into the AU, *see* note 7.

[22] Rachel Murray, Human Rights in Africa: From the OAU to the African Union (2004); Adrien Katherine Wing & Tyler Murray Smith, *The New African Union and women's rights*, 3 Transnat'l. L. & Contemp. Probs. 33 (2003); Ben Kioko, *The African Union and the implementation of the decisions of the African Court on Human and Peoples' Rights*, 15 Interights Bulletin 7, *available at* http://www.interights.org/document/49/index.html (accessed September 3, 2011); George Mukindi Wachira, Report, *African Court on Human and Peoples' Rights: Ten years on and still no justice*, *available at* http://www.unhcr.org/refworld/pdfid/48e4763c2.pdf (accessed October 17, 2011); Mutua, *supra* note 4.

promotion of gender equality." The existing African Women Committee on Peace and Development was changed into the AU Women's Committee (AUWC) by a July 2004 decision of the AU's Executive Council.[23] The AUWC was established as an advisory body to the chairperson on gender and development.[24] The Committee is composed of twenty African women of "high moral standing and proven integrity"[25] who are appointed by the chairperson of the commission. The AUWC's main function is to watch over progress and make recommendations toward gender equality on the continent, within the framework of the Solemn Declaration on Gender Equality in Africa (SDGEA).[26]

In addition, this AU gender policy was pursued through the adoption of a gender parity policy within the Commission. The Commission is the Secretariat of the AU entrusted with executive functions. It represents the AU and protects its interest under the auspices of the Assembly of Heads of State and Government, as well as under the Executive Committee. It is composed of ten officials: a chairperson,[27] a deputy chairperson, and eight commissioners.[28]

According to the *Gender Is My Agenda* campaign website, gender parity in the African Commission is the direct result of the lobbying of a network of African women's organizations.[29] So is the landmark decision to adopt the African Women's Protocol during the Second Ordinary Session of the Assembly in Maputo, Mozambique, 2003.

In an article published by the African Centre for Gender and Development posted on the website of the United Nations Economic Commission for

[23] African Union's Concept Note, fourth meeting of African Union Women's Committee (AUWC), April 29 2009, Addis Ababa, Ethiopia. *Available at* the Gender Directorate website, http://www.africa-union.org/structure_of_the_commission/women,%20gender%20and%20development.htm (accessed October 29, 2012).

[24] "The Women, Gender and Development Directorate (Gender Directorate) is the vehicle via which the Commission advances the principle of gender equality through gender mainstreaming." *Id.*

[25] *Id.*

[26] At the Third Ordinary Session of the African Union (AU) Assembly of Heads of State and Government in Addis Ababa, Ethiopia, in July 2004, the Heads of State and Government adopted the Solemn Declaration on Gender Equality in Africa (SDGEA), *available at* http://www.africa-union.org/root/au/conferences/past/2006/October/WG/doc.htm (accessed October 29, 2012).

[27] A woman, former South African Home Affairs Minister Dr. Nkosazana Dlamini Zuma, is the incoming chairperson of the African Union (AU) Commission. She was elected July 15, 2012.

[28] See the African Union Commission official website: http://www.au.int/en/commission (accessed August 12, 2012), and arts. 5 and 20, African Union Constitutive Act.

[29] *Available at* http://www.genderismyagenda.com/campaign/previous.html (accessed October 29, 2012).

Africa, tribute is expressly paid to the African women's movement: "Thanks to the concerted action of non-governmental organizations, including the International Commission of Jurists (ICJ), the organization 'Women in Law and Development in Africa' (WiLDAF) land the African Centre for Democracy and Human Rights Studies in Banjul, international seminars were held on women's rights in Africa, in close cooperation and/or under the auspices of the African Commission."[30]

More than a decade ago, the same players organized a seminar in Lomé, in March 1995, on the topic, "The African Charter on Human and Peoples' Rights and the African Woman."[31] Among the recommendations of the Lomé seminar is the adoption by the OAU of a protocol to the African Charter on the Rights of Women; another is the appointment by the African Commission of a Special Rapporteur on Women's Human Rights. Both recommendations were endorsed first by the Commission and later by the June 1995 OAU Conference of Heads of State and Government. Following this approval, the African Commission established a Working Group on the Protocol to the Charter on the Rights of Women in Africa,[32] and, in 1998, appointed Commissioner Julienne Ondziel-Gnelenga (Congo–Brazzaville) to the post of Special Rapporteur on the Rights of Women.[33] Drafting the Protocol was the main task of the Special Rapporteur. She enlisted support from various African women's organizations.[34]

30 Mubiala, *supra* note 7.

31 *Id.*

32 The Working Group held its first session on the draft Protocol in Banjul, January 26–28, 1998. Mubiala, *supra* note 7.

33 "On the occasion of its 25th Ordinary Session held in Bujumbura, Burundi, from 26 April to 5 May 1999, the African Commission adopted resolution ACHPR/res. 38 (XXV) 99 on the appointment of a Special Rapporteur on the Rights of Women in Africa. The Resolution appointed the first Special Rapporteur in May 1999 retroactively as from October 1998," *available at* the African Commission website, http://www.achpr.org/mechanisms/rights-of-women/about/ (accessed October 29, 2012). Commissioner Julienne Ondziel Gnelenga served from 1998 to 2001 and retired. When her time with the Commission ended, Commissioner Angela Melo served from October 2001 to November 2007. The current Special Rapporteur on Women's Rights is Soyata Maïga.

34 These organizations include WiLDAF and FEMNET. WiLDAF is a pan-African network conceived through a conference entitled *Women, Law and Development: Networking for Empowerment in Africa* held in Harare, Zimbabwe, in 1990. The aim of the conference was to establish an organization that promotes and strengthens a society that strives to empower women and improve their status in Africa. Official WILDAF website: http://www.WiLDAF.org/index.php/whoweare/history (accessed October 29, 2012). The African Communications and Development Network (FEMNET) was set up in 1988 to share experiences, information and strategies among African women's non-governmental organizations through advocacy, training and communications in order to advance African women's development, equality, and other human rights. Official FEMNET website: http://femnet.co/index.php/en/ (accessed September 3, 2013).

The Association for Women's Rights in Development (AWID) interviewed Fazia Jama Mohamed, director of Equality Now, about the Solidarity for African Women's Rights (SOAWR) campaign for the ratification and implementation of the African Women's Protocol.[35] When asked to recount how the African Women's Protocol was developed and how women's groups mobilized to get it adopted, she outlined the fact that the African Communications and Development Network (FEMNET) raised concern that the draft Protocol was weak and that experts had adopted it with the exception of three provisions that they agreed to revisit after country consultations.[36] She also pointed out that after consultations with FEMNET, WiLDAF, and the African Centre for Democracy and Human Rights Studies (ACDHRS), Equality Now, an organization based in New York, showed solidarity with the African-based nongovernmental organizations (NGOs) by convening a two-day consultative meeting of women's organizations in January 2003, in Addis Ababa. Massan d'Almeida of AWID reports that, "Following that meeting, we generated a mark-up of the draft Protocol showing areas of weaknesses that needed to be improved, also providing stronger language for provisions that the participants found to be of lower standard than CEDAW."[37]

Gender ministers[38] adopted the Protocol with most of the recommended changes. However, Massan adds, the AU had difficulty in getting a quorum to convene the second meeting of experts, a meeting that was to conclude adoption of the Protocol.

In a private interview, Said Djinnit, who was then Deputy General Secretary for Political Affairs of the OAU from 1999 until 2003, explained how he struck a deal with African women from FEMNET to overcome that challenge. In exchange for his support of the Beijing platform, the African leaders' consensus on the issue of women's rights as well as on "plus

[35] Massan d'Almeida, *African women's organizing for the ratification and implementation of the Maputo Protocol*, AWID website, http://awid.org/eng/News-Analysis/Friday-Files/African-Women-s-Organizing-for-the-Ratification-and-Implementation-of-the-Maputo-Protocol (accessed October 29, 2012).

[36] Said Djinnit was Deputy General Secretary for Political Affairs of the OAU from 1999 until 2003; he is presently the Special Representative of the UN Secretary General for West Africa and has been head of the UN Office for West Africa since 2007. He said in a private interview (June 3, 2011, UNOWA office in Dakar) that at the meeting of the group of experts that took place in 1999, all provisions were approved except three critical ones: (1) the monitoring process, (2) the issue of polygamy, and (3) the right to safe abortion.

[37] d'Almeida, *supra* note 35.

[38] The Gender Ministry's role is to facilitate the implementation of National Gender Policies and Plans of Action to ensure effective gender mainstreaming and full participation of women in all activities related to the socioeconomic development of the nation. Its aim is to promote equality and equity for both men and women.

questions,"[39] they would lobby the relevant ministers and request that the commission of experts in charge of drafting the protocol on women's rights would actually meet (by that time, the meeting had already been cancelled three times). He recalls the impact of this intense African women's movement lobbying as having been successful because the experts' meeting finally took place and was followed by a meeting of the AU Executive Council.

The draft Protocol was adopted by the Executive Council in the presence of Said Djinnit, who, holding to the deal he made with the women's groups, wholly supported it. The last hurdle was the Heads of States and Governments summit. The Protocol was adopted on July 11, 2003, during the Second Ordinary Heads of States and Governments Summit held in Maputo, Mozambique.

One year after its adoption, only one African state, the Union of the Comoros, had ratified the Protocol, and there was a concern that its ratification and domestication would take time. Consequently, in 2004, the SOAWR coalition began its campaign for the ratification and implementation of the African Women's Protocol. According to Faiza Mohamed, the campaign was quite aggressive:

> In the beginning, in order to get the 15 ratifications needed for the Protocol to enter into force, SOAWR focused on AU Summits and engaging media to show which states had ratified, not ratified and those who had not signed on to the Protocol at all. For example we handed out red, green and yellow cards to Member States, in the presence of the Press. At the beginning this strategy was useful because in 2003, only one country has ratified the Protocol, so there was need for very aggressive advocacy at the Summit level. At national levels, we have mobilized our members and other CSOs to put pressure on their governments to ratify the Protocol.[40]

This campaign was also successful.[41] The African Women's Protocol made history by breaking all records for the ratification of continental human rights instruments in Africa.[42] By December 2011, of the fifty-four AU member countries, forty-nine had signed the protocol; thirty-one of those countries

[39] The Protocol contains very progressive provisions – which are not even in CEDAW – mainly women's rights to control their fertility and to access safe medical abortion (art. 14) and gender parity at all levels in electoral processes (art. 9). The Protocol also addresses specific harmful cultural practices such as female genital mutilation (art. 5).

[40] d'Almeida, *supra* note 35.

[41] *See Update on the campaign on ratification, domestication and popularization of the Protocol on the Rights of Women in Africa, Pambazuka News*, January 17, 2001, Issue 238, *available at* http://pambazuka.org/en/category/wgender/31284 (accessed August 13, 2012).

[42] The African Charter for Human and Peoples' Rights was adopted in 1981 but only came into force in 1986. The Protocol establishing the African Court on Human and Peoples' Rights

had ratified it (58.5 percent of AU member states);[43] and only four countries have not yet signed the Protocol. The only countries that have not signed the AU African Women's Protocol are Botswana,[44] Egypt, Eritrea, and Tunisia.[45]

Implementation of the rights enshrined within the Protocol is the current challenge.[46] However, history teaches us that African women have overcome equally daunting challenges in times that were no less trying than the present. There is indeed a long tradition of feminist activism or feminist social entrepreneurship[47] in Africa. As has been noted in an article analyzing the

came into force in 2004, six years after its adoption in 1998. The African Charter on the Rights and Welfare of the Child, which was adopted in 1990, came into force nine years later.

43 "Some of the provisions preventing some countries from ratifying the Protocol are those on inheritance, equal rights in marriage and reproductive rights. Kenya and Uganda for example have ratified the Protocol with reservations on article 14 related to reproductive rights, in particular women's rights to control their fertility and to access safe, medical abortion." Massan d'Almeida, November 11, 2011, comments on AWID's article, *African women's organizing for the ratification and implementation of the Maputo Protocol*, posted on AWID's website, http://awid.org/eng/News-Analysis/Friday-Files/African-Women-s-Organizing-for-the-Ratification-and-Implementation-of-the-Maputo-Protocol (accessed October 29, 2012).

44 According to the Africa for Women's Rights, Ratify and Respect! website: "The Coalition of the Campaign is particularly concerned about the following continued violations of women's human rights in Botswana: application of discriminatory customary laws; access to property; violence against women; access to decision-making positions; access to employment and health services; and the persistence of discriminatory stereotypes and patriarchal attitudes." *Available at* http://www.africa4womensrights.org/public/Dossier_of_Claims/BotswanaENG.pdf (accessed August 13, 2012).

45 One can infer from the following facts the reason why Tunisia has not signed or ratified the African Women's Protocol: "Although Tunisia has ratified the Convention on the Elimination of All Forms of Discrimination against Women (CEDAW), it entered a general declaration stating that only those provisions that are consistent with the Tunisian Constitution will be applied. Tunisia also entered reservations to the following articles: art. 9(2) concerning transmission of nationality; art. 16 concerning marriage and inheritance; and art. 15(4) concerning the choice of residence. The Coalition of the Campaign underlines that these reservations violate international law in that they are incompatible with the object and purpose of the Convention." Africa for Women's Rights, Ratify and Respect!, *available at* http://www.africa4womensrights.org/public/Dossier_of_Claims/TunisiaENG.pdf (accessed August 13, 2012).

46 *See generally* Kristin Davis, *supra* note 9.

47 Roger L. Martin & Sally Osberg, *Social entrepreneurship: The case for definition*, Stan. Soc. Innov. Rev. 29–36 (Spring 2007), *available at* http://www.ngobiz.org/picture/File/Social%20Entrepreneur-The%20Case%20of%20Definition.pdf (accessed October 28, 2012): "We define social entrepreneurship as having the following three components: (1) identifying a stable but inherently unjust equilibrium that causes the exclusion, marginalization, or suffering of a segment of humanity that lacks the financial means or political clout to achieve any transformative benefit on its own; (2) identifying an opportunity in this unjust equilibrium, developing a social value proposition, and bringing to bear inspiration, creativity, direct action, courage, and fortitude, thereby challenging the stable state's hegemony; and (3) forging a new, stable equilibrium that releases trapped potential or alleviates the suffering of the targeted group, and through imitation and the creation of a stable ecosystem around the new equilibrium ensuring a better future for the targeted group and even society at large." *Id.* at 35.

meaning of social entrepreneurship, "the language of social entrepreneurship may be new, but the phenomenon is not. We have always had social entrepreneurs, even if we did not call them that. They originally built many of the institutions we now take for granted."[48]

In Africa and on the other continents where they were deported as slaves, African women have accomplished social missions with innovation,[49] determination, and discipline. It is important for present-day female African women's rights activists to emphasize the fact that they are only putting their feet on the path their female ancestors repeatedly cleared for them centuries ago. Therefore, one might argue that women in Africa were "social entrepreneurs" and "feminists" long before the terms were invented.

A Process Anchored in African Women's Social Entrepreneurship Tradition

Comparing the situation of freed "Circassian" (White) slaves[50] to that of freed "Abyssinian" (Black) slaves ("the negresses"),[51] Lucy M. J. Garnett describes the latter in the following way: "It is only the negresses who always remain a class apart, and fall not infrequently into penury and want. As a rule, however, they are themselves chiefly to blame for their misfortunes. For, after they have been freed and married, it not infrequently happens that their ungoverned tempers cause them to quarrel with, and separate from, their husbands, when they are obliged to support themselves as best they can by hawking parched peas and such trifles about the streets."[52]

[48] "Social entrepreneurs are one special breed of leader, and they should be recognized as such. This definition preserves their distinctive status and assures that social entrepreneurship is not treated lightly. We need social entrepreneurs to help us find new avenues toward social improvement as we enter the next century." Gregory Dees, *The meaning of social entrepreneurship, available at* http://www.caseatduke.org/documents/dees_sedef.pdf (accessed September 3, 2013).

[49] "Entrepreneurs are innovative. They break new ground, develop new models, and pioneer new approaches. However, as Schumpeter notes, innovation can take many forms. It does not require inventing something wholly new; it can simply involve applying an existing idea in a new way or to a new situation. Entrepreneurs need not be inventors. They simply need to be creative in applying what others have invented." *Id.*

[50] "At the present day the white slaves are brought chiefly from Circassia, the rest being Yezidis from Kurdistan, or Georgians though, since the occupation by Russia of that former happy hunting-ground of the slave-dealer, this traffic has only been carried on clandestinely." Lucy M. J. Garnett, The Turkish People, Their Social Life, Religious Beliefs and Institutions and Domestic Life 224, *available at* http://www.archive.org/stream/turkishpeopletheoogarnrich/turkishpeopletheoogarnrich_djvu.txt (accessed December 24, 2011).

[51] "A considerable number of negroes, as also of Abyssinians and other Africans of both sexes, are, however, still annually smuggled into the country." *Id.* at 225.

[52] *Id.* at 226.

What is meant as a criticism is in fact the observation of a cultural trait common to many African communities: women's autonomy, whether or not they are married.[53] In a paper with the revealing title, "The Myth of the Inferiority of the African Woman," Thelma Awori states: "African women have always been an economic asset to both their husbands and their fathers and this single factor made her subjugation and domination a little more difficult. … Amongst agricultural people her work in the fields was responsible for much of what was the family wealth. … It is not unknown in traditional African society for women to achieve great independence through their own economic activities."[54]

Another cultural feature common in many African cultures is the setting up of "sororities"[55] (women's associations). This tradition of forming associations along gender lines can be documented in various times and in different African societies.[56] In Turkey, Garnett informs us that the Black women's associations are each headed by a priestess, "the Kolbashi," whose role is not only to perform African religious rituals, but also to manage the property of the group. The way this property is amassed exactly reflects the practice called "tontine" in Senegal and "Esusu" by the Yoruba in Nigeria. Every day, week, or month (according to what has been decided by the group), each member of the sorority makes a contribution. The destination of the capital thus collected is agreed upon beforehand by all members. In the case of the Black women in Turkey, Garnett notes that the Kolbashi is expected to use the funds "to purchase the freedom of negress slaves who are on bad terms with their owners, as also to receive in her house freed women who are sick or without employment."[57] Although Black men are also entitled to receive assistance from the sororities, Garnett points out that

[53] Fatou K. Camara & Saliou S. M. Kanji, L'UNION MATRIMONIALE DANS LA TRADITION DES PEOPLES NOIRS (2000).

[54] Sow, *supra* note 17, at 35, 36.

[55] They are called *mbootaay* (in Wolof orthography "oo" reads as in the "o" in "tort") by the Wolof in Senegal. It is a term derived from the verb "boot," which means to carry someone on one's back, the way African women carry babies.

[56] See Tarikhu Farrar, *supra* note 19, at 588; Simi Afonja, *Nigerian women in traditional public affairs*, *in* CIVILIZATION OF THE WOMAN supra note 17, at 367–76; Josephine Dikeble & Madeleine Hiba, *The woman in the traditional political life of societies in the center, east and south-east of the Ivory Coast States*, *id.*, 377–88; Cheikh Anta Diop, BLACK AFRICA: THE ECONOMIC AND CULTURAL BASIS FOR A FEDERAL STATE 33 (1987); Fatou Kiné Camara, *Women and political power in the Black African tradition: Maat and matriarchy*, 18, 19, 20 ANKH, JOURNAL OF EGYPTOLOGY AND AFRICAN CIVILIZATIONS, 143–55 (2009–2010–2011).

[57] Garnett, *supra* note 50, at 226.

they take no part in the rites and ceremonies that are led by the Kolbashi,[58] a fact that demonstrates that these women are totally in control of their institution.

The African women held captive and brought as slaves in Turkey took with them what their captors could not take from them: their culture. Once freed, African women resumed their tradition of forming associations with the mission not only to educate, help, and protect their members, but also to have a positive transformative impact on their society.[59]

African women's economic role has not been confined to the household. As a matter of fact, even to date, the African societies engaged in subsistence agriculture see women playing the major role in food production and processing (with a lot of surplus) and, in the craft industries, becoming major traders both at the local and regional levels.[60] In most of West Africa, marketplaces

[58] *Id.*

[59] B. S. Diouf gives an example of how those gendered organizations ensured a society where women had the means to uphold their rights to respect and fair treatment peacefully: "Suka Mbul was married to Njem Selbe Naadi (the mother of Coumba Ndofène Diouf II, king of Sine-Sereer kingdom in pre-colonial Senegal – from 1898 to 1924). The couple had irreconcilable differences and in order to solve them, Njem Selbe Naadi took up residence at the village's well where the women of 'Ngulook' (the association of women initiates) joined her, out of gender solidarity. For three days and three nights, they danced and sang, deserting their homes completely. Then the men of the 'Kasak' (the association of men initiates), with Suka at the head, came to ask for reconciliation with the 'Ngulook.' They brought an ox as a peace offering. And peace returned in the homes when the ox was cut up and cooked, the couscous of renewed alliance and mutual respect was consumed while the drums were beating." Babacar Sedikh Diouf, "La dimension genre dans le 'vivre ensemble' africain" (Gender in the African way of Life), unpublished article.

[60] Such is the case in Yoruba country. It is so much so that Bolanle notes: "The instinct to trade is almost inborn and is nurtured from childhood; a Yoruba girl learns not only to produce a particular commodity but also how to market it." Awe Bolanle, *The economic role of women in a traditional African society, the Yoruba example*, CIVILIZATION OF THE WOMAN, *supra* note 17, at 268; Amadiume gives a list of the wide variety of products women traded on the many marketplaces they created and controlled: "The internal trade was an autonomous economy based on agricultural and craft products, such as salt, grain, cloth, cotton thread, textiles, shea butter, dried fish, kola nuts, tobacco, iron and gold, spices, scents and perfumes, dyes, medicinal herbs, roots and fresh steroids from certain trees, medicinal and mystical knowledge, secrets, etc." Amadiume, *supra* note 18, at 96. She concludes: "Europeans had nothing to do with this extensive network of distribution and trade. Consequently, when historians refer to Europeans in Africa as traders, we wonder what they mean, since the evidence shows that what the Europeans exchanged for land and slaves were no more than gun powder, muskets, alcohol and sometimes amber and coral beads. These were goods directed at the local rulers. They were therefore exchanging nothing that was of benefit to African people; on the contrary, by the time the Europeans were through with their mission, they had appropriated the people's lands, flooded the place with European consumer goods, undermined the agricultural economy and colonized Africans." *Id.* at 96.

served not only as places to exchange goods but also to socialize, discuss events, and, when needed, organize collective actions.[61]

This social organization allowed African women to participate very effectively in anticolonial struggles. For instance, the two-month resistance movement called the "Aba Women's War," which took place across southeastern Nigeria in 1929, was led by market women.[62] Such was again the case in 1940, with the Abeokuta[63] market women's protests.[64] These determined and organized women had tremendous mobilizing power, and they demonstrated it in Nigeria.[65] Women also joined postcolonial struggles such as the Ugandan National Resistance Movement. Their active participation in the civil war, on the winning side, is given as an explanation for the quota system that reserves a certain number of legislative seats for women.[66] In South Africa, Black women organized campaigns against the "pass laws."[67] In 1933, at the annual African National Congress (ANC) conference, ANC president Pixley ka Isaka Seme acknowledged, "No national movement can be strong unless the women volunteers come forward and offer their services to the nation."[68] Later the same year, the ANC general secretary reiterated those comments, saying, "No

[61] *Id.* at 102. In Senegal, the Wolof have a saying that illustrates the social role of markets: "*Ku dee ci marse yaa tàgge sa bopp*" ("the one who dies in a market has made his/her own media death announcement").

[62] Sokari Ekine & Emem Okon, *Conversation-building alliances in the women's movement: The challenges of feminist mobilisation in Nigeria, in* The Challenges of Change, Building Feminist Political Influence in Africa, *available at* http://www.boell.org.za/downloads/Perspectives_2.11_web.pdf (accessed December 16, 2011).

[63] Southwest Nigeria.

[64] Ekine & Okon, *supra* note 62.

[65] Ekine & Okon note the following about the Aba Women's War: "The women – some twenty-five thousand strong in places – attacked the colonial system: prisons, courts and European-owned shops, as well as the warrant officers themselves. They were able to force the colonial authorities to drop the taxes and curb the warrant officers." *Id.*

[66] "Uganda's system of reserved seats for women, established in 1986, [has been interpreted] as President Yoweri Museveni's acknowledgment of women's contributions to the victory of his National Resistance Movement in the Ugandan civil war. Women harboured and fed soldiers, hid weapons in their homes, and fought alongside the men against Milton Obote's forces." M. Y. Yoon, Explaining women's legislative representation in sub-Saharan Africa, 29 (3) LEGISL. STUD. Q. 447–68, cited in van Wyk, *supra* note 17.

[67] "In July 1913 a crowd of six hundred women had handed in their passes to the Mayor of Bloemfontein, refusing to carry them in future. Similar demonstrations took place in Jagersfontein, Fauresmith, and Winburg. The women were arrested and given sentences of imprisonment and hard labour. Despite the privations they suffered during their stay in prison, they declared they would never buy passes even if they had to return to prison." Judy Kimble & Elaine Unterhalter, "*We opened the road for you, you must go forward*": *ANC Women's Struggles,* 1912–1982, 12 FEMINIST REV. 11 (1982). In 1918, Charlotte Maxeke started the first formal women's organization (Bantu Women's League), which was created to resist the pass laws.

[68] *Id.* at 20.

people or nation can rise to its legitimate aspirations without the aid of the women."[69]

Although the reality and the legitimacy of female political power in ancient and precolonial Africa is disputed by some scholars,[70] the very fact that the first queens recorded in history are Africans tells its own story.[71] Queenship is an undeniable fixture of Africa's history. In addition, all through African history, from earliest times, women have risen as commanders-in-chief when their countries were under attack or met with troubled times. In ancient Egypt, c. 1200 BCE, in an era when her country needed powerful leadership, queen Tausret was "the Powerful One," according to Egyptologists.[72] In ancient Soudan, it was the *Kandake* (title of the "queen mother" in Kush/Meroe) who fought the Roman army, the most powerful army in the world (25–21 BCE); she was described by the Greek historian Strabo as having been a formidable opponent.[73] In the Wolof and Sereer kingdoms of precolonial Senegal, the *lingeers* (*lingeer* is the title of the "queen mother") Yaasin Bubu (17th c.),[74] Ngoné Lattir (17th c.)[75], Njombot Mbooj (19th c.), and Ndatte Yàlla (19th c.)[76] made history as outstanding political and military leaders in difficult times. In Angola, Queen Nzinga is equally remembered as the leader who stood up against Portuguese colonial conquest.[77] In Ghana, Queen

[69] *Id.*

[70] Liz Dimock, *Women's leadership roles in the early Protestant Church in Uganda: Continuity with the old order*, 25 (2) AUSTRALASIAN REV. AFRICAN STUD. 8 (2003); John K. Thornton, *Legitimacy and political power: Queen Njinga, 1624–1663*, 32(1) J. AFRICAN HISTORY 25–40 (1991).

[71] The Kandake of Kush and Meroe; Queen Sheba of Ethiopia and Yemen; Queen/Pharaohs Nitocris and Hatshepsut of Ancient Egypt. Angelika Lohwasser, *Queenship in Kush: Status, role and ideology of royal women*, 38 J. AM. RES. CTR. EGYPT 61–76 (2001); Miriam Ma'At-Ka-Re Monges, *Reflections on the role of female deities and queens in ancient Kemet*, 23 (4) J. BLACK STUD. 561–70 (June 1993); Barbara S. Lesko, *Women's monumental mark on ancient Egypt*, 54 (1) BIBLICAL ARCHAEOLOGIST 4 (March 1991).

[72] Vivienne G. Callender, *Queen Tausret and the end of dynasty* 19, Bd. 32 STUDIEN ZUR ALTÄGYPTISCHEN KULTUR 81, 88 (2004); TAUSER: FORGOTTEN QUEEN AND PHARAOH OF EGYPT (Richard H. Wilkinson ed., 2012).

[73] See Molefi Kete Asante & Ama Mazama, ENCYCLOPEDIA OF BLACK STUDIES 302 (2004).

[74] She opposed an army of the "Muslim party" who wanted to impose sharia law in the kingdom. Majhemout Diop, 2 HISTOIRE DES CLASSES SOCIALES DANS L'AFRIQUE DE L'OUEST 34–35 (1985).

[75] She is recorded in oral history as having led the army of her father, the ailing king/*damel* Lat Sukkaabe, to victory in the fight against an invading army.

[76] Boubacar Barry, LE ROYAUME DU WAALO 263, 275 (1985). Njombot Mbooj and Ndatté Yàlla were sisters who succeeded each other to the throne of Waalo (Senegal) as *lingeer*. They both fought valiantly against the French colonial occupation.

[77] Thornton, *supra* note 70, John K. Thornton, *Elite women in the kingdom of Kongo: Historical perspectives on women's political power*, 47 (3) J. AFRICAN HIST. 437(2006).

Mother Yaa Asantewaa (c. 1830s–1921) was celebrated for commanding Asante military forces in the 1900 Asante uprising against the British colonial army.[78] In Niger, in 1899, the Azna people's resistance to the deadly French war machine was led by Queen Sarraounia.[79]

Mama says of these legacies, "They suggest that women on the African continent did not derive their impulses for freedom from those eccentric and well-intentioned Western women who travelled south to educate and uplift us. Indeed, it might be worth considering the reverse possibility: that African women's various actions may well have served to inspire European and North American women, and so contributed to the genesis of modern feminism."[80]

Present-day African women's rights activists should carry out their advocacy programs with the clear knowledge of all that has been done in past centuries by women on the African continent. They will carry the torch with a firmer hand with such knowledge. For instance, affirmative action as a way to advance the gender equity and equality agenda is quite a controversial measure; however, African feminists must include in their analysis of this measure the evaluation of the gender-sensitive institutions that existed in precolonial Africa.

THE PROVISION FOR EQUAL PARTICIPATION OF MEN AND WOMEN IN DECISION-MAKING BODIES: A CULTURAL HERITAGE

Article 9 of the African Women's Protocol makes it mandatory for states and parties to take specific positive action to promote the equal participation of women in the political life of their countries and to ensure increased and effective representation and participation of women at all levels of decision making through affirmative action.

In many precolonial African communities, gender parity in political institutions was mandatory. Indeed, giving women a voice and a place in decision-making bodies is a fixture of precolonial African laws and institutions that should be appropriated as another contribution to modern feminism. In Senegal, from 2005 to 2010, a women's rights movement successfully

[78] T. C. McCaskie, *The life and afterlife of Yaa Asantewaa*, 77 (2) Africa 151–79 (2007).

[79] Ousmane Tandina & Richard Bjornson, *Sarraounia, an epic?* 24 (2) Res. African Lit., Special Issue on Oral Literature 23, 23, 26 (Summer 1993).

[80] Amina Mama, 4 Feminist Africa – Women Mobilised (2005) Editorial, *available at* http://www.feministafrica.org/index.php/regional-networking (accessed December 16, 2011).

campaigned for gender parity in electoral assemblies, anchoring its advocacy discourse on the slogan "Gender parity is our heritage."[81]

The Lead Taken by African Countries in Implementing Affirmative Action Programs for Female Representation

In Rwanda, the Constitution has provisions that grant women "at least thirty per cent of posts in decision making organs."[82] As a result, after the elections in October 2004, women held 48.8 percent of the seats in the National Assembly, and Rwanda became the country with the biggest percentage of women in a national assembly; Sweden was a close second, with women holding 45 percent of the seats in the national parliament.[83] Rwanda's second parliamentary elections since the 1994 genocide took place on September 15–18, 2008. Women secured forty-five out of the eighty available seats, making the Rwandan parliament the first in the world to have women in the majority with 56.2 percent.[84]

Shirley Randell makes the noteworthy observation that raising women's status in decision-making bodies is solely a matter of political will.[85] In support of that statement, she gives the following argument: "Rwanda's achievement outshines that of wealthy countries with huge investments in gender equality spanning decades, and it demystifies the perception that poverty or underdevelopment equals women's marginalisation and disempowerment."[86]

Milandré Van Wyck shares the same analysis, which she backs with the following statistics (from a 2010 paper): "A focus on socio-economic development does not fully explain the obstacles to female political representation, as a comparison between countries such as Canada (where 20% of

[81] Conseil sénégalais des femmes (COSEF), Council of Senegalese Women and the Steering Committee of the campaign "Let's Consolidate Democracy with Gender Parity."

[82] Constitution of the Republic of Rwanda, chapter 2, arts. 9, 76, 82, *available at* http://www.rwandahope.com/constitution.pdf (accessed August 12, 2012).

[83] UNDP Newsroom, *Rwanda's Parliament now leads world in gender parity*, *available at* http://content.undp.org/go/newsroom/choices-rwandas-parliament-now-leads-world-in-gender-parity-2004–12.en (accessed January 2, 2012).

[84] *Rwandan Women secure 56% of parliamentary seats in historic election result*, U.N. Women website: http://www.unifem.org/news_events/story_detail.php?StoryID=736 (accessed January 2, 2012); Shirley Randell, *Report from Rwanda: Rebuilding in the wake of catastrophe*, Communication for Social Change Consortium, *available at* http://www.communicationforsocialchange.org/mazi-articles.php?id=388 (accessed October 30, 2012).

[85] *Contra* Kristin Davis who holds that Rwanda's achievement is a direct consequence of the disproportionately high deaths of men during the 1994 Rwandan genocide; Davis, *supra* note 9, at 981, note 220.

[86] Randell, *supra* note 84.

Parliamentarians are women), the United States (13%) and South Africa (30%) clearly illustrates. In sub-Saharan Africa, one of the world's poorest regions, 13 out of 39 states' Parliamentary seats are filled with at least 15% women[87]. In other words, some 'poor' countries currently have more women representatives in government that some 'rich' countries do."[88]

So it is indeed political will and not socioeconomic factors that determines gender equality in decision-making bodies. The African Women's Protocol upholds that point of view and so do the African women's movements that advocate for its ratification and implementation. The attempt to explain Rwanda's achievement in electing a parliament that is 50 percent female as a consequence of its particular situation due to the genocide is negated by the fact that other African countries are successfully implementing affirmative action programs.

In South Africa, women's representation in the National Assembly increased to 45 percent at the June 2009 legislative election, putting South Africa third in the ranks of nations with the highest proportion of women in parliamentary bodies, behind Rwanda and Sweden.[89] According to a Johannesburg-based NGO, Gender Links, "this achievement has come about as a result of voluntary party quotas as opposed to legislated quotas."[90]

In Senegal, the latest legislative elections (July 1, 2012) gave women 65 of the 150 seats of the National Assembly. This result puts Senegal in the top ten of countries with more than 40 percent of women in Parliament. It was achieved thanks to the campaign for gender parity in electoral assemblies led by a

[87] Eileen Connolly, *Women's representation in national parliaments in sub-Saharan Africa: An ideational framework for investigation*, Working Papers in International Studies Centre for International Studies Dublin City University. Working Paper 2 of 2005, *available at* http://doras.dcu.ie/2128/1/2005–2.pdf (accessed November 6, 2012).

[88] van Wyk, *supra* note 17; Aili Mari Tripp, *Regional networking as transnational feminism: African experiences*, 4 Feminist Africa – Women Mobilised (2005), *available at* http://www.feministafrica.org/index.php/regional-networking (accessed December 16th 2011): "Africa has some of the highest rates of female representation in the world today. Rwanda became the country with the largest percentage of women parliamentarians in the world after women claimed almost 49% of the seats in the country's 2003 parliamentary elections. Women held 46% of parliamentary seats in Seychelles between 1991 and 1993. Today, women in South Africa, Mozambique, and Seychelles hold one-third of parliamentary seats; women in Swaziland hold one-third of the seats in the upper house of parliament; in Namibia, women hold 42% of seats in local government; and in Uganda, they hold one-third."

[89] Bathandwa Mbola, *Women in parliament on the rise*, SouthAfrica.Info, May 6, 2009, *available at* http://www.southafrica.info/about/democracy/parlyw-060509.htm#.UI_SXLF2uO8 (accessed October 30, 2012).

[90] Gender Links spokesperson Kubi Rama cited by Bathandwa Mbola, *id.*

women's rights' association, COSEF (Conseil Senegalais des Femmes/ Council of Senegalese Women).[91]

In 2005, COSEF launched a nationwide campaign for gender parity in all political assemblies with the slogan, "With parity, let us consolidate democracy" ("*Avec la parité, consolidons la démocratie*").[92] The campaign was undertaken in partnership with political parties' women's movements, civic organizations, and the media. The partnership started with five civic organizations and seventeen political party-based women's organizations; it expanded over time to more than fifty organizations. The COSEF campaign has not only been based on legal arguments, such as the obligation for the state to implement article 9 of the African Women's Protocol, but it also uses the language of culture, invoking Senegal's most famous queens and female leaders prior to the relatively short period of French occupation. The first advocacy leaflet for the gender parity campaign bears the slogan "Gender Parity Is Our Heritage."

In support of gender parity on electoral lists of candidates, the president of the Republic of Senegal sent his prime minister to read a message to the members of parliament at the National Assembly. The content of the message mirrors almost word for word the advocacy arguments of COSEF: "In doing so, we will, in some way, restore Senegalese women to their historical role in the exercise of power and in the defense of freedom, dignity and honor. Let us revisit our history and think of Ndieumbët Mbodj, Yacine Boubou, Ndaté Yalla, Aline Sitoé Diatta. These famous names demonstrate that the quality of leadership is not just the prerogative of the male gender. Remaining faithful to our history, we are also in line with our international commitments. . . . Our history ties us to it. Our traditional values allow it. International standards recommend it."[93]

As a result of this campaign, an organic law was passed (Law No. 40/2007)[94] that made the following amendment to the Senegalese Constitution in Article

[91] See generally, http://cosef.org/

[92] COSEF has published two books tracing the various stages of the campaign. They are available in French on the COSEF website: COMBATS POUR LA PARITE: LA CAMPAGNE "AVEC LA PARITE, CONSOLIDONS LA DEMOCRATIE," http://cosef.org/IMG/pdf/COMBATSPARITEIMPRIMTOUTDV_8avril.pdf; COMBATS POUR LA PARITE: ACTES DU SEMINAIRE D'ELABORATION D'UN MODELE DE LOI SUR LA PARITE, http://cosef.org/IMG/pdf/COSEFPublicationCOUV_1_.pdf

[93] Message from the President of the Republic of Senegal to the National Assembly, December 8, 2006, *Fighting for parity, proceedings of the seminar to develop a model law on parity*, 109–10 (COSEF, AECID 2011) (document on file with author).

[94] The Constitutional Council of Senegal declared unconstitutional the law 23/2007 of March 27, 2007, which made mandatory an equal number of candidates of both sexes in the proportional representation list for the legislative elections (Decision No 1/c/2007 Apr. 27, 2007), which copies a 1982 decision by the French Constitutional Council. In 1982, the French Parliament

7, Paragraph 5: "The law favors the equal access of women and men in offices and positions."[95]

A law was passed on May 28, 2010, establishing total parity between men and women in wholly or partly elective institutions of the Republic:[96]

> Article 1 – Total gender parity is established in Senegal in all institutions wholly or partly elective.
> Article 2 – Lists of candidates are alternately composed of persons of both sexes.
> Lists of candidates must comply with the above provisions to be accepted.

On June 16, 2011, the practical issues of these provisions were defined in the decree on the implementation of the act:

> Article 1 – According to Law No. 2010–11 of 28 May 2010, establishing total gender parity in all institutions wholly or partly elected, the lists of candidates for election in such institutions are, in turn, composed of both sexes under penalty of inadmissibility.
> Article 2 – Institutions wholly or partly elective concerned are:
> – Regional Councils, municipal and rural as well as their boards and commissions;
> – The Senate, its Bureau and its Committees;
> – The National Assembly, its Bureau and Commissions;
> – The Congress and its Bureau;
> – The Economic and Social Council, its Bureau, and its Committees.
> For the post of senator, deputy, or councilor vacancy, the replacement must be of the same sex.[97]

Criticisms of affirmative action programs for female representation abound. They are mostly based on the arguments that such provisions are paternalistic and protective, that they entrench the vision of women as the weak sex in need

adopted an amendment to the French electoral law under which "lists of candidates may not contain more than 75% of persons of the same sex," the French Constitutional Council declared that provision unconstitutional on the grounds that it discriminates citizens along gender lines (decision no. 82–146 DC, November 18, 1982). *See* Fatou K. Camara, La parité au Sénégal, entre modèle autochtone et modèle importé, 80 REVUE INTERNATIONALE DE DROIT AFRICAIN EDJA 63–80 (Janvier-Février-Mars 2009).

95 Constitution of Senegal, art. 7 §5 "La loi favorise l'égal accès des femmes et des hommes aux mandats et fonctions," *available at* http://www.gouv.sn/-Constitution-du-Senegal-.html (accessed October 30, 2012).

96 Law No. 2010–11 Journal Officiel No. 6544 of September 4, 2010.

97 Decree No. 2011–819 of June 16, 2011 implementing the Act establishing total Gender Parity, Journal Officiel No. 6614 of Saturday September 17, 2011.

of a sheltered status instead of an equal status.[98] It is true that mandatory equal representation of women and men does not guarantee full gender equality on all fronts; still, it is a step in the right direction.[99] Why? Because in modern democratic states (based on the gendered social contract established during the liberal enlightenment), gender-blind systems systematically underrepresent women due to societal inequality, and this undermines women candidates. Krystof and WuDunn illustrate this point with village chiefs in India after 1993, when the constitution was amended to provide that one-third of the positions of village chief would be reserved for women. A study was conducted to evaluate that program. One of its conclusions was, "This does suggest that women politicians, at least in India, face a hurdle: Even if they do better than men at providing services, they initially are judged more harshly." However, "[f]ollow-up research did find that after a village had once had a female leader, this bias against women chiefs disappeared. Women leaders were then judged by gender-neutral standards."[100]

Considering those results, Krystof and WuDunn point out that "such research suggests that quotas for local female leaders may be worthwhile, because they overcome the initial hurdle that blocks women candidates."[101] They add, "An Indian-style quota of women officeholders seems to break down gender barriers so that afterward the political system becomes more democratic and open."[102]

One ancient tale tells the whole story of the systemic inequality that hides behind "nondiscriminatory" gender-blind laws:

> At one time the Fox and the Stork were on visiting terms and seemed very good friends. So the Fox invited the Stork to dinner, and for a joke put nothing before her but some soup in a very shallow dish. This the Fox could easily lap up, but the Stork could only wet the end of her long bill in it, and left the meal as hungry as when she began. "I am sorry," said the Fox, "the soup is not to your liking."

[98] "Portraying women as in need of protection and coddling affirms the image of women as weak and subordinate." Kristin Davis, *supra* note 9, at 982.

[99] Mi Yung Yoon, *More women in the Tanzanian legislature: Do numbers matter?*, 29 (1) J. CONTEMP. AFRICAN STUD. 83; Claire Devlin & Robert Elgie, *The effect of increased women's representation in parliament: The case of Rwanda*, 61 (2) PARLIAMENTARY AFFAIRS 237 (2008); Shireen Hassim, *A virtuous circle? Gender equality and representation in South Africa*, State of the Nation: South Africa 2004–2005 (2005) 336–59, *available at* http://www.safhr.org/index.php?option=com_docman&task=cat_view&gid=131&Itemid=570 (accessed October 30, 2012).

[100] Nicholas Kristof & Sheryl WuDunn, HALF THE SKY, TURNING OPPRESSION INTO OPPORTUNITY FOR WOMEN WORLDWIDE 197 (Knopf, 2009).

[101] *Id.*

[102] *Id.*

> "Pray do not apologize," said the Stork. "I hope you will return this visit, and come and dine with me soon." So a day was appointed when the Fox should visit the Stork; but when they were seated at the table all that was for their dinner was contained in a very long-necked jar with a narrow mouth, in which the Fox could not insert his snout, so all he could manage to do was to lick the outside of the jar.
>
> "I will not apologize for the dinner," said the Stork:
>
> "One bad turn deserves another."[103]

What is the lesson the Stork gives the Fox? "What is done for you and without you will be done against you!" Representation in the decision-making bodies is key. That is how many African communities understood the concept of the representative council or assembly. A brief overview of African institutions demonstrates that equal representations of all gender, territories, and professional guilds in decision-making bodies is indeed the norm.

Gender Parity in African Decision-Making Institutions: The Precolonial Precedents

A common feature of ancient and precolonial African political structures, from local levels to the highest echelons, is an assembly in which all social groups are present, according to age, gender, and profession (caste). Ifi Amadiume accurately highlights the philosophy underlying this form of assembly: "The democratic principles governing these assemblies meant that all social groups were present, including the youth, who were usually organized in age-grades or age-sets. Every human being had the right to voice an opinion. Those who showed a gift of oratory became very popular or [became] spokespersons. The system was geared to work by consensus."[104]

This kind of political organization has been documented at very early times in African history, as illustrated by Cheikh Anta Diop's account of the political system in the empire of Ghana: "The emperor governed through a council of ministers made up of representatives of the diverse classes of society, that is to say the castes."[105]

It is important to pay careful attention to the observation Diop makes as to the truly ancient character of this political organization: "Now, Ghana was not

[103] *Available at* http://etc.usf.edu/lit2go/35/aesops-fables/595/the-fox-and-the-stork/ (accessed August 11, 2012).
[104] Amadiume, *supra* note 18, at 97.
[105] Diop, *supra* note 18, at 120–21.

a beginning but a continuation: the level of political organization involved (constitutional monarchy) implies an older system."[106]

The same point of view is developed by Munson, who argues that the empire of Ghana arose from the remains of an earlier prehistoric system.[107] This system was not only ancient, it was also robust because it survived the fall of the empire of Ghana. The empire of Mali[108] rose from the ashes of Ghana and retained the same constitutional characteristics. Those were reflected in 1236 in the Charter of Kurukan Fuga,[109] also called the Manden Charter. The orally transmitted Charter outlined the basis of the legal system of the empire of Mali.[110] The Manden Charter illustrated the intricate workings of a web of associations in which membership was defined by age,[111] by profession (professional fraternities/castes),[112] and by gender: "Article 16: The

[106] *Id.*

[107] "Archaeological investigations in southern Mauritania have revealed a wealth of rather spectacular stone masonry villages which were occupied by prehistoric cultivators as early as 1000 B.C. It is argued that the inhabitants of these villages were Negro and very probably Soninke, and that the basic elements of their culture had developed without major influences from outside the area. The apparent sophistication and complexity of this cultural manifestation, combined with the close fit of developments in this area with Carneiro's theory of state formation, suggests that this prehistoric complex represented at least a powerful chiefdom which embodied many of the characteristics of subsequent West African states." Patrick J. Munson, *Archaeology and the prehistoric origins of the Ghana Empire*, 21 (4) J. AFRICAN HIST. 457 (1980).

[108] At its peak, it covered most of West Africa and was equal to the size of Western Europe.

[109] Full text available in English at http://www.africaknowledgeproject.org/index.php/war/article/view/931 (accessed January 1, 2012). Siriman Kouyaté, WEST AFRICAN REVIEW, No. 15 (2009).

[110] The Charter was not originally set down in writing, but its content has been orally transmitted from one generation to the next thanks to the *dyelis*, the traditional archivists of Mandingo society. A regional workshop of dialogue between communicators and Maninka traditionalists from Senegal, Mali, Niger, Burkina Faso, and the Republic of Guinea took place in Kankan (Republic of Guinea), March 3–12, 1998. At the end of the workshop, a draft of the forty-four articles of the Charter was made available. Read more about it in *Africa drafted its declaration on the rights of man in 1236*, LES AFRIQUES – THE AFRICAN FINANCE JOURNAL, July 24, 2008, *available at* http://www.lesafriques.com/en/mali/africa-drafted-its-declaration-on-the-rights-of-man-in-1236.html?Itemid=35 (accessed January 1, 2012).

[111] *Id.*, art. 4: "The society is divided into age groups. At the head of each age group there will be an elected leader. The people (men and women), born within the course of three consecutive years belong to the same age group.

"The Kangbes, the intermediate class between the young people and the old men must be invited to take part in the important decisions making processes concerning the society."

[112] *Id.*, art. 1: "The society of the great Mande Kingdom is divided into sixteen (16) quiver carriers, five (5) classes of Marabouts, four (4) classes of Nyamakalas ("griots" = traditional jurists/archivists, and artisans: weavers, smiths, shoemakers). Each of these groups has an activity and a specific role." The roles of the Nyamakalas and the marabouts are defined in articles 2 and 3 of the Charter. Art. 2: "The Nyamakakas have a duty to tell leaders the truth, be their advisers and defend them (meaning orally, as a lawyer does in court) with the rules laid down, and law and

women, in addition to their daily occupations, must be associated to all our governments."[113]

A society organized along gender lines from its base to its top positions has the advantage of acknowledging gender duality in a way that guarantees both sexes equal rights and opportunities. In Senegal, or Siin-Gànna "the southern province of the empire of Ghana,"[114] the Seereer communities were organized in the following way: girls and boys underwent separate initiation rites. A man presided over the training of male initiates, and a woman took over the training of women. National coordination was ensured at the top by a female head of state (the queen mother, the *lingeer*)[115] and by her male counterpart (the king – not the *lingeer*'s husband but a next of kin on his maternal lineage – called the *maad* or *buur*).[116] The *lingeer* participated in the Crown Council, where her political advice carried weight; she performed important religious duties; and she served in the judiciary in litigations involving women.[117]

In Akan society (Ghana, Ivory Coast), the same rule applied, as noted by Tarikhu Farrar: "Every office in the Akan political hierarchy (in all its variants) has female and male counterparts. This practice of maintaining separate, parallel political hierarchies for the female and male sections of the population is a fundamental and presumably ancient feature of Akan political organization."[118]

Farrar goes on to point out a fact that has also been remarked upon concerning the Seereer's political organization and the role of the *lingeer* (Senegal): "In the day-to-day affairs of government in pre-colonial Akan society, women did not normally come under the authority of men. All issues pertaining primarily or exclusively to women (and there were many political,

order on the whole territory"; art. 3: "The Morikanda Lolu (five classes of Marabouts) are our masters and our teachers in Islam. Everyone owes them respect and consideration."

[113] *Id.*

[114] SALIOU KANDJI, SÉNÉGAL N'EST PAS SUNUGAL, OU DE L'ÉTYMOLOGIE DU TOPONYME SÉNÉGAL (2006).

[115] For the *lingeer*'s role and potent political power, *see* JEAN BOULÈGUE, LE GRAND JOLOF (XIIIE-XVIE SIÈCLE) 61–62 (Ed. Façades, diffusion, 1987); HENRY GRAVRAND, COSAAN 267(1983).

[116] B. S. Diouf. *Le genre dans le vivre ensemble africain*, unpublished presentation at the workshop for a law on gender parity in electoral assemblies organized by COSEF. The Wolof kingdoms also have powerful *lingeer*, and the Wolof language puts gender duality in all functions even inside the familial sphere. In Wolof, fatherhood is a function that is bestowed both on men (*baay* – father) and on women (*bàjjan* – paternal aunt, contraction of *baay jigéen*, which literally means "female father"; mothers are also of both sexes, the female mothers are called *yaay* and the male mothers are the *nijaay* a deformation of *ni yaay* which means "like a mother" – the maternal uncle).

[117] Gravrand, *supra* note 115.

[118] Farrar, *supra* note 19, at 588.

economic, and cultural) and all conflicts between women were addressed within the context of this female political hierarchy. Furthermore, issues involving both females and males – issues like adultery, rape, marital conflict, and so forth – were also handled by female stool-holders."[119]

Such societal organization along gender, age, and professional lines ensured that each of these groups had equal access to justice and decision-making bodies. Simi Afonja provides confirmation of the effectiveness of this constitutional law in Nigeria by stating that, in cities and villages, women were represented in the council of leaders in the executive and the judiciary.[120] She also states that in each Ibo village, women had their own council.[121]

In the kingdom of Dahomey (Benin), there was an assembly for women and one for men. Cheikh Anta Diop writes the following about this African gender-based dual-chamber system:[122] "A study of our past can give us a lesson in government. . . . Women participated in running public affairs within the framework of a feminine assembly, sitting separately but having the same prerogatives as the male assembly."

Diop goes on to underline the following points:[123] "The aforementioned facts remained unaffected until colonial conquest took place, particularly in such non-Islamised States as the Yoruba and Dahomean. Behanzin's military resistance to the French Army under colonel Dodds is said to have resulted from a decision of the women's assembly of the kingdom, meeting at night after the men had met during the day and countermanding them by ordering mobilization and war – after which, the men ratified the decision."

One can infer from all these historical facts that, in ancient African culture, the need to involve women in all decision-making processes at all levels is quite specifically addressed. Two Wolof sayings stress the importance of women's participation in all decision-making processes: *Jigéen ku ko sóoraa-léwul ndi nga yekk ñamu mbaam* ("If you do not involve women in what you are cooking, you will serve a dish only fit for pigs"), and *Jigéen ay suñu asamaan fu ñu xiinul du taw* ("Women are our clouds, it does not rain where they are not assembled in great numbers").[124]

[119] *Id.*
[120] Afonja, *supra* note 56, at 371.
[121] *Id.* at 373.
[122] Diop, *supra* note 56, at 33.
[123] *Id.*
[124] Ismael Lô, Senegalese singer, put these two sayings in the lyrics of one of his hit songs, "Jigéen" ("Woman").

CONCLUSION

In conclusion, this chapter has worked to redefine the quest for women's rights and gender-parity in Africa not so much as ground-breaking, but rather as a renaissance of the equitable decision-making norms that were in place prior to colonial conquest and as an affirmation of the robust, democratic, precolonial societies that saw gender parity as a given. Empowered by this cultural background, African women's organizations have aggressively pursued the equality agenda.

The quest for gender parity by African women's movements is not revolutionary; instead, it has been a result of the rediscovery of traditions lost to colonial conquest. The reification of democracy by the 50/50 parity campaigns throughout Africa has unveiled the tacit democratic cultural norms already in place in various and far-reaching precolonial traditional African societies. African democracy includes respect and celebration of variance and assortment. The participation of women in decision making, from politics to family choices, was quite specifically addressed. It is then logical for African women not to look toward modern democratic states because those states' gender-blind systems systematically underrepresent women. It is also logical for African women to trust into the age-old gender-sensitive system that allowed them to have a voice and to hold political leadership in their communities, before the colonial conquest and paternaltarianism swept it all away.

6

Law, Peace-Construction, and Women's Rights in Africa: Who Will Safeguard Abeena and Afia?

Jeremy I. Levitt

INTRODUCTION

Since the end of the Cold War, African states have become the testing grounds for Western conflict resolution experiments, particularly transitional political power-sharing agreements that are supposedly intended to end deadly conflict, secure peace, and build democracy in divided societies.[1] One of the most troubling aspects of deadly armed conflict is the disparate impact it has on women. Seventy percent of deaths in internal conflict are noncombatants – the majority of whom are women and children. Maternal death is the "highest lifetime risk" of women in conflict-ridden and postconflict states. It is estimated that more than 600,000 women have died of pregnancy or childbirth complications during armed conflict in Africa over the past decade and a half, one-fifth of whom were young girls. As Aili Tripp observes, "[c]ivil conflict breaks open, pathologizes, distorts and can even transform societal rifts,"[2] splits that simultaneously systematize violence against women and pervert gender-neutral conflict resolution devices. Conflict resolution, peacebuilding, and "peace construction" processes – that is, how peace is conceptualized,

[1] The terms *power sharing*, *political power sharing*, *transitional political power sharing*, and *power-sharing arrangements* are used interchangeably. For purposes of this chapter, *power sharing* is broadly defined to mean the range of peace processes that seek to construct (e.g., mediate and negotiate) and apportion (e.g., share power) political power in peace deals. In this context, transitional political power sharing takes place between contesting groups (warlords, rebels, and junta) and national governments for a fixed and impermanent period of time, until elections take place. Power-sharing accords and provisions seek to outline and codify into law decision-making mandates that allocate political power and authority. Although military and economic power sharing are important, this chapter primarily focuses on transitional political power sharing birthed during violent internal armed conflict, not on those forms of power sharing that have been solely written into legislation or constitutions during peacetime.

[2] Aili Mari Tripp, *Gender, agency and peace negotiations in Africa*, *in* GENDERED INSECURITIES: HEALTH AND DEVELOPMENT IN AFRICA 170 (Howard Stein & Amal Hassan Fadlalla eds., 2012), at 170.

negotiated, normatively institutionalized, and operationalized – have given birth to power-sharing models that structure gender inequality into political transitions, ultimately disenfranchising women in the transitional and postconflict orders. Although women represent the global majority – meaning that they represent the group with the largest stake in peace – they have had the smallest voice in shaping it. Women and women representing women's interests are rarely included in peace negotiations because the "enterprise" of peacebuilding is unfortunately "owned" by men and male-centered institutions. Women infrequently benefit from transitional peace agreements that restructure power, and rarely do they secure any positions in transitional governments, let alone influential positions. The "orderly" exclusion of women and women's issues in peace processes during peace negotiations and in the postconflict transitional political apparatus is a global human rights problem that arguably affects the longevity of peace deals because the opinions, welfare, and interests of the majority are not represented.[3] Nowhere is this wretchedly unlawful condition more apparent than in power-sharing peace agreements, which brings us to the question: Who will safeguard Abeena and Afia?[4]

Despite these realities, African women have vociferously advocated to end armed conflict and participate in peace processes and transitional justice practices. Within the broad conception of peacemaking and peace construction, women's participation is vital to sustainable peace, security, and the realization of fundamental rights. Power sharing is the most important component of any peace agreement because such arrangements determine who will have a seat at the table of power, in what capacity, and for how long. They determine the constitution of the new political order and the distribution of political, legislative, and judicial power to elites, and hence control the nature and character of future political transitions, as well as choosing those who rule

[3] That said, the author is cognizant of the fact that women advocates and decision makers may have malevolent rather than benevolent intentions; hence, prescriptions for their inclusion should not be underwritten by "benign" paradigms. Despite the imminent need for gender equality in peace construction, women also serve as combatants, obstructionists, and peace spoilers. Like men, they engage in corrupt behavior aimed at derailing peace processes and leveraging the greater cause of gender equality for personal gain.

[4] In the Akan language in Ghana Abeena (Tuesday) and Afia (Friday) are girls' names representing the days of the week in which they were born. I use the names Abeena and Afia as metaphors to symbolize African women and girls, as well as the days of the week in which the Convention against All Forms of Discrimination against Women (CEDAW) (adopted Tuesday, December 18, 1979, entered into force on September 3, 1981), the Protocol to the African Charter on Human and Peoples Rights on the Rights of Women in Africa (adopted Friday, July 11, 2003, entered into force on Friday, November 25, 2005), and UN Security Council Resolution 1135 (adopted unanimously Tuesday, October 31, 2000), were adopted.

the peace. Too often, women are disenfranchised during peace transitions and subjugated to the rule of human rights abusers and unsympathetic leaders. Nonetheless, their collective efforts have significantly shaped the dynamics of peace arrangements and, perhaps more importantly, the legal framework in which they are supposed to operate. Consequently, the subject of this chapter, law, power sharing, and women's rights in Africa, presents a vibrant opportunity to examine the various operative and normative roles Black women have played in peace construction, from marginalized victims to innovative activists. What is abundantly clear is that the various waves of African women's movements in the 1990s stirred a seething brew of activism that has shaped and is shaping the normative tide against their orderly exclusion in peace construction.

Power sharing has become far more than a tool of conflict resolution. It is a graphic enterprise with the capacity to rebuild or ruin societies emerging from deadly conflict and/or coups. It is a commonly practiced "fine art" that broad-brushes society in a way that inhibits sustainable peace because it disregards controlling rules intended to safeguard human rights, women's rights, and democracy. The recent coups or extraconstitutional seizures of power in the Central African Republic (2008), Guinea (2008), Kenya (2008), Madagascar (2009), Mauritania (2009), Niger (2010), Burkina Faso (2011), and the Central African Republic (2012) exhibit the precarious record of power-sharing schemes in Africa. Women played negligible roles as decision makers in all of these peace processes, which may lend insight into their categorical failure. It thus should come as no surprise that, to varying degrees, these states also have troublesome human rights records and traditions of discouraging women from participating in government and governance. It follows that the international community – regional and international organizations – must embrace more artful, inclusive, and effective conflict-resolution models in societies seeking to end deadly conflict and ensure women's active participation in peace processes. In this sense, the traditional orthodoxy of placing a higher premium on peace and conflict resolution than on human rights and justice should be considered an unacceptable tradeoff with the principle of the rule of law that intends to shield people, especially women, from the arbitrary edicts of male-centered groups holding discretionary power.

How to construct a just and sustainable political order, share power, and ensure gender equality and justice in societies emerging from armed conflict is one of the most arduously understated and complex issues confronting contemporary international law and politics in the twenty-first century. During peace negotiations, in the transitional regime, and in the postconflict order, women are systematically alienated and discriminated against in Africa, Eastern Europe, South and Central Asia, Latin America, and the South Pacific. Power sharing is also challenging because, at the most fundamental level, it significantly impacts the human rights and democracy entitlements of women, given that impunity, whether through amnesty or inaction, curbs rights-based claims and participatory governance and reconstitutes political power and its future disposition. Consequently, peace agreements that do not sufficiently include or consider the welfare and interests of women run afoul of settled regional and international law norms such as, for example, the Convention on the Elimination of All Forms of Discrimination against Women (CEDAW, 1988), United Nations Security Council Resolution 1325 (2000), and the Protocol to the African Charter on Human and People's Rights on the Rights of Women in Africa (African Women's Protocol, 2003). These legal instruments, among others, underwrite the most fundamental principles in the international human rights of women related to power sharing, including the rights of women to participate in peace negotiations and processes as decision makers, partake in the formulation and implementation of government policy, hold public office, and perform government functions at all levels, including regionally and internationally. The significance of this largely unaddressed problem was identified by the Secretary-General pursuant to Security Council Resolution 1325 (2000):

> Women are under-represented in formal peace negotiations, whether as local participants representing warring factions, or as representatives of international authorities overseeing or mediating deliberations and institutions invited to the negotiating table. In addition, central issues of concern to women, including their participation in post-conflict political, social, civil, economic and judicial structures, do not always reach the negotiating table, in part because of the exclusion of women from formal peace negotiations. Women not only call for issues specific to themselves but raise issues that affect society as a whole, such as land reform, access to loans and capacity-building. All actors committed to equality and non-discrimination – whether male or female – should have the responsibility and capacity to ensure that peace agreements incorporate gender equality issues.[5]

Notwithstanding, to date, not a single national government in Africa has heeded the UN's call to formally and forthrightly study the gendered impacts of peace processes, and less than a handful of scholars and academic institutions worldwide have formally initiated research programs on the impact of

[5] *Women, Peace and Security*, study submitted by the Secretary-General pursuant to Security Council resolution 1325 (2000), 61.

peace agreements on women. Very few of the academics who have initiated projects/programs have seriously considered the gendered dimensions of power sharing. Essentially, African women have been forced to challenge the unlawful status quo produced by illegal peace deals, which makes them both objects and subjects of conflict resolution doctrine and the "Law on Power Sharing."[6]

Nevertheless, the object–subject dichotomy only reveals a part of the complexity presented by transitional political power sharing. Power-sharing governments are a dependent appendage of an externally located ideal: an imaginative democratic and gender-neutral entity composed of peace-loving "bandits of the law." It is alien to women and other victims of conflict; the overall rebel–woman subject dichotomy contains several nesting dualities: man/woman, inclusion/exclusion, ruler/ruled, victim/victimizer, peace/war, impunity/justice, and lawful peace/unlawful peace. Its inner logic is fashioned by the vocation of male domination and multilateral institutional collusion, which has led to women's movements that reject the legitimacy of power-sharing agreements. It follows that, since women are the most adversely affected by exclusionary power-sharing deals that reward warlords, rebels, and juntas with sovereign power and authority, women contest the legitimacy and legality of these deals even as they advocate for the adherence to rules that protect participatory rights during peacemaking and work to author a new normative order that safeguards their long-term interests in peace construction.

This chapter seeks to address this seemingly dichotomous phenomenon in conflict resolution: the orderly exclusion of women from peace construction and particularly from power-sharing processes and the catalytic role women play in advancing peacebuilding norms. The proposed research is comparative, normative, interdisciplinary, and qualitative, drawing from international human rights law, peace, and conflict resolution studies and from the conceptual propositions of women's studies. It employs what I refer to as an African rights-based approach to examine the legality and political efficacy of power-sharing agreements that exclude, alienate, or disenfranchise women, and it assesses the normative impact, if any, that African women have had on the development of equality rules, doctrine, norms, and jurisprudence in peace construction, with a focus on power sharing.[7] The chapter

6 Jeremy I. Levitt, Illegal Peace?: An Inquiry into the Legality of Power-Sharing with African Warlords and Rebels 238–43 (2012).

7 The African rights-based approach is based on law, norms, doctrine, and jurisprudence that contests gender inequality and necessitates the empowerment of women as individual and collective subjects of law with equal and affirmative rights, duties, and responsibilities that

comparatively references peace deals birthed in the post–Cold War era in Africa and evaluates both the extent to which they provide specific protections for African women and whether Black women have influenced the gendered dimensions of what the author refers to as "peace construction" and its doctrinal progeny, the "Law of Power Sharing".[8] Consequently, it contemplates the role that law indicates for itself to play in informing, shaping, and regulating gender equality in transnational political power-sharing deals. What role does law indicate for women, and what roles do women indicate for themselves to play in fashioning, observing, and safeguarding women's rights in peace agreements? Are the aims of peace, gender equality and justice, rule by law, and democracy attainable, let alone compatible, when women are excluded from peace construction and simultaneously forced to live under unlawful power-sharing agreements and transitional governments ruled by the amnestied warlords, rebels, and juntas responsible for committing atrocities against them?

LAW, POWER SHARING, AND WOMEN'S RIGHTS

Problems with Power Sharing

About 50 percent of peace agreements fail within five years.[9] I have argued elsewhere that a major reason for this failure rests in their extralegal or unlawful anatomy, which is precipitated by expediency, necessity, and a smug disregard for the rule of law and historical experientialism.[10] Their illegality occurs at the national, subregional, regional, and international levels, where predominant law, doctrine, and norms that protect women's rights are intentionally flouted. However, nowhere is such infringement more apparent than in the international human rights of women. One analyst argues that only 5 out of 111 peace agreements "signed between the adoption of UN Security

must be guaranteed, promoted, and protected by states and by regional and international institutions.

8 Levitt, *supra* note 6, at 237–43.

9 Thomas Reuters Foundation, *Half of peace accords fail in five years*, March 14, 2011, *available at* http://www.trust.org/item/?map=half-of-peace-accords-fail-within-five-years/

10 In this sense, historical experientialism philosophically connotes that law's internal logic is derived from historical experiences of either people, states, or institutions, which in turn generates knowledge of its central purpose (e.g., the adoption of the Genocide Convention on December 9, 1948, by the UN General Assembly was a consequence of the Holocaust perpetrated by Nazi Germany during World War II). Consequently, it is important to understand the historical rationale for rule existence or history of law, particularly in the area of human rights, in order to ascertain the probable impacts of ignoring it.

Council Resolution 1325 in October 2000 and the end of December 2008 ... included provisions linked to accountability for gender-based violence."[11] To make matters worse, none of them mandated gender equality in peace negotiations or in transitional or permanent allocations of political power. The systematic exclusion of women from peace processes and peace negotiations is a form of "democratic impunity," and I suspect this is why domestic violence, alcoholism, and drug abuse substantially increase in postconflict environs; these are problems that intersect, conflate, and disproportionately affect women but remain ignored in peace-construction processes. Moreover, the general exclusion of women from conflict prevention, management, and resolution serves as a root cause of conflict in and of itself. First, it excludes the societal majority and those with the greatest stake in peace: women. Second, such marginalization sidelines the group with debatably the most successful track record of peacebuilding and bottom-up postconflict reconstruction, despite being undermined by gender discrimination. Third, it is no secret that during and after armed conflict, families with large numbers of women and children, female-headed families, and women and girls impacted by armed conflict are increasingly affected by homelessness, poverty, landlessness, joblessness, and inadequate access to food and potable water. These conditions ultimately produce fractured families and distressed children who are physically and ideologically vulnerable, disadvantaged, and highly susceptible to "recruitment" by would-be rebels. The exclusion of women from peace processes, coupled with gender-neutral power-sharing agreements that codify rules and structures that exacerbate and concretize gender disparities, creates a nexus of circular causation with power sharing, societal distrust, discrimination, and the resumption of deadly conflict as permanent features.

Consequently, whether UN-sanctioned or not, womenfolk are horribly underrepresented in peace processes as peace negotiators, signatories, and chief mediators.[12] For example, women were almost entirely absent from all seven of the negotiations and peace deals that preceded the Juba peace talks between the government of Uganda and the Lord's Resistance Army (LRA)

[11] The five peace agreements are the 2006 Darfur Peace Agreement of Sudan (DPA), the 2007 Agreement on Accountability and Reconciliation in Uganda and its 2008 Annexure to the Agreement, the 2003 Inter-Congolese Negotiation, the final Act of the Democratic Republic of the Congo (DRC), and, finally, the 2006 Regional Pact on Security, Stability and Development in the Great Lakes Region. *See* Sahla Aroussi, *Women, peace and security: Addressing accountability for wartime sexual violence*, 13 (4) INT'L FEMINIST J. POL. 576, 581.

[12] *See generally*, UN Development Program for Women (UNIFEM), WOMEN'S PARTICIPATION IN PEACE NEGOTIATION: Connections between Presence and Influence (August 2010).

that produced the 2008 Final Peace Agreement (Juba Peace Agreement).[13] Only one LRA female mediator participated in the negotiations leading to the gender-neutral Juba Peace Agreement, which means that neither the UN nor the Ugandan government appointed women negotiators. For some time, women peace activists have argued that "formal mediation processes include no women – not at the table representing national interests, not in mediation support teams, not within observer delegations," and rarely are their perspectives solicited.[14] Rather, women spend the bulk of their time seeking to be included in peace processes rather than "focusing their time and attention on service as equal participants in efforts to set a comprehensive and inclusive agenda for peace."[15] On this point, Tripp notes that, despite the fact that "women have demanded a seat at peace talks, in transitional governments," and "on constitutional commissions engaged in drafting new constitutions" and have also "pushed for increased representation in legislative bodies", "[i]t is still rare to find women leading official peace negotiations."[16] This essentially means that conventional conflict resolution and transitional governance processes are systematically flawed because they bar women from holding decision-making positions during peace negotiations and consequently exclude them from the power-sharing governments they establish. Accordingly, women's concerns, issues, and needs are left to the whims of violent, male-centered groups that hold discretionary power, whether these are political elites in incumbent regimes, warlords, or rebels engrossed with haggling over control of the body politic and the economy.

As already noted, armed conflict affects women more than any other group. Power sharing exacerbates and accentuates the negative impacts of armed conflict on women in transitions to peace, meaning it lengthens transitional

[13] All seven agreements were entered into between 2006 and 2008 and, according to the Juba Peace Agreement, are listed as follows: the Cessation of Hostilities Agreement and its six addenda; the agreement on comprehensive solutions and its protocol (that address security arrangements, power and wealth sharing); the agreement on accountability and reconciliation and its annexure (that address issues of war crimes and crimes against humanity, including how to deal with the International Criminal Court's [ICC] indictments on LRA leaders); the agreement on a permanent ceasefire; the agreement on disarmament, demobilization, and reintegration; the agreement on implementation and monitoring mechanisms; and the implementation schedule that shall be signed with and attached to the final peace agreement.

[14] Theresa de Longis, *Across conflict lines: Women mediating for peace*, 12th Annual Colloquium Findings, The Institute for Inclusive Security 3 (2011). One clear exception is Betty Bigombe, a long-time political player in Uganda and current minister of state for water resources, who served as chief mediator between the Ugandan government and LRA (2004–2005) prior to the Juba Peace Agreement. It is widely believed that her efforts, which did not resolve the conflict, set the stage for the Juba peace process.

[15] *Id.*

[16] Tripp, *supra* note 2, at 177.

periods between war and peace, on the one hand, and delays peace and reconstruction, on the other. For example, gender-based violence exponentially increases in transitional and transnational postconflict environs; however, very few safeguards have been conceived that (1) protect women from lurking predatory forces in the transitional postconflict milieu, (2) seek retributive and reparative justice for sex crimes, and (3) institutionalize gender training into demobilization and reintegration schemes. Although women are pioneers in the development of informal and formal grassroots peacebuilding processes, they remain largely invisible at the negotiating table when major decisions are taken, when policy is framed, and when the new constitution of order is adopted. Hence, they function in an oppressive conundrum where "invisibility and activity, victimhood and agency run parallel."[17] As has been previously noted, the situation for women worsens when there is political power sharing because such power sharing "usually improves the situation of the rebel group relative to the status quo" and inevitably leads to a perverse arrangement in which women victims of war are forced to live under the rule of opulent and oppressive warlords and rebels.[18] This may explain why there were spikes in sexual violence in postconflict power-sharing states such as, among others, Liberia and Sierra Leone. On this point, a prominent study on sexual violence and armed conflict concluded, "A number of countries emerging from armed conflict report a very high and/or increasing incidence of criminal and family violence. Impunity for acts of sexual violence committed during the conflict, postconflict poverty, lack of livelihood opportunities and the weakened rule of law, may combine to foster increased inter-personal and sexual violence, and to make women and girls particularly vulnerable to sexual exploitation and trafficking."[19] Moreover, power dynamics expressed through sexual violence may be more prevalent as the strength of "bandits of the law" increases through power sharing.[20] In addition, power sharing and impunity send a potent psychological message to demobilized or former rebels, suggesting that armed violence is a viable path to political and economic power. For example, Liberia's Prince Y. Johnson, a brutal former warlord turned senator and presidential contestant in the 2012

[17] Elisabeth Porter, *Why women's contribution to peacebuilding matters*, 10 (3) INT'L. STUD. REV. 632 (2008) (reviewing Sanam Naraghi Anderlini, WOMEN BUILDING PEACE: WHAT THEY DO, WHY IT MATTERS [2007]).

[18] Stephen E. Gent, *Relative rebel strength and power-sharing in intrastate conflicts*, 37 INT'L. INTERACTIONS 215, 218 (2011).

[19] Megan Bastick, Karin Grimm, & Rahel Kunz, SEXUAL VIOLENCE IN ARMED CONFLICT: A GLOBAL OVERVIEW AND IMPLICATIONS FOR THE SECURITY SECTOR 10, 155–67 (2007).

[20] The terms African warlords, rebels, and juntas; bandits of the law; and *pirates de la loi* are used interchangeably.

elections, has never been held accountable for his barbarous and serial rape, torture, and murder of Liberians while a commander in Charles Taylor's wicked National Patriotic Front of Liberia. Johnson also served as the notorious leader of the brutal splinter faction, the Independent National Patriotic Front of Liberia, during Liberia's vicious civil war (1990–1997), which was directly responsible for killing thousands of Liberians. Johnson is allowed to hold office and roam free with impunity: one wonders what message this sends to desperate youth and would-be rebels.

In this context, it is important to note that impunity for sexual crimes and/or the social repression of women may serve as initial indicator(s) of the probability of gendered violence during and after armed conflict. It has also been argued that states with high levels of gender inequality produce more internal armed conflict.[21] Societies that relegate women to second-class status during peacetime have greater proclivities for gendered violence not simply because of widespread abuses of discretionary power in the private and public spheres, but also because of how normative violence impacts women's images of themselves and the dogma about them. Subjugation reinforces exploitive patterns of patriarchy and masculinity that, for example, constrain feminine enterprise or women's labor power and the ability of women to participate in and shape peace processes. Again, one clear example is that during and immediately after armed conflict, women bear the brunt of family obligations, which makes them largely immobile, less knowledgeable about transitional peace initiatives, and hence ineffective advocates for themselves, for their children, and for restorative and retributive justice. This, in turn, reduces the likelihood of their participation in grassroots or other peace movements and processes, and it increases the probability that they will only be viewed as victims. In essence, the livelihood of women declines more than that of any other group during and immediately after armed conflict. Therefore, women have a vested interest and a vital role to play in both early warning and prevention of conflict and in conflict resolution and postconflict justice. Women also have the greatest incentives to mitigate the harsh impacts of conflict on their families by ensuring that shelter, medical care, food, water, and education are accessible during episodes of conflict. In this way, individually and collectively, women become human safety nets that create protective webs during crises and build strategic alliances with similarly situated women across sociocultural lines: Liberia, Rwanda, South Africa, Sierra Leone, and Sudan are prime examples. In these countries, women organized

[21] Mary Caprioli, *Primed for violence: The role of gender inequality in predicating internal conflict*, 49 INT'L. L. STUD. Q. 161, 172 (2005).

across racial, ethnic, political, and religious lines to protect the vulnerable and effectuate peace.

African Women's Movements: Building Normative Architecture

As the introduction to the volume indicates, African women have a rich legacy of national leadership that dates back to antiquity. They have, among other things, been revered as gods, ruled and built nations as pharaohs and queens, led vast armies, pioneered in science and technology, fashioned law and religion, established vast enterprises,[22] and served as peacemakers. In the modern era, African women have been visibly active in global governance since the 1970s and served as the primary mobilizing force behind the establishment of the African Training and Research Center for Women (ATRC) within the UN Economic Commission for Africa. The ATRC served as a base for women's advocacy within the UN system and ensured that women's issues were represented in the formulation of international law and policy.[23] Such advocacy led to the 1982 Lagos Plan of Action, which included a comprehensive section on women and development, a section that promoted women's equality and advancement in the public and private spheres.[24] In this sense, African women were actively engaged in global governance processes long before women from other regions. These efforts spurred paradigm-shifting women's conferences, beginning with the 1985 Nairobi Conference and climaxing with the 1995 Beijing Conference, which called for an increase in the "participation of women in conflict resolution at decision-making levels, the protection of women living in situations of armed and other conflicts or under foreign occupation" and for taking "measures to ensure women's equal

[22] *See generally* David Sweetmen, Women Leaders in African History, African Historical Biographies (1984). It is also interesting to note that African women pioneered and evolved the regime on microfinance. *See generally* Women's World Banking, available at http://www.swwb.org/about/about-wwb (last visited November 27, 2012).

[23] *See generally* Report on the Fourth Meeting of the African Regional Coordinating Committee for the Integration of Women in Development, UN Economic Commission for Africa-Silver Jubilee Anniversary Meetings, Fourth Meeting of the Technical Preparatory Committee of the Whole, Addis Ababa, Ethiopia, April 14–22, 1983, Item 8(a) of the provisional agenda, E/ECA/TPCW.4//8 (April 18, 1983).

[24] Lagos Plan of Action for the Economic Development of African 1980–2000, Organization of African Unity, Lagos, Nigeria, April 28–29, 1980. The Lagos Plan of Action identified several areas where women should be advanced, including "agriculture and nutrition, handicrafts and small-scale industries, employment, education and training, science and technology, trade, natural resources (especially water supply), energy, health and family life, population, research, mass media, and establishment of national and sub-regional machineries for integration of women in development." *Id.*

access to and full participation in power structures and decision-making."[25] The Beijing Conference, which reinforced CEDAW, created the normative architecture for women's continued activism in human rights protection and peacebuilding that culminated in the adoption of the African Women's Protocol and UN Security Council Resolution 1325.

African women and girls have also fought, both willingly and unwillingly, in domestic and regional wars, and, unfortunately, the post-Cold War surge in internal armed conflict in Africa has significantly amplified their presence on the battlefront, particularly in Burundi, the Democratic Republic of the Congo, Liberia, Mozambique, Sierra Leone, and Uganda. Women comprised about 9 percent of combatants in Sierra Leone's brutal Revolutionary United Front (RUF) and 25 percent of Charles Taylor's savage National Patriotic Front of Liberia (NPLF). In the 1970s and 1980s, women served in subsidiary roles and as combatants "in armed liberation and guerilla movements in Mozambique, Zimbabwe, Guinea-Bissau, Eritrea, Uganda and elsewhere."[26] Their dual roles as combatants and peace stewards explains why their appeal for greater recognition and participation in peace construction is gaining normative expression. As one female combatant in Liberia noted, "We fight better than the men and make peace better than them too, so why are we kept outside?"[27] Although African women have played double roles on Africa's killing fields as victims and victimizers,[28] their marginalization in transitional peace and justice processes has unleashed waves of women's movements throughout the continent.[29]

Consequently, the twenty-first century has ushered in a new era of "ebony movements" that have triggered lawmaking processes in the domestic and international realms. At the domestic level, "Africa has some of the highest rates of female legislative representation in the world, with women claiming over 30 percent of the parliamentary seats in Mozambique, South Africa, Tanzania, Uganda, and Burundi."[30] Women claimed 56 percent of lower house seats and 38 percent of upper house (senate) seats in Rwanda

[25] Women in Armed Conflict Diagnosis, Strategic Objective E1, Platform for Action, The UN Fourth World Conference on Women, Beijing, China, September 1995, *available at* http://www.un.org/womenwatch/daw/beijing/platform/armed.htm (last visited June 11, 2013).

[26] Tripp, *supra* note 2, at 176.

[27] Interview with female ex-combatant of the Liberians United for Reconciliation and Democracy (LURD) faction in Monrovia, January 25, 2009.

[28] *See generally* Hillary Charlesworth, *Are women peaceful? Reflections on the role of women in peace-building*, 15 FEMINIST L. STUD. (2008).

[29] Aili Mari Tripp, Isabel Casimiro, Joy Kwesiga, & Alice Mungwa, AFRICAN WOMEN'S MOVEMENTS: CHANGING POLITICAL LANDSCAPES (2009). This volume is one of the most comprehensive studies of African women's movements ever published.

[30] *Id.* at 17.

(September 2008 elections), and in Senegal 42 percent of legislative seats and 40 percent of upper house seats are held by women (July 2012 elections). This does not include an estimated 42 percent of lower house and 32 percent of senate seats held by women in South Africa (April 2009 elections). Women are also being elected to key government posts, as typified by the 2005 and 2012 presidential victories of Ellen Johnson-Sirleaf of Liberia and the peaceful transition of power to Joyce Banda in Malawi in 2012; they are using their positions to lobby for constitutional reforms and general legislation to protect women's rights, ensure gender equity, and alleviate gender discrimination.[31] New women's rights law and policy are also being adopted by more gender-balanced legislatures. It appears that African women have seized upon new political space opened up by armed conflict and/or state collapse in the legislative and executive realms. At the regional level, it is thus not surprising that Gertrude Mongella, chairperson of the 1995 Fourth World Conference of Women, became the first president of the Pan-African Parliament of the African Union.[32] Ironically, in March 2004, a year and a half after she took office, the Protocol to the African Charter of Human and Peoples' Rights on the Rights of Women in Africa entered into force (November 2005). African women are increasingly relying on the Protocol to contest impunity in power-sharing peace agreements that place warlords and rebels in authoritative positions. They also regularly assert its equality provisions, among other rules, to justify and legitimize their participation in peace negotiations.

African women have mobilized all over the world (Burundi, Democratic Republic of the Congo, Liberia, Mozambique, Rwanda, Sierra Leone, Somalia, South Africa, and Uganda) to influence peace processes because peace deals often have longer lasting impacts on the rights and well-being of women than does armed conflict. Women have known for decades that society cannot genuinely recover from the evils of armed conflict if they are not actively involved as equal stakeholders and their issues are not forthrightly addressed in the design and implementation of transitional regimes: this knowledge is only beginning to find normative expression in law and policy. For example, women's rights verbiage, from victim to stakeholder classifications, can be identified in about 90 percent of the peace agreements that have resolved internal armed conflict between 1990 and 2012. African

[31] *Id.* The authors note that there have been six female prime ministers in Africa since the mid-1990s. Other notable examples include Luisa Dia Diogo's tenure as prime minister of Mozambique since 2004 and Specioza Wandera Kazibwe's election as vice president of Uganda (1994–2003).

[32] *Pan-African President: Gertrude Mongella*, AFRICA RESEARCH NEWS BULLETIN, Mar. 1–31, 2004, at 15667.

women have taken holistic approaches to conflict, prevention, management, and resolution that draw on local culture and custom, such as instituting Gacaca courts in Rwanda and Palava Hut tribunals in Liberia, and at times also incorporate Western peacemaking theory and modeling. Women, more than any other group, understand that their participation in peace construction is necessary to address and inform vital transitional and postconflict issues that disproportionately impact women, particularly mothers. These issues range from access to food, water, shelter, medical treatment, and sanitation to the need for security, justice, reparation, and employment opportunities. As one analyst noted, "[w]omen's participation in and influence over the terms of peace is therefore both a precondition for addressing a range of postconflict issues and to long-term prevention of armed conflict and of the harms that war inflicts disproportionally on women."[33] This is precisely why it is imperative that they participate in every phase of peace construction, including the conceptual, drafting, interpretive, and operative stages, and serve as peace negotiators, brokers, technicians, and transitional government officials. When women participate as decision makers in political processes, the character of the body politic and the content of political outcomes arguably change for the better.[34]

"African womanist" approaches arguably accelerate gender equality during and immediately after armed conflict more effectively than Western feminist attitudes.[35] This is often because their approaches and the new rules that follow reflect the views of local women, unlike the law and conflict resolution models developed by international consultants and specialists, which largely ignore them. Gwendolyn Mikell rightly notes that African feminism "owes its origins to different dynamics than those that generated Western feminism" because it "has largely been shaped by African women's resistance to Western hegemony and its legacy within African culture."[36] This dichotomy in oppositional approaches is accentuated during war and explains why "African

[33] Margaret E. McGuinness, *Women as architects of peace: Gender and the resolution of armed conflict*, 15 MICH. ST. J. INT'L. L. 63, 64 (2007).

[34] Sue Thomas, *The impact of women on state legislative policies*, 53 J. POLITICS 974 (1991).

[35] African womanists embrace incremental rights-based approaches that leverage and manipulate traditional pathologies and patriarchies to achieve women's equality without robustly disturbing nonviolent and nonoppressive social and cultural practices to which their societies subscribe. African womanists are not preoccupied with attacking African culture, the cultural dynamics of masculinity, or the idea of male dominance of women: rather, they focus on achieving women's equality in all spheres of life by leveraging, not threatening, conventional verities. The end goal is not to become men, replace men, or destroy masculine constructions, but rather to work with and lead men as coequals in human development while amplifying feminine ideals and creations.

[36] AFRICAN FEMINISM: THE POLITICS OF SURVIVAL IN SUB-SAHARAN AFRICA 4 (Gwendolyn Mikell ed., 1997).

womanism" is markedly different; it is "distinctly heterosexual, pro-natal, and concerned with many 'bread, butter, culture, and power' issues."[37] This organic approach in some ways illuminates why African womanist methods that employ intercultural leveraging have been effective. This approach seeks to consciously manipulate or leverage traditional authority structures, social interaction norms, patriarchal modes of communication, and social relations in order to sway "spoils" or "winner-take-all" approaches.[38] As Sylvia Tamale wisely observes:

> For many African women the sustainable solutions to their oppression, exploitation and subordination hardly lie in vague, alien legal rights, but in a careful and creative deployment of the more familiar cultural norms and values. Thus far, the blunted tools of human rights have had a very limited effect on the lives and realities of African women. While the top-down constitutional and legal framework is necessary as a foundational touchstone of women's rights, our activism must begin from the assumption that bottom-up approaches anchored in local cultures and traditions are more likely to succeed than those working from without.[39]

It follows that bottom-up approaches to conflict resolution and peace construction that integrate women's concerns and needs seem to produce more holistic and enduring peace agreements because the legitimacy of womanist-centered peace deals increase when women, the numerical majority in civil society, embrace them.

Consequently, African women activists are intentionally and unintentionally constructing independent approaches to African diplomacy and conflict prevention, management, and resolution that may disturb conventional multi-track diplomacy typologies.[40] One African womanist approach, which I refer to as "intracultural leveraging"' has been successfully used by African women's groups in peacemaking processes for decades. This form of advocacy naturally synthesizes informal and formal advocacy approaches and leverages social networks, cultural practices and norms, technical knowledge, and activism with political elites and/or war contestants. Intracultural leveraging embraces culture as a basis of engagement and integrates advantageous analytical and advocacy strategies rather than replicating West-centric feminist approaches,

[37] *Id.* at 5.

[38] For a pioneering study on African feminism, *see* African Feminism, *supra* note 36.

[39] Sylvia Tamale, *The right to culture and the culture of rights: A critical perspective on women's sexual rights in Africa*, Urgent Action Fund-Africa 165 (2007).

[40] *See generally* Multi-Track Diplomacy: A Systems Approach to Peace (Louise Diamond & John McDonald eds., 1996).

making it a variegated example of "situated judgment."[41] This approach appears to be most effective when used by a broad cohort of women ranging from homemakers to professional executives (e.g., market women, teachers, seamstresses, traditional leaders, lawyers, doctors, mediators, bankers, and diplomats). To emphasize this point, Sanam Anderlini notes that some women's rights movements approach peace construction "with an explicit message of equality and demands for the right to participate in decision-making and the firm belief that peace processes should promote more equitable relations between men and women. Others build on their socially accepted identities as mothers, daughters, or along ethnic, religious, or tribal lines, and focus on critical peace and security issues."[42]

Intracultural leveraging seems to balance equality claims while embracing traditional sociocultural identities. Hence, African women have employed social identities to promote their right to participate as decision makers in vital peace and security issues that affect their existence. They see themselves as durable actors in forging law, norms, doctrine, and jurisprudence aimed at achieving equality and reinforcing positive cultural traditions in the private and public spheres and, for the purpose of this analysis, in peace processes.[43] For example, African women in South Africa not only served as the nucleus of the antiapartheid movement, but also fiercely contested the conscription of children into the South African National Defense Force (SANDF) and freedom-fighting groups such as *UmkhontoweSizwe* (MK). African women activists such as Angelina Atyam avidly protested against the abduction of children in Uganda by the Lord's Resistance Movement, thereby bringing national and international attention to the issue. Liberian activists established the Liberian Women's Initiative (LWI) to represent the voices of those affected by the Liberian civil war. Led by a former school teacher, Mary Bromwell, the group engaged in community messaging and sensitization while advocating for an end to the war, the inclusion of women in the peace process, a comprehensive peace agreement, and democratic elections, using nonviolent demonstrations and media campaigns to influence war contestants. In fact, Liberian women have been credited for "perfecting the art of 'corridor lobbying'" by petitioning domestic, regional, and international mediators to ensure that their intellectual and policy-related concerns influenced

41 Margaret Jane Radin, *The pragmatist and the feminist*, 63 S. Cal. L. Rev. 1699, 1718–19 (1990).

42 Sanam Naraghi Anderlini, Women Building Peace, What They Do, Why It Matters 62 (2007).

43 See *generally* African Women's Movements, *supra* note 29.

Liberia's various peace talks between 1994 and 2003.[44] Notwithstanding, in 1996, even Ruth Perry, Liberia's incoming transitional head of state, was barred from directly participating in peace talks because she was not "accredited" to partake in them,[45] a situation that vividly illustrated how women, irrespective of their qualifications and standing, are more welcomed in the hallways of peace than in the boardrooms of peace construction.

Nevertheless, African women continue to strive to ensure gender equality in all aspects of peace construction, particularly in the areas of power sharing and retributive justice.[46] One reason for their unrelenting advocacy stems from the realization that armed conflict "accentuates existing differences of power and access to resources, weakening the position of those who are already without power," namely women.[47] Local women understand all too well the disproportionate impact that war has on their families. For example, in 1996, after her fourteen-year-old daughter Charlotte was abducted, raped, and forced into marriage by the LRA in Northern Uganda (along with 138 other girls) after a night raid on their boarding school, Angelino Atyam established the Concerned Parents Association (CPA) to advocate for the protection and rights of children, peace, and reconciliation.[48] Although the LRA's diabolical leader, Joseph Kony, attempted to acquire Atyam's silence with the return of her daughter, she refused Kony's offer.[49] Atyam became a champion of children and women's rights in Uganda's peace process; she was eventually appointed to the six-person delegation that represented her country in meetings with international stakeholders seeking to end the conflict.[50] Another illuminating example is that of Asha Hagi Elmi Amin (Asha Amin). In 2000, after women were systematically excluded from a series of peace talks aimed at ending clan warfare in Somalia, Amin, founder of Save Somali Women and

[44] *Id.* at 63.

[45] African Women and Peace Support Group, LIBERIAN WOMEN PEACEMAKERS: FIGHTING FOR THE RIGHT TO BE SEEN, HEARD, AND COUNTED 26–31 (2004). It is interesting to note that Ruth Perry was Africa's first female head of state and Ellen Johnson-Sirleaf its first democratically elected female president.

[46] African women launched several prominent regional institutions and networks primarily concerned with peacebuilding including the Femmes Africa Solidarité (FAS), African Women's Committee for Peace and Development and the (AWCDP) (now African Unions Women Committee and Federation of African Women's Peace Networks [FERFAP]).

[47] Judy El Bushra, *Feminism, gender, and women's peace activism*, 38 DEVELOPMENT AND CHANGE 131, 136 (2007).

[48] Anderlini, *supra* note 42, at 68. See also, Jonathan Wilson-Hartgrove, *A nonviolent response to Joseph Kony*, March 9, 2012, *available at* http://www.patheos.com/blogs/jonathanwilsonhartgrove/2012/03/a-nonviolent-response-to-joseph-kony/, last visited October 30, 2012.

[49] *Id.*

[50] *Id.*

Children (SSWC), demanded that they be included.[51] Although the UN allowed her to attend the peace negotiations as an observer, she was plainly ignored by the leaders of all five participating clans, which were led by men. As a result she "decided to both play by and subvert the rules" by forming "a sixth clan, the women's clan," or SSWC, because she believed that women would be stronger bridges for peace.[52] SSWC "put pressure on clan elders, religious leaders, Islamic scholars and politicians to put women at the negotiating table as equal partners and decision-makers."[53] In January 2004, she represented the women's clan as the only woman cochair of the final phase of the Somali National Reconciliation Conference, ultimately becoming the first Somali woman to sign the peace accord.[54] Hagi's efforts ultimately led to gender mainstreaming in the Somalia National Peace Process and gender quotas in the Federal Parliament, among other reforms.[55]

One unique development unearthed in this study is the special ability of African women to organize and to build capacity during armed conflict, during transitions from war to peace, and in the postconflict environment. This new activism can be attributed to several factors including, at the national level, women's ability to develop alliances during peace negotiations irrespective of race, ethnicity, clan, religion, or party affiliation; an increase of women in national parliaments; and donor support for women's empowerment programs. At the regional level, new norm-generating dynamics include the subregional, regional, and international normalization of the women's rights movement after the 1995 Beijing Conference, the domestication of women's rights norms in national systems, the codification of human rights and democracy conventions at the regional level, and the debility of authoritarianism and one-party rule in Africa.

[51] Founded in 1991, SSWC seeks to stop violence against women by empowering them to become human rights advocates, to provide humanitarian relief to war victims and war-torn communities, and to promote a peaceful transition to constitutional democracy. *See Peace Direct: Supporting local action against conflict, save Somali women and children*, Somalia, *available at* http://www.peacedirect.org/peacebuilders/past-projects/somalia/ (last visited October 30, 2012).

[52] Anderlini, *supra* note 42, at 69.

[53] *Peace Direct, supra* note 51.

[54] The peace accord was the *Declaration on the Harmonization of Various Issues Proposed by the Somali Delegates at the Somali Consultative Meetings* (January 29, 2004, State House, Nairobi, Kenya). Save Somali Women and Children, *available at* http://www.sswc-som.com/index.php?page=accomlishments (last visited October 30, 2012); *See also* Anderlini, *supra* note 42, at 69; *Somalia wins "alternative Nobel,"* BBC News, October 1, 2008, *available at* http://news.bbc.co.uk/2/hi/africa/7646771.stm (last visited October 30, 2012).

[55] *Save Somali women and children, available at* http://www.sswc-som.com/index.php?page=accomlishments (last visited October 30, 2012).

Perhaps one of the most compelling examples of such capacity building was the establishment of the Mano River Women's Peace Network (MARWOPNET) in 2000. This network aimed, among other things, to bring peace to the region of West Africa by organizing and mobilizing women's groups to be full stakeholders in peacemaking, democratization, and development processes.[56] MARWOPNET was a formidable subregional movement of women in West Africa, namely Liberia, Sierra Leone, and Guinea-Bissau, that very effectively used "intracultural leveraging" to lobby at the local, national, and international levels for women to be included in conflict prevention, management, and resolution, and particularly for them to be included as stakeholders during peace talks. In August 2003, MARWOPNET's efforts were bolstered by the Women in Peace Building Network (WPBN), a small women's refugee organization, which, in a show of courage and desperation in protest of ongoing hostilities, threatened to strip naked and lock negotiators behind closed doors until a comprehensive peace agreement was agreed upon and signed. On August 18, 2003, MARWOPNET officially witnessed the signing of the Accra peace agreement that ended armed conflict in Liberia. One of its signature accomplishments was that it secured women's participation in the Accra peace process – albeit at the periphery of power – and sternly protested against any "UN-sponsored peace agreement that basically rewarded leaders of the armed factions with positions in the transitional government while doing little to disarm them."[57] Consequently, disarmament became a precondition to power sharing, to the chagrin of rebel leaders. Interestingly, as the MARWOPNET example shows, women have found ways to shape debates and influence peace outcomes even when they have been excluded from peace processes. Their actions and efforts have had significant political and legal impacts on peace-construction processes. Consequently, the "peace industry" has been forced to accept that gender equality is a critical aspect of peace construction and consequently to adopt rules, norms, and doctrine aimed at ensuring women's participation – particularly the right to play a part in peace negotiations, inform peace deals, and partake in transitional governance structures as decision makers. MARWOPNET's peace activities illustrate the growing trend in African women's advocacy networks (AWANs) or regional advocacy networks (RANs) that have significantly contributed to and fashioned conflict resolution processes; other AWANs have actively influenced the development

[56] *See Mano River Union Women's Peace Network*, *available at* http://www.marwopnet.org/objectives.htm

[57] Tripp, *supra* note 2, at 182.

of regional and international law and doctrine, including the design and adoption of the African Women's Protocol[58] and UN Security Council Resolution 1325.[59]

Hence, the orderly exclusion of women from peace negotiations, power-sharing deals, and the transitional regimes such arrangements ratify has birthed tenacious activism, which in turn has significantly impacted legal developments at the regional and international levels. On this point, referencing the impact of women on the development of UN Security Council Resolution 1325, which aims to ensure women's full participation in all phases of peacebuilding, Anderlini notes: "So the strategic targeting of the Security Council and push for a resolution that endorsed women's inclusion in peacemaking was not only a deliberate attempt at shifting the paradigm and the norms governing peace processes, but also a means of ensuring that they had a chance to determine the future – theirs and their society's – at the point in time when foundations were being laid."[60] African women and women's groups were key participants – as victims, advocates, and technicians – in the foundational thinking behind UN Security Council Resolution 1325, as well as in

[58] Melinda Adams & Alice Kang, *Regional advocacy networks and the protocol on the rights of women*, 3 Politics and Gender 451–74 (2007). Examples of such regional groups include, among many others, the Inter-African Committee on Traditional Practices Affecting the Health of Women and Children (IAC), African Women's Development and Communication Network (FEMNET), Women in Law and Development in Africa (WiLDAF), and Solidarity for African Women's Rights (SOAWR). In 1984, IAC was established in Addis Ababa, Ethiopia, to advocate "for the removal of harmful traditional practices that affect the health of women and children"; it is comprised of "National Committees in 28 African countries and 15 Affiliates/Group Sections in Europe, USA, Canada, Japan and New Zealand." *See Inter-African Committee on Traditional Practices Affecting the Health of Women and Children, available at* http://www.iac-ciaf.net/index.php?option=com_content&view=article&id=10&Itemid=3 (last visited November 19, 2012). In 1988, FEMNET was created in Nairobi, Kenya to "share experiences, information and strategies among African women's non-governmental organizations (NGOs) through advocacy, training and communications so as to advance African women's development, equality and other human rights" and includes numerous individual and nonprofit members throughout Africa. FEMNET, *available at* http://femnet.co/index.php/en/background-history (last visited November 19, 2012). In 1990, WiLDAF was created to promote women's rights in Africa. It is comprised of 500 organizations and more than 1,200 individual members in thirty-one countries. WiLDAF, *available at* http://www.wildaf.org/index.php/whoweare/history (last visited November 15, 2012). In 2004, SOAWR was established in Nairobi and "is a coalition of 36 civil society organizations across the continent working to ensure that the Protocol to the African Charter on the Rights of Women in Africa remains on the agenda of policy makers and to urge all African leaders to safeguard the rights of women through ratification and implementation of the Protocol." SOAWR, *available at* http://www.soawr.org/en/ (last visited November 25, 2012).

[59] African Women's Movements, *supra* note 29, at 204.

[60] Anderlini, *supra* note 42, at 71.

other core women's rights law, including CEDAW and the African Women's Protocol.[61] All three documents concretely pronounce on the unlawfulness of women's exclusion during peace construction and, more formidably, on the illegality of power sharing as a tool of conflict resolution. It is not farfetched to argue that UN Security Resolution 1325 and the African Women's Protocol would not have been adopted but for the near-universal recognition of the cruel and exclusionary impacts of war and peacebuilding on African women. Such law has been emboldened by doctrine and jurisprudence emanating from human rights commissions and courts and international criminal law tribunals such as the International Criminal Tribunal for Rwanda (ICTR).[62]

This section provides insight into the multifarious ways in which African women and women's groups have conceived and contributed to the development of peacebuilding law, which is an important component of the international women's rights protective regime; the next section examines the legality of transitional political power sharing through the prism of CEDAW, the African Women's Protocol, and Resolution 1325.

LAW AND LAWLESSNESS: NORMATIVITY AND EXCLUSIVITY

The International Human Rights of Women in Peace Construction

The exclusion of women as key actors in peace construction tramples on the civil liberties that are protected in most national constitutions in Africa; such exclusion is unlawful under regional and international law.[63] Peace agreements that include political power-sharing provisions are often the most offensive to human rights law and democratization processes, especially the international human rights of women in Africa, as exemplified in CEDAW, UN Security Council Resolution 1325, and the African Women's Protocol, each of which normatively builds on the other. Transitional political power-sharing agreements operate in a nebulous legal realm because they are

[61] For example, Femmes Africa Solidarité (FAS) has been one of the most effective African women's peacebuilding organizations that aims, among other things, to ensure women's active participation and leadership in conflict prevention, management and resolution processes as well as other peacebuilding activities. The Femmes Africa Solidarité (FAS), *available at* http://www.fasngo.org/ReportsActivities.html (last visited November 29, 2012).

[62] Human Rights Watch, GENDER, WAR CRIMES & CRIMES AGAINST HUMANITY: DIGEST OF THE CASE LAW OF THE INTERNATIONAL CRIMINAL TRIBUNAL FOR RWANDA (2010), at 126–134. Democratic Republic of the Congo v Burundi, Rwanda and Uganda (2004) AHRLR 19 (African Commission on Human and People's Rights, 2003), *available at* http://www1.chr.up.ac.za/index.php/browse-by-subject/227-burundi-democratic-republic-of-the-congo-v-burundi-rwanda-and-uganda-2004-ahrlr-19-achpr-2003.html

[63] This section draws heavily from an earlier work of the author. Levitt, *supra* note 6, at 154–59.

typically shaped by political necessity and expediency and are principally concerned with ending deadly intrastate armed conflict rather than with protecting rights and delivering justice. In this sense, they consciously ignore the prevailing domestic, regional, and international legal norms that are intended to shape and inform them. As the earlier discussion notes, political power sharing too often has a broad and disproportionate impact on the human rights and democracy entitlements of women, given that impunity, whether through amnesty or inaction, curbs rights-based claims and reconstructs or reorders the framework of governance and its future disposition. In Cote d' Ivoire, the Democratic Republic of the Congo, Guinea-Bissau, Liberia, Rwanda, and Sierra Leone, to name a few examples, women were largely absent as "players" from the negotiating tables that birthed their respective peace agreements, despite, for example, the ardent advocacy of the Mano River Women's Peace Network (MAROWET) in Liberia and a small collective of women's groups in Sierra Leone.[64] Notwithstanding, although women and women's groups may have informed the aforementioned peace processes to varying degrees, it is popular myth that they were key players in what remained male-dominated enterprises.[65] In each instance, the collective interests of women stood virtually ignored during peace negotiations and peacebuilding processes. As a result, women's issues were also largely overlooked in the postconflict order. This troubling phenomenon is symptomatic of a perplexing global pattern of discrimination that harms the welfare and interests of women in direct contravention of CEDAW.

CEDAW mandates that states parties must condemn discrimination against women in all forms and prescribes policy to ensure their equality with men in national constitutions, legislation, and other law.[66] Although CEDAW's equality model discounts intracultural leveraging approaches, its parity requirement directly applies to peace agreements because they form a part of domestic, regional, and international law and are often sanctioned by legislation. CEDAW requires member states to safeguard the rights of women on an equal basis with men and to ensure, through tribunals, courts, and other public institutions, that women are effectively protected from any act of discrimination.[67] Thus, the mere adoption of power-sharing peace

64 *Women, peace and security*, study submitted by the secretary-general pursuant to Security Council Resolution 1325 (2000), U.N. Publ. (2002), at 61–62.

65 UN Development Program for Women (UNIFEM), WOMEN'S PARTICIPATION IN PEACE NEGOTIATION: CONNECTIONS BETWEEN PRESENCE AND INFLUENCE (August 2010), at 1–10.

66 41 Convention on the Elimination of All Forms of Discrimination against Women, G.A. Res. 34/180, art. 2(a), 34 U.N. GAOR Supp. (No. 46) at 193, U.N. Doc. A/34/46 (December 18, 1979), entered into force September 3, 1981 (hereinafter CEDAW).

67 *Id.* at art. 2(c).

agreements – ad hoc political mandates accorded the weight of super law – abrogates CEDAW. This means that the disparate impact of power sharing – whether hard, moderate, or soft – on women must be carefully weighed during peace negotiations,[68] and women must be afforded judicial reprieve when such impacts are ignored. CEDAW also prohibits states and, by extension, international institutions from engaging in any act or practice that discriminates against women and specifically directs state parties to take all appropriate measures, including legislation, to amend or eradicate any existing law, regulations, customs, or practices that likewise discriminate.[69] Hence, national legislatures – whether transitional or not – have a legal duty to reject agreements that discriminate against women, particularly when women are excluded from negotiations and issues specific to their welfare that are not sufficiently recognized. Public authorities and institutions, including besieged government officials and warlords and rebels, that have acquired some measure of legal personality arguably have a duty to comply with CEDAW. Finally, these important rights and duties underwrite the most fundamental principles in CEDAW related to power sharing: the right of women to participate in the formulation and implementation of government policy, to hold public office, to perform government functions at all levels, and to represent their governments at the regional and international levels.[70]

The right of women to actively participate in peace processes was reaffirmed by UN Security Council in Resolution 1325, which stresses the "importance of their equal participation and full involvement in all" peacemaking efforts, especially their role in "decision-making" with regard to conflict prevention and resolution,[71] and it affirms the need for full implementation of international human rights law and international humanitarian law, which are aimed at protecting women and girls during and after armed conflict.[72] The resolution recognizes that full participation of women in peace processes "can significantly contribute to the maintenance and promotion of international peace and security" and urges all member states to increase the numbers of women at all levels of decision making in national, regional, and international institutions, including peace construction.[73] It also calls on all actors – whether state or nonstate – to adopt gender perspectives "when negotiating and implementing peace agreements" and to end impunity and protect

[68] Levitt, supra note 6, at 154–58.

[69] *Id.* at art. 2(d), (f).

[70] *Id.* at arts. 7(a), (b), and 8.

[71] Preamble, UN Security Council Resolution 1325, adopted by the Security Council at its 4213th meeting on October 31, 2000.

[72] *Id.*

[73] *Id.* at arts. 1 and 2.

women and girls from gender-based violence during armed conflict by prosecuting perpetrators.[74] Consequently, Resolution 1325 provides a firm veil of legality and legitimacy of principles in CEDAW concerning the right of women to participate in, make, and implement government policy and execute government functions at all levels. However, unlike CEDAW, the resolution specifically applies to armed conflict and the rights of women to partake in every phase of peacemaking, including the design and operation of transitional power-sharing arrangements. Hence, the protective and participatory principles in UN Security Council Resolution 1325 should influence the character of all peace processes. Unfortunately, the UN and regional and subregional actors – all of whom play informative roles in ending armed conflict in Africa – do little to operationalize such law and to make certain that woman actively play a part in peace negotiations as decision makers or serve as senior officials in transitional governments. Notwithstanding, Resolution 1325 amplifies the equality paradigm and serves as a catalyst for women and women's groups to organize and demand representation in conflict management and resolution structures, particularly in peacebuilding arrangements in Burundi, Democratic Republic of the Congo, and Sudan.[75]

Although Resolution 1325 amplifies CEDAW's platform for women's rights during armed conflict, the 2013 adoption of General Recommendation No. 30 on Women in Conflict Prevention, Conflict and Postconflict Situations, of the Committee on the Elimination of Discrimination against Women, emboldens and crystalizes Resolution 1325. General Recommendation No. 30 is the most authoritative interpretation of the applicability of CEDAW during and after armed conflict and other imminent situations that threaten the well-being of women. It intends to bolster states parties compliance with CEDAW's equality and protective principles during and after armed conflict and "other situations of concern" including the "war on terrorism" and "internal disturbances."[76] It provides states parties with authoritative guidance "on legislative, policy and other appropriate measures to ensure full compliance with their obligations under the Convention to protect, respect and fulfil

[74] *Id.* at arts. 8, 10, and 11. The UN Security Council also asked the Secretary-General to conduct a study on the "impact of armed conflict on women and girls and the role of women in peacebuilding and the gender dimensions of peace processes and conflict resolution." *Id.* at art. 16.

[75] UN Department of Public Information, Facts and Figures on Women, Peace and Security, U.N. Doc. DPI/2409 (2005).

[76] Comm. on the Elimination of Discrimination against Women, General Recommendation No. 30 on Women in Conflict Prevention, Conflict and Post Conflict Situations, Paragraph 26, 56th Sess., September 30–October 18, 2013, U.N. Doc. CEDAW/C/GC/30 (September 4, 2013).

women's human rights"[77] General Recommendation No. 30 explicitly and authoritatively concludes that CEDAW necessitates women's participation at every level of conflict, prevention, management, and resolution, including the shaping, development, and implementation of peace agreements and transitional justice initiatives.[78] It provides no leeway for devolutionary reinterpretation and seems to place a positive duty on state and nonstate actors to refrain from engaging in any conduct or activities that abrogate CEDAW's protective mandate. In this context, any form of transitional political power sharing that nullifies predominant or controlling rules (domestic constitutions, regional and international women's rights norms) and excludes women from actively participating in peace processes at every level of decision making from peace negotiations to transitional governance and justice arrangements to disarmament and demobilization, is woefully unlawful. Not only is their exclusion in peace construction distressingly unlawful, but it is also arguably the greatest indicator of their long-term political disenfranchisement and gender-specific violence and poverty in the postconflict environment.

General Recommendation No. 30 equality provisions were sternly and immediately backed by UN Security Council Resolution 2122, which assertively recognizes the importance of women's participation and leadership in peacemaking and firmly establishes as a matter of doctrine the critical role of gender equality to long-term peace and stability.[79] It seems to acknowledge the need to track, study, and address the full scope of gender-based violence and harms against women during armed conflict. Recommendation No. 30 is by far the UN's most fervent call to action of member states, UN entities, international financial institutions, and nonstate actors to strengthen the capacity of institutions to sustainably assist "women and girls affected by armed conflict and post conflict situations."[80] It also calls upon states parties to end impunity and "to thoroughly investigate and prosecute persons responsible for war crimes, genocide, crimes against humanity or other serious violations,"[81] which is a welcome call, given the unacknowledged but never-ending nexus of circular causation between impunity, power sharing, and deadly conflict. Essentially, this means that the UN Security Council must take affirmative efforts to comply with its own dictates by ending the practice of sanctioning or endorsing unlawful power-sharing peace deals that

77 *Id.* at Paragraph 1.
78 *Id.* at Paragraphs 45–47.
79 *See generally*, UN Security Council Resolution 2122, adopted by the Security Council at its 7044th meeting, on October 18, 2013.
80 *Id.* at Paragraph 11.
81 *Id.* at Paragraph 12.

discriminate against and disenfranchise women, a practice deeply entrenched in the ethos of UN conflict management and resolution practice.

The systematic exclusion of women and women's issues in peace agreements – both during negotiations and in the transitional political apparatus – is a global human rights problem that detrimentally affects the longevity of peace because the opinions, welfare, and interests of those most affected by armed conflict are not represented. On this point, the UN Secretary-General reported:

> Women are under-represented in formal peace negotiations, whether as local participants representing warring factions, or as representatives of international authorities overseeing or mediating deliberations and institutions invited to the negotiating table. In addition, central issues of concern to women, including their participation in post-conflict political, social, civil, economic and judicial structures, do not always reach the negotiating table, in part because of the exclusion of women from the formal peace negotiations. Women not only call for issues specific to themselves but raise issues that affect society as a whole, such as land reform, access to loans and capacity-building. All actors committed to equality and non-discrimination – whether male or female – should have the responsibility and capacity to ensure that peace agreements incorporate gender equality issues.[82]

Despite this clear message, the UN, African Union (AU), and other African regional institutions continue to sanction or legitimize political power-sharing agreements that prevent women from being full stakeholders in their creation and implementation. African governments in (for example) Burundi, Liberia, Sierra Leone, Guinea-Bissau, and Rwanda, along with the UN and other peace brokers and peace guarantors, failed to ensure that women were accorded decision-making seats at "all" tables of power during and after peace negotiations and did not consider the impact of power sharing on women generally. In these cases and many others, government and international institutions have routinely failed to guarantee or secure women positions of authority in transitional governments or to provide domestic venues (e.g., courts and tribunals) to challenge the legality and legitimacy of peace arrangements that flagrantly contravene international law. Because, in Africa, a right to justice, internal self-determination, and democracy exists, power sharing without consideration of women's rights flouts them woefully. Furthermore, impunity through explicit (e.g., Burundi, Cote d'Ivoire, Sierra Leone) or implicit (e.g., Liberia and Guinea-Bissau) amnesty is too often a scandalous tradeoff, a malevolent

[82] *Women, peace and security*, study submitted by the Secretary-General pursuant to Security Council Resolution 1325 (2000), U.N. Publ. (2002), Para. 191 at 61.

feature of power-sharing arrangements that discriminates against women and subverts retributive justice.

The justice component of human rights is paramount because women disproportionally suffer from sexual violence, displacement, and other forms of violence during armed conflict even as they bear the brunt of family responsibilities. Women's family commitments are too often lopsided during peace time, but during armed conflict they are unbearable: women take on additional work as caregivers, as well as fulfilling duties traditionally reserved for men and caring for the sick, wounded, and disabled. Access to courts is another major problem in many countries, especially in postconflict environments in which justice for women is virtually nonexistent. As a result, women are too often left to fend for themselves and their families without any form of social assistance and redress. As already noted, the failure of peace accords to include, let alone contemplate, women's justice affirmatively disenfranchises them. What's more, the consequential interplay among making peace during armed conflict, postconflict justice, and development deserves special attention, given that the bulk of donor aid for postconflict construction is controlled and directed by men. This not only means that women are denied seats at tables of power during peace negotiations and transitions, but also that their developmental and reparatory needs, such as health, nutrition, education, literacy, psychological services, security, and justice are arrogantly flouted, not made equal with those of similarly situated men. As such, power sharing systemically disenfranchises women in the preconflict and postconflict order – an outcome that only societies and institutions with an ingrained pathology of violence against women can tolerate. From this background, there is a systematic practice in the structure and operation of power sharing that boldly discriminates against and impinges on the fundamental human rights and democratic entitlements of women, rights that are enshrined in CEDAW, UN Security Council Resolution 1325, and regional human rights norms in Africa.

The Protocol to the African Charter on Human and Peoples' Rights on the Rights of Women in Africa was adopted on July 11, 2003, and entered into force on November 25, 2005.[83] The African Women's Protocol reinforces and expands the Banjul Charter and the Grand Bay Declaration and also comprehensively addresses disparities engendered by power sharing.[84] It is the first regional human rights treaty to focus exclusively on women's rights,

[83] *Protocol to the African Charter on Human and Peoples' Rights on the Rights of Women in Africa*, adopted by the Second Ordinary Session of the Assembly of the Union in Maputo on July 11, 2003.

[84] African Women's Protocol, supra note 77, at art. 8–11.

particularly on the elimination of discrimination against them.[85] In this sense, it also claims, restates, reinforces, and reinstitutionalizes equality and non-violent precepts and doctrine in CEDAW and Resolution 1325.[86] The Protocol requires member states to actively mainstream gender equality in law, doctrine, and policy and to integrate gender perspectives in rules, policy decisions, and programs in all spheres of life, including, presumably, peace agreements.[87] It mandates that states have a positive duty to safeguard the dignity of women, as well as to protect them from all forms of violence. This includes, among other things, the duty to prevent and eliminate such violence by ensuring equal and effective access to justice and legal services, including legal aid, and to guarantee enforcement of equality rights and the investigation, prosecution, and punishment of perpetrators of violence.[88] Furthermore, it requires states to provide adequate budgetary resources to curb violence against women and to establish mechanisms and accessible services for redress, rehabilitation, and reparation.[89] The African Women's Protocol directs member states to guarantee that women are equally represented in the judiciary and to take "specific positive action" to promote equal participation in governance, including, as previously noted, equality in the distribution of positions in power-sharing deals.[90] Despite these legal rules and mandates, state compliance has been lackluster, deepening the disparity of protection between women and men.

The "responsibility to include" falls on governments, insurgent groups, and, by extension, other actors actively participating in peace negotiations, including, again, the UN and African regional organizations.[91] In fact, the African Women's Protocol mandates states parties to take appropriate measures to ensure women's participation in the "structures and process of *conflict prevention, management and resolution* at the local, national, regional, continental and international levels" and in all "aspects of planning, formulation and implementation of post-conflict reconstruction and rehabilitation."[92] Although the participation of civil society in the negotiation and implementation of the Accra Agreement in Liberia was limited, such participation,

[85] Adrien Wing, *Women's rights and Africa's evolving landscape: The Women's Protocol of the Banjul Charter*, in AFRICA: MAPPING NEW BOUNDARIES IN INTERNATIONAL LAW 27–33 (Jeremy I. Levitt ed., 2008).

[86] *Id.*

[87] African Women's Protocol, *supra* note 83, at art. 2.

[88] *Id.* at arts. 3, 4, 8, and 11.

[89] *Id.* at arts. 4 and 25.

[90] *Id.* at art. 9.

[91] The terms IGAD and SADC mean the Inter-Governmental Authority on Development and the Southern African Development Community, respectively.

[92] *Id.* at art. 10 (emphasis added).

especially among women, provided the agreement with greater legitimacy than the agreements reached in Lomé and Abuja, which included remedial to virtually no participation by women's organizations, respectively. That said, women's participation in Liberia, and to some extent in Sierra Leone, was more participatory than technical. It follows that prevailing rules dictate that women's contributions to peacemaking processes should not be "participation neutral," meaning that their quantitative contribution must be complemented by the opportunity for qualitative input. Some analysts attribute stronger civil society involvement in the Accra peace process to its apparent transition to democracy, arguing that

> the stark contrast in Liberia between the outcomes of the 1996 Abuja Accords and the 2003 Accra Agreement is telling in this regard. After early roles in the 1996 peace process, Liberian civil society groups were excluded and deals were made among the factional armies leading to the emergence of Charles Taylor as president the following year. Taylor's predatory government teetered for several years before collapsing in resumed civil war. The 2003 peace process, on the other hand, saw strong civil society participation, with the [women's] groups even signing the final agreement as witnesses. Credible elections followed, leading to the emergence of Ellen Johnson-Sirleaf as president, who has governed with broad civil society input and has begun moving Liberia forward. The two series of negotiations for Sierra Leone similarly illustrate this point.[93]

Anecdotal evidence from this study and others suggests that peace processes are more sustainable when women actively participate in them as equals, supporting Hillary Charlesworth's call to "revive the equality framework as the basis of the claim that women should be involved in conflict resolution and formal peace-building" while being "cautious" about "invoking" affinity and utility arguments.[94] This may be because women are the most affected by armed conflict and are consequently the greatest stakeholders in peace. As such, the African Women's Protocol explicitly and normatively addresses the global pathology of violence against women during times of peace and war and, in the field of conflict resolution and intervention, decrees that women should actively participate in the design and implementation of peace arrangements. This essentially means that male-centered spheres of discretionary power that dominate peace processes are inconsistent with and prohibited by the law as it currently stands.

[93] Anthony Wanis-St. John & Darren Kew, *Civil society and peace negotiations: Confronting exclusion*, 13 (1) INT'L. NEGOTIATION 11, 27, 30 (2008) (emphasis added).

[94] Charlesworth, *supra* note 28, at 359.

CONCLUSION: WHO WILL PROTECT ABEENA AND AFIA?

Waves of African women's movements in the 1990s stirred activism that struggled against the normative tide that abetted their orderly exclusion from peace construction. Still, even now, law, doctrine, and norms that purport to protect women from the evils of illegal peace and impunity are largely ignored, particularly by the UN and regional organizations. On this point Hillary Charlesworth aptly notes, "The need to involve women in peace-building is regularly ignored by the UN and other international institutions. Sanam Anderlini talks of the UN's 'Triple-A' syndrome with respect to women and peace: apathy, ad hoc practices and amnesia. The Security Council has made reference to Resolution 1325 in just 25% of its country-specific resolutions from 2000 to 2006, and the Secretary-General has rarely appointed women to leadership roles in peace-building."[95] In essence, UN inaction forces women to suffer the indignities of war, to quietly succumb to the illegality of peace through the arbitrary political edicts of either misdirected or evil men during peace negotiations and transitions to peace, and, finally, to live under the nonjusticiable rule of the various warlords and rebels who brutalized them.

The systematic exclusion of women in peace construction is a form of "democratic impunity" and contributes to domestic violence, alcoholism, and drug abuse in postconflict environs; these are problems that disproportionately affect women but remain ignored in peacemaking and peacebuilding processes, and they arguably serve as a root cause of conflict itself. Notwithstanding their marginalization, women bear the greatest burden and incentive to neutralize the exacting impacts of war on their families by ensuring that shelter, medical care, food, water, and education are accessible during episodes of conflict. In this way, they become safety nets that create protective webs during crises and forge alliances with similarly situated women across sociocultural lines. In this sense, African womanist approaches seem to accelerate the aim of gender equality during and immediately after armed conflict more effectively than Western feminist attitudes or West-centric multitrack models. Their methods – especially intracultural leveraging – and the new norms and rules that echo them derive from African women with a tradition of resistance to the legacy of Western hegemony within African culture.

African women have proven to be a potent normative force. As they have in the past, they will continue to informally and formally monitor, evaluate, and

[95] Charlesworth, *supra* note 28, at 358–59.

report the legality of peace agreements, and when states and institutions falter in their commitment to women's rights issues, they will continue to advocate for "legal" peace processes or those that necessitate their inclusion and safeguard women's rights. This not only requires gender mainstreaming in the design, development, and implementation of peace agreements but, more importantly, "gender balance" or equitable participation in peace construction (i.e., mediation, negotiation, technical and implementation teams) and transitional governance processes is necessary as well.[96] And, although gender parity may be difficult to achieve in some societies or circumstances, states, regional, and international institutions and NGOs have a legal duty to prioritize women's issues by making them more formidable stakeholders in peace construction and peacebuilding, including the validation and inclusion of informal conflict-resolution approaches in which women play prominent roles. They can amplify their participation through the recruitment of local women as mediators and advisors, funding of women and women's groups to participate in peace negotiations, including the provision of childcare, transportation, and, when necessary, security. International negotiators and mediators should not advance peace deals that blatantly contravene regional and international human rights norms intended to safeguard the rights of women. Subregional, regional, and international organizations should likewise refrain from endorsing peace prescriptions that infringe their own rules, norms, standards, and jurisprudence – rules intended to protect women's rights – in the service of nonsensical and politically expedient rationales.

In conclusion, the UN, AU, the Economic Community of West African States, and other African regional institutions, as well as the member states that comprise them, have demonstrated an uncanny schizophrenia when protecting (or failing to protect) the rights of women to be full stakeholders in conflict prevention, management, and resolution processes. This study highlights the extreme efforts that African women have been forced to make to effectuate their participatory rights as citizens with the most vested interest in sustainable peace. They have been vociferous advocates for peace, lobbying for the normative inclusion of women's issues at the design and implementation phases of peace construction and thereby reinforcing normative gains with systematic practice, where one movement influences the character and content of others, as vividly demonstrated by the cases of Liberia and Sierra Leone, among others. The transnational nature of African women's movements has been a potent force in the development of a "Law of Power Sharing"

96 Christine Chinkin, *Gender, Human Rights and Peace Agreements*, 18 Ohio St. J. on Disp. Resol. 867, 870–71 (2003).

that seeks to safeguard women's rights. Hence, until the UN and other moral guarantors of peace approach women's rights issues in conflict management and resolution attentively, as prescribed by law, African women will continue to suffer under illegal peace agreements while simultaneously serving as Abeena and Afia's principal guardians.

7

African Women Leaders and the Advancement of Peacebuilding in International Law

Anna Spain

INTRODUCTION

The twenty-first century is bearing witness to critical shifts in international law, as the preferences of civil society and local peoples are reshaping global values.[1] One area in which local practices have advanced such international understanding is in efforts to promote peace in postconflict societies in Africa.[2] As the site of numerous wars, genocides, and humanitarian crises over the past two decades, Africa has become the nexus for advancements in peace promotion.[3] Such efforts have contributed to the development of international law in the areas of international criminal law, international humanitarian law, and

Anna Spain, Associate Professor, University of Colorado Law School. The author expresses her gratitude for the opportunity to contribute this chapter in honor of Judge Gabrielle K. McDonald, whom she appeared before at the Iran-U.S. Claims Tribunal during the B/61 hearings.

[1] For discourses on the changing nature of international law *see generally* James Crawford, INTERNATIONAL LAW AS AN OPEN SYSTEM (2004) (discussing the rise of new actors and responsibilities); Rafael Domingo, THE NEW GLOBAL LAW 173–94 (2010) (discussing the principles of solidarity, subsidiarity, and democratization in a global legal framework); Gareth Evans, THE RESPONSIBILITY TO PROTECT (2008) (discussing the development of the Responsibility to Protect doctrine and its nature as an emerging legal norm); Thomas Franck, THE EMPOWERED SELF: LAW AND SOCIETY IN THE AGE OF INDIVIDUALISM 21 (1999) (arguing that people are asserting their individual rights in ways that bring "about the disintegration of multinational civil societies and established states"); and Charles Beitz & Robert Goodin, GLOBAL BASIC RIGHTS (2009) (considering the role of rights in addressing myriad moral challenges including human rights, security, and economic development).

[2] *See generally* DURABLE PEACE: CHALLENGES FOR PEACEBUILDING IN AFRICA (Taisier Mohamed Ahmed Ali & Robert O. Matthews eds., 2004); PEACEBUILDING, POWER, AND POLITICS IN AFRICA (Devon Curtis & Gwinyayi A. Dzinesa eds., 2012).

[3] Jeremy Levitt, ILLEGAL PEACE IN AFRICA 1 (2012) (arguing that "[s]ince the end of the Cold War, Africa has become the testing ground for Western conflict-resolution experiments intended to forestall deadly conflict, secure peace, and build democracy"); Lise Morjé Howard, UN PEACEKEEPING IN CIVIL WARS 1 (2008) ("Civil war is the most important and troubling problem in international life today").

human rights.[4] However, although the contributions made by actors at the international level are well known,[5] scant attention has been directed toward the ways that local actors have advanced the theory and practice of peace promotion in international law.

Predicated upon the idea that local action advances developments in international law, this chapter explores the contributions that women operating in postconflict societies in Africa have made to the development of peacebuilding. Furthermore, it suggests that understanding these contributions is essential to understanding the evolution of the normative purpose of peacebuilding in international law. The chapter tells the stories of several women-led peacebuilding efforts in postconflict African communities and describes how such efforts embody five principles of right action for peacebuilding: reconciliation, reintegration, protection of women, subsidiarity, and sustainability. This chapter posits that these contributions are reshaping the ways in which the international community conceptualizes peacebuilding and its effectiveness, given the complexities of armed conflict today. Thoroughly understanding such women-led innovations and how they are advancing a broader normative agenda for the peacebuilding field can help us better understand both the foundations and the evolution of peace as a first principle of international law.

The Development of Peacebuilding in International Law

Promoting global peace and security is a fundamental aim of international law.[6] Before the development of peacebuilding per se, law has long sought to advance the cause of peace. In Ancient Egyptian and Roman law, for example,

4 *See, e.g.*, Jennifer Moore, Humanitarian Law in Action within Africa 2 (2012) (arguing that Africa has been a testing ground for humanitarian law); The Changing Face of Conflict and the Efficacy of International Humanitarian Law (Helen Durham & Timothy McCormack eds., 1999) (arguing that the changing nature of armed conflict, as witnessed in Africa in addition to other locations, demands reconsidering how international humanitarian law seeks to protect vulnerable groups); Ruti Teitel, Humanity's Law 8–11 (2011) (discussing the how developments in international criminal law, including the tribunals in Rwanda and Sierra Leone, are a part of a broader normative paradigm shift in international human rights toward the prioritization of human security).

5 *See, e.g.*, Howard, *supra* note 3; Thorsten Benner, Stephan Mergenthaler, & Philipp Rotmann, The New World of UN Peace Operations: Learning to Build Peace? (2011); Jus Post Bellum: Towards a Law of Transition from Conflict to Peace (C. Stahn & J. K. Kleffner eds., 2008).

6 *See, e.g.*, U.N. Preamble ("We the peoples of the United Nations, determined to save succeeding generations from the scourge of war . . . unite our strength to maintain international peace and security."), *available at* http://www.un.org/en/documents/charter/preamble.shtml.

restrictions existed on the use of force.[7] During the Middle Ages in Europe, Hugo Grotius introduced the concept of *jus ad bellum* and *jus in bello* as bodies of law that could temper the human tendency to engage in war.[8] During the Hague Peace Conferences of 1899 and 1907, the international community of states sought to strengthen the collective capacity to promote peace and prevent war by adopting the Convention for the Pacific Settlement of International Disputes and establishing the Permanent Court of Arbitration.[9] After World War II, the United Nations was established to "maintain international peace and security."[10] In pursuit of this aim, the second half of the twentieth century has witnessed the proliferation of international courts and tribunals and the normalization of adjudication as nations continue to promote peaceful mechanisms for the resolution of disputes as a means of discouraging war.[11]

This historical narrative of peace promotion efforts in international law continues with the introduction of peacebuilding as a means for bringing about sustainable peace in postconflict societies after the end of the

7 *See, e.g.*, the "Treaty of Kadesh" *in* S. Langdon & Alan Gardiner, *The treaty of alliance between Hattusili, King of the Hittites, and the Pharaoh Ramesses II of Egypt*, 6 J. Egyptian Archaeology 179 (1920); J. G. Manning, *The representation of justice in ancient Egypt*, 24 Yale J. L. & Human. 111 (2012); Adolf Berger, *Encyclopedic Dictionary of Roman Law*, 43 Trans. Am. Philosoph. Ass'c. 333–808 (1953). (In Roman law *humanitas* means "the human tendency as an ethical commandment, benevolent consideration for others.")

8 Hugo Grotius, On the Law of War and Peace (1625) (Francis W. Kelsey trans., 1925); Hersch Lauterpacht, *The Grotian tradition in international law*, 23 British Yearbook Int'l. L. 1 (1946); Derek Croxton, *The peace of Westphalia of 1648 and the origins of sovereignty*, 21 Int'l. Hist. Rev. 569, 570 (1999).

9 The Hague Conventions and Declarations of 1899 and 1907 (James Brown Scott ed., 1918); Convention for the Pacific Settlement of International Disputes, art. 1, July 29, 1899, 32 Stat. 1779, *available at* http://avalon.law.yale.edu/19th_century/hague01.asp; Ruth Mackenzie et. al, The Manual on International Courts and Tribunals (2010) at ix (noting that the Convention "marked a turning point in favour of international adjudication before standing bodies" and describing the formation of the PCA as the first standing body for international adjudication).

10 U.N. Charter art. 1, para. 1. See also U.N. Charter art. 2, para. 4 (calling for nations to refrain from the threat or use of force); art. 33, paras. 1–2 ("[t]he parties to any dispute, the continuance of which is likely to endanger the maintenance of international peace and security, shall, first of all, seek a solution by negotiation, enquiry, mediation, conciliation, arbitration, judicial settlement, resort to regional agencies or arrangements, or other peaceful means of their own choice"); art. 40 and art. 51, *available at* http://www.un.org/en/documents/charter/); Ruth Russell & Jeannette Muther, A History of the United Nations Charter 210 (1954); and Bernard Boxill, *The duty to seek peace*, 27 Soc. Philosoph. Pol'y. (2010).

11 Jacob Bercovitch & Richard Jackson, Conflict Resolution in the Twenty-first Century: Principles, Methods and Approaches 8–14 (2009); Oliver Richmond, Maintaining Order, Making Peace (2002).

Cold War.[12] In 1989, the UN Transitional Assistance Group (UNTAG) was created to assist in building the democratic sovereign nation of Namibia.[13] UNTAG's operations have been recognized as an early demonstration of peacebuilding; through governance creation, election reform, and confidence-building measures, it sought to establish long-term peace.[14] A few years later, in 1992, UN Secretary-General Boutros Boutros-Ghali identified and defined peacebuilding as the fourth tenet of his *Agenda for Peace* (in addition to preventive diplomacy, peacemaking, and peacekeeping).[15]

Thus, peacebuilding can be understood as a conceptual framework for the emerging range of activities taking place in postconflict environments that help end war and bring about long-term peace. It is a "holistic concept aimed at no less than the complete transformation of the political, economic, and social structures within a nation that can lead to violent conflict."[16] The International Peace Academy defines peacebuilding as "action to identify and support structures which tend to strengthen and solidify peace to avoid a relapse into conflict."[17] The Canadian Peacebuilding Coordinating Committee states that peacebuilding is "the effort to promote human security in societies marked by conflict. The overarching goal of peacebuilding is to strengthen the capacity of societies to manage conflict without violence, as a means to achieving sustainable human security."[18] A critical addition to the definition of peacebuilding was added by the African Union (AU), which highlighted the importance of gender.[19]

[12] Bercovitch, *supra* note 11, at 8–9. *See, e.g.*, United Nations, Report of the Panel on United Nations Peace Operations, A/55/305-S/2000/809 (2000) (describing the peacebuilding as a hybrid of political and development activities targeted at the sources of conflict); John Burton, Resolving Deep-Rooted Conflict: A Handbook (1987); Necla Tschirgi, Peacebuilding as the Link between Security and Development: Is the Window of Opportunity Closing? (2003).

[13] United Nations Transitional Assistance Group (UNTAG), *available at* http://www.un.org/en/peacekeeping/missions/past/untag.htm. *See also* Richard Ponzio, Democratic Peacebuilding: Aiding Afghanistan and Other Fragile States 71 (2011); Virginia Page Fortna, *United Nations transition assistance group in Namibia* in The Evolution of UN Peacekeeping 362 (W. J. Durch ed., 1994).

[14] Ponzio, *supra* note 13, at 71.

[15] Report of the U.N. Secretary-General Boutros Boutros-Ghali, *An Agenda for Peace*, UN A/47/277 – S/24111 (June 17, 1992), *available at* http://www.un.org/docs/SG/agpeace.html

[16] Bercovitch, *supra* note 11, at 168.

[17] International Peace Academy, *Towards comprehensive peacebuilding*, 2 (2001), *available at* http://www.ipacademy.org/publication/meeting-notes/detail/203-towards-comprehensive-peacebuilding.html.

[18] David Last, *Organizing for effective peacebuilding*, 7 Int'l. Peacekeeping 80 (2000).

[19] African Union, *Post-Conflict Reconstruction and Development Framework* (2006) (identifying 'women and gender' as one of six elements of its Post-Conflict Reconstruction and Development Policy), *available at* http://www.africa-union.org/root/AU/AUC/Departments/PSC/

Drawing from the fields of international relations, peace and conflict studies, and international development, scholars have further defined peacebuilding in the following ways. Bush conceptualizes peacebuilding as initiatives that promote sustainable infrastructure for peaceful coexistence and deter armed conflict.[20] Adelman and Masciulli define peacebuilding as a decentralized political process capable of addressing the causes of conflict and peace in postconflict societies.[21] Tripp, Casimiro, Kwesiga, and Mungwa emphasize the importance of maintaining a "localized focus" when engaging in peacebuilding.[22] Cousens argues that peacebuilding's defining priority is its ability to provide means by which a nation can resolve internal conflict without violence.[23] A survey of governments and intergovernmental organizations revealed that most understand peacebuilding as the creation of a positive peace through the elimination of root causes of conflict.[24] There have also been a number of empirical studies on peacebuilding, such as the report by Doyle and Sambanis, which provides an extensive dataset of peacebuilding outcomes in civil wars since 1944.[25] Thus, although there is no one definition or dimension that encompasses the meaning and practice of peacebuilding, it can be understood as a comprehensive process with overlapping spheres of engagement in social, economic, political, and legal realms.[26]

Peacebuilding takes place in relationship to armed conflict. Political scientists traditionally define "armed conflict" as ongoing violent conflict between two or more groups that results in a certain threshold of death and/or casualties.[27]

PCRD/PCRD%20Main%20Web%20Source/index.html, including gender), http://www.africa-union.org/root/au/Conferences/2007/july/PCRD/pcrd1.htm.

[20] Kenneth Bush, *Toward a balanced approach to rebuilding war-torn societies*, 3 (3) CAN. FOR. POL'Y. 49 (1996).

[21] Howard Adelman, *Cultures of violence*, *in* BUILDING SUSTAINABLE PEACE 303–330 (Tom Keating & Andy W. Knight eds., 2004); Joseph Masciulli, *From a culture of violence to a culture of peace: Evolving cosmopolitan politics and ethics*, in BUILDING SUSTAINABLE PEACE 331–354.

[22] Aili Mari Tripp, Isabel Casimiro, Joy Kwesiga, & Alice Mungwa, AFRICAN WOMEN'S MOVEMENTS: TRANSFORMING POLITICAL LANDSCAPES 66 (2009).

[23] Elizabeth Cousens, *Introduction*, in PEACEBUILDING AS POLITICS: CULTIVATING PEACE IN FRAGILE SOCIETIES 4 (Elizabeth Cousens & Chetan Kumar eds., 2001).

[24] Michael Barnett et al., *Peacebuilding: What is in a name?* 13 GLOBAL GOVERNANCE 44 (2007).

[25] Michael Doyle & Nicholas Sambanis, MAKING WAR & BUILDING PEACE: UNITED NATIONS PEACE OPERATIONS (2006).

[26] *See* Michael Lund & Andreas Mehler, PEACE-BUILDING & CONFLICT PREVENTION IN DEVELOPING COUNTRIES: A PRACTICAL GUIDE (1999); FROM WAR TO DEMOCRACY: DILEMMAS OF PEACEBUILDING (Anna K. Jarstad & Timothy D. Sisk eds., 2008).

[27] Meredith Reid Sarkees & Frank Whelon Wayman, RESORT TO WAR 1816–2007 9 (2010) (categorizing armed conflict as events that reached a threshold of at least 1,000 deaths directly resulting from battle).

Conflict is further defined by the context in which it occurs, as interstate, intrastate (civil or internal), or nonstate.[28] Several empirical studies have confirmed that intrastate conflict has outpaced interstate war in recent decades.[29] For example, the University of Maryland's Peace and Conflict report found that, in 2008, all 26 active armed conflicts in the world occurred in the intrastate context.[30] A study of 121 conflicts occurring between 1989 and 2005 identified 90 as intrastate and seven as interstate and noted that, in 2005, all 31 ongoing conflicts were intrastate.[31] Legal scholars, focusing on the changing nature of war as it moves from militarized battles between nations into new contexts, have distinguished between international armed conflicts (involving two or more states) and noninternational armed conflicts (between governmental and nongovernmental armed forces or between two or more nongovernmental armed groups).[32] Noninternational armed conflicts involve different actors, interests, and priorities, and they are on the rise.[33] They are characterized by asymmetrical warfare methods that pit weaker combatants against stronger ones; the stronger combatant is usually a state's military.[34]

[28] *Id.* at 6 (defining the types of war as interstate conflict, occurring between "[s]tates or members of the interstate system"; extrastate conflict, occurring between a state and a nonstate entity outside of the state's borders; intrastate conflict, occurring between the state and nonstate entities (civil) or entirely between nonstate armed groups (internal) within a state's boundaries; and nonstate conflict, occurring between nonstate armed groups in nonstate territory or across state borders).

[29] *Id.* at 45–70, 562 (The COW dataset included 655 wars between 1816 and 2007 and defines intrastate war as "sustained combat between or among organized armed force taking place within the territorial boundaries of a state system member and leading to 1000 battle-related deaths per year" recognizing three subcategories: civil war, regional internal war, and intercommunal war).

[30] *See* J. Joseph Hewitt, *Trends in global conflict, 1946–2007*, *in* PEACE AND CONFLICT 2010 27, 27 (J. Joseph Hewitt et al. eds., 2010) (graphically demonstrating the negative correlation between extrastate and intrastate war onsets and finding that "[a]t the beginning of 2008 . . . [all armed conflicts worldwide] were civil conflicts between the government of a state, on the one hand, and at least one internal group on the other").

[31] Lotta Harbom et al., *Armed conflict and peace agreements*, 43 J. PEACE RES. 617, 618 table 2 (2006).

[32] International Committee of the Red Cross, Opinion Paper (March, 2008), *available at* http://www.icrc.org/eng/assets/files/other/opinion-paper-armed-conflict.pdf.

[33] *See* Mary Kaldor, NEW AND OLD WARS: ORGANIZED VIOLENCE IN A GLOBAL ERA (1999); Nicolas Lamp, *The "new war" challenge to international humanitarian law*, 16 J. CONFLICT & SECURITY L. 225, 227 (2011); Sarkees, & Wayman, *supra* note 27, at 562 (stating that intrastate wars began to rise by the mid-1960s); Monty G. Marshall & Ted Robert Gurr, CIDCM, Peace and Conflict 2003: A Global Survey of Armed Conflicts, Self-Determination Movements, and Democracy 1 (2003), *available at* www.systemicpeace.org/PC2003.pdf; N. P. Gleditsch et al., *Armed conflict 1946–2001: A new dataset*, 39 J. PEACE RES. 615 (2002).

[34] Daniel Thürer, *International humanitarian law: Theory, practice*, Context, *in* RECUEIL DES COURS, COLLECTED COURSES OF THE HAGUE ACADEMY OF INTERNATIONAL LAW 2008 199–201 (2011).

Changes in the nature of armed conflict have driven changes in the practice of peacebuilding in the twenty-first century.[35] Intrastate conflicts are difficult to prevent and to resolve. They are characterized by identity and ethnic disputes, cyclical violence, the lack of clear victors, and a high probability of recurrence.[36] Such conflicts are most common in countries with poor economies, insufficient political freedom, and dysfunctional public institutions.[37] To address these new conflicts, the concept of peace has been redefined. During World War II and the Cold War, peace was understood as the absence of war.[38] Today, it is marked by the positive progression toward societal reconciliation and state-building.[39]

Another important change has been the identification of women as an essential component of peacebuilding. On October 31, 2000, the UN Security Council adopted Resolution 1325, "reaffirming the importance of women in the prevention and resolution of conflicts and in peacebuilding."[40] The resolution calls upon member states to increase the representation of women in key roles, to support training for women, and to adopt a gendered perspective in the negotiation of peace agreements, among other things. In 2007, the Secretary-General published a Report on Women, Peace, and Security that provides a seven-point plan for implementing these obligations.[41]

[35] *See* Changing Face of Conflict, *supra* note 4; Stahn, *supra* note 5; Noah Weisbord, *Conceptualizing aggression*, 20 Duke J. Comp. & Int'l. L. 1, 7–11 (2009) (discussing future scenarios of aggression and noting the rise of intrastate conflicts); Eric De Brabandere, *The responsibility for post-conflict reforms: A critical assessment of jus post bellum as a legal concept*, 43 Vand. J. Transn'l. L. 119 (2010); Council on Foreign Relations, *State Department needs "clear guidelines" on engaging with nonstate armed groups* (Council on Foreign Relations, Working Paper, 2011), *available at* www.cfr.org/nonstate_armed_groups_paper.

[36] Charles Call, Why Peace Fails: The Causes and Prevention of Civil War Recurrence 9–15 (2012).

[37] *Id.* at 6.

[38] *See* Hans Kelsen, Peace Through Law 1 (1944) ("Peace is a state characterized by the absence of force"); Turbulent Peace: The Challenges of Managing International Conflict (Chester Crocker, Fen Osler Hampson & Pamela Aall eds., 1996); Peacemaking in International Conflict: Methods and Techniques (I. William Zartman & J. Lewis Rasmussen eds., 1997) (providing examples of conflict management approaches during this era).

[39] Richmond, *supra* note 11, at 79 ("negative peace is characterized by the absence of direct violence and preventing war, while positive peace encompasses the broader issues relating to human security").

[40] S.C. Res. 4213th Sess. U.N. Doc. S/Res/1325(October 31, 2000), *available at* http://www.un.org/events/res_1325e.pdf.

[41] Report by the Secretary-General on Women and Peace and Security U.N. Doc. S/2007/567 (September 19, 2007), *available at* http://daccess-dds-ny.un.org/doc/UNDOC/GEN/N07/503/69/PDF/N0750369.pdf?OpenElement; Report by the Secretary-General on Women and Peace and Security U.N. Doc. S/2010/498 (September 19, 2007), *available at* http://daccess-dds-ny.un.or g/doc/UNDOC/GEN/N10/540/24/PDF/N1054024.pdf?OpenElement; See also, Kofi Annan, *Causes of conflict and the promotion of durable peace and sustainable development in Africa*,

WOMEN'S APPROACHES TO PEACEBUILDING IN AFRICA

Women living in postconflict African countries have led advancements in the practice of peacebuilding in the twenty-first century. Due to the prevalence of armed conflict in Africa since the end of World War II, they have had many opportunities to do so. According to one study, of the 343 armed conflicts that took place between 1945 and 2003, more (28.3 percent) occurred in Africa than in any other geopolitical region.[42] The following chart documents the instances of armed conflict (defined as civil wars and recurrence events) that have occurred in Africa between 1946 and 2007:[43]

Nonrecurrent Civil Wars
Angola 1975–2002
Mozambique 1976–95
Sierra Leone 1991–2000
South Africa 1983–94

New Civil War, Same Country or Territory
Algeria 1962–63, 1992–present
Chad 1965–2002, 2005–present
Democratic Republic of Congo 1960–65, 1977–78, 1996–2001, 2006–present
Ethiopia 1974–92, 1997–present
Kenya 1963–67, 1991–93
Nigeria 1967–70, 1980–85

Civil War (and Internal Armed Conflict Recurrences)
Burundi 1972, 1988, 1993–2006
Central African Republic 1996–97, 2001–02
Liberia 1989–96, 1999–2003
Mali 1989–94, 2007
Rwanda 1962–65, 1990–2002
Senegal 1971, 1983–2002, 2003–present
Somalia 1981–2002, 2006–present
Sudan 1963–72, 1983–present
Zimbabwe 1972–79, 1983–87

Secretary-General's Report to the UN Security Council (Apr. 16, 1998); *Beyond victimhood: women's peacebuilding in Sudan, Congo and Uganda*, International Crisis Group, Africa Report No. 112 (June 28, 2006), *available at* http://www.crisisgroup.org/en/regions/africa/horn-of-africa/112-beyond-victimhood-womens-peacebuilding-in-sudan-congo-and-uganda.aspx.

[42] Jacob Bercovitch, REGIONAL GUIDE TO INTERNATIONAL CONFLICT AND MANAGEMENT FROM 1945–2003 (2004) at 9, table 2: *Incidence of conflict by geopolitical region* (Africa 28.3%, Americas 13.1%, East Asia & Pacific 19%, SW Asia 11.4%, Europe 8.7%, Middle East 19.5%).

[43] Call *supra* note 36, at 14–15 (table I.1, All civil wars and recurrences 1946–1999, plus recurrences as internal armed conflict 1999–2007).

Between 2007 and 2011, armed conflict in Africa spiked, with civil wars raging in the Central Africa Republic (2012–13), Cote d'Ivoire (2002–07, 2010–11), Guinea (2013), Libya (2011–present), Mali (2012–present), and Sudan (2009). Taken together, these armed conflicts have placed peacebuilding practice and doctrine center stage in international relations since World War II and consequently at the forefront of international peace promotion activities.[44]

The UN, AU, North Atlantic Treaty Organization (NATO), and other intergovernmental and regional organizations have often led such efforts. In addition, subregional organizations such as the Economic Community of West African States (ECOWAS) have also been instrumental in promoting peace in Africa.[45] These organizations are recognized as leaders in advancing the normative framework for peacebuilding. The AU, for example, has adopted innovative mechanisms for early warning, preventive diplomacy, mediation, peace support operations, intervention, humanitarian action, and peacebuilding.[46] The West African Network for Peacebuilding (WANEP) is an example of a regional peacebuilding entity that has emphasized the practice of empowering local participants.[47]

International and regional institutions are not the only purveyors or innovators of peacebuilding. Indeed, it is often the case that the survivors of armed conflicts, working in their individual capacity or together in civil society groups, are leading the way as peacebuilders. This chapter posits that African women, as survivors and peacebuilders, are also contributing to the development of international law by advancing a novel normative framework for peacebuilding. This section shares the stories of how several African women peacebuilders have contributed to and advanced new visions and

44 International Crisis Group Report, *available at* http://www.crisisgroupblogs.org/africanpeacebuilding/ (describing the variety of peacebuilding efforts taking place in post-conflict countries in Africa).

45 Ponzio, *supra* note 13, at 95–97.

46 African Union, Peace and Security Council Protocol, art 6, paras (a)–(f) (July 9 2002); African Union, Constitutive Act, art. 4(h) ("the right of the Union to intervene in a Member State pursuant to a decision of the Assembly in respect of grave circumstances, namely: war crimes, genocide and crimes against humanity"); *See* Jeremy Levitt, *The Peace and Security Council of the African Union and the United Nations Security Council: The case of Darfur Sudan, in* THE SECURITY COUNCIL AND THE USE OF FORCE 213–252 (N. M. Blokker & N. J. Schriver eds., 2005).

47 West African Network for Peacebuilding (WANEP), *Operating principles, available at* http://www.wanep.org/wanep/about-us-our-story/operating-principles/19-operating-principles.html. ("Local ownership of peacebuilding processes. Those who directly or indirectly are involved in a conflict situation are critical to peacebuilding efforts. Third party must ensure that they are empowered to make decisions and not making decisions for them. WANEP's strategy is to locate, empower, support and accompany local actors as they respond to conflicts of their communities.")

methods for building peace in postconflict societies. Although these examples do not provide a comprehensive study of African women engaged in peacebuilding activities after conflict, they do illustrate the emergence of five guiding principles of peacebuilding: reconciliation, reintegration, protection of women, subsidiarity, and sustainability. This chapter identifies these contributions as a necessary first step to describing their normative impact.

Reconciliation

African women peacebuilders have advanced understandings about the importance of reconciliation as a component of effective peacebuilding. Reconciliation is the act of "restoring friendship or harmony,"[48] which, in the peacebuilding context, may aim to reestablish relations between disputing ethnic groups.[49] This aim is achieved through processes that promote truth-telling, forgiveness, and healing. Reconciliation is essential to establishing sustainable peace because it facilitates conflict resolution and social rehabilitation. The Truth and Reconciliation Commissions (TRCs) popularized in South Africa,[50] Liberia, and Sierra Leone[51] and the use of Gacaca courts in Rwanda are well-known examples of reconciliation models.[52]

Two notable African women proponents of reconciliation as a principle of effective peacebuilding were the joint recipients of the 2011 Nobel Peace Prize, Ellen Johnson Sirleaf and Leymah Gbowee (along with the Yemeni activist Tawakkol Karman).[53] The award was given to them "for their

48 Webster's Dictionary (2012). *See also* Building Peace: Sustainable Reconciliation in Divided Societies (John Paul Lederach ed., 1997).

49 Donna Pankhurst, *Issues of justice and reconciliation in complex political emergencies: Conceptualising reconciliation, justice and peace* 20 (1) Third World Q. 239, 240 (1999).

50 Government of South Africa, Promotion of National Unity and Reconciliation Act 34 (July 19, 1995), *available at* http://www.justice.gov.za/legislation/acts/1995–034.pdf.

51 Lomé Peace Accord, art. 26, *available at* http://www.sierra-leone.org/lomeaccord.html; *Republic of Liberia Truth and Reconciliation Commission*, Volume II: Consolidated Final Report (June 30, 2009), *available at* http://trcofliberia.org/resources/reports/final/volume-two_layout-1.pdf; Priscilla Haynor, *The Sierra Leone Truth and Reconciliation Commission: Reviewing the first year*, International Center for Transnational Justice Case Study Series (2004), *available at* http://ictj.org/sites/default/files/ICTJ-SierraLeone-Justice-Review-2004-English.pdf; William A. Schabas, *Conjoined twins of transitional justice? The Sierra Leone Truth and Reconciliation Commission and the Special Court*, 2 J. Int'l. Crim. J. 1082 (2004).

52 See Roelof H. Haveman, *Gacaca in Rwanda: Customary law in case of genocide*, *in* The Future of African Customary Law 387–422 (Jeanmarie Fenrich, Paolo Galizzi, & Tracy Higgins eds., 2011); Geetanjali Mukherjee, *Achieving reconciliation through prosecution in the courts: Lessons from Rwanda*, 28 Conflict Resol. Q. 331 (2001).

53 The Nobel Foundation, 2011 *Nobel Peace Prize Winners*, *available at* http://www.nobelprize.org/nobel_prizes/peace/laureates/2011/.

non-violent struggle for the safety of women and for women's rights to full participation in peace-building work."[54] Leymah Gbowee is a Liberian mother who became the coordinator of the Liberian Women's Network. During the Second Liberian Civil War in 2003, she was the spokesperson for the peace movement, known as the Women of Liberia Mass Action for Peace, which brought Christian and Muslim women together for nonviolent demonstrations to protest the presidency of Charles Taylor. After the war, she helped draw attention to the long-term impacts and the need for healing, saying:

> A war of fourteen years doesn't just go away. In the moments we were calm enough to look around, we had to confront the magnitude of what had happened in Liberia. ... A whole generation of young men had no idea who they were without a gun in their hands. Several generations of women were widowed, had been raped, seen their daughters and mothers raped, and their children kill and be killed. Neighbors had turned against neighbors; young people had lost hope, and old people, everything they had painstakingly earned. To a person, we were traumatized.[55]

Gbowee was instrumental in bringing about trauma healing for women in Liberia who had been affected by the war. She is credited with introducing a "peace-church" philosophical orientation developed from the Eastern Mennonite tradition.[56] Her contributions promoted understanding about the long-term consequences of war and the necessity of reconciliation through healing for long-term peace.

Working with Gbowee and other women in Liberia, Ellen Johnson Sirleaf has been instrumental in raising awareness about the importance of reconciliation in peacebuilding. In 2005, she was elected president of Liberia, becoming the first female president of an African nation.[57] Her political success has provided an important platform for raising awareness about the centrality of women leadership in peacebuilding, as well as for other social and economic initiatives.

Alongside Gbowee and Sirleaf, many other women were instrumental in building peace and security in Liberia in 2003 after the country had been ravaged by the First and Second Liberian Civil Wars. Women leaders helped bring about an end to the armed conflict by working to establish the initial ceasefire. Written by women leaders, the Golden Tulip Declaration, for example, provided terms for peace that were guided by the principles of

[54] *Id.*

[55] Leymah Gbowee (with Carol Mithers), Mighty Be Our Powers, 168, 171 (2011).

[56] *Id.* at 171.

[57] Tripp et al., *supra* note 22, at 196 (describing the impact of Johnson-Sirleaf's election for peace movements in Africa).

gender equality.[58] These were later incorporated into the Comprehensive Peace Agreement, which, among other initiatives, established the TRC.[59] After the war, women held important decision-making positions, through which they had a direct influence on peacebuilding[60] They raised awareness about the unique impacts of the conflict on women, the long-term nature of traumas endured, and the need for protection and security.[61] As one survivor, Naomi Saydee of the Liberian Women's Media Action Committee, remarked, "So if the TRC can give women preference when it comes to the process there would be genuine reconciliation. Because if the women all come up to talk about the things that happened to them, and the things that they did during the conflict [there would be genuine reconciliation]."[62]

An effort by African women to integrate reconciliation as a component of peacebuilding has proved important in other postconflict contexts as well. In Eritrea, for example, author Abeba Tesfagiorgis wrote about the importance of empathy and forgiveness as tools for reconciliation in peacebuilding.[63] In her novels *Woi Ane Dekai* (*My Poor Children*, 1969) and *Nemenye Zenegro* (*Who Am I Going to Tell*, 1974), Tesfagiorgis described the violence and injustices occurring in Eritrea and the need for societal healing. She then went on to found an organization that aimed to promote reconciliation, The Relief and Rehabilitation Association of Eritrea, which spread the message that forgiveness was essential to the future of Eritrea because it would allow adversaries to work together to find solutions to political difficulties. These activities, which were deemed political, led to her arrest by the Eritrean authorities and a subsequent six-month imprisonment. Confronted with threats to her personal safety, as well as to the safety of her husband and children, she fostered her vision for building peace. Modeling this behavior in her work, she represents an early pioneer of the purpose of empathy and forgiveness as essential components of reconciliation and peacebuilding. In her words, "It would be

[58] *Golden Tulip Declaration*, 30 Peacewomen E-news 1325 (September 5, 2003), *available at* http://www.peacewomen.org/portal_resources_resource.php?id=749749.

[59] Comprehensive Peace Agreement between the Government of Liberia, the Liberians United for Reconciliation and Democracy and the Movement for Democracy in Liberia and Political Parties (August 18, 2003), U.S. Institute of Peace, Comprehensive Peace Agreement, *available at* http://www.usip.org/sites/default/files/file/resources/collections/peace_agreements/liberia_08182003.pdf.

[60] Republic of Liberia TRC Volume II, Consolidated Final Report, supra note 51.

[61] Karen Campbell-Nelson, *Liberia is not just a man thing: Transitional justice lessons for women, peace and security*, International Center for Transnational Justice 20–22 (2008), *available at* http://www.ictj.org/sites/default/files/ICTJ-IFP-Liberia-Gender-Cluster-2008-English.pdf.

[62] *Id.*; *See also* Naomi Saydee, Statement, Monrovia, Liberia (June 9, 2008).

[63] Michael Henderson, ALL HER PATHS ARE PEACE: WOMEN PIONEERS IN PEACEMAKING 43–53 (1994).

a disservice to our heroic *tegadelti* who fall in battle, to the mothers who suffer in silence the loss of their husbands and children, to our children who die pot-bellied due to malnutrition, to our pregnant women whose stomachs were slit . . . to all those who lives are a constant nightmare – it would be a disservice to all – if we did not forgive and love one another."[64]

African women peacebuilders advanced a similar paradigm of reconciliation as a component of peacebuilding in postconflict Burundi, the site of a civil war that lasted more than a decade. Working at the local level in their villages and communities, these women advocated the use of *ubushingantahe*, a village-level conciliation process led by a local council of elders.[65] They, alongside their male counterparts, also spoke out in favor of providing amnesty for former combatants, which became a component of the Uganda Amnesty Act.[66] The issue of amnesty is controversial, with the UN and the AU taking the formal position that amnesty should not be granted for those who have committed international war crimes.[67] However, these women countered this international view with their local view: that reintegrating and accepting former combatants into their communities is essential to maintaining long-term peace. Such a position underscores the local benefits of amnesty when coupled with reconciliation.

Reintegration

A second principle of effective peacebuilding advanced by African women is the concept of reintegration, which seeks to promote social rehabilitation by offering a process through which former combatants can reenter society. As the Burundi example illustrates, reintegration often requires a reconciliation process of some kind that offers individuals an opportunity to admit their prior acts and offer apologies and compensation to the communities they seek to reenter. The importance of reintegration is a practical one as well as a moral one. The lived experience of many survivors of war is that victims must often reside alongside their perpetrators.[68] The process of having former combatants lay down their arms and publicly commit to living peaceably in a community creates public accountability. This is vitally important to the survivors of wars where

64 *Id.* at 46.

65 Moore, *supra* note 4, at 199–200.

66 The Amnesty Act 2000, Ch. 294 (2000), *available at* http://www.ulii.org/ug/legislation/consolidated-act/294; UN Position on Uganda's Amnesty Act 2000, http://www.jlos.go.ug/uploads/UN%20Position%20on%20Uganda%20Amnesty%20Law%20.pdf.

67 United Nations Secretary-General Report on the Establishment of the Special Court for Sierra Leone, U.N. Doc S/2000/915, para. 22–23 (October 4, 2000) ("the United Nations has consistently maintained the position that amnesty cannot be granted in respect of international crimes").

68 Moore, *supra* note 4, at 199.

community-enforced security is often the only security mechanism because formal policing institutions do not exist. Reintegrating people back into a community has become an essential component of peacebuilding.[69] In Sierra Leone, for example, there was an unexpectedly high turnout of former combatants who sought to disarm, demobilize, and reintegrate through the UN's Disarmament, Demobilization, and Reintegration (DDR) program.[70]

Betty Bigombe, a native of Gulu, Uganda, raised awareness about the importance of reintegration in building sustainable peace.[71] A Harvard graduate and former government minister for the pacification of the North in Uganda, Bigombe initiated negotiations with Joseph Kony, the leader of the Lord's Resistance Army (LRA), that sought the demilitarization of his army.[72] Though these efforts were ultimately not successful, she was able to negotiate the release of some child soldiers, which she argued was essential for long-term peace in the region. Her vision for the negotiations was inspired by her belief that child soldiers were not the enemy; they were children who had been terrorized and had become refugees.[73] Bigombe explained that because of her identity as a local resident of the region where the violence was taking place and as a woman, she viewed the child soldiers of the LRA as victims who were conscripted into war against their will.[74]

Some reintegration efforts have been the product of former combatants themselves. Jacinta Jorge, a combatant turned peace activist in Mozambique, has advanced important new perspectives about how to conduct reintegration efforts in a manner that contributes to long-term peace. Jorge established Propaz (ProPeace) whose mission is to promote the effective reintegration of former combatants, in part by recognizing the different needs of women and men.[75]

[69] Tripp et al., *supra* note 22, at 199–200.

[70] Benner et al., *supra* note 5, at 7; United Nations, *DDR in Peace operations: A retrospective* (September 2010), *available at* http://www.un.org/en/peacekeeping/documents/DDR_retrospective.pdf.

[71] *Africa's peace seekers: Betty Bigombe*, Christian Science Monitor (September 13, 2005), *available at* http://www.csmonitor.com/2005/0913/p01s04-woaf.html/(page)/5.

[72] Kasaija Phillip Apuuli, *Amnesty and international law: The case of the Lord's Resistance Army insurgents in Northern Uganda*, 5 African J. Conflict Resol. 35 (2005); Billie O'Kadameri, *LRA/government negotiations 1993–94, in* Protracted Conflict, Elusive Peace: Initiatives to End the Violence in Northern Uganda 35–41 (Okello Lucima ed., 2002).

[73] *See generally* Mark Drumbl, Reimagining Child Soldiers (2012) (discussing the humanity of those children who are armed combatants).

[74] Daniel Fischlin & Martha Nandorfy, The Concise Guide to Global Human Rights 127–28 (2007).

[75] Tripp et al., *supra* note 22, at 200 (based on January 12, 2005 interviews with Jacinta Jorge in Maputo, Mozambique); Helen Scanlon & Benilde Nhalevilo, "*Many truths were not revealed*":

By emphasizing the centrality of reintegration to long-term peace, these leaders, among numerous others, have contributed both to their local peacebuilding efforts and to the broader project of considering how the international community conceptualizes peacebuilding. Their voices and actions have a vital role to play in how the UN conceives of reintegration as a formal element of its peace operations.[76] Furthermore, scholars must not ignore the ways in which the experiences of African women peacebuilders give explanatory power to important research questions, such as when and why reintegration helps prevent conflict from recurring.[77]

Protection of Women

A third component of effective peacebuilding advanced by African women peacebuilders is the protection of women during and after armed conflict. Recent decades have witnessed important advancements in international law with regard to the protection of women.[78] For example, the women who bravely provided testimony during the International Criminal Tribunal for Rwanda (ICTR) in the *Akayesu* case were instrumental in bringing about the development of international laws that protect women and girls from sexual violence during armed conflict. Women are uniquely targeted during wartime through the use of sexual violence and rape as means of aggression. As Van Schaack explains, "[w]omen experience armed conflict and repression in ways that are different from men" because they are victims of the unique weapon of rape during war.[79] Such sexual violence can lead to death by rape, torture,

the case of Mozambique, in WOMEN AND SECURITY GOVERNANCE IN AFRICA, 116 (Funmi Olonisakin & Awino Okech eds., 2011). (For example, Jorge criticized the disarmament, demobilization, and reintegration efforts led by the UN Operations in Mozambique for only providing men's clothes, shoes, and underwear in their reintegration kits.)

[76] United Nations Department of Peacekeeping Operations, *DDR in peace operations: A retrospective* (September 2010), *available at* http://www.un.org/en/peacekeeping/documents/DDR_retrospective.pdf; http://www.un.org/en/peacekeeping/documents/DDR_retrospective.pdf.

[77] *See, e.g.*, Michael Wessells, *Psychosocial issues in reintegrating child soldiers*, 37 CORN. INT'L. L. J. 513 (2004); Macartan Humphreys & Jeremy Weinstein, *Demobilization and reintegration*, 41 J. CONFLICT RESOL. 531 (2007); Save the Children, *When children affected by war go home: Lessons learned from Liberia* (2003), *available at* http://www.essex.ac.uk/armedcon/story_id/000169.pdf.

[78] Christine Chinkin, *Women: The forgotten victims of armed conflict, in* CHANGING FACE OF CONFLICT, *supra* note 4, at 36–44 (discussing recent advancements in international law – i.e., *Aydin v. Turkey* – as "strong evidence of a changed understanding of human rights violations that incorporate the violence experienced by women," at 40).

[79] Beth Van Schaack, *Endangering genocide: The Akayesu case before the International Criminal Tribunal for Rwanda, in* HUMAN RIGHTS ADVOCACY STORIES 193–227, at 208 (Deena Hurwitz, Margaret Satterthwaite, & Doug Ford eds., 2009). *But see* Jelena Batinic, *Feminism,*

mutilation, and unwanted pregnancies or *enfants de mauvais souvenir* (children of bad memories).[80]

During the *Akayesu* trial, the unnamed Witness J testified about her escape from death during the violence committed against the Tutsi population in Taba Commons. She shared with the Tribunal the fact that her six-year-old daughter had been raped and that, during the course of the investigation and trial, no judge or lawyer had ever asked about rape.[81] Rape – of women or girls – was not at that time among the possible acts included in the definition of genocide.[82] Witness J's testimony before the panel of predominantly male judges (with the exception of female Judge Navi Pillay) led the court to question later witnesses about acts of sexual violence.[83] As the trial proceeded, the testimony of a large number of acts of sexual violence against women and girls came to light. As a result, the ICTR amended the indictment against Akayesu to include rape and acts of sexual violence.[84]

Although rules against rape during wartime existed – for example, the 1863 Lieber Code includes rape as a war crime[85] – sexual violence had not been actively prosecuted prior to *Akayesu*. *Akayesu*, along with *Prosecutor v. Kunarac*,[86] which was the first international indictment focused exclusively on sexual violence (rape, sexual slavery, crimes against humanity), established the groundwork for including substantive law as well as procedural rules that were inclusive of sexual crimes in the Rome Statute.[87] Articles 8(2)(b)(xxii) and (e)(vi) enumerate the crimes of rape, sexual slavery, enforced prostitution, forced pregnancy, enforced sterilization,

nationalism, and war: The 'Yugoslav case' in feminist texts, 3 J. INT'L. WOMEN'S STUD. 2 (2001) (identifying the struggle between unity based on gender vs. nationality for rape victims of war).

80 *Id.*

81 *Akayesu*, Case No. ICTR-96-4-T, Testimony by Witness J (January 27, 1997). *See also* Van Schaack, *supra* note 79, at 199 (describing the testimony).

82 *Id.*

83 Van Schaack, *supra* note 79, 199–200. (In March 1997, two months after Witness J's testimony, Witness H testified that she was raped, and Judges Pillay and Aspegren asked the witness about the attack.)

84 Van Schaack, *supra* note 79, 217. ("It was not until *Akayesu* that the idea was first litigated and ultimately grounded in the jurisprudence of international criminal law.")

85 Francis Lieber, INSTRUCTIONS FOR THE GOVERNMENT OF ARMIES OF THE UNITED STATES IN THE FIELD, art. 47 (April 24, 1863) ("Crimes punishable by all penal codes, such as arson, murder, maiming, assaults, highway robbery, theft, burglary, fraud, forgery, and rape, if committed by an American soldier in a hostile country against its inhabitants, are not only punishable as at home, but in all cases in which death is not inflicted, the severe punishment shall be preferred"), *available at* http://avalon.law.yale.edu/19th_century/lieber.asp.

86 Prosecutor v. Kunarac, Case No. IT-96-23 & 23/1-T, Judgment (February 22, 2001).

87 Van Schaack, *supra* note 79, at 225.

and other forms of sexual violence as war crimes in armed conflict. Thus, the contributions of Witness J and her fellow witnesses helped bring about the development of international law that recognizes rape as a component of genocide and sexual violence as a crime not only against women, but also against peace.[88]

A second example of the advancement of prioritizing protection of women as a component of peacebuilding took place during the transition to postapartheid South Africa, where South African women sought to redefine societal values about the use of force and peace by advancing women-led development of security policies. Operating in local community groups, these women were instrumental in drafting the *South African White Paper on Defence*, which introduced a new conceptualization of security.[89] The paper identified the need to reject the "military-masculinity nexus"[90] of security in order to reframe young men's views about the benefits of engaging in the use of force. Instead, the paper advocates the promotion of opportunities for these men, and women, to engage in peacebuilding in order to prioritize "human security in societies experiencing or emerging from armed conflict."[91] Women peacebuilders further identified and promoted awareness about the important role women enjoy as the center of family units in fostering postconflict stabilization by shaping future generations' views on peace.[92] These contributions have provided a new doctrinal and normative perspective on the definition of peace. They have also introduced new ways of engaging in peacebuilding. For example, South African women's organizations demonstrated the effectiveness of using decentralized networks, referred to as "meshworks," that create social bonds among participants and foster solidarity and connectedness.[93] These novel methods – employed through decentralized sources of authority, minimal hierarchy, and horizontal forms of organizing – emphasize the

88 Van Schaack, *supra* note 79, at 226–27. *See also* Kelly Dawn Askin, *Gender crimes jurisprudence in the ICTR: Positive developments*, 3 J. Int'l. Crim. J. 1007 (2005) (discussing the ICTR's contributions to the development of gender jurisprudence).

89 Nomboniso Gasa, Women in South African History: They Remove Boulders and Cross Rivers 275 (2007). *See also* Peter Batchelor, Jacklyn Cock, & Penny Mckenzie, Conversion in South Africa in the 1990s: Defence Downsizing and Human Development Challenges 254 (2000).

90 Daniel Conway, *Masculinity, citizenship and political objection to military service in apartheid South Africa, in* (Un)thinking Citizenship: Feminist Debates in Contemporary South Africa 91–116 (Amanda Gouws ed., 2005).

91 Gasa, *supra* note 89, at 259 (defining peacebuilding).

92 *Id.* at 262.

93 *Id.* at 273. *See also* Sidney Tarrow, Power in Movement: Social Movements and Contentious Politics (2003).

value of women-led contributions to the field of peacebuilding and international law.[94]

Subsidiarity

The fourth component of effective peacebuilding advanced by African women peacebuilders is the concept of subsidiarity. Subsidiarity is the principle of "locating governance at the lowest possible level" so that those most affected by decisions can be involved in making them.[95] This principle has been recognized as being essential to the effective resolution of disputes. For example, in the International Court of Justice's *Gabčíkovo-Nagymaros Project* case, Judge Christopher Gregory Weearmantry emphasized the importance of adopting local practices in resolving resource disputes.[96] The principle of subsidiarity is also essential to effective peacebuilding. It promotes the use of culturally and contextually appropriate practices and encourages inclusion of local people as essential actors in developing national peace.[97] In postconflict African societies, women are most often the survivors of war. They are the ones who assume primary responsibility for rebuilding peace at the local level. Thus, because of their experiences, they offer valuable perspectives and lessons learned.

The Sudanese Women's Voice for Peace (SWVP), a nongovernmental organization (NGO) conducting peacebuilding efforts in the Sudan, embraced the principle of subsidiarity as a criterion for selecting mediators. Departing from the practice of choosing mediators based on expertise and experience, the typical practice in the United States, SWVP selected mediators from local communities who, as elders or family members, enjoyed authority and standing.[98] As referenced earlier, Bigombe argued that, following the principle of subsidiarity, her identity as a local was an important reason

[94] Jacklyn Cock, *"Another mother for peace": Women and peace building in South Africa, in* WOMEN IN SOUTH AFRICAN HISTORY 272–73 (2007).

[95] Anne Marie Slaughter, A NEW WORLD ORDER 30 (2004) (defining subsidiarity as "a principle of locating governance at the lowest possible level – that closest to the individuals and groups affected by the rules and decisions adopted and enforced").

[96] Gabcikovo-Nagymaros Project (Hung. v. Slovk.) 1997 I.C.J. 197 (September 25), para. 7; *Id.* (separate Opinion of Weeramantry, J.) paras. 88–119 (emphasizing the importance of subsidiarity in referencing local customary law and negotiation practices on traditional water management in Bali as guidance for the case). *See also* Eyal Benvenisti, *Asian traditions and contemporary international law on the management of natural resources*, 7 CHIN. J. INT'L L. 273, 277 (2008).

[97] Call, *supra* note 36, at 6.

[98] Anna Snyder, SETTING THE AGENDA FOR GLOBAL PEACE, CONFLICT AND CONSENSUS BUILDING 125 (2003).

that her efforts in reintegrating child soldiers as a component of peacebuilding in Uganda were successful. Gbowee is also an advocate of subsidiarity. She has noted that, "people who have lived through a terrible conflict may be hungry and desperate, *but they're not stupid* [Gbowee's emphasis]. They often have very good ideas about how peace can evolve, and they need to be asked."[99] Gbowee advocated involving Liberian civil society, especially women's organizations, in restoring the country. She critiqued the way that the "UN was spending many millions of dollars in Liberia, but most of it was on [their own] staffing resources. ... If they had just given some of that money to the local people, it would have made a real difference."[100]

Recognizing the importance of local practices is one of the key normative implications of adopting subsidiarity as a guiding principle in peacebuilding in Africa. For example, in Sierra Leone, the October 2004 final report of the TRC found that government corruption and the betrayal of public trust were two causes of the war there.[101] In response, restorative justice approaches were adopted alongside traditional ones. The Special Court of Sierra Leone was set up to prosecute violations of international humanitarian law.[102] At the same time, a local process known as the Fambul Tok ("Family Talk"), which consists of truth telling, cleansing rituals, and cooperative development initiatives, was adopted.[103] Similarly, as this chapter previously described, women-led peacebuilding efforts in Burundi advocated the use of the traditional and locally based dispute resolution mechanism of *ubushingantahe*.[104] These examples illustrate the importance of subsidiarity as an aspect of effective peacebuilding in postconflict societies.

Sustainability

The fifth component of essential peacebuilding described in this chapter is environmental sustainability. Environmental degradation is a consequence of war, and restoring a healthy natural environment is essential to long-term peace. The late Kenyan activist Wangari Maathai recognized the importance of sustainability as a principle of peacebuilding. She was awarded the 2004 Nobel Peace Prize for her groundbreaking work in promoting environmental

[99] *Id.* at 173.
[100] *Id.* at 177.
[101] Moore, *supra* note 4, at 198–99.
[102] Statue of the Special Court for Sierra Leone, Art. 1.1 (2000), *available at* http://www.sc-sl.org/LinkClick.aspx?fileticket=uClnd1MJeEw%3d&tabid=70.
[103] *Id.*
[104] Moore, *supra* note 4, at 199–200.

protection. She founded the Green Belt movement to mobilize Kenyans to work for a "greener, cleaner Kenya."[105] This movement employed planting trees as a form of protest against government policies that created conditions of oppression across the country. Maathai was labeled a "mad woman and a threat to the order and security of the country" by the then President Daniel Moi.[106] She risked her life in these acts of protest because she believed that they were necessary to expose the injustices of the existing system where "[t]he rights of those at the bottom of the pyramid are violated every day by those at the top."[107] Her vision for promoting peace involved protecting Kenya's precious resources, both human and natural: the trees, the water, the earth, the children and their mothers. In doing so, Maathai helped to solidify environmental protection as an essential component of peacebuilding.[108]

Another promoter of sustainability in peacebuilding is Emem Okon, a community mobilizer in Niger Delta, Nigeria. Her work seeks to address oil pollution by Exxon-Mobil and other oil companies that are causing environmental degradation. Like Wangari Maathai, Okon recognized the integral connection between environmental degradation, resource scarcity, and armed conflict. She also highlighted the disparate impact that such conflicts have on women and girls. She has advocated for the critical importance of including women in peacebuilding efforts at all levels, which is not the common practice of either the oil companies or the Nigerian government. Okon explains why women are necessary to successful peacebuilding: "We believe that women, as mothers and wives and lovers, are in a better position to talk to the men who are perpetuating the acts of violence. And we're causing the violence to go down. Since 2007, we've gotten more than 1,600 boys and young men to surrender their weapons to the police and to make the decision not to be involved in violence."[109] Okun's work has highlighted why including women at all levels of decision making is essential to developing peacebuilding capacity in fragile states and postconflict nations.[110]

[105] Anita Price Davis & Marla J. Selvidge, Women Nobel Peace Prize Winners 196 (2006) (explaining the mission statement of the Green Belt movement); Judith Hicks Stiehm, Champions for Peace: Women Winners of the Nobel Peace Prize 201–16 (2006).

[106] *Id*. at 198.

[107] Wangari Muta Maathai, The Bottom is Heavy Too 13 (1994).

[108] Stiehm, *supra* note 105, at 212–14 (2006).

[109] Beverly Bell, *Birthing justice: Women in peace-building: Peace amidst war for resource control* (April 2, 2012), *available at* http://www.allianceforpeacebuilding.org/news/88406/BIRTHING-JUSTICE-Women-in-Peace-Building-Peace-amidst-War-for-Resource-Control.htm.

[110] *Id*.

Advancing the African Women-Developed Normative Paradigm of Peacebuilding

This chapter has been critical of the lack of attention and recognition that mainstream international law scholars and practitioners have paid to the specific contributions that local actors, including African women, have made to international legal frameworks for peace promotion. As the stories shared here illustrate, women peacebuilders in fragile and postconflict African nations have advanced reconciliation, reintegration, protection of women, subsidiarity, and sustainability as guiding principles of peacebuilding. Witness J and her fellow witnesses brought attention to the need to understand that women are vulnerable in unique ways during and after armed conflict and thus need special protection. Tesfagiorgis and Gbowee highlighted the importance of reconciliation in promoting healing from physical, emotional, and psychological trauma. Bigombe emphasized the necessity of reintegrating former combatants back into society, often because there is no other place for them to go.

However, identifying and examining specific contributions is not enough. The contributions of these women, and others like them, are representative of a broader normative vision for what peacebuilding is and ought to be.[111] As survivors of conflict and as women, their insights and perspectives offer important intelligence about what works, when, and why. Therefore, it is vital that policymakers, institutions, and scholars alike strive to consider the full impact that such contributions are having on the practice and theory of peacebuilding.[112]

One reason that these contributions remain underrecognized is that such views are not captured and promulgated in the prevailing models that standardize peacebuilding practices.[113] The following overview of several prominent models illustrates how they advance a framework for understanding the values and perspectives that guide the selection and application of

[111] *See* Tripp et al., *supra* note 22, at 3 (arguing that women-led peacebuilding efforts have contributed to the changing international norms) and at 196 (arguing that peacebuilding practices employed in Mozambique and Uganda have contributed to broader trends).

[112] For examples of scholarship discussing the normative goals described here, *see generally* John McDonald with Noa Zanolli, THE SHIFTING GROUNDS OF CONFLICT AND PEACEBUILDING 278–79 (2008) (describing the author's participation in drafting a UNGA resolution on trauma, healing, and reconciliation in response to lessons learned in Liberia); Benner et al., *supra* note 5, at 146 (discussing the importance of reintegration in Sierra Leone). For examples of scholarship discussing peacebuilding models with little or no reference to the contributions described here, *see* Uzi Rabi, INTERNATIONAL INTERVENTION IN LOCAL CONFLICTS (2010); Howard, *supra* note 3; and Ponzio, *supra* note 13.

[113] Bercovitch, *supra* note 11, at 6. *See generally* Howard, *supra* note 3, and Benner et al., *supra* note 5.

peacebuilding techniques, such as political inclusion, power sharing, development of national identities, pursuing legitimacy of the state, economic development, and social reform. However, they do not recognize and integrate the guiding principles identified in this chapter that have emerged from the African women's view of peacebuilding and thus fail to provide comprehensive and effective models.

Peacebuilding frameworks can be categorized according to the following typology developed by Call. Liberal peacebuilding aims to promote democracy and market-based economies. This includes the promotion of civil and political rights, the liberalization of markets, and the development of governance institutions.[114] Republican peacebuilding is understood as a legitimacy-focused approach that aims to create stability among groups in discord based on the principles of deliberation, representation, and constitutionalism.[115] Peacebuilding through state-building is a third approach that emphasizes the development of self-sustaining peace through state-building as the remedy for fragile states, based on experiences in Rwanda and Angola.[116] A fourth category of peacebuilding is defined by critical theory that argues against intrusive measures adopted by the other theories.[117] These categories are not inclusive of reconciliation, subsidiarity, the protection of women, and the other principles identified in this chapter.

An overview of several prominent peacebuilding frameworks further illustrates the point. The Democratic Reconstruction Model (DRM) is a peacebuilding framework adopted by UN-led efforts in East Timor and Kosovo, by NATO in Bosnia, and by the United States in Iraq.[118] DRM was credited with bringing about the decline of violence in intrastate political disputes, increasing capacity for governance and humanitarian assistance, and increasing political participation and the creation of

[114] *See generally* Doyle & Sambanis, *supra* note 25.

[115] Call, *supra* note 36, at 33. *See also* Michael Barnett, *Building a republican peace: Stabilizing states after war*, 30 INT'L. SEC. 87–112 (2006).

[116] Call, *supra* note 36, at 33–35. *See also* Francis Fukuyama, STATE-BUILDING: GOVERNANCE AND WORLD ORDER IN THE 21ST CENTURY (2004); and MAKING STATES WORK: STATE FAILURE AND THE CRISIS OF GOVERNMENT (Simon Chesterman, Michael Ignatieff, & Chandra Thakur eds., 2005).

[117] *Id. See also* David Chandler, EMPIRE IN DENIAL: THE POLITICS OF STATE-BUILDING (2006) (arguing that state-building does not work); PALGRAVE ADVANCES IN PEACEBUILDING: CRITICAL DEVELOPMENTS AND APPROACHES (Oliver P. Richmond ed., 2010), Ian Taylor, LIBERAL PEACE, LIBERAL IMPERIALISM: A GRAMSCIAN CRITIQUE (2010) (featuring essays critical of liberal approaches to peacebuilding).

[118] Ponzio, *supra* note 13, at 205–07.

conditions that support socioeconomic recovery.[119] DRM is considered costly and complex, and it has the potential to destabilize postconflict societies.[120] The Institutionalization Before Liberalization (IBL) approach prioritizes developing political stability through the creation of effective institutions before engagement in significant economic and democratic reform.[121] An IBL approach advocates postponing elections until political parties and electoral structures are well formed. It also promotes economic policies that build the market economy alongside government and legal systems capable of providing effective regulations.[122] A third model, described by Lakhdar Brahimi, UN Special Representative for Afghanistan, is the Light Foot Approach (LFA). LFA seeks to avoid extensive international infrastructure and personnel and emphasizes engagement with local stakeholders to build indigenous capacity.[123] As peacebuilding through LFA in Afghanistan has shown, this approach requires high-level commitment and resources to be effective.[124] These peacebuilding models form the basis for the normative dialogue about what peacebuilding is and what it should be. The perspectives of African women peacebuilders are not captured in these frameworks and are therefore absent from mainstream conversations about peacebuilding.

One model that does capture some of the guiding principles discussed in this chapter is the Democratic Peacebuilding Approach (DPA), described as a "dynamic, long term process of institutionalizing and expanding democratic legal authority within a weak state or territory to reduce the propensity toward violent conflict."[125] DPA emphasizes the use of local authority structures to legitimize reforms essential for peacebuilding[126] and emphasizes the importance of subsidiarity in order to promote "innovative governance models" that work well in non-Western societies.[127] This model has placed renewed emphasis on using multidimensional approaches that are inclusive of local perspectives.[128] For example, nonstate actors, such as tribal groups in Afghanistan or

[119] *Id.* at 206.
[120] *Id.*
[121] *Id.* at 211.
[122] *Id.* at 212.
[123] *Id.* at 213–14.
[124] *Id.* at 215.
[125] *Id.* at 216.
[126] *Id.* at 217.
[127] *Id.* at 219. *See also* Charles Call & Susan Cook, *On democratization and peacebuilding*, 9 Global Gov. 233 (2003) at 242–43.
[128] Bercovitch, *supra* note 11, at 8–10. *See also* Karen Aggestam, *Quasi-informal mediation in the Oslo Channel: Larsen and Holst as individual mediators*, *in* Studies in

armed groups in Sierra Leone, have been recognized as necessary stakeholders in various peace initiatives in recent years.[129]

As the examples provided in this chapter illustrate, women-led peacebuilding in Africa has advanced a vision that peace and security are best achieved after armed conflict by prioritizing reconciliation, reintegration, protection of women, subsidiarity, and sustainability. These women, given their identities as survivors of war and as mothers endeavoring to rebuild a life for their children, offer distinct and important perspectives about the causes of war and peace.[130] Women often find themselves at the bottom of societal power structures; although this renders them particularly vulnerable to the consequences of war, it also makes them effective advocates for peace. During the movements that sought an end to apartheid in South African, a slogan, "Another mother for peace," developed to represent the belief that women are naturally expert peacebuilders because they learn to be facilitative, cooperative, and capable of mediating conflicts: all qualities useful in peacebuilding.[131] Empowering women empowers peacebuilding; it is toward achieving this goal that the world must now turn.

Conclusion

This chapter acknowledges the remarkable contributions of African women who, after the traumas of war and against all odds, have advanced the cause of peace. In addition, it highlights the importance and value of the perspectives and contributions of those embedded at the bottom of societal structures, whose voices are often unheard. It is essential that the international community recognize these often undocumented and ignored contributions, which have advanced forms of peacebuilding that prioritize social rehabilitation, forgiveness, and healing through reconciliation and reintegration. The contributions of these women have also highlighted the necessity for subsidiarity, sustainability, and increased protection of women during and after war. In doing so, these women peacebuilders have advanced a normative framework for defining the concept of peacebuilding and showing how it can be achieved in today's complex world.

INTERNATIONAL MEDIATION 57–79 (Jacob Bercovitch ed., 2002); Nicolas Sambanis & Michael Doyle, *International peacebuilding: A theoretical and quantitative analysis*, 94 AM. POL. SCI. REV. 779 (2000); UN Peacebuilding Commission (established in 2005), *available at* http://www.un.org/en/peacebuilding/.

[129] Ponzio, *supra* note 13, at 3–5. Lakhdar Brahimi, *The Situation in Afghanistan: Briefing to the UN Security Council*, *available at* http://www.un.org/news/dh/latest/afghan/brahimi-sc-briefing.htm.

[130] Snyder, *supra* note 98, at 132.

[131] Batchelor et al., *supra* note 89, at 267.

PART II

BLACK WOMEN’S MOVEMENTS

8

African-American Women on the World Stage: The Fourth World Conference on Women in Beijing

Linda Sheryl Greene

INTRODUCTION

This chapter examines whether the participation of African-American women affected the outcome of the Platform for Action of the 1995 Fourth World Conference on Women in Beijing[1] (Beijing World Conference). At that conference, a delegation of African-American women organized by the Lawyers' Committee for Civil Rights under Law,[2] as well as other African-American women,[3] constituted themselves an African-American Women's Caucus. There, they successfully advocated for a gender equality framework called *intersectionality*,[4] a framework that emphasizes the manner in which a woman's other circumstances – such as poverty, race, or immigrant status – exacerbate gender inequality and render it more resistant to eradication. In the section "The Genesis of the Fourth World Conference on Women: From Nairobi to Beijing," I trace the multidecade process leading up to Beijing and Beijing's objective of a Platform for Action, a platform intended

Linda Sheryl Greene Vice Chancellor, Equity, Diversity and Inclusion, University of California San Diego; former Evjue Bascom Professor, University of Wisconsin Law School.

[1] *Beijing and its Follow-up*, U.N. Women, *available at* http://www.un.org/womenwatch/daw/beijing/index.html (last visited October 11, 2011). For a list of the official report and other official documents and statements, see *Fourth World Conference on Women: Beijing, China – September 1995 Action for Equality, Development and Peace*, U.N. Women, *available at* http://www.un.org/womenwatch/daw/beijing/fwcwn.html (last visited October 11, 2011).

[2] Lawyers' Committee For Civil Rights Under Law, *available at* http://www.lawyerscommittee.org/ (last visited October 11, 2011).

[3] A contemporaneous article on the role of African-American women at the Fourth World Conference appeared in Ebony Magazine, the magazine of record for the African-American community in the United States. *Black Women and the World Conference*, Ebony 42 (December 1995), http://www.highbeam.com/doc/1G1-17934730.html (last visited October 12, 2012).

[4] *See infra* note 30.

to serve as a blueprint for the elimination of discrimination against women worldwide. In the section "Historical and Theoretical Antecedents of African-American Participation in the Fourth World Conference," I review the historical involvement of African-American women in human rights activities in which an intersectionality framework was implicit, as well as the late-twentieth-century emergence of the theoretical construct of intersectionality. In the section "African-American Women Advocate the Incorporation of the Intersectionality Framework in the Beijing Platform of Action," I discuss the Lawyers' Committee preparatory conference[5] in Washington, DC, that laid the groundwork for both the intersectionality-focused critique of the Platform for Action and the formation of a Beijing African-American Women's Caucus. In the last section, "African-American Women and Intersectionality: From the Margins to the Center," I show that African-American women successfully advocated for the incorporation of an intersectionality framework in the Beijing Platform for Action. Since Beijing, the domestic and international discourse about equality for women incorporates an intersectionality framework. This is the story of that development.

THE GENESIS OF THE FOURTH WORLD CONFERENCE ON WOMEN: FROM NAIROBI TO BEIJING

The United Nations Commission on the Status of Women organized the Fourth World Conference on Women in Beijing, which took place in August 1995.[6] The Commission on the Status of Women, established by the UN Economic and Social Council in 1946,[7] focuses exclusively on gender equality and the advancement of women.[8] The Commission previously organized

5 African-American Women and the Law: Exerting Our Power – Reclaiming Our Communities, Washington, DC (June 15–18, 1995) (Lawyers' Committee for Civil Rights under Law, Washington, DC) [hereinafter Lawyers' Committee Conference].

6 United Nations Fourth World Conference on Women, Beijing, China, September 4–15, 1995, U.N. Doc. A/CONF.177/20/Rev.1 (1996) [hereinafter Report of the Fourth World Conference].

7 United Nations Economic and Social Council, *available at* http://www.un.org/en/ecosoc/index.shtml (last visited October 11, 2011).

8 For a brief history of the commission, *see Overview-Short History of the Commission on the Status of Women*, U.N. Women, *available at* http://www.un.org/womenwatch/daw/csw/ (last visited October 11, 2011). The commission, *inter alia*, "evaluate[s] progress on gender equality, identi[ies] challenges, set[s] global standards and formulate[s] concrete policies to promote gender equality and women's empowerment worldwide." *Id.*

three world conferences on women: Mexico (1975),[9] Copenhagen (1980),[10] and Nairobi (1985).[11]

These conferences, as well as the 1979 UN International Convention on the Elimination of All Forms of Discrimination against Women,[12] laid the foundation for the Beijing Conference. The primary objective of the Beijing Conference was "to build on consensus and progress made at previous UN conferences and summits ... [and] to [a]chieve the full and effective implementation of the Nairobi Forward-looking Strategies for the Advancement of Women."[13] The aim of the Beijing Conference was the production of a Platform for Action[14] in which participating nations agreed to continue to work to eliminate discrimination against women.

HISTORICAL AND THEORETICAL ANTECEDENTS OF AFRICAN-AMERICAN PARTICIPATION IN THE FOURTH WORLD CONFERENCE

It is not surprising that African-American women would be interested in the work of this international conference. For more than 150 years, African-American women pursued human rights concerns both domestically and abroad. In addition, for close to fifty years, African-American women have argued that gender *and* race combine to disadvantage Black women in a manner that is distinct from the effects of race or gender alone.

The participation of African-American women in the Beijing Conference had its antecedents in the past activities of African-American women. African-American women were engaged in human rights activities during the nineteenth and early twentieth century, as for example, anti-slavery activists. In addition, African-American women had been involved in international affairs prior to the Beijing Conference. Finally, African-American female law

[9] World Conference of the Women's Year, Mexico City, Mexico, June 19–July 2, 1975, U.N. Doc. E/CONF.66/34 (1976).

[10] World Conference of the United Nations Decade for Women: Quality, Development and Peace, Copenhagen, Denmark, July 14–30, 1980, U.N. Doc. A/CONF.94/30 (1980), *available at* http://www.un.org/womenwatch/daw/beijing/otherconferences/Copenhagen/Copenhagen%20Full%20Optimized.pdf (last visited October 12, 2012).

[11] World Conference to Review and Appraise the Achievements of the United Nations Decade for Women: Quality, Development and Peace, Nairobi, July 15–26, 1985, U.N. Doc. A/CONF.116/28/Rev.1 (1986).

[12] U.N. Convention on the Elimination of All Forms of Discrimination against Women, December 18, 1979, 1249 U.N.T.S. 13.

[13] Implementation of the Nairobi Forward-looking Strategies for the Advancement of Women, G.A. Res. 48/108, U.N. Doc. A/RES/48/108 (February 28, 1994).

[14] G.A. Res 49/161, A/RES/49/161 (February 9, 1995).

professors had developed a discourse of "intersectionality" focused specifically on the subordination of African-American women as distinct from other women and African-American men. These were antecedents to the development of a delegation of African-American women who would express a distinctive voice at the 1995 Fourth World Conference on Women in Beijing.

Historical Antecedents: Human Rights Activities of African-American Women in the Nineteenth and Twentieth Centuries

African-American women have long been involved in human rights activities. The antislavery activities of Sojourner Truth and Harriet Tubman must be viewed through a human rights lens.[15] In addition, African-American women were prominently involved in human rights efforts at the National Emigration Convention of 1854, from which emerged an uncompromising and bold statement of human rights that included a specific reference to the rights of female children.[16] In 1895, Mrs. Joseph St. Pierre Ruffin convened the First National Conference of Colored Women in Boston, Massachusetts,[17] at which she urged African-American women to "talk over not only those things which are of vital importance to us as women, but also the things that are of special interest to us as colored women."[18] In 1900, African-American leaders Anna Julia Cooper and Anna H. Jones addressed the 1900 gathering of the Pan

[15] For a biography of Sojourner, *see Sojourner Truth: Online Resources*, *available at* Library of Congress, http://www.loc.gov/rr/program/bib/truth/ (last visited October 12, 2011). For a biography of Harriet Tubman, *see* Africans in America, *Harriet Tubman*, PBS Online, *available at* http://www.pbs.org/wgbh/aia/part4/4p1535.html (last visited October 12, 2011).

[16] *See* 2 Black Women in America: An Historical Encyclopedia 1312 (Hine et al. eds., 1993) (noting the presence of 29 black women, one-third of delegates to the National Emigration Convention and election of Mary E. Bibb as second vice president) [hereinafter 2 Black Women in America]; Proceedings of the National Emigration Convention of Colored People: Held at Cleveland, Ohio, on Thursday, Friday, and Saturday, the 24th, 25th, and 26th of August, 1854 (1854), *available at* http://books.google.com/books?id=i50-AAAAYAAJ&printsec=frontcover&source=gbs_ge_summary_r&cad=0#v=onepage&q&f=false. At the outset of the proceedings of this effort for freedom, in 1854, a Platform and Declaration of rights for Blacks of all descriptions, including a specific state of rights on behalf of Black female children was outlined. *Id.* at 26–27, para. 26 ("That the potency and respectability of a nation or people, depends entirely upon the position of their women; therefore, it is essential to our elevation that the female portion of our children be instructed in all the arts and sciences pertaining to the highest civilization").

[17] Wilson Jeremiah Moses, The Golden Age of Black Nationalism, 1850–1925 106 (1978).

[18] (1895) Josephine St. Pierre Ruffin, Address to the First National Conference of Colored Women, *available at* http://www.blackpast.org/?q=1895-josephine-st-pierre-ruffin-address-first-national-conference-colored-women.

African Conference in London,[19] and Ida Gibbs Hunt attended the 1919 Pan African Congress organized by W. E. B. Dubois.[20] The antilynching work of the activist Ida Wells, which she pursued in the United States, England, and Scotland, is worthy of note,[21] as was the work of Mary McLeod Bethune,[22] who advised the United States at the 1945 founding conference of the UN in San Francisco.[23]

Bethune's successor, Dorothy Height, continued the human rights legacy. She was known as the "arbiter of the gender and racial divide,"[24] and her work at both the YWCA and the National Conference of Negro Women provided a unique perch from which to view the intersection of race and gender. She specifically addressed these issues in the 1930s when she called international attention to the existence of New York street markets for the services of African-American maids.[25] Later, she addressed the intersection of race and gender in her work as director of the Center for Racial Justice of the YWCA.[26]

[19] 1 BLACK WOMEN IN AMERICA: AN HISTORICAL ENCYCLOPEDIA 278 (Hine et al. eds., 1993) [Hereinafter 1 BLACK WOMEN IN AMERICA]. *See also* Bettye Gardner, AFRICAN-AMERICAN WOMEN AS AGENTS OF CHANGE: AN HISTORICAL OVERVIEW 15 (1990).

[20] *Id.*; ORGANIZING BLACK AMERICA: AN ENCYCLOPEDIA OF AFRICAN-AMERICAN ASSOCIATIONS 478 (Nina Mjagkij ed., 2007), *available at* http://books.google.com/books?id=cfESrcLSbCcC&pg=PA479&lpg=PA479&dq=Women+Delegates+to+1919+pan+african+congress+Delegates+to&source=bl&ots=E2XPbvUWdB&sig=cx1p5LmGaDeKGKa9JhJlwPDaHHI&hl=en&ei=cqrSTsa9AoS3twe839mrDQ&sa=X&oi=book_result&ct=result&resnum=5&ved=0CDwQ6AEwBA#v=onepage&q=Women%20Delegates%20to%201919%20pan%20african%20congress%20Delegates%20to&f=false (last accessed November 27, 2011); Dorothy Sterling, BLACK FOREMOTHERS: THREE LIVES 86 (2d ed. 1988).

[21] The Post-Beijing Declaration of the African-American Women's Caucus specifically mentioned the foundation laid by women such as Ida B. Wells Barnett for their activities in Beijing. *See* Letter from Barbara Arnwine, Executive Director of the Lawyers' Committee for Civil Rights under Law, and Adjoa Aiyetoro to African-American Women Caucus Participant and attached Declaration of the African-American Women's Caucus Beijing 1995 (October 30, 1995) (on file with author).

[22] Joyce Ann Hanson, MARY MCLEOD BETHUNE AND BLACK WOMEN'S POLITICAL ACTIVISM (2003); MARY MCLEOD BETHUNE: BUILDING A BETTER WORLD, ESSAYS AND SELECTED DOCUMENTS xiii (Audrey Thomas McCluskey & Elaine M. Smith eds., 1999) (farewell address to the World Assembly for Moral Rearmament).

[23] 1 BLACK WOMEN IN AMERICA, *supra* note 17, at 118. Also in attendance at the Conference were W. E. B. Dubois and Walter White of the NAACP. *Id.* Bethune united twenty-six African-American women's groups into the National Conference of Negro Women.

[24] MARY MCLEOD BETHUNE: BUILDING A BETTER WORLD, *supra* note 22, at xiv. Bethune's role took her many places throughout the world, including Caux in Switzerland, a visit to the pope in Vatican City, Liberia, and Scotland. *Id.* at 8, 33, 45. Her successor at the National Conference of Negro Women, Dorothy Height, traveled widely throughout the world for her work to "rise above the limitations of race and sex."

[25] Margalit Fox, *Dorothy Height, largely unsung giant of the civil rights era, dies at* 98, NEW YORK. TIMES (April 20, 2010), *available at* http://www.nytimes.com/2010/04/21/us/21height.html.

[26] *Id.*

Height traveled abroad extensively during the 1930s to international conferences and undertook training missions to further the work of the YMCA and the National Conference of Negro Women in Africa, Europe, Latin America, Asia, and Caribbean.[27]

Height joined efforts to influence United States foreign policy. She was a member of the Delegation to the UNESCO Conference on Women in 1974 and a participant in the Tribunal at the International Women's Conference of the UN in Mexico City in 1975, and she addressed the National Convention of the Black Women's Federation of South Africa in Johannesburg in 1977.[28]

Other African-American women were involved in governmental international affairs prior to Beijing. Patricia Roberts Harris served as ambassador to Luxembourg during the administration of Lyndon B. Johnson in 1965 and was an alternate delegate to the UN. Jewel Lafontant-Mankarious, a 1946 University of Chicago Law School graduate, had been a Council on Racial Equality activist in her early years; she was U.S. Ambassador at Large and U.S. Coordinator for Refugee Affairs.[29]

Thus, for 150 years, African-American women have understood the importance of international fora in the pursuit of their own full citizenship. It is equally important to note that they have not been content to focus on limited or parochial aims, but rather have been ambitious in the pursuit of the global stage in their search for empowering norms.

Theoretical Antecedents: The Emergence of the Intersectionality Framework in Litigation, Judicial Opinions, and Scholarship

A critique of equality law grounded in a rejection of race essentialism, intersectionality provided a theoretical foundation for the work of the African-American Women's Caucus in Beijing. Intersectionality rejects race

[27] Crystal Hayes, *Remembering Dr. Dorothy Height*, San Francisco Bay View (May 10, 2010), *available at* http://sfbayview.com/2010/remembering-dr-dorothy-height/.

[28] Dr. Dorothy I. *Height: Chair and President Emerita, National Council of Negro Women*, National Council of Negro Women, *available at* http://www.ncnw.org/about/height.htm (last visited October 12, 2011).

[29] *Id.* at 689–90.

Other prominent African-American women on the world stage during this time were athletes. They included Alice Coachman Audrey Patterson (track and field), who won medals in the 1948 Olympic Games; Wilma Rudolph (track and field), who won medals in the 1956 and 1960 Olympic Games (Bronze), 2 Black Women in America, *supra* note 16, at 457–58; Willye White (track and field), who competed in Olympic Games from 1956 through 1972, *available at* http://www.sports-reference.com/olympics/athletes/wh/willye-white-1.html (last accessed November 27, 2011); and Althea Gibson, who won Wimbledon in 1957–1958, 3 Black Women in America: An Historical Encyclopedia 182 (Hine et al. eds., 2005).

essentialism in favor of more nuanced concerns about the ways in which other circumstances of a women's identity, such as poverty, determine the extent of her equality.[30] Intersectionality holds that the interaction of multiple factors shapes unique experiences for women at those intersections and that generalized explorations of gender do not capture the particularities of the barriers that pose obstacles to full equality for women. African-American women were the pioneers of this perspective, upon which many other racial, ethnic, and other groups have relied.

Early writings, such as Pauli Murray's 1971 "The Negro Women's Stake in the Equal Rights Amendment,"[31] provide firm evidence of the early emergence of an intersectionality equality framework. Murray spoke of the importance of the ratification of the Amendment in order to end discrimination against African-American women: "Black women remain the lowest and most vulnerable social and economic group in the United States. ... Nor has the movement for black liberation improved their situation for they must still contend with prejudice based on their sex. ... The dual victimization creates special problems of educational disadvantage, lack of employment opportunities, low income, poverty, and general powerlessness. ... They cannot be remedied by policies directed solely against racial discrimination."[32]

As early as 1971, a federal district court recognized that racial discrimination against African-American women might be distinct from racial discrimination against African-American men. A class of African-American women alleged that an employer's reliance on referrals to fill jobs discriminated against

[30] For primers on intersectionality theory in the United States context, see Kimberlé Crenshaw, *Mapping the margins: Intersectionality, identity politics, and violence against women of color*, 43 STAN. L. REV. 1241 (1991); Angela P. Harris, *Race and essentialism in feminist legal theory*, 42 STAN. L. REV. 581 (1990); and Kimberlé Crenshaw, *Demarginalizing the intersection of race and sex: A Black feminist critique of antidiscrimination doctrine, feminist theory and antiracist politics*, 1989 U. CHI. LEGAL F. 139 (1989). *See generally* Symposium, *Black Women Law Professors: Building a Community at the Intersection of Race and Gender*, 6 BERKELEY WOMEN'S L. J. 1 (1990–91). The Lawyers' Committee Conference included content related to the concept of intersectionality. Panel: Vision of Unity: Combating Sexism in the African-American Community, Lawyers' Committee Conference, *supra* note 3, at 32; Panel: Jurisprudence on Race and Gender, Lawyers' Committee Conference, *supra* note 3, at 19 (with Taunya Banks, Linda Greene, and Stephanie Moore).

[31] Pauli Murray, *The Negro woman's stake in the Equal Rights Amendment*, 6 HARV. C.R.-C.L. L. REV. 253 (1971). Pauli Murray gained national publicity when, in 1938, with the support of the NAACP, she began a campaign to enter the all-White University of North Carolina. She was also arrested and imprisoned for refusing to sit at the back of the bus in Virginia. In addition, Murray was a writer, poet, and founding member of the Congress of Racial Equality. Pauli Murray Project, *Biography*, Duke Human Rights Center, *available at* http://paulimurrayproject.org/pauli-murray/biography/ (last visited October 12, 2011).

[32] Murray, *supra* note 31, at 254.

African-American women more significantly than it did African-American men because the company had only recently lifted its historical policy against hiring African-American women. The company had very few African-American female employees,[33] and thus the policy disproportionately affected African-American females.[34] Later, some courts recognized that employers often forced African-American women into the most underpaid and marginalized work, behind White men, White women, and African-American men.[35]

The concept of intersectionality gained further traction in 1971. Judith Trent Ellis,[36] who had litigated employment discrimination cases with the U.S. Justice Department, published an article in which she discussed the intersection and interplay of race and gender employment discrimination in the context of sexual harassment.[37] Moreover, the National Conference of

33 *Lea*, 301 F. Supp. at 97–98.

34 Lea v. Cone Mills Corp., 301 F. Supp. 97 (M.D.N.C. 1969), *aff'd in part, vacated in parton other grounds*, 438 F.2d 86 (4th Cir. 1971).

35 Thereafter, many courts implicitly recognized discrimination at the intersection of race and gender, Lewis v. Bloomsburg Mills, Inc., 773 F.2d 561 (4th Cir. 1985); Parker v. Secretary, HUD, 891 F.2d 316 (D.C. Cir. 1989); Proffitt v. Anacomp, Inc., 747 F. Supp. 421, 65 Fair Empl. Prac. Cas. (BNA) 1481 (S.D. Oh. 1990). Other cases explicitly recognized claims at the intersection of race and gender. *See* Brooms v. Regal Tube Co., 881 F.2d 412 (7th Cir. 1989); Hall v. Gus Constr. Co., Inc., 842 F.2d 1010 (8th Cir. 1988); Moore v. Hughes Helicopters, Inc., 708 F.2d 475 (9th Cir. 1983) (representation of class of African-American women); Prince v. Commissioner, INS, 713 F. Supp. 984 (E.D. Mich. 1989); Jefferies v. Harris Cnty. Cmty. Action Ass'n, 615 F.2d. 1025 (5th Cir. 1980); Judge v. Marsh, 649 F. Supp. 770 (D.D.C. 1986); Chambers v. Omaha Girls Club, Inc., 629 F. Supp. 925 (D. Neb. 1986), *aff'd*, 834 F.2d 697 (8th Cir. 1987); Graham v. Bendix Corp., 585 F. Supp. 1036 (N.D. Ind. 1984); Good v. U.S. West Commc'ns, Inc., 1995 U.S. Dist. LEXIS 1968, 1995 WL 67672 (D.Or. 1995); Payne v. Travenol Laboratories, Inc., 673 F.2d 798 (5th Cir. 1982) (affirming lower court recognition of Black female class); Hicks v. Gates Rubber Co., 833 F.2d 1406 (10th Cir. 1987) (allowing aggregation of evidence of racial hostility with evidence of sexual hostility); Anthony v. Cnty. of Sacramento, 898 F. Supp. 1435 (E.D. Cal. 1995) (finding that claims of race and sex discrimination constituted a continuing violation and therefore were not time barred); Stingley v. Arizona, 796 F. Supp. 424 (D. Ariz. 1992) (allowing aggregation of evidence of racial hostility with evidence of sexual hostility in determining the extent to which work environment is hostile to Title VII plaintiff); Cardona v. Skinner, 729 F. Supp. 193 (D.P.R. 1990); Jew v. Univ. of Iowa, 749 F. Supp. 946 (S.D. IA 1990); Lam v. Univ. of Hawaii, 40 F.3d 1551 (9th Cir. 1994); Arnett v. Aspin, 846 F. Supp. 1234 (E.D. Pa. 1994); Mosley v. Gen. Motors, 497 F.2d 1330 (8th Cir. 1974). *Contra*, Shannon v. Ford Motor Co., 72 F.3d 678 (8th Cir. 1996); Robinson v. Adams, 847 F.2d. 1315 (9th Cir. 1987), *cert. denied*, 490 U.S. 1105 (1989); Rogers v. Am. Airlines, Inc., 527 F. Supp. 229 (S.D.N.Y. 1981); Sogg v. Am. Airlines, Inc., 603 N.Y.S.2d 21(N.Y. App. Div. 1993). *But see* DeGraffenreid v. Gen. Motors Assembly Div., 413 F. Supp. 142 (E.D. Mo. 1976), *aff'din part, rev'din part on other grounds*, 558 F.2d 480 (8th Cir. 1977) (claims of race and sex discrimination do not state a claim upon which relief may be granted).

36 Judy Trent Ellis is now Professor Judith Trent Scales at SUNY Buffalo School of Law.

37 Judy Trent Ellis, *Sexual harassment and Race: a legal analysis of discrimination*, 8 J. LEGIS. 30 (1981).

Black Lawyers[38] convened a Conference For and About: Black Women and the Law,[39] attended by more than 200 women,[40] to address both race and gender discrimination and the "critical role [of law] in shaping and defining the positions of women and Blacks in the United States."[41] The conference explored a variety of topics relevant to the legal status of African-American women under U.S. law and the extent to which the law recognized their claims as distinct from those of White women and Black men.[42]

By 1995, the intersectionality framework was well established[43] and had been expanded to contexts beyond the intersection of race and gender.[44] Against this intellectual background, a group of African-American women

[38] The National Conference of Black Lawyers [hereinafter NCBL] was formed in 1968, in Cappahosic, Virginia. The purposes of the organization were "(1) to analyze and study problems facing black attorneys in the United States. (2) To encourage black youth to study law, (3) to work for the elimination of racism in the law, (4) to give attention to the root problem of the black community and (5) to analyze and study problems of black attorneys in the United States in their legal practices." Conference Brochure, National Conference of Black Lawyers, Conference For and About Black Women and the Law, March 13–15 1981, Fisk University Nashville, Tennessee (on file with author) [hereinafter Conference Brochure].

[39] *Id.*

[40] Telephone interview with Adjoa Aiyetoro, Professor of Law, University of Arkansas – Little Rock (June 28, 2011); Interview with Barbara Arnwine, Executive Director of Lawyers' Committee for Civil Rights under Law (July 27, 2011).

[41] Conference Brochure, *supra* note 38, at 1.

Those honored included Septima Clark, a South Carolina educator and civil rights activist; Dr. Pauli Murray, a "civil rights activist, lawyers, minister, and scholar"; and Reverend Willie T. Barrow, a minister and National Director of People United to Serve Humanity (PUSH). Conference Brochure, *supra* note 38, at 10–11.

[42] Topics included: The Black Women in the Family: Past Present and Future; Health, Politics, and the Laws of Reproduction; Employment Rights and Affirmative Action for Black Women; Black Women in the Workplace; Criminal Justice/Injustice: Black Women as Offenders; and Criminal Justice in Justice: Black Women as Victims. Conference Brochure, *supra* note 38, at 5–8.

[43] For primers on intersectionality theory in the U.S. context, *see* footnote 30.

[44] *See, e.g.*, Elvia R. Arriola, *Gendered inequality: Lesbians, gays, and feminist legal theory*, 9 Berkeley Women's L. J. 103 (1994); Robert Westley, *Lat crit theory and the problematics of internal/external oppression: A comparison of forms of oppression and intergroup/intragroup solidarity*, 53 U. Miami L. Rev. 761 (1998–99); Mary Jo Wiggins, *The Future of Intersectionality and Critical Race Feminism*, 11 Journal of Contemporary Legal Issues 677 (2000–01); Johanna E. Bond, *International intersectionality: a theoretical and pragmatic exploration of women's international human rights violations*, 52 Emory L. J. 71, 73 (2003) ("The predominant narrow, relatively static notion of women's human rights does not adequately reflect the experience of women within minority racial or ethnic communities, lesbians, disabled women, or other women who may experience discrimination or human rights violations as a result of both gender and another ground"); Kevin R. Johnson, *Racial restrictions on naturalization: The recurring intersection of race and gender in immigration and citizenship law*, 11 Berkeley Women's L. J. 142 (1996); Frank Rudy Cooper, *Against bipolar Black masculinity: Intersectionality, assimilation, identity performance, and hierarchy*, 39 U.C. Davis L. Rev. 853 (2005–06).

gathered in Washington, DC, to prepare to present their equality arguments as international human rights concerns on the world stage at Beijing.

AFRICAN-AMERICAN WOMEN ADVOCATE THE INCORPORATION OF THE INTERSECTIONALITY FRAMEWORK IN THE BEIJING PLATFORM OF ACTION

Preparation for Beijing: The 1995 National Conference on African-American Women and the Law

In June 1995, the Lawyers' Committee for Civil Rights under Law mounted the National Conference on African-American Women and the Law,[45] which served as a preparatory conference for an African-American Women's Caucus destined for Beijing.[46] Convened by Lawyers' Committee Executive Director Barbara Arnwine,[47] the Conference enjoyed the support and oversight of the prestigious Lawyers' Committee Board, two members of which agreed to serve as co-chairs of the high-profile Conference Advisory Committee, which was established to provide oversight, advice, and assistance on critical matters relating to the Conference, such as fundraising.[48] The conference took place in Washington, DC, June 15–18, 1995, "seeking just solutions to the problems of race and gender."[49] The conference was attended by more than a thousand African-American women lawyers, social scientists, politicians, and activists.[50]

[45] Conference Brochure, *supra* note 38.

[46] Conference Brochure, *supra* note 38.

[47] Conference Brochure, *supra* note 38.

[48] *See* Letter from Barbara Arnwine, Executive Director of Lawyers' Committee for Civil Rights under Law, to Brooksley Born (February 6, 1995) (on file with author). The advisory board included Lawyers' Committee co-chairs Michael A. Cooper and Herbert J. Hansell, as well as board members Brooksley Born (then of Arnold and Porter) and Myles Lynk (then of Dewey Ballentine) who served as co-chairs of the Advisory Committee. The additional members of the Lawyers' Committee Advisory Committee Board were Peter J. Connell, Sara-Ann Determan, Margaret Marshall, and Carroll Rhodes.

[49] *Id.* at 15. The National Planning Committee included, inter alia, Adjoa Aiyetoro, former National Director of the National Conference of Black Lawyers, the organization that held the First National Conference at Fisk University in 1981. Ms. Aiyetoro served as a special consultant to the Lawyers' Committee on the Conference, as well as on the Beijing effort. In addition, the committee included Dr. Mary Frances Berry, Chair of the U.S. Commission on Civil Rights; Dean Alice Gresham Bullock of Howard University Law School; the author; Dr. Dorothy Height, President of the National Council of Negro Women; Gay McDougall, Executive Director of the International Human Rights Law Group; and Dr. C. Delores Tucker, National Chair, National Political Congress of Black Women. *See* Memorandum, National Planning Committee Members List (Mar. 29, 1995) (on file with author).

[50] Barbara Arnwine, *Upholding the sky: Perspectives on African-American women and the law*, VOICES OF VISION: AFRICAN-AMERICAN WOMEN ON THE ISSUES 274 (1996).

Arnwine and her committee obtained support from notable contributors[51] and prominent organizations.[52] Headline-grabbing speakers were in plentiful supply: the first African-American U.S. Senator Carol Moseley Braun; U.S. Representative from the District of Columbia Eleanor Holmes Norton (also former chair of the Equal Employment Opportunity Commission); Dr. Dorothy Height of the National Council of Negro Women; Mrylie Evers Williams, widow of Medgar Evars and chair of the NAACP Board,[53] and the venerable National Political Congress of Black Women chair, C. Delores Tucker.[54]

As important as these celebrity activist speakers were, it was the scholars and experts whose work would provide the intellectual foundation for the conference. They were there to "provide an in depth exploration" of the "historical and contemporary experience"[55] of African-American women, as well as "an examination of the race and gender dualism African-American women live through ... in workshops on rape, employment discrimination, sexism, politics ... health issues ... crime, housing, drugs, education, the environment, [and] political empowerment."[56] Moreover, the Conference also explored "the international legal dimensions of African-American Women's domestic experience" and was officially dubbed a preparatory conference to enable "African-American women leaders ... to participate vigorously in the Fourth World Conference."[57]

[51] Major financial contributors included foundations such as Ford Foundation and the Rockefeller Family Fund and corporations such as Sara Lee, Fannie Mae, and Nabisco. Conference Brochure, *supra* note 38, at 53. The Ford Foundation provided a grant of $100,000 to support the Conference on African-American Women and the Law and for preparatory activities for the Fourth World Conference. Letter from Diane Galloway, Ford Foundation, to Barbara Arnwine, Executive Director of the Lawyers' Committee for Civil Rights under Law (December 30, 1994) (on file with author). The Carnegie Foundation contributed $20,000. *See* Letter from Dorothy Willis Knapp, Secretary, Carnegie Foundation to Barbara Arnwine, Executive Director Lawyers' Committee for Civil Rights under Law (September 15, 1995).

[52] A partial list of other organizations that provided financial support includes the American Bar Association, the National Bar Association, Howard University School of Law, and the National Women's Law Center. *Id.*

[53] *Id.* at 16.

[54] *Id.* at 52.

[55] *Id.* at 16.

[56] *Id.*

[57] *Id.* The participation in the NGO Forum and Fourth World Conference was part of an overall objective to develop a National Network for African-American Women and the Law with an "action agenda" designed to maximize the political clout of African-American women. The action agenda was to emerge from the substance of the conference and the conference working papers. The Network for African-American women and the Law, "*Sisters*"' *Voices from the United States* (Summer 1995) (on file with author).

Although the Lawyers' Committee Conference included a wide range of topics designed to illuminate and critique the progress of African-American women toward full equality, it was also deliberate in its focus on preparations for Beijing. Ms. Arnwine was motivated to organize the Conference to create an organization that would qualify to participate formally in both the non-governmental organization (NGO) forum and World Conference. On the basis of her own attendance at the Third UN World Conference on Women in Nairobi in 1995 and her research on the experience of African-American women at the 1985 Mexico Conference, she concluded that only a very well-organized delegation could hope to achieve a visible presence at the conference as well as an effect on its ultimate platform.[58] To this end, she sought and received funding from the Ford Foundation to mount a nation-wide effort to organize African-American women and organizations into a Network of African-American Women. The Network would "identify and examine our experiences, assess the effectiveness of . . . existing legal frameworks, and propose creative and workable solutions for the future."[59] The aim was a conference that would provide a broad-based understanding of domestic issues as well as international law and international organizations.[60] In addition, she thought it essential that prospective members of the delegation become familiar with the documents and processes specifically relevant to the upcoming Fourth World Conference.[61]

Arnwine also convened a series of conference calls with other leaders of organizations for women of color in order to lay the foundation for a unified effort among women of color to ensure that they shared her interest in a platform that would be broad enough to encompass the needs of their diverse

[58] Dorothy Gilliam, *Where Race and Gender Meet*, Unity 99 Report from Beijing: The 1995 U.N. Fourth World Conference on Women and the Non-Governmental Organizations Forum as seen by US. Journalists of Color 54, 58 (1996) (on file with author).

[59] Conference Brochure, A National Conference, Thursday June 15–Sunday June 18, 1995 African-American Women and the Law: Exerting our Power-Reclaiming our Communities 16 (1995) (on file with author).

[60] *See, e.g.*, Panel: African-Women Claiming Rights, Lawyers' Committee Conference, *supra* note 38, at 33 (with Gay McDougall, International Human Rights Law Group; Mona Papillon, Amnesty International; Penelope Andrews, CUNY School of Law); Panel-Exploring the Common, Global Nature of Key Conference Themes, *id.* at 39 (with Gay McDougall, International Human Rights Law Group; Abdullabhi An-Na'im, Human Rights Africa and Human Rights Watch; Julianne Cartwright Taylor, Human Rights Advocates).

[61] *See* Panel-Human Rights and the Fourth World Conference on Women: Equality, Development, and Peace (with Gay McDougall, International Human Rights Law Group; Benaifer Nowrajee, Human Rights Watch-Women; Wandra G. Mitchell, U.S. Agency for International Development; Mumbi Mathangangi, The Fund for Peace) and Panel-Beijing '95 (with Gay McDougall, International Human Rights Law Group; Dr. Sarah Moten, National Council of Negro Women; Laura Blackburne, NAACP), *id.* at 21, 27.

constituents.[62] Arnwine was keenly aware that the platform failed to grasp the significance of intersectionality. Prior to Beijing, one human rights lawyer observed that despite many preparatory meetings, the Draft Platform for Action still "failed to address the intersection of race, gender, class, and ethnic subordination in its definition of discrimination."[63] Arnwine was determined to lead a delegation that would call attention to that defect: "We go to Beijing prepared to challenge the policy of ignoring women of color. Our unique circumstances and realities must be recognized."[64]

The Work of the African-American Women's Caucus in Beijing

After the Lawyer's Committee for Civil Rights Preparatory Conference in Washington, DC, more than one hundred African-American women traveled to Beijing to attend and participate in the UN Fourth World Conference. There were two delegations, composed predominantly of African-American women: one numbering fifty-two and organized by the National Conference of Negro Women,[65] and another comprising forty-eight women organized by the Lawyers' Committee on Civil Rights under Law.[66] The two delegations worked together to add their experience, voice, and perspective to the gender and human rights dialogue.[67] Arnwine and the author were official delegates

[62] Memorandum from Barbara Arnwine, Executive Director of the Lawyers' Committee for Civil Rights under Law, to Honorable Delois Blakley et al., re: Conference Call with Leaders of Women of Color Delegations to Beijing (July 21, 1995) (on file with author). Interview with Barbara Arnwine, Executive Director of the Lawyers' Committee for Civil Rights under Law (June 29); Gilliam, *supra* note 58, at 57, 58.

[63] Gilliam, *supra* note 58, at 58 (quoting Professor Celina Romany, former co-director of the Women's International Human Rights Program at the City University of New York Law School).

[64] Press Release, *Lawyers' Committee heads delegation to Beijing UN Conference* (August 18, 1995) (on file with author).

[65] Barbara Arnwine, *Beijing experiences-NGO Forum in Huairou, China* (October 1995) (on file with author).

[66] The National Council of Negro Women was organized by Mary McLeod Bethune to secure full civil rights for African-American women. *National Council of Negro Women (1935–)*, BlackPast.org, *available at* http://www.blackpast.org/?q=aah/national-council-negro-women-1935 (last visited October 13, 2011). *See also* Dorothy D. Height, Open Wide the Freedom Gates: A Memoir (2003); Tracey A. Fitzgerald, The National Council of Negro Women and the Feminist Movement, 1935–1975 (1985). The Lawyers' Committee delegation was composed predominantly of lawyers and law professors but both delegations included lawyers and law professors, civil rights workers, social workers, writers, journalists, government employees, and others.

[67] Valeria Davis-Humphrey, *Madison women test rights conference: Challenge to seek world equity*, Wisc. St. J. October 1, 1995, at IB.

to the UN Conference,[68] and the author chaired the Caucus Platform Committee.[69]

Women from both delegations participated in the NGO forum that preceded the Fourth World Conference,[70] but they focused their attention on influencing the final draft of the Platform for Action, the document that would outline efforts that state and nonstate actors would undertake after the conference to improve the status of women.

Upon arrival in Beijing, the two delegations formed an African-American Women's Caucus[71] [hereinafter "the Caucus"], which spent a week of twenty-hour days networking with other women, especially women of color from the United States and other nations, and analyzing the draft of the Platform for Action to ensure that it addressed the concerns of diverse women in the United States and abroad.[72] In addition, the Caucus undertook significant efforts to coordinate with other delegations, including the International Network of Women of Color and the U.S. Women of Color Delegation.[73] Myriad logistical problems complicated these efforts,[74] and there were also legitimacy issues. Some African-American women expressed concern about

68 Memorandum from Barbara Arnwine, Executive Director of the Lawyers' Committee for Civil Rights under Law, to Attendees of National Conference on African-American Women in the Law (August 28, 1995) (on file with author).

69 Barbara Arnwine, *Beijing experiences-NGO Forum in Huairou, China*, at 3, October 1995 (on file with author). *See* Memorandum to Barbara Arnwine, *infra* note 70, at 7.

70 Between August 31 and September 7, 1995, the National Council of Negro Women mounted six workshops: Networking Strategies: Empowerment Dynamics; Role of the Young African-American Woman in a Global Community; Violence Has No Borders: Violence against African/African-American Women; Women and the Environment: DataGap/Issues and Dilemma; International Partners: Educating and Broadening the Awareness of People of Color about Environmental Pollutants; and African-American Women and Children; Global Issues on Empowerment. The African-American women's sorority, Alpha Kappa Alpha, presented a workshop on Africa Diaspora Women and Volunteerism: Initiatives for the 21st Century. The Lawyers Committee for Civil Rights under Law presented a workshop on Violence against Women, one on Multiple Forms of Discrimination against African-American Women, and one on African-American Women: Exerting Our Power, Reclaiming Our Communities. *See* Memorandum to Barbara Arnwine, executive director of the Lawyers' Committee for Civil Rights under Law, from Adjoa Aiyetoro, re: Final Report of Consultant (May 6, 1996) (on file with author). *See also* Schedule of Activities, NGO Forum on Women – Look at the World Through Women's Eyes Forum on Women, Beijing, August 30–September 8, 1995.

71 Barbara Arnwine, executive director of the Lawyers' Committee for Civil Rights under Law, presided over the delegation.

72 More than 200 African-American women attended the meeting of the Caucus despite transportation and logistical difficulties. The first five meetings were attended by 60–150 African-American women.

73 Gilliam, *supra* note 58, at 61.

74 Memorandum to Barbara Arnwine, *supra* note 70, at 4, 7.

the influence of the Lawyers' Committee-led Caucus, whereas other women of color were troubled by what they perceived to be the African-American domination of the U.S. Women of Color Caucus.[75]

The limited time in Beijing to sort out these trust issues required tenacious diplomatic efforts.[76] Through it all, the African-American Women's leadership remained convinced that it had a propitious opportunity to influence the platform by quickly developing position papers would clearly communicate the views of the Caucus. It would be important to pursue this objective, and, whenever possible, to collaborate with other women of color, including Native American/Indigenous women, Asian Americans, and Latinas.[77]

In the short week preceding the opening of the Fourth World Conference, the Caucus drafted three position papers[78] that emphasized the racial nuances and other complexities embedded in gender inequity. These papers were the Consensus Statement of the African-American Women's Caucus at the NGO Forum of the UN Fourth Conference on Women, the African-American Women's Caucus Recommendations on the Bracketed Text in the Fourth World Conference on Women Draft Platform for Action, and

[75] Memorandum to Barbara Arnwine, *supra* note 70, at 5; Gilliam, *supra* note 58, at 60. *See* Interview with Barbara Arnwine, *supra* note 40; Mallika Dutt, *Some reflections on U.S. women of color and the United Nations Fourth World Conference on Women and NGO Forum in Beijing, China*, 22, Feminist Studies 519, 521–24 (1996) (detailing fragility and fragmentation of the U.S. Women of Color network and limited utility of framework of color as a basis for international alliances). *See also* Kimberlé Williams Crenshaw, *Gender-related aspects of race discrimination*, Background Paper Submitted to the Expert Group Meeting on Gender and Racial Discrimination, U.N. Doc. EGM/GRD/2000/WP.1, at 3 (November 2000). ("Because the nature of group-based discrimination varies widely around the world, there is no uniform way to name the women who are victimized by compound discrimination. In some contexts, the term 'women of color' may be appropriate, in others, 'ethnic women' or 'minority women' is more descriptive and in still others, none of these terms is apt.") These tensions were alive and well in Beijing.

[76] Gilliam, *supra* note 58, at 61. ("Before the International Network of Women of Color could generate enough passion for a demonstration, however, the group had to address ... issues of trust and process ... So Arnwine and Linda S. Greene, a professor at the University of Wisconsin and chair of the African-American Women's Caucus Platform Committee, worked through many leadership and inclusion issues with Margaret Prescod of the International network of Women of Color and others.")

[77] Memorandum to Barbara Arnwine, *supra* note 70, at 6.

[78] These papers included *The African-American Women's Caucus Recommendations on the Bracketed Text in the Fourth World Conference on Women Draft Platform for Action; Consensus Statement of African-American Women's Caucus at the NGO (Non-Governmental Organization) Forum of the United Nations Fourth Conference on Women*; and *The African-American Women's Caucus Amendments to the Beijing Declaration of the G-77*. The author, formerly Counsel to the U.S. Senate Judiciary Committee, chaired the Caucus Platform Committee.

the African-American Women's Caucus Amendments to the Beijing Declaration of the G-77. Throughout, these documents emphasized the complex nature of gender discrimination.[79] The Caucus urged attention to its priorities for the advancement of women domestically and worldwide; those priorities included poverty, unequal access to health care and related services, inequality in economic structures and policies, inequality in power sharing and decision making, stereotyping of women in all communication systems, gender and environmental justice issues, discrimination, and violation of the rights of the girl child.[80]

In addition, the Caucus used intersectionality to frame its concern about the debilitating effects of poverty on women in developing and developed

[79] Indigenous women formed a caucus as well and held a related view about the heterogeneity of women's experience, explicitly adopting a framework of intersectionality as well. "We have been and are continuing to suffer from multiple oppression; as indigenous peoples, as citizens of colonised and neo-colonial countries, as women, and as members of the poorer classes of society." Beijing Declaration of Indigenous Women, *available at* http://www.twnside.org.sg/title/dec-ch.htm. (last accessed May 27, 2013). *See* Zainab Qureshi, *The Beijing Declaration of Indigenous Women*, 1995, Lums Student Law Review Blog (December 2010), *available at* http://lumsstudentlawreview.blogspot.com/2010/12/beijing-declaration-of-indigenous-women.html. ("In this sense, the indigenous women frame their claims through a 'politics of intersectionality.'")

> The concept of intersectionality constitutes a theoretical and methodological approach to a non-essentialized identity politics and provides a basis for justice cause action. "Intersectional approaches start from the analytical premise that people's identities, i.e., gender, race, class, sexuality, nation, etc., are not mutually exclusive, but rather multiple, layered, and inter-related and, as such, produce unique and specific experiences that are not easily essentialized" [Parisi, Laura, and Jeff Corntassel. "In pursuit of self-determination: Indigenous women's challenges to traditional diplomatic spaces," Canadian Foreign Policy. 1–18]. Intersectional approaches go beyond simplistic binary gender-based analysis, which examines only one relationship of power (universal system of patriarchy assumed by "First World"), to highlight how social categories " . . . gain meaning and power by reinforcing and referencing each other". Indigenous women, claim to experience violence and discrimination based on multiple identities, and thus use the notion of 'intersectionality' to locate themselves in their "families, clans, communities or nations, host states, and the transnational and in the international arena." They argue that the structural gender inequality is inextricably linked to other forms of inequality such as racism, capitalism and colonialism, and hence can only be understood through its interactions with the latter forms.
>
> Therefore, by their rejection of the frame of "Woman" and its corresponding assumption of a universal sameness of experience/oppression, the indigenous women of the Beijing Declaration develop their own framework and language for understanding themselves which allows them (and their constituencies) to reclaim the aspects of their cultures and histories lost within the predominant hegemonic neo-liberal legal discourse.

Id.

[80] *See supra* note 30.

countries. It noted that "[t]he consequences of the intersection of gender and other forms of discrimination have relegated many women, in developed and developing countries, to the lowest rungs of poverty."[81] The Caucus urged nations to commit to the elimination of poverty and the "[e]asing of debt burdens ... [to]allow those countries to reset their priorities to achieve sustained economic growth ... [and] enhance programs ... to eliminate poverty ... [and] promote the advancement and prosperity of women."[82]

The development of these papers unified the Caucus and furthered its advocacy work. They served as a framework for dialogue with other NGOs during the NGO forum, including those that joined as a U.S. Women of Color caucus, to frame common concerns.[83] The Caucus used the papers to guide discussions with the official U.S. Delegation to the Fourth World Conference,[84] co-organizing and participating in three meetings with that delegation.[85] In those discussions, the Caucus urged the United States to

[81] *Id.*

[82] *Id.*

[83] Dorothy Gilliam, *Building trust and bridges*, WASHINGTON POST, September 9, 1995, at B1, B5. Latinas from the United States also submitted proposed language. *See Proposed Language on Platform for Action by Latinas from the U.S.* (on file with author); *U.S. Latinas Caucus Amendments to the Beijing Declaration of the G-77* (on file with author).

[84] Interview with Barbara Arnwine, *supra* note 40. The author was also the primary draftsperson of these documents and participated in the discussions for which the document provided the African-American Women's Caucus talking points.

The U.S. delegation's honorary chair was Hillary Clinton, and its chair was UN Ambassador Madeleine K. Albright. Other members of the delegation included its co-chair, U.S. Secretary for Health and Human Services Donna Shalala; alternate chair, Undersecretary of State for Global Affairs Timothy Wirth; deputy chair, former U.S. Representative Marjorie Margolies-Mezvinsky; vice chair, former assistant to the president Veronica Biggins; Lynn Cutler; Maria Antonietta Berriozabal; Arthenia Joyner; Dorothy Lamm; Linda Tarr-Whelan, and others. U.S. Department of State, *Focus on 4WCW Update on Preparations*, Bureau of Public Affairs, 95/06/16 (June 16, 1995), *available at* http://dosfan.lib.uic.edu/ERC/intlorg/conference_women/950616.html.

[85] The U.S. Delegation to the UN Fourth World Conference was composed of the Honorable Hilary Rodham Clinton; Madeleine K. Albright, chair and head, U.S. ambassador to the United Nations; the Honorable Carol Browner, co-chair, administrator of the Environmental Protection Agency; the Honorable Donna Shala, co-chair, secretary of Health and Human Services; the Honorable Timothy Wirth, alternate chair and alternate head, undersecretary of state for Global Affairs; the Honorable Marjorie Margolies Mezvinsky, deputy chair, former member of Congress from Pennsylvania; and the Honorable Veronca Biggins, vice chair, executive search consultant, honorary chair. The African-American Women's Caucus representatives to the U.S. Delegation meeting were Barbara Arnwine, Linda Greene, Lind Burnham, Marian Kramer, and Vernice Guthrie with Eleanor Hinton Hoytt of the National Council on Negro Women as an alternate. Memorandum to Barbara Arnwine, *supra* note 70. *See* Gwen McKinney, *African-American women organize around themes of race, gender at UN*, ATLANTIC INQUIRER, October 14, 1995; Gilliam, *Building trust and bridges, supra* note 83; 7, *Madison women test rights conference, supra* note 63.

support the intersectionality framework in the final Platform for Action and to agree that U.S. commitments for actions to be made after Beijing would be undertaken with a focus on the intersectionality approach.[86]

Beijing Platform for Action Incorporates the Intersectionality Framework

The final documents of the Fourth World Conference did incorporate the intersectionality framework and the concerns of the African-American Women's Caucus.[87] For example, the final Platform for Action included a commitment to "[i]ntensify efforts to ensure equal enjoyment of all human rights and fundamental freedoms for all women and girls who face multiple barriers to their empowerment and advancement because of such factors as their race, age, language, ethnicity, culture, religion, or disability, or because they are indigenous people."[88] The Platform also explicitly "recognizes that women face barriers to full equality and advancement because of such factors as their race, age, language, ethnicity, culture, religion[,] ... disability [or] ... because they are indigenous ... [or] their socio-economic status"[89] and that "these diverse factors isolate or marginalize such women."[90] With respect to health, the Platform for Action noted the importance of collecting statistical data in a manner that recognized diverse groups of women, noting that absence of statistical data "disaggregated and analysed by age, sex and socio-economic status and by established demographic criteria used to serve the interests and solve the problems of subgroups ... [including] the vulnerable and the marginalized."[91] In addition, in the context of violence against women, it noted that certain subgroups of women are more vulnerable to violence, including "women belonging to minority groups, indigenous women, refugee women ... [and] women in poverty."[92] Hence, the Platform called on governments to "enhance the self-reliance of special groups of women, such as ... women belonging to racial and ethnic minorities."[93] The inclusion of an intersectionality framework in the

86 Barbara Arnwine, *Beijing experiences-NGO Forum in Huairou, China* at 3 (October 1995) (on file with author).
87 Report of the Fourth World Conference, *supra* note 6.
88 Fourth World Conference on Women, Beijing, China, September 4–15, 1995, *Fourth World Conference on Women Beijing Declaration*, U.N. Doc. A/CONF.177/20/Rev. 1, Annex 1 (1996).
89 Report of the Fourth World Conference, *supra* note 6, at ¶ 46.
90 *Id.* at ¶ 31.
91 *Id.* at ¶ 104.
92 *Id.* at ¶ 116.
93 *Id.* at ¶ 175(d).

Platform for Action of the Fourth World Conference on Women was a powerful framework for a robust and inclusive vision of gender equality.[94] These results are consistent with the Caucus's conclusion that it did make a difference in Beijing.[95]

Since Beijing, the framework of intersectionality has gained traction. It is a theme incorporated into other areas of international human rights law discourse.[96] It provides the framework for the UN-mandated post-Beijing five-year reviews of progress as the UN Commission on the Status of Women assesses Platform for Action outcomes through an intersectionality lens.[97] In 2006, a commentator confirmed the centrality of the intersectionality framework in international human rights discourses on gender:

> Intersectional analysis of social divisions has come to occupy central spaces in both sociological and other analyses of stratification as well as in feminist and other legal, political and policy discourses of international human rights. There has been a gradual recognition of the inadequacy of analysing various social divisions, but especially race and gender, as separate, internally homogeneous, social categories resulting in the marginalization of the specific effects of these, especially on women of colour.[98]

Moreover, during the March 10, 2010, UN Global Review Process on the fifteenth anniversary of the Beijing Platform for Action, the Chair's summary shows that the intersectionality framework remains salient: "In the design, planning and monitoring of laws, policies and programmes to achieve gender equality, it is important to fully address the multiple forms of discrimination and marginalization that particular groups of women continue to face,

94 *See, e.g.*, Bond, *supra* note 44.

95 Barbara Arnwine & Adjoa Aiyetoro, *Declaration of the African-American Women Caucus Beijing* 1995 (October 30, 1995) (on file with author).

96 UN World Conference against Racism, Racial Discrimination, Xenophobia and Related Intolerance, Durban, South Africa, August 31–September 8, 2001, *Declaration and Programme Action*, ¶ 69, U.N. Doc. A/CONF.189/12 (2001) (emphasizing multiple forms of discrimination). Navi Pillay, United Nations High Commissioner for Human Rights stated, "[i]t is . . . not surprising that the intersection of discrimination based on race and gender has widespread and devastating effects." *Double odds: Women overcoming multiple discrimination*, United Nations Office of the High Commissioner for Human Rights (April 2009), *available at* http://www.ohchr.org/EN/NewsEvents/Pages/DoubleOdds.aspx (last visited October 14, 2011). *See also* Bond, *supra* note 44, at 144–45.

97 G.A. Res.23/3, U.N. Doc. A/RES/S-23/3 (November 16, 2000)(on the report of the Ad Hoc Committee of the Whole of the Twenty-third Special Session of the General Assembly, A/S-23/10/Rev.1 (2000)).

98 Yuval-Davis, *Intersectionality and feminist politics* 13 EUR. J. WOMEN'S STUD. 193, 206 (2006); *see also* Nura Taefi, *The synthesis of age and gender: Intersectionality, international human rights law and the marginalisation of the girl-child*, 17 INT'L. J. CHILDREN'S RTS. 345–76 (2009).

including rural, indigenous and older women, women belonging to ethnic minorities and women with disabilities."[99]

AFRICAN-AMERICAN WOMEN AND INTERSECTIONALITY: FROM THE MARGINS TO THE CENTER

The participation of the African-American women at the Fourth World Conference on Women was not an anomalous event. Rather, it grew out of the long-standing involvement of African-American women in human rights efforts in both domestic and international settings. The African-American women who traveled to Beijing under the auspices of the Lawyers' Committee for Civil Rights under Law did so after careful preparation, including Executive Director Arnwine's participation in UN preparatory conferences, her organization of a National Network of African-American Female Lawyers, and her organization, with her colleagues, of a domestic preparatory conference devoted to a thorough exploration of relevant legal issues, as well as a thorough review of Beijing documents and processes. The group journeyed to Beijing to raise their voices in the international debate over the content of gender equality and urge a normative nonessentialist framework for gender equality.

At the Fourth World Conference, African-American women effectively advocated for the inclusion in the Beijing Platform for Action of an intersectionality framework across a range of issues. They prepared several documents incorporating their perspective including a "Consensus Statement" of the Caucus, a detailed markup of the proposed Platform for Action, a response to the position of the C-77, the Caucus of Developing Nations,[100] and the Caucus amendments to the Beijing Declaration. Throughout the NGO Forum and the World Conference, they caucused alone, with women of color from the United States and abroad, and with the U.S. Delegation to the Fourth World Conference. This participation resulted in the addition of the intersectionality perspective to the international law discourse about both gender and racial equality. Since then, intersectionality human rights discourse has thrived.

[99] "High-level round table on the implementation of the Beijing Declaration and Platform for Action and the outcomes of the twenty-third special session of the General Assembly and its contribution to shaping a gender perspective in the realization of the Millennium Development Goals," United Nations Commission on the Status of Women E/CN.6/2010/CRP.5 (March 10, 2013).

[100] The Group of 77 at the United Nations, *available at* http://www.g77.org/ (last accessed May 27, 2013).

African-American women, grounded in a long tradition of participation in international and human rights efforts,[101] contributed a distinct and empowering voice to a world community committed to gender equality. Women worldwide may not experience the disadvantage at the intersection of race and gender in the manner in which it manifests in the United States. But women throughout the world share our interest in the elimination of all circumstances that exacerbate the effects of gender discrimination. The conceptual framework advanced by African-American women in Beijing broadened the discourse of gender equality and cemented the relevance of intersectionality in that discourse.

[101] Since 1995, the presence of African-American women in international law–related posts, if not ubiquitous, is much more visible. For example, Gay McDougall, already a prominent international human rights lawyer, served as the United Nations Independent Expert on Minority Issues at the Office of the High Commissioner for Human Rights from 2005 until July 2011. *Independent Expert on Minority Issues*, Office of the High Commissioner for Human Rights, *available at* http://www2.ohchr.org/english/issues/minorities/expert/index.htm (last visited October 14, 2011). Condoleezza Rice was National Security Advisor from 2001 to 2005 and has served as Secretary of State from 2005 through 2008. Hoover Institution, *Fellows: Condoleezza Rice*, Stanford University, *available at* http://www.hoover.org/fellows/10078 (last visited October 14, 2011). Gabrielle Kirk McDonald, a former federal judge, was selected by the UN as one of 11 judges for the International Criminal Tribunal for the Former Yugoslavia in 1993, and she presided over the three-judge panel that heard the first criminal trial of that international court. She remains one of three American arbitrators on the Iran–United States Claims Tribunal. *Gabrielle Kirk McDonald*, Iran–United States Claims Tribunal, available at http://www.iusct.org/english/page18/mcdonald.html (last visited October 14, 2011). Finally, Ambassador Susan E. Rice, who had been in line to become secretary of state until the Benghazi aftermath, continues to serve the nation as the U.S. Permanent Representative to the UN, *available at* http://usun.state.gov/leadership/c31461.htm (last accessed May 27, 2013).

9

African Descendant Women and the Global Reparations Movement

Adjoa A. Aiyetoro

INTRODUCTION

African descendant women[1] have played a vital role in the development and progression of national and international reparations movements. Callie House, born into slavery in 1861, was the spokesperson for the Ex-Slave Mutual Relief, Bounty & Pension Association, which advocated for freed Africans and their descendants.[2] Queen Mother Dorothy Benton Lewis was a leader in the movement for reparations for Africans and African descendants in the United States and throughout the world.[3] The successes of African and African descendant women can be measured qualitatively and quantitatively; however, this chapter primarily focuses on the rich and normative

This chapter is dedicated to Queen Mother Dorothy Benton Lewis, an avid reparationist for more than thirty years. I met Dorothy in 1987, prior to the founding of the National Coalition of Blacks for Reparations in America. Her passion for obtaining reparations was infectious. It was fueled by her love for African peoples and her commitment to seeing justice done for the crimes against humanity that they suffered at the hands of European governments, the thirteen colonies founded by European settlers in North America, and the United States of America. Dorothy was a renowned leader of the global reparations movement. Her unswerving commitment to obtaining reparations for African peoples was seen in virtually every conversation she had, in her travels that took her to any country that had even a budding reparations movement, and to her indefatigable leadership of organizations committed to reparations for African descendants in the Diaspora. Her bodily presence is missed, yet her spirit continues to lift up the righteousness of the demand for reparations and to energize those who continue to work for reparations for African peoples.

1 "African descendant" refers to Black people who are descendants of Black Africans.

2 *See generally*, Mary Frances Berry, My Face Is Black Is True: Callie House and the Struggle for Ex-Slave Reparations (2005).

3 *See* Adjoa A. Aiyetoro & Adrienne D. Davis, *Historic and modern social movements for reparations: The National Coalition of Blacks for Reparations in America (N'COBRA) and its antecedents*, 16 Tex. Wesleyan L. Rev. 686, 746–51 (2010); Sam Anderson, Muntu Matsimela, & Yusuf Nuruddin, *The reparations movement: An assessment of recent and current activism, in* Redress for Historical Injustices in the United States 427, 434 (Michael T. Martin & Marilyn Yaquinto eds., 2007).

contributions they have made to the reparations movement in the United States and England, with comparative reference to reparations work in Africa. It is intended for a wide audience, not simply scholars, and draws heavily on the author's experience, including her work as a reparations activist for descendants of Africans enslaved during the transatlantic slave trade;[4] systematic *de jure* racial discrimination and oppression, including the genocidal attacks on Black communities in the United States;[5] and the continuing vestiges of these violations of the rights of Africans and their descendants.

The author became a reparations advocate while working at the Department of Justice. One day, while walking to my office in the Department of Justice on Tenth Street in Washington, DC, in 1980, I saw an African National Reparations Organization (ANRO) poster that had a picture of "Uncle Sam" pointing at me with the words, "Black people, Uncle Sam owes you $3 trillion." The poster struck that unrelenting chord in my heart for justice for African descendant people, resulting in an immediate response of "Yes!" It reminded me that although African descendants had made and were making major contributions to the economic and cultural development of the United States and the world despite being brutalized by horribly violent and racist systems, there was a debt owed to them that needed to be paid.[6] Although it is beyond the scope of this chapter to examine the normative contributions of African women on the continent to the global reparations movement, their work

[4] Although this term is commonly used, it was not a "trade" in "slaves." It was the kidnapping, forced relocation, sale, and forced labor of African peoples by European and U.S. businessmen for profit.

[5] On the latter point, I am specifically referring to the well-documented genocides of African Americans in Arkansas, Florida, and Oklahoma, including the premeditated massacres in Elaine, Arkansas; Rosewood, Florida; and Tulsa, Oklahoma. Grif Stockley, BLOOD IN THEIR EYES (2001) (discussing the Elaine, Arkansas massacre); Kenneth Nunn, *Rosewood*, *in* WHEN SORRY ISN'T ENOUGH, 435 (Roy L. Brooks ed., 1999); Albert Brophy, RECONSTRUCTING DREAMLAND (2001) (discussing the Tulsa, Oklahoma massacre). There are a number of other massacres or racially motivated acts of violence against Black communities including those that took place during what is called the Red Summer of 1919 (Cameron McWhirter, RED SUMMER: THE SUMMER OF 1919 AND THE AWAKENING OF BLACK AMERICA [2011]); the forced exclusion of Blacks from communities in the South and Midwest (Elliot Jaspin, BURIED IN THE BITTER WATERS: THE HIDDEN HISTORY OF RACIAL CLEANSING IN AMERICA [2007]); and violence instigated by Whites to thwart the democratic process in elections where Blacks exercised or were attempting to exercise their right to vote. *See* 1898 Wilmington Race Riot Report, 1898 Wilmington Race Riot Commission, LaRaeUmfleet (Principal Researcher, May 31, 2006) and Paul Ortiz, *Ocee, Florida: Remembering "the single bloodiest day in modern U.S. political history" – 90 years after the Ocoee Election Day race riot*, The Institute for Southern Studies, *available at* www.southernstudies.org/2010/05/ocoee–florida-remembering-the single bloodi est-day.

[6] Randall Robinson describes this debt eloquently in his 2001 book, THE DEBT.

has left an indelible mark.[7] The famous organizing statement "all politics are local" applies to the character of reparations work in the Diaspora and Africa. The term "local," in this instance, connotes the relationship between those seeking reparations in a specific country and those from whom reparations are sought. In this sense, voices for reparations are muted when those seeking reparations and those responsible for giving reparations due to their victory over the oppressive government, as is the case in South Africa, are the same people. The demand is loudest and more strident when it comes from the descendants of a conquered and abducted people, living as oppressed minorities in lands controlled by their abductors and the abductors' progeny. African descendant women in the Diaspora, living in countries still controlled by their ancestral abductors, have played an indefatigable role in the African descendant reparations movement, and, in that process, they have influenced the discourse and policy outcomes of reparations advocacy and claims nationally and internationally.

African descendant women's work for reparations generally flows from their commitment to addressing the racial oppression of African descendants.[8] Their voices emanate from a national focus yet are heard beyond the borders of specific countries, invigorating reparations movements worldwide. African descendant women in the Diaspora seek reparations for the enslavement of Africans in the Diaspora and the pernicious vestiges of that enslavement.[9] The issue of reparations, specifically reparations for official government abuse and international crimes, has attained normative status. The right to a remedy and to reparations under international law is not only

[7] *See, e.g.*, WHAT HAPPENED TO THE WOMEN? GENDER AND REPARATIONS FOR HUMAN RIGHTS VIOLATIONS (Ruth Rubio-Martin ed., 2006), in which various authors discuss the role women in South Africa, Rwanda, and Sierra Leone played in advocating for reparative remedies for violations of the human rights of their people.

[8] Although a number of African descendant women have taken leadership roles in movements to end racial oppression, some of the most noted women, for example, Dorothy Height, Maxine Waters, and Assata Shakur, were not vocal advocates for nor leaders in the reparations movement. Assata Shakur did issue a statement from Cuba in July 2001 that supported the reparations agenda that was to be presented at the World Conference against Racism in South Africa, August 31–September 7, 2001. In that statement, she acknowledged that she embraced the idea of reparations prior to 1971. *Available at* http://www.murchisoncenter.org/reparations/speakers.htm.

[9] African women on the continent participate in seeking reparations either because of their general commitment to justice for their people, as in South Africa, or as a result of their involvement in women's issues, as in Sierra Leone. *See* Beth Goldblatt, *Evaluating the gender content of reparations: Lessons from South Africa, in* WHAT HAPPENED TO THE WOMEN, *supra* note 7, *at* 48; and Jamesina King, *Gender and reparations in Sierra Leone: The wounds of war remain open, in* WHAT HAPPENED TO THE WOMEN at 246.

well settled in regional and international law, but is also arguably a norm of customary international law.[10]

REPAIRING THE INJURY: SEEKING WHOLENESS

International Law and Reparations

Reparations are an internationally accepted principle of recompense for injuries caused to individuals by gross human rights violations.[11] Although the various restorative principles in the United Nations conventions and guidelines to date have not provided reparations to African descendants for historical wrongs and for the continuing legacies of those wrongs, international law, doctrine, and jurisprudence have given energy to the reparations movements in the Diaspora in obtaining recognition and remedy for legacies of enslavement, for example in the development of Truth and Reconciliation Commissions (TRCs).[12]

In 1997, the Oklahoma legislature established the Tulsa Race Riot Commission to examine the 1921 destruction of the Greenwood District, the primarily Black community known as Black Wall Street. It was in form and purpose a TRC. The Commission issued its final report in 2001 and called for reparations for the survivors, a demand that has yet to be met.[13]

[10] There are a number of international instruments that affirm the right to remedy for violations of human rights including the Universal Declaration of Human Rights (GA res. 217A (III), U.N. Doc A/810 at 71 (1948), art. 8), the International Covenant on Civil and Political Rights (GA res. 2200A (XXI), 21 U.N. GAOR Supp. (No. 16) at 52, U.N. Doc. A/6316 (1966); 999 U.N.T.S. 171; 6 ILM 368 (1967), art. 2[3]), the International Convention on the Elimination of All Forms of Racial Discrimination (660 U.N.T.S. 195; G.A. res. 2106 (XX), Annex, 20 U.N. GAOR Supp. (No. 14) at 47, U.N. Doc. A/6014 (1966), art. 6), the Convention against Torture and other Cruel, Inhuman or Degrading Treatment or Punishment (GA res. 39/46, annex, 39 GAOR Supp. (No. 51) at 197, U.N. Doc. A/39/51 (1984); 1465 U.N.T.S. 85, art. 14[1]), and the Convention on the Rights of the Child (GA res. 44/25, annex, 44 U.N. GAOR Supp. (No. 49) at 167, U.N. Doc. A/44/49 (1989); 1577 U.N.T.S. 3; 28 ILM 1456 (1989), art. 39). In 2005, the UN Commission on Human Rights approved the Basic Principles and Guidelines on the Right to a Remedy and Reparation for Victims of Gross Violations of International Human Rights Law and Serious Violations of International Humanitarian Law. Resolution 2005/35 (U.N. Doc. E/CN.4/2005/L.48).

[11] Ruth Rubio-Marin, *Introduction: The gender of reparations: Setting the agenda*, *in* WHAT HAPPENED TO THE WOMEN, *supra* note 7, 24.

[12] *See generally*, Priscilla B. Hayner, *Truth commissions: A schematic overview*, 88 INT'L. REV. RED CROSS 295 (2006). Although South Africa's TRC is perhaps the most well known, TRCs have been vehicles to redress "widespread abuses" including disappearances, murder, torture, massacres, kidnapping, arbitrary detention, sexual violence, and violation of collective rights since at least 1983. *Id.* at 295, 300–07.

[13] 1921 Tulsa Race Riot Reconciliation Act of 2001, Okla. Sess. Law Serv. ch. 315 (West) (codified at Okla. Stat. Ann. tit. 74, 8000.1 (3) (2002).

Greensboro, North Carolina, formed a TRC in 2005 to examine the "context, causes, sequence and consequences" of and to make recommendations for community healing around the tragedy occurring there on November 3, 1979, which resulted in the deaths of five anti-Klan demonstrators.[14] There are other examples of commissions that, although not citing international conventions and guidelines, represent an aspect of the burgeoning creation of TRCs following the creation of these commissions in the international community, as discussed by Hayner. The Florida legislature's investigation of the 1923 massacre of the African-American community in Rosewood, Florida, including the destruction of homes, bodily injury and death – a vestige of enslavement – led to reparations being given to the African-American descendants of families who lost property and lives.[15]

The UN's formal consideration and adoption of reparations as a specific remedy for violations of international human rights laws also provided an international law framework and support for reparations movements in the United States. Although the *Basic Principles and Guidelines on the Right to a Remedy and Reparation for Victims of Gross Violations of International Human Rights Law and Serious Violations of International Humanitarian Law* were not approved by the UN Commission on Human Rights until 2005,[16] drafts of the *Basic Guidelines* circulated in the 1990s and early 2000s and were used to advance the demand for reparations for African descendants.[17] These *Guidelines* reflect the international community's commitment to having a specific formulation for providing a reparative remedy. Although they are not specifically directed at group victimization, reparations of the types sanctioned by the *Guidelines* were given to individuals involved in some of the most notable cases of gross human rights violations that occurred due to an attack on them because of their group identity. For example, reparations programs were developed for Jewish victims of the Nazi Holocaust, including financial compensation, consistent with Principle 20 of the *Guidelines*.[18] Japanese Americans interned in the United States during World War II were provided reparations consistent with Principle 19, Restitution (restoring to the

[14] Greensboro Truth and Reconciliation Commission Report 2 (May 25, 2006), *available at* www.greensborotrc.org.

[15] Nunn, *supra* note 5, at 435.

[16] UN Commission on Human Rights, *supra* note 10.

[17] Adjoa A. Aiyetoro, *The development of the movement for reparations for African descendants*, 3 J. L. Soc'y. 133 (2002)

[18] Roy L. Brooks, *A reparations success story?*, *in* When sorry Isn't Enough, *supra* note 5, at 17; In re Holocaust Victim Assets Litigation, 105 F. Supp. 2d 139 (E.D.N.Y. 2000) (authorizing distribution of $1.25 billion payment from Swiss banks to Jewish Holocaust survivors and heirs); Bodner v. Banque Paribas, 114 F. Supp. 2d 117 (E.D.N.Y. 2000) (a global settlement in favor of Holocaust survivors and heirs against banks doing business in France during World War II).

status before the violation inclusive of citizenship, employment, and return to place of residence); Principle 20, Compensation (although the compensation, $20,000, was a token rather than payment for "economically assessable damage" including physical and mental injury, lost opportunities, loss of wage); and Principle 22, Satisfaction (exposure of the truth, including declaration or apology).[19] Likewise, families of the "disappeared" in Argentina,[20] the Aborigines in Australia,[21] Native Americans,[22] victims of apartheid in South Africa,[23] victims of genocide in Rwanda;[24] and victims of the civil war in Sierra Leone[25] were given or promised reparations that were consistent with the forms recommended by the *Guidelines*. International law, custom, and practices have flowed from the need to remedy gross violations of human rights based on group identity and provide legal, political, and moral arguments for reparations to African descendants for the injuries caused by slavery and its continuing vestiges. An understanding of African women's involvement in demanding and obtaining reparations, although not the focus of this chapter, provides some context for a discussion of the normative impact of African descendant women in the reparations movements in the United States and England.

The Diaspora

African women's leadership role in reparations efforts in South Africa, Rwanda, and Sierra Leone differs significantly from African descendant

19 Roger Daniels, *Relocation, redress, and the report: A historical appraisal*, *in* WHEN SORRY ISN'T ENOUGH, *supra* note 5, at 183–86; Civil Liberties Act of 1988, Pub. L. No. 100–383; 102 Stat. 903(1).

20 *See* Graciela Louis & Margarita Lacabe, *In search of vindication: Reparations for human rights violations in Argentina*, *available at* http://www.derechos.org/koaga/vii/lois.html.

21 Barbara McMahon, *Tasmania to pay "stolen generation" of Aborigines £2.2m in reparations*, THE GUARDIAN (January 22, 2008), *available at* http://www.guardian.co.uk/world/2008/jan/23/australia.international/print; Unrepresented Nations and Peoples Organization, *The West Australia government has announce the payment of up to £2000 to those who fell under the "stolen wages" regime*, reprinting SYDNEY MORNING HERALD article (March 7, 2012), *available at* http://www.unpo.org/article/13987; Unrepresented Nations and Peoples Organization, *Aboriginals of Australia: Granted native title over lake*, reprinting article published by ABC News (May 23, 2012), *available at* http://www.unpo.org/article/14320.

22 Ronald L. Trosper, *American Indian Reparations*, Poverty & Race, Poverty & Race Research Action Council (November/December 1994) (describing three forms of reparations to American Indians including [1] cash payments, [2] land, and [3] tribal recognition). There is a strong argument that Native Americans have not and should not receive reparations. Rather, what they have received and should receive flows from the enforcement of treaty rights. *See, e.g.*, William C. Bradford, *Beyond reparations: An American Indian theory of justice*, 66 OHIO ST. L. J., 1, 8 (2005).

23 Goldblatt, *supra* note 7, at 48, 50.

24 Heidy Rombouts, *Women and reparations in Rwanda: A long path to travel*, *in* WHAT HAPPENED TO THE WOMEN, *supra* note 7, at 194, 199–200.

25 King, *supra* note 9, at 246, 248.

women's roles in the Diaspora. African women often assumed a leadership role because they were appointed to commissions in postconflict governments that focused on reparations for injuries caused during conflict.[26] In other instances, African women were in leadership roles because they were working with nongovernmental organizations (NGOs) focused on repairing injuries caused by armed conflict.[27] Finally, African women involved in the effort to obtain reparations in South Africa, Sierra Leone, and Rwanda were part of the winning side of the conflict in their countries.

Still, there are some similarities across countries in terms of injuries for which reparations are sought. The injuries to African people in the United States, England, South Africa, Rwanda, and Sierra Leone all include physical violence perpetrated on the affected communities of African peoples by those in power based on identifiers of race or ethnicity, including rape of women; physical maiming of men, women, and children; and loss of life. The affected groups were also either denied the right to own property (in the case of slavery in the United States) or had property destroyed or taken away. In the United States and England, African descendants were denied the right to participate fully in civil society.

It is the dissimilarities between African women and African descendant women working for reparations, however, that give rise to the force, passion, and strategies embraced by African descendant women in their leadership roles in the reparations movements in the Diaspora. If there are any similarities between African and African descendant women's voices in the demand for material reparations, these arise from the legend of Nana Yaa Asantewaa, the queen mother of the Edweso tribe in Asante.[28] Nana Yaa Asantewaa took on a leadership role to reclaim and protect African artifacts from British appropriation. She is credited with leading the 1900 Asante resistance against the British who colonized Asante[29] and other adjacent African kingdoms.[30]

[26] Goldblatt, *supra* note 7, at 55. (Seven of the seventeen South African TRC commissioners were women, four of whom served on the Reparations and Rehabilitation Committee. This Committee was chaired and co-chaired by women, Hlengiwe Mkhize and Wendy Orr, respectively.)

[27] King, *supra* note 9, at 246–48, 250, 253, 254–57. (Although the laws of Sierra Leone disadvantaged women, who were particularly vulnerable during the civil war, women took a leadership role in pressing for peace and returning the country to a democracy. The Women's Forum and a number of women leaders were particularly instrumental in the push for peace, expressing the views of women in this process.)

[28] Brempong Arhin, *The role of Nana YaaAsantewaa in the 1900 Asante war of resistance*, 8 LE GRIOT 1, 1 (2000), *available at* http://www.ucalgary.ca/~taarn/LeGriot/articlec4.pdf). PDF is unpaginated.

[29] Asante was a part of Kumase, seized by the British in 1896. It is now known as Ghana. T. C. McCaskie, *The life and afterlife of YaaAsantewaa*, 77 AFRICA 151, 153 (2007); *see also*, Arhin, *supra* note 28.

[30] McCaskie, *supra* note 29, at 153; Arhin, *supra* note 28.

The British determined that securing the Golden Stool, a symbol of Asante kingship and unity, would solidify their control of the Asante and break their allegiance to the Osei-Poku Dynasty by assuring the Asante that the dynasty was gone forever.[31] The British demanded the Golden Stool in a speech delivered by the Governor of the Gold Coast, Sir Frederick Hodgson, on March 28, 1900. Nana Yaa Asantewaa was among those attending the meeting, and she spoke to the Asante rulers, who seemed to be in shock, chiding them to not act like women and do nothing about these edicts.[32] In response to her challenge, Nana Yaa Asantewaa was chosen by the Asante rulers to lead the resistance, and, in this role, she initiated the development and implementation of the war effort, including creating strategies and tactics in consultation with other rulers and organizing the resources necessary to sustain the war effort.[33] The British eventually defeated the Asante, captured Yaa Asantewaa, and exiled her to the Indian Ocean archipelago of Sychelles, where she died in 1921.[34] The British took the Golden Stool; however, in 1935, they made reparation for that theft by returning it to the Asante when they recognized the Ashanti Confederacy as a political entity.[35]

Nana Yaa Asantewaa's demonstration of leadership, courage, and outspokenness in attempting to protect what rightfully belonged to the Asante from appropriation by the British has been a model for the leadership, courage, and outspokenness of many leaders of the reparations movements in the Diaspora.[36] Of additional significance, and a fact that distinguishes Nana Yaa Asaantewaa from the African women supporting reparations in South Africa, Sierra Leone, and Rwanda, is that she and the Asante confrontation was with the British, as is the struggle for reparations for African decendents in the Diaspora; the United States also began as a British colony.

[31] Arhin, *supra* note 28.

[32] *Id. See also*, McCaskie, *supra* note 29, at 158, note 7 (indicating that YaaAsantewaa was defending the cultural norms of the Asante by her call to Asante men to fulfill their male responsibility).

[33] Arhin, *supra* note 28 (citing Sir Francis Charles Fuller, A VANISHED DYNASTY – ASHANTI 189 (1921); McCaskie, *supra* note 29, at 161 (Asante troops were led by a woman: YaaAsantewaa)

[34] McCaskie, *supra* note 29, at 159.

[35] UNHCR, *Refworld*, Chronology for Ewe in Ghana, *available at* http://www.refworld.org/type,CHRON,,GHA,469f388fc.ohtm; Wonders: Ashanti Kingdom in Wonders of the African World – the SLAVE KINGDOMS, *available at* http://www.pbs.org/wonders/Episodes/Epi3/3_wondr1.htm; GHANA TIMELINE – THE GOLD COAST, *available at* http://crawfurd.dk/africa/ghana_timeline.htm.

[36] A number of African descendant women, including this author, for example, chose or were given Nana YaaAsantewaa's name when they received African names. McCaskie, *supra* note 29, 153, 162, 172.

England

Esther Stanford-Xosei is a leader in the reparations movement in England. She is from Lewisham, south London. Ms. Stanford-Xosei is the co-vice chair of the Pan-African Reparations Coalition in Europe.[37] Her leadership focuses on linking the history of slavery and race discrimination to the current conditions faced by African descendants in England today. Like some of her comrades in the United States, she believes that the links must be shown between slavery and present-day disabilities and disparities experienced by African descendants in order to build a broad-based movement for reparations. The tenet of the reparations movement in the Diaspora echoed by Stanford-Xosei is that the problems faced by African descendants today in health, criminal punishment, and housing, for example, are linked to the history of slavery. Active in the leadership of the reparations movement in England since the 1990s, Ms. Stanford-Xosei brought a legal action against the Queen of England based on the language of the World Conference against Racism (WCAR) Declaration, "We acknowledge that slavery and the slave trade, including the trans-Atlantic slave trade ... and further acknowledge that slavery and the slave trade are a crime against humanity and should always have been so, especially the transatlantic slave trade and are among the major sources and manifestations of racism, racial discrimination," to expose the legal system as being inadequate and to highlight the importance of strengthening the resolve for political action.[38] She has taken the importance of the demand internationally. She consciously reached out to the National Coalition of Blacks for Reparations in America (N'COBRA) in the 1990s, at which time the author met and spoke with her about the global reparations movement. She worked with Queen Mother Dorothy Benton Lewis, discussed later, who was the chair of N'COBRA's International Commission, and Stanford-Xosei became an active member of that commission.[39] She was involved with WCAR and participates on panels discussing the need for reparations to be addressed globally.[40]

Ms. Stanford-Xosei's greatest contribution to the global reparations movement is her focus on education about the importance of the demand in the Diaspora generally, in Africa, and in her home country, England. It is particularly important to an understanding of the status of African descendants

[37] Google Profile, *available at* https://profiles.google.com/estherstanfordxosei; Adam Lusher, *Slaves at the root of the fortune that created Richard Dawkins' family estate*, TELEGRAPH, February 19, 2012, *available at* http://telegraph.co.uk/news/uknews/9091007/Slaves-at-the-root-of-the-fortune-that-c ...

[38] PARCOE Mau Mau Discussion, *available at* www.YouTube.com/watch?v=mx8hyRaR700.

[39] *Id.*

[40] *Id.*

worldwide that she links the history of slavery and its legacy to present-day conditions and to the advocacy of reparative remedies, including advocating for reparations. She is a broadcaster on Britain's first licensed Afrikan community radio station, Voice of Africa Radio, facilitating weekly discussions to educate the public on reparations-related topics. She is a founder and the general secretary of the Rendezvous of Victory, an antislavery abolitionist heritage "learning" movement that seeks to educate about the past in order to provide examples of the achievements that are reached through united action. Stanford-Xosei participates as a birth coach in a program designed to educate expectant mothers about health-related problems of African descendant people that are connected to the history of human rights violations and to encourage them to create an in vitro and postbirth environment for their child that will combat these health problems.[41] Her leadership in the reparations movement also led to the British government's adoption of August 23 as the UK's Slavery Memorial Day and the introduction of teaching about the transatlantic slave trade as a compulsory curriculum topic.[42]

The United Kingdom's decision to adopt August 23 as the UK Slavery Memorial Day demonstrates the timely, fortuitous combination of a number of events. On June 8, 2006, MP Dawn Butler "submitted an Early Day Motion to Parliament for a National Day of Remembrance of Victims of Slavery."[43] Butler, not associated with the grassroots movement for reparations, proposed March 25, the day the slave trade became illegal in England. This was to be in commemoration of the 200th anniversary of England's abolition of the slave trade in 2007. Esther Stanford-Xosei and activists in the reparations movement stridently opposed this resolution. She and others demanded material reparations rather than a symbolic day of recognition. This struggle coincided with UNESCO's decision to make August 23 a day to memorialize resistance to slavery in Haiti. Stanford-Xosei and the grassroots movement for reparations in England supported this date because of its association with "resistance," as well as the concomitant introduction of the TransAtlantic Slave Trade as a compulsory curriculum topic.[44] This outcome is consistent with Stanford-Xosei's stridency in the demand for reparations.

[41] The C.O.W.S. with Esther Stanford-Xosei: It Takes a Village, *available at* www.youtube.com/watch?v+NZG_pjROHuY.

[42] Google Profile, *available at* https://profiles.google.com/estherstanforxosei

[43] Raymond Enisuoh, *MP Dawn Butler under fire over slavery memorial day proposal*, *available at* http://vuesdumonde.forumactif.com/t4078-mp-dawn-butler-under-fire.

[44] *Id.*; Stephen Farrell, *Driving change through Parliament*, *available at* http://www.bbc.co.uk/history/british/abolition/parliament_article_01.shtml, Anti-Slavery, *UK establishes National Slavery Memorial Day*, *available at http://www.antislavery.org/english/press_and_news/news_and_press_releases_2008/2008_press_and_news/280108_uk_national_slavery_memorial_day1.aspx*

The United States

This stridency and daring to demand reparations are traits reflected also in the advocacy of reparations by African descendant women in the United States. Immediately after the Civil War, Sojourner Truth organized "a petition seeking free public land for former slaves. 'America owes to my people some of the dividends, ... I shall make them understand that there is a debt to the Negro people which they can never pay. At least, then, they must make amends.'"[45]

Since the end of the Civil War, African descendant women have often used the international arena to voice their demands for racial justice in the United States. These women sought international allies to put additional pressure on the United States to end the oppression and brutalization of African descendants. Ida B. Wells-Barnett, Queen Mother Audley Moore, Queen Mother Dorothy Benton Lewis, and women members of the WCAR African and African Descendant NGO caucus, who will be discussed later, are primary examples of African descendant women who took the message of racial oppression and its remedy to international bodies.

However, the first African descendant woman[46] to gain prominence in the demand for reparations in the United States focused only on the national stage, rather than taking her demands to the international community. In 1896, Callie House and Isaiah Dickerson organized the Ex-Slave Mutual Relief, Bounty & Pension Association. It had two purposes: (1) to serve as a benevolent organization and provide mutual aid to its members and (2) to mobilize and organize support for a federal bill providing a pension to ex-slaves.[47] House was the "field secretary" and traveled throughout the United States mobilizing and organizing ex-slaves, their families, and their supporters to lobby Congress for the passage of a pension bill. House became the face of reparations for formerly enslaved Africans in the United States. More than 600 people joined the Association. In addition to organizing to obtain a pension bill, the Association, under House's leadership, filed an unsuccessful lawsuit against the federal government for collection of the "southern cotton tax" as reparations for African descendants.[48] The federal government, feeling threatened by the Association's legislative and litigation efforts to obtain reparations, prosecuted and convicted House and other

[45] Robin D. G. Kelley, *A day of reckoning: dreams of reparations, in* REDRESS FOR HISTORICAL INJUSTICES, *supra* note 3, at 203, 205.

[46] The first known call for reparations to African descendants came from David Walker in 1829. David Walker, DAVID WALKER'S APPEAL at 80 (Black Classic Press 1993) (1830).

[47] Berry, *supra* note 2, at 61.

[48] Johnson v. McAdoo, 45 App. D.C. 440 (1916).

Association leaders on charges of mail fraud without any evidence, purportedly for leading African descendants to believe that it was possible to pass a pension bill.[49]

Despite her almost twenty years of reparations advocacy throughout the United States with a focus on passage of a pension bill in the United States Congress, there is no evidence that House's work included the involvement of the international community or that it even received international attention. A contemporary of House, Ida B. Wells, who does not appear from the research to have known or been influenced by House, is well known for her trips to England to garner support and assistance from the English people for the passage of antilynching legislation.[50] Although Wells mentioned on occasion that the victims' families should be given some form of recompense, her involvement in and leadership of the antilynching campaign was primarily focused on legislative actions to punish the perpetrators of lynching. The first African descendant woman in the United States to take the demand for reparations to the international arena was Audley Moore, known as Queen Mother Moore, an honorific she received in 1972 when she attended the funeral of the Ghanaian leader and pan-Africanist Kwame Nkrumah in 1972.[51]

Queen Mother Moore was a lifelong advocate for racial justice. Her advocacy began when she became a Garveyite and joined the New York United Negro Improvement Association (UNIA).[52] Moore's activism for reparations became known in 1955 when she authored a pamphlet, *Why Reparations? Money for Negroes*.[53] However, her resolve that reparations were needed for African descendants in the United States is best reflected in a poem, "What's the Hour of the Night?," which she wrote in 1950. It has been recited and reprinted on a number of occasions, urging that whatever progress has been made in the lives of African descendants, it was time for reparations for slavery and its vestiges. Moore was not satisfied with the progress made in the United States to obtain reparations for African descendants. In 1957 and 1959, the International Committee for Reparations for Descendants of U.S. Slaves and

[49] Berry, *supra* note 2, at 83, 124, 190, 192, 202–04, 235–37 (House's conviction on charges of mail fraud was a forerunner to the same treatment by Marcus Mosiah Garvey in 1923, also because of success in galvanizing grassroots African descendants in advocating for self-help reparations. In 1919, Garvey led the UNIA, which raised money for a Black Star Line of ships, the purpose of which was to repatriate African descendants to Africa.)

[50] *See, e.g.*, Paula J. Giddings, IDA: A SWORD AMONG LIONS (2008).

[51] Kelley, *supra* note 45, at 210.

[52] *Id.* at 203.

[53] Aiyetoro & Davis, *supra* note 3, at 687, 707.

the Association of Ethiopian Women, both led by Moore, took the demand for reparations to the international arena, filing petitions with the UN that raised the issues of self-determination and reparations.[54]

Queen Mother Moore's engagement of the international community did not stop in 1959. She made numerous international trips before her physical health would no longer allow such travel. According to Raymond Winbush, she also influenced leaders of the African descendant community to make reparations part of their message. For example, he indicates that Queen Mother Moore influenced a speech Malcolm X made in Paris in 1964 incorporating a demand for reparations:

> If you are the son of a man who had a wealthy estate and you inherit your father's estate, you have to pay off the debts that your father incurred before he died. The only reason that the present generation of white Americans are in a position of economic strength ... is because their fathers worked our fathers for over 400 years with no pay. ... We were sold from plantation to plantation like you sell a horse, or a cow, or a chicken, or a bushel of wheat. ... All that money ... is what gives the present generation of American whites the ability to walk around the earth with their chest out ... like they have some kind of economic ingenuity. Your father isn't here to pay. My father isn't here to collect. But I'm here to collect and you're here to pay.[55]

During her many international trips, Queen Mother Moore brought the message of reparations to African descendants, some of whom would later become leaders in the reparations movement.[56] Charles Ogletree, co-founder of the Reparations Coordinating Committee, the group that brought the reparations lawsuit on behalf of the survivors and descendants of victims of the 1921 Tulsa Race Massacre, *Alexander v. Oklahoma*, credits Queen Mother Moore with planting the seed for his embrace of reparations during a trip to Senegal.[57] Indeed, her influence may have been partly responsible for the legal team taking the case to the Inter-American Court.[58]

[54] *See* www.ncbsonline.org/ncbs_statement_on_the_international_year_of_people_of_african_descent.

[55] Raymond A. Winbush, *And the earth moved: Stealing black land in the United States, in* Should America Pay? Slavery and the Raging Debate on Reparations 46–56, at 42–43 (Raymond A. Winbush ed., 2003).

[56] *Id.* at 43.

[57] Charles J. Ogletree, Jr., All Deliberate Speed: Reflections on the First Half Century of *Brown v. Board of Education* 280–81 (2004).

[58] Global Rights and Charles J. Ogletree, Jr., Petitioners, on behalf of John Melvin Alexander, et al., Victims v. The United States of America, Member of the Organization of American States, Respondent, Petition Alleging Violations of the Human Rights of John Melvin Alexander et al. by the United States of America, filed October 26, 2005.

Queen Mother Moore inspired Dorothy Benton Lewis after Lewis moved to Washington, DC, in the mid-1970s. Lewis hosted discussions on reparations in her home in Potomac, Maryland, and Queen Mother Moore was a guest at one of these discussions. Lewis, however, became a reparationist in the 1960s in Alaska, when the "restitution for involuntary servitude" became an issue for the NAACP chapter to which she belonged.[59] Lewis stayed the course, keeping her focus on reparations throughout her life. Her interest in the international arena was sparked when she began working with the late Irving B. Davis. In 1978, Lewis and Davis formed the Black Reparations Commission. They decided to focus the organization's agenda on both Africa and the United States, given Davis's international work and relationships with African leaders. For example, Davis worked with Julius Nyere, the first president of Tanzania. In Lewis's eyes, it seemed natural to divide the responsibilities for the organization; Davis would lead the international work of the Commission, and Lewis would lead the domestic efforts. After Davis's death, Queen Mother Lewis added international work to her agenda and continued the Commission's focus on getting domestic and international organizations to support the demand for reparations.

Lewis was a founding member of N'COBRA. When N'COBRA went to a commission structure in 1993, Lewis became the chair of the International Commission. Under her leadership, the Commission engaged with reparations activists in Jamaica, England, and Ghana. These relationships led to the formation of N'COBRA chapters in Ghana and Jamaica and to a strong, collaborative relationship with a leader of England's reparations movement, Esther Sanford. As discussed earlier, Ms. Stanford-Xosei became a member of N'COBRA and attended some N'COBRA conferences. Queen Mother Lewis attended the WCAR in Durban, South Africa, in 2001. She continued collaborations with reparationists from England, Brazil, the Caribbean, and Africa after the WCAR and attended the African and African Descendant Caucus's post-WCAR conference held in Barbados in 2002. Lewis was elected the U.S. representative to the Global African Congress (GAC) that was formed at the Barbados meeting.[60]

Queen Mother Lewis remained the U.S. representative to the GAC until her transition on March 23, 2012. In 2005, acting in both this capacity and as chair of the N'COBRA International Commission, she was a primary organizer of an international conference in Ghana on reparations for Africans and African descendants in the Diaspora (the conference focused on slavery,

[59] Much of the information about Dorothy Benton Lewis is taken from a December 2009 interview that is reproduced in Aiyetoro & Davis, *supra* note 3, at 746–51.

[60] Anderson et al., *supra* note 3, at 427, 434.

colonialism, and their legacies). Until her transition, Queen Mother Lewis continued to chair the N'COBRA International Commission and traveled extensively, particularly to England, South Africa, and other African countries, where she worked with reparationists in those countries to strengthen the demand for reparations.

Queen Mother Moore and Queen Mother Lewis expanded the discussion of reparations for African descendants in the United States by taking that discussion to the international community. Much like Stanford-Xosei, they educated those in the United States as well as in Africa and in the wider Diaspora about the importance of the demand and the connectedness of the injuries caused by enslavement, slavery, and segregation. Lewis also was a voice for that part of the reparations movement that looked to creating healing modalities for the injuries caused by the violations of human rights of African descendants "on the way to reparations," as she would say. She advocated for healthy (physical and mental) living, buying from and using the services of Africans and African descendants, and hosting educational fora on reparations to the mainstream community, including Whites. Lewis's involvement in the formation of N'COBRA and its ongoing work led to her interactions with U.S. Congressman John Conyers (D-MI) who introduced the Reparations Study bill in 1989 and has reintroduced it every Congressional session since then.[61]

Conyers (D-MI) praised Queen Mother Dorothy Benton Lewis as a truly strong and dedicated spokesperson

> for the issue of Reparations for the centuries of injustice endured during and following the United States era of enslavement of African peoples. As a founding member of the National Coalition of Blacks for Reparations in America, she played a tremendous role in mainstreaming the Reparations debate, and making the word Reparations a household word. Out of all the issues that I have championed during my years of service on Capitol Hill, the issue of Reparations has generated more letters from across the country than any other. I thank and honor Queen Mother Dorothy Benton Lewis for her part in this effort, and for her tireless fight for Reparations. Her energy cannot be surpassed, but her contributions shall live on for the movement.[62]

[61] In 1989, Conyers was lobbied by N'COBRA activist "Reparations Ray" Jenkins, a Detroit supporter of Conyers, resulting in the drafting of the Reparations Study bill that was sent to N'COBRA in 1989 for review and comment. Adjoa A. Aiyetoro, *The National Coalition of Blacks for Reparations in America (N'COBRA)*, *in* SHOULD AMERICA PAY?, *supra* note 55, at 209, 217.

[62] Representative John Conyers Jr. (D-MI), Tribute to Queen Mother Moore in the program, "Celebrating the Life and Homegoing of Dorothy Faye Benton-Lewis," March 31, 2012.

African Descendant Women at the World Conference against Racism

The Africans and African descendants who participated in preparatory meetings and in the WCAR formed an African and African Descendant Caucus initiated by Roger Wareham of the December Twelfth Movement in the United States; this organization was among the leading groups lobbying at the UN for a world conference on racism. All caucus members were members of NGOs that met the necessary criteria to participate in the World Conference. There was no dissent in the Caucus for support of reparations as a part of the Declaration and Programme of Action developed by the government delegates, although there were differences concerning what might constitute reparations. Women had a strong presence at the WCAR, and African and African descendant women from various countries in Africa, as well as from Brazil, Canada, the Caribbean, Central and South America, England, and the United States, actively participated. They made important contributions to the dialogue, strategy, and implementation at NGO conferences, as well as in meetings with governmental delegations. The author of this chapter, a leader of the reparations movement in the United States,[63] was asked by the Women's International League for Peace and Freedom (WILPF) to represent it at WCAR. I participated in all the preparatory meetings and was chosen to be a co-chair of the African and African Descendant Caucus. The author made presentations at NGO meetings held at the UN headquarters; these were preparatory meetings on the importance of reparations. As a leader of the caucus, and at the invitation of the South African organizers, I spoke on two panels at the NGO conference that immediately preceded the WCAR governmental meeting. The caucus also selected me to make a presentation on reparations before the governmental delegate body on August 31, at the beginning of the governmental conference.[64] Interestingly, at a session of the governmental delegates meeting on September 1, the Cuban president, Dr. Fidel Castro Ruz, chose to focus his comments specifically on reparations, a topic only

[63] The author was a founding member of N'COBRA, served as its first woman co-chair, chaired N'COBRA's Legal Strategies Commission, and chaired the Reparations Coordinating Committee with Randall Robinson and Charles J. Ogletree Jr.

[64] Speakers were listed in the report by the NGO they represented not by the caucus. I was representing the Women's International League for Peace and Freedom. *See* Annex III, Roundtable of Heads of State and Heads of Government, point 6, 164, Documents World Conference against Racism, Racial Discrimination, Xenophobia and Related Intolerance, *available at* www.unhchr.ch/Huridoca/Huridoca.nsf/0/.../N0221543.doc.

presented by me as a representative of the African and African Descendant Caucus.[65]

Kimberlé Crenshaw was the leader of the African and African Descendant Women's Caucus. She was also a member of the African and African Descendant Caucus, and worked with it to develop language for WCAR documents. Under her leadership, the African Descendant Women's Caucus lobbied government delegations for support of reparations language in the documents. Indeed, through the work of the African and African Descendant Caucus and the African and African Descendant Women's Caucus, many caucuses supported reparations for African and African descendants, joining them in a demonstration in front of the building where the government delegates were meeting. This support was significant in getting language into the Declaration and Programme of Action that supported the call for reparations.

The African Caucus was the government delegation that put forward reparations language; it was supported by a number of other government delegations. Delegates from countries that participated in the enslavement of Africans and the colonization of Africa, including England, Portugal, France, and Belgium, although resistant to the process, did not abandon the process, as did the United States. The United States was a major stumbling block in the effort to get language in the WCAR documents advocating reparations. In informal discussions with members of the U.S. delegation in some of the early preparatory meetings, we were told that one reason the U.S. delegation opposed reparations was because of the potentially large liability. The U.S. delegation eventually walked out. This walkout was attributed to language in the initial drafts of the document that equated Zionism with racism and to slavery reparations language. The U.S. representatives told the government delegations that the "mention of trans-Atlantic slavery in the proposed Durban drafts is extreme and unbalanced." And, although it agreed to language expressing regret for historic injustices such as slavery, the U.S. view was that the conference should focus on "contemporary manifestations

[65] Keynote address by Dr. Fidel Castro Ruz, President of the Republic of Cuba at the World Conference against Racism, Racial Discrimination, Xenophobia and Related Intolerance, Durban, South Africa, September 1, 2001, *available at* http:www.un.org/WCAR/statements/01 09cubaE.htm. Among other things President Castro said, "Cuba speaks of reparations, and supports this idea as an unavoidable moral duty to the victims of racism, based on a major precedent, that is the indemnification being paid to the descendants of the Hebrew people.... The irrefutable truth is that tens of millions of Africans were captured, sold like a commodity and sent beyond the Atlantic to work in slavery.... After the purely formal slave emancipation, African-Americans were subjected during one hundred more years to the harshest racial discrimination, and many of its features and consequences still persist."

of racism and intolerance," and it wanted a "future-oriented approach."[66] The U.S. representatives expressed no understanding that the "historic injustices such as slavery" were the cause of many "contemporary manifestations of racism."

The work of the African Descendant Caucus and the African (governmental) Caucus, with the support of other delegates to the conference and NGO caucuses, led to language in the WCAR documents that (1) call slavery and slave trade, especially the transatlantic slave trade, a crime against humanity and acknowledge that it should always have been seen as such;[67] (2) affirmed that colonialism led to (rather than was caused by) racism and suffering;[68] and, (3) recognized apartheid and genocide as crimes against humanity.[69] The Programme of Action supported reparations, particularly in Paragraph 158 of the document, calling for a number of actions including debt forgiveness, return of stolen art objects, and return of African descendants.[70] Paragraph 5 of the Programme of Action focuses on Africans and African descendants and suggests reparations in the form of, among other things, investments, health care systems, and education.[71]

The work of the African and African Descendant Caucus and the African and African Descendant Women's Caucus was pivotal in obtaining language in the UN's WCAR Declaration and Program of Action that is used to educate people throughout the world about the egregiousness of the crimes perpetrated against Africa and African descendants in the Diaspora. These documents serve to support the claims for reparations and are excellent organizing tools, although, as Esther Stanford-Xosei found, they do not provide a basis for litigation in countries that signed it.

CONCLUSION

African descendant women have been a major force in the global reparations movement. The national and international impact of raising and sustaining the call for reparations is seen in the work of Queen Mother Audley Moore,

[66] Congressional Research Service Report for Congress, the 2009 U.N. Durban Review Conference: Follow-up to the 2001 UN World Conference against Racism, Luisa Blanchfield, Analyst in International Relations, Order Code RL34754 (November 20, 2008), *available at* www.fas.org/sgp/crs/row/RL34754.pdf; Kelley, *supra* note 45, at 204.

[67] Report of the World Conference against Racism, Racial Discrimination, Xenophobia and Related Intolerance, 31 August–8 September 2001, Declaration, para. 13, at 11–12.

[68] *Id.*, para. 14, at 13.

[69] *Id.*, para. 15, at 13.

[70] *Id.* at 61.

[71] *Id.* at 28.

who was the first African descendant to take the claim for African descendant reparations from the United States to the international community; Queen Mother Dorothy Benton Lewis, to which this chapter is dedicated; Kimberlé Crenshaw; Esther Stanford-Xosei; and the author. African descendant women have counterparts in Africa who have participated in developing reparations for victims of sustained oppression and conflicts in their countries. Yet, unlike those in the Diaspora, they have been members of the winners' group in ending the oppression and resolving the conflict in their countries. African descendants in the Diaspora are citizens of countries in which members of the oppressor class responsible for the enslavement of Africans in the Diaspora and for the pernicious vestiges of that enslavement remain in control.

The reparations work of African and African descendant women, whether in Africa or in the Diaspora, is challenging to quantify – but is normative in scope. Such work has led to worldwide debate about the legitimacy and importance of reparations for Africans and African descendants. Reports by international bodies on the essentiality of reparations for Africans and African descendants are in part a reflection of the work of the women discussed herein and of the organizations with which they work and which they often lead.

Although their activism has not resulted in reparations for African descendants, it has maintained the visibility of that call, contributed to honoring the resistance to enslavement, led to the creation of a curriculum on the transatlantic slave trade in England, and led to the inclusion in the documents of the WCAR language that indicts the TransAtlantic Slave Trade and supports the call for reparations. Indeed, it was the leadership of Dorothy Benton Lewis that led to the formation of N'COBRA, the only grassroots organization in the United States that is devoted to organizing and leading the demand for reparations for African descendants in the United States, an organization that has influenced congressional leaders to support reparations for African descendants in the United States. The work of African descendant women has contributed to keeping alive the demand for reparations, work that can be seen in the number of fora focused on this issue, as well as in publications that are written concerning the legitimacy of reparations.[72] This work serves as the basis for continuing efforts to create reparative remedies that may one day lead to the ultimate goal of reparations: healing human-created injury that is based

[72] *See, e.g.*, Redress for Historical Injustices, *supra* note 3; What Happened to the Women, *supra* note 7; Conference on Truth and Reconciliation at University of Massachusetts at Amherst, November 13, 2012, sponsored by the History Department, at which the author will speak.

on race or ethnic identity. Just as our African and African descendant ancestors maintained focus on the call for abolition of slavery, we also will continue the work for reparations for African descendants, and our focus on reparations for slavery and its vestiges will lead to some form of reparations beyond those granted for specific incidents, as in Rosewood, Florida.

10

The Challenge of Climate Change and the Contribution of African Women to Engendering International Environmental Law

Erika George

Today we are faced with a challenge that calls for a shift in our thinking, so that humanity stops threatening its life-support system. We are called to assist the Earth to heal her wounds and in the process heal our own – indeed, to embrace the whole of creation in all its diversity, beauty and wonder. This will happen if we see the need to revive our sense of belonging to a larger family of life, with which we have shared our evolutionary process.

– Wangari Muta Maathai, Nobel Laureate

The impacts of climate change will be differently distributed among different regions, generations, ages, classes, income groups, occupations and sexes.

– The Intergovernmental Panel on Climate Change

INTRODUCTION

There is strong scientific consensus that the climate of the earth is changing and that human activities are substantially contributing to the change in

Erika R. George is Professor of Law at the University of Utah's S. J. Quinney College of Law, where she teaches constitutional law, international human rights law, international environmental law, civil procedure, and seminar courses on corporate citizenship and human rights. She earned her B.A. with honors from the University of Chicago and her J.D. from Harvard Law School, where she served as articles editor of the Harvard Civil Rights-Civil Liberties Law Review. She also holds an M.A. in International Relations from the University of Chicago. Her current research explores the responsibilities of multinational corporations to respect international human rights and various efforts to hold corporations accountable for alleged rights violations. The BBC, The Economist, NBC News, CNN, and the Christian Science Monitor, among other media outlets, have reported on her human rights investigations. She dedicates this chapter to the daughters and sons of Africa and the African Diaspora committed to eradicating the adverse impacts of unhealthy environments.

climate.[1] The causes of climate change are multifaceted, and the projected consequences potentially catastrophic. The impacts of climate change are projected to be particularly devastating for Africa, African women, and women of the African Diaspora in ways that are sure to compound the existing inequalities they already confront.

Atmospheric concentrations of greenhouse gases that cause climate change continue to increase, exceeding previously recorded record highs.[2] In addition to greenhouse gases from natural sources, emissions from the use of fossil fuels, land uses that lead to environmental degradation, and deforestation all contribute to causing climate change.[3] Although the rate of warming varies from one year to the next due to natural weather cycles and solar variation, global temperatures have continued to rise as human-induced emissions of greenhouse gases have continued. The decade 2001–10 was the warmest on record.[4] Average temperatures were elevated on every continent. There is scientific consensus that changes in weather and pressure patterns and recent extreme weather events are also consistent with the projected impacts of climate change.[5] Extreme weather events are expected to increase as temperatures rise and the climate changes.

While scientists continue to study how the earth will respond over time and across different regions, the Intergovernmental Panel on Climate Change (IPCC) has confirmed that climate change will disproportionately affect "less developed countries and people living in poverty in all countries, exacerbating inequalities in well-being and in access to food, clean water and other resources."[6] Africa, the birthplace of humanity, stands to bear a heavy burden if the international community fails to curb human-induced climate change. African women will bear the greatest weight of the burden.

[1] World Meteorological Organization, *Information note: A summary of current climate change findings and figures*, WMO (March 2013), *available at* http://www.wmo.int/pages/mediacentre/factsheet/documents/ClimateChangeInfoSheet2013–03final.pdf, last visited December 22, 2013.

[2] *Id.*

[3] *Id.*

[4] *Id.*

[5] *See, e.g., Joint science academies' statement: Global response to climate change, available at* http://www.nationalacademies.org/onpi/06072005.pdf, last visited January 26, 2014.

[6] The United Nations Environmental Program (UNEP) and the World Meteorological Organization (WMO) created the IPCC to study scientific, technical, and socioeconomic information relevant to understanding the effects of climate change and alternatives for adaptation and mitigation.

Climate change presents a complex challenge for international environmental law. Initially, women and their issues were virtually invisible to policymakers. Rights were not a central consideration in conversations concerning the climate. When governments gathered in Stockholm in 1972 to discuss the environment, they were not talking about women's rights. When women gathered in Nairobi in 1985 for the World Conference to Review and Assess the Achievements of the United Nations Decade for Women, they were talking about their rights as well as the environment. Today, the right to a healthy environment is now enshrined in the constitutions of many countries. Women's issues and interest are gaining ground in global policy arena as an appreciation of the interconnections among human rights, economic development, and environmental sustainability is growing.

African women played a critical role in placing issues of gender on the global climate change agenda and in increasing the international community's appreciation of the interrelationship among rights, economic development, and environmental sustainability. A large and growing body of literature examines the challenging consequences that climate change will present for African women. Fewer works explore the agency that African women have shown in facing challenges, finding innovative solutions, and fostering sustainable development.

This chapter considers the contributions of Black women and women of African descent to the development of a more inclusive body of international environmental law. First, it explains the projected impacts of climate change with particular reference to the African continent and the challenges climate change presents for African women. The difference gender makes during natural disasters and in the aftermath of extreme weather events for women of the African Diaspora is also discussed. Next, it examines the evolution of the international environmental law of climate change and the increasing inclusion of women's concerns in recent years. Then it explores how African women's mobilization has successfully moved the discussion of climate change to now mandate that gender issues enter the mainstream of climate change law and policymaking. It is argued that the activism and adaptive strategies of African women could serve, and women's human rights should command, greater attention from policymakers in the development and climate arenas. Finally, it concludes with an examination of the ways the activism of African women has served to highlight the importance of appreciating the interrelationship among environmental conservation, human rights, and human security.

The Impact of Climate Change and Environmental Disasters on Africa, African Women, and Women of the African Diaspora

The threats associated with climate change will likely widen gaps between the privileged and the poor; these threats stand to erase gains in economic development and erode progress toward respect for human rights as conflicts over increasingly scarce resources increase.[7] The UN Climate Development Program (UNDP) has called climate change the "defining human development issue of our generation."[8] Current struggles over natural resources on the African continent are rooted in abuses that occurred generations ago. Human activity impacts ecological systems without regard for political boundaries or national borders. Political boundaries in Africa often are not directly aligned with national borders due to the legacy of colonial partition of the continent. African politics are still shaped by the European "Scramble for Africa," and responsible resource control and allocation have remained problematic in the postcolonial period.

European colonial powers at the 1884 Berlin Conference or *Kongokonferenz* divided the African continent to ease the extraction of economic and natural resources, the expansion of political influence, and the exploitation of African peoples.[9] Colonialism eroded and distorted existing forms of African autonomy and governance. The political partition of the continent at the Berlin Conference served to separate African peoples and reorganized political power in ways that disrupted community networks and reduced the political capital of chieftainships and kingdoms. Alternatively, African political power structures were corrupted and co-opted to serve European colonial interests over those of African peoples. By the early 1900s, approximately 90 percent of the African continent was effectively under European control.[10]

The Berlin Conference divided the continent, leaving it to this day with a patchwork of political frontiers that often do not reflect realities of the lived

[7] For a discussion of disparity and adverse environmental impacts *see, e.g.*, Abigail H. Neely, *Blame it on the weeds: Politics, poverty and ecology in the new South Africa*, J. SOUTHERN AFRICAN STUD. 36:4, 869(2010) (In January of 2000, spectacular fires burned in the natural veld of Cape Town, South Africa. This article places the fires of 2000 in a longer history of postapartheid policy and science surrounding invasive alien floral species, arguing that the fires allowed for a synergy between concerns over poverty relief, nature conservation, and scientific research).

[8] United Nations Development Programme, *Resource guide on gender and climate change* 3 (2009) (citing United Nations Development Programme, Human Development Report (2007).

[9] *See generally* Stig Förster, Wolfgang Justin Mommsen, & Ronald Edward Robinson, eds., BISMARCK, EUROPE, AND AFRICA: THE BERLIN AFRICA CONFERENCE 1884–1885 AND THE ONSET OF PARTITION (1988).

[10] Elizabeth Heath, *Berlin Conference of 1884–1885*, *in* ENCYCLOPEDIA OF AFRICA (Henry Louis Gates & Kwame Anthony Appiah eds., 2010), *available at* http://www.oxfordreference.com/view/10.1093/acref/9780195337709.001.0001/acref-9780195337709-e-0467 (last visited January 26, 2014).

experience of communities.[11] The legacy of peoples lacking effective sovereignty over the natural resources in their surrounding environment can contribute to perpetuating environmental problems and conflict over or competition for resources. The influence of European colonial expansion left lasting consequences for the continent that have contributed to problems of corruption in some contemporary African states and the loss of positive cultural practices that were protective of the environment.[12] Corruption and weak governance regimes can have negative impacts on the natural environment when policies are put in place to profit the privileged rather than to protect public resources.

The colonial period also served to repress several African cultural practices, including some practices that emphasized a relationship with land that contributed toward more conscious conservation and husbandry efforts. While rejecting harmful cultural practices inconsistent with gender equality, many African women environmental activists are embracing positive aspects of culture that connect communities to land. African women environmental activists in Kenya called out the corruption of Daniel Arap Moi for passing rapacious land use policies that convert common public natural resources into private profits for the personal gain of an unrepresentative elite. The ecosystems and social systems of contemporary Africa were shaped by colonialism and are being reshaped by African women exercising their power and influence to adapt to the coming changes.

Climate Change and the African Continent

Climate change will impact ecosystems and social systems of Africa and will likely widen gaps between the privileged and the poor. The African continent is vulnerable to desertification. Many communities depend on natural resources that are becoming increasingly scarce due to climate change. According to the UN Environment Program (UNEP) most climate models predict drier conditions for the region in the future. The IPCC expects that the West African Sahel and Central Africa will experience among the highest temperature increases as the Earth's climate changes.[13]

In particular, climate change is placing tremendous strain on the already fragile ecosystem and social systems of the Sahel region of sub-Saharan Africa.

11 *See* M. E. Chamberlain, The Scramble for Africa (1974, 2nd ed.).

12 *See, e.g.*, Pierre Englebert & Denis Tull, *Post-conflict reconstruction in Africa: Flawed ideas about failed states*, Int'l Sec. 32:4, 106 (Spring 2008).

13 Integrated Regional Information Network, *Sahel: Backgrounder*, June 2, 2008, *available at* http://www.irinnews.org/report/78514/sahel-backgrounder-on-the-sahel-west-africa-s-poorest-region (last visited December 22, 2013).

A semi-arid area of land that spans nine African nations, the Sahel covers 3 million square kilometers and contains a population of approximately 58 million.[14] Senegal, Mauritania, Mali, Burkina Faso, Niger, Chad, Sudan, Somalia, Ethiopia, and Eritrea are the countries that currently make up the Sahel region.[15] The northern portions of Togo, Benin, Nigeria, and Ghana also all share Sahel-type terrain and climate.[16] In addition to the rise in temperatures, the population of the region is also projected to increase. The Permanent Interstates Committee for Drought Control in the Sahel (CILSS) projects that the region will be home to 100 million people by 2020.[17]

The CILSS estimates that a majority of the population of the Sahel is engaged in or depend on agriculture.[18] Agricultural production makes up more than 40 percent of the regions gross domestic product (GDP).[19] Vital food crops include millet, sorghum, various peas, and groundnuts.[20] The majority of low- and middle-income households in the region are subsistence farmers.

The subsistence farmers of the Sahel region depend on only three to four months of summer rainfall for agricultural production.[21] Climate change is expected to exacerbate existing water shortages. According to UNEP, the river basins of Senegal, Niger, and Chad have experienced a total water decrease of 40–60 percent. The "lean season," which normally spans from June to September, seems to be starting earlier and lasting longer.[22] When rain does fall, it falls with great intensity for a short time, causing floods that destroy crops and farming community settlements.[23]

In addition to lower and erratic rainfall volumes, the land degradation caused by deforestation, overgrazing, and desertification also contribute to challenges in areas dependent on agricultural production.[24] The Food and Agriculture Organization (FAO) has declared that 80 percent of the land in the Sahel is now degraded.[25]

[14] *Id.* The Sahel is "the Shore" in Arabic.

[15] Syngenta Foundation for Sustainable Agriculture, *available at* http://www.syngentafoundation.org/index.cfm?pageID=47 (last visited December 22, 2013).

[16] IRIN, *supra* note 13.

[17] *Id.*

[18] *Id.*

[19] *Id.*

[20] *Id. See also* Syngenta Foundation, *supra* note 15.

[21] IRIN, supra note 13.

[22] *See also* Africa Renewal Online, *Sahel: Surviving the lean season, available at* http://www.un.org/africarenewal/web-features/sahel-surviving-lean-season (last visited April 3, 2014).

[23] IRIN, supra note 13.

[24] *Id.*

[25] *Id.*

Long and persistent periods of drought in the Sahel and accompanying conflict in some countries have led to forced migration and displacement of the region's population. The violent conflict in Northern Mali has further complicated efforts to relieve food insecurity.[26] As farmers are forced out of the countryside and move to cities, additional pressures are put on urban infrastructure and sanitation.

Changes in the climate conditions of the Sahel have severe implications for food security and a range of human rights. Hunger is increasing across the region because rains are increasingly erratic, reducing pasture for livestock and the irrigation available for crops. Crop yields are down significantly as a consequence of drought conditions. Food prices are increasing. A 2011 World Food Program postharvest food security assessment in Chad determined that up to 3.5 million people were "food insecure."[27] Cereal production in Chad fell by 50 percent in one year.[28] In Mali an estimated 1.7 million people are at risk of hunger.[29] Conditions in Mali are further complicated by the violent conflict in the north of the country because thousands of refugees are flowing out of the country and fleeing to neighboring nations. According to the World Food Program, households in Senegal are reducing the number of meals.[30] Global Acute Malnutrition rates are above the "serious" threshold in some regions of Cameroon.[31] In the Gambia, overall crop production is estimated to have dropped by 62 percent since 2010.[32] Women and children in the region will be most affected by these expected ecosystem changes and the risk to rights that climate change presents.

The Consequences of Climate Change for African Women

Climate change is not neutral. The changing climate will have gendered effects.[33] Women in developing nations are among the poorest and least

26 UN World Food Programme, *Sahel crisis: 8 questions answered, available at* http://www.wfp.org/stories/sahel-crisis-8-questions-answered (last visited April 3, 2014).

27 UN. World Food Programme, *Sahel crisis: Country by country, available at* http://www.wfp.org/stories/sahel-crisis-by-country (last visited April 3, 2014).

28 *Id.*

29 *Id.*

30 *Id.*

31 *Id.*

32 *Id.*

33 For a discussion of the differential impact gender difference makes in climate change adaptation and mitigation *see, e.g.*, Ann Kobia Makena, *Climate change in Kenya is changing women's lives*, Third World Network (Climate change and its impacts have drastically affected the lives of rural women pastoralists in Kenya); Wendy Annecke, *Gender and climate change adaptation, available at* http://www.indigo-dc.org/documents/Adaptationandbeyond04small.pdf (last visited April 14, 2014); Jeannette D. Gurung, *Gender and desertification*, IFAD, *available*

privileged social groups. Worldwide, 70 percent of the 1.3 billion people living in poverty are women.[34] Of the "960 million illiterate people in the world, two-thirds . . . are women."[35] Women's poverty is caused by a myriad of factors: less pay, more work caring for others, less support, more vulnerability to violence, less access to education and economically gainful employment, and more gender discrimination.[36] Women's poverty can be further exacerbated by discriminatory codes of law or discriminatory social customs that erect barriers to equal opportunities to advance. Around the world, women's poverty and women's inequality will place them at greater risk and limit their capacity to respond to risks associated with a changing climate. Many African women already experience poverty and gender discrimination.

The social consequences of climate change are compounded by the poverty and discrimination that African women encounter in society. African women are vulnerable to the impacts of climate change because they are vulnerable to discrimination. From the division of labor in daily life to laws and customs that limit life chances by constraining access to education and economic opportunities, African women and girls confront barriers to their ability to enjoy basic human rights on equal terms with men.

at http://www.ifad.org/pub/gender/desert/gender_desert.pdf (last visited April 14, 2014); Constance Okollet, *Climate change is killing our people*, GUARDIAN, September 23, 2009.

34 UN Development Programme, *Resource guide on gender and climate change* 30 (2009), *available at* http://www.undp.org/content/undp/en/home/librarypage/womens-empowerment/resource-guide-on-gender-and-climate-change/ (last visited April 14, 2014) [hereinafter UNDP 2009].

35 *Id.* at 30 citing UNFPA (2008).

36 The Convention on the Elimination of All Forms of Discrimination against Women (CEDAW), which a number of African nations have ratified, offers the following definition of discrimination:

> [A]ny distinction, exclusion or restriction made on the basis of sex which has the effect or purpose of impairing or nullifying the recognition, enjoyment or exercise by women, irrespective of their marital status on a basis of equality with men and women of human rights and fundamental freedoms in the political, economic, social, cultural, civil or any other field.

See also UNDP *Resource guide on gender and climate change*, 2006 edition, at 26 (explaining: "Equality is achieved by means of gender equity understood as justice in how women and men are treated according to their respective needs. Gender equity means fairness of treatment for women and men, according to their respective needs"). UNDP uses gender equality in its publications, but explains that the reference also encompass the concept of equity as adopted in the framework of the human development paradigm. The shift to an understanding of equity "implies the possibility of differential treatments to correct inequalities: measures that are not necessarily equal but that result in equality in terms of rights, benefits, obligations and opportunities." *Available at* http://www.un.org/womenwatch/downloads/Resource_Guide_English_FINAL.pdf (last visited April 14, 2014) (citing UNDP 2006).

The gender discrimination African women confront in the division of labor and under certain customs and laws compromise their ability to avoid risk during disaster and their ability to adapt to climate change or to mitigate its impacts on their lives and livelihoods, as described next.

DISCRIMINATION AGAINST WOMEN. According to some estimates, women make up almost 90 percent of Africa's agricultural sector, yet they remain poor.[37] In large part, women's poverty is due to discriminatory laws. In Kenya, for example, until 2012, property laws restricted women's ability to own and control productive resources that could empower women to confront the challenges associated with climate change.[38] Until 2012, women in Botswana were not able to inherit property.[39] According to World Bank estimates published in 2011, there were 25 countries in Africa that recognized legal differences based on gender that may serve to limit women's economic opportunities and access to credit.[40]

Kenyan Nobel Laureate Wangari Maathai fought discrimination and deforestation by founding a women's social movement that planted trees, yet efforts by women to mitigate climate change impacts alone will not be sufficient unless systems of discrimination are confronted and dismantled. As African woman environmentalist Fatima Denton has observed: "There is little logic in involving women in environmental conservation and tree planting schemes when only a small percentage of women have control over land. Development policy has still not addressed the structural constraints that curtail women's access to control and ownership over resources. Nor has it been able to ensure that women's expertise in land or resource management is recognized or their

37 *See* UN WomenWatch, *Fact sheet: Women, gender equality and climate change* (2009), *available at* http://www.un.org/womenwatch/feature/climate_change/ (last visited April 14, 2014).

38 The International Women's Human Rights Clinic, Georgetown University Law Center, *Women's land and property rights in Kenya-moving forward into a new era of equality: A human rights report and proposed legislation*, 40 GEORGETOWN J. INT'L LAW 1 (2009); Janet Walsh, Human Rights Watch, *Double standards: Women's property rights violations in Kenya* (2003), *available at* http://www.hrw.org/sites/default/files/reports/kenya0303.pdf (last visited April 14, 2014).

39 *See* BBC, *Botswana women allowed to inherit*, October 12, 2012, *available at* http://www.bbc.co.uk/news/world-africa-19924723 (last visited April 14, 2014); and Pumza Fihlani, *The four sisters who took on Botswana's chiefs and won*, October 22, 2013, *available at* http://www.bbc.co.uk/news/world-africa-24623692 (last visited April 14, 2014).

40 UNDP, *Gender and climate change Africa Policy Brief 4: Gender, climate change and food security* (2012) [hereinafter UNDP 2012], *available at* http://www.undp.org/content/dam/undp/library/gender/Gender%20and%20Environment/Gender%20and%20Agriculture%20Policy%20Brief%204%20FNL.pdf (last visited April 14, 2014) (citing World Bank (2011).

efforts compensated through ownership of that land or resource."[41] Denton also says, "Gender inequalities continue to exist in terms of access to land, control over resources, ability to command and access paid labor, capacity, and strategies for income diversification."[42]

When given opportunities and access to resources, women are more apt to opt for a more equitable distribution of the benefits of their production. A UN Food and Agriculture Organization study on closing the gender gap in agriculture projects that the number of hungry people in the world could be reduced by up to 150 million people by providing women equal access to resources and financing opportunities.[43] Women are the recipients of just 5 percent of agricultural extension services worldwide, and women's ability to access credit is lower than that of men.[44] Women in Africa predominate in food production but own less than 10 percent of the land due to discriminatory laws and customs. With fewer economic resources, African women must work harder to adapt to the changes climate change will bring to the continent. Women's inequality will leave communities insufficiently equipped to adapt and vulnerable to food insecurity. Frequently, men are more mobile and can migrate, leaving farms to find employment elsewhere when crops fail. Women often remain behind to care for family members and are underresourced.

Women's inequality can also be a contributing factor in environmental degradation. For example, there is ample evidence that economically insecure individuals often resort to survival strategies that can take a negative toll on the environment, such as slash and burn agriculture or wildlife poaching.[45]

DIVISION OF LABOR: WOMEN'S WORK. The gendered division of labor will also contribute to the disparate impact climate change is expected to have on African women and girls. African women work long and hard hours to secure sustenance for themselves and for their families.

More than 100 million people in the developing world do not have access to safe drinking water. The UNDP reports that women in sub-Saharan Africa spend up to 40 billion hours annually working to find and transport water.[46]

[41] Fatma Denton, *Climate change vulnerability, impacts, and adaptation: Why does gender matter?*, GENDER AND DEVELOPMENT 10:2, 10(Jul. 2002) at 13.

[42] *Id.* at 17.

[43] Food and Agriculture Organization of the UN, *The state of food and agriculture: Women in agriculture-closing the gender gap* (2011), *available at* http://www.fao.org/publications/sofa/2013/en/ (last visited April 14, 2014).

[44] UNDP 2012, *supra* note 41.

[45] United Nations Environmental Program, Women at the Frontlines: Gender Risks and Hopes A Rapid Response Assessment (2011).

[46] UNDP 2009, *supra* note 34.

This is equivalent to a year's worth of labor by the entire workforce in France.[47] Water sources are increasingly scarce in the Sahel and elsewhere in Africa due to climate change, desertification, and deforestation. This means women will have still more work. As sources of water become more difficult to locate, women will have to look longer and go farther to find water resources. Women will be at greater risk of waterborne diseases.

Approximately 2 billion people in the world do not have access to energy sources.[48] In Africa, as elsewhere, it is women who find and gather firewood and other biomass products for fuel, spending up to nine hours each day finding fuel sources. According to UN estimates, nearly 60 percent of rural women in Africa are now facing a shortage of firewood.[49] This means more work for women.

Girls are often kept at home and out of school to help fetch and find water and fuel in rural areas. These girls will be at greater risk of missing educational opportunities as their workloads at home increase due to ecosystem changes. Education will be imperative for creating the capabilities to access employment and opportunities that can protect them from the impacts of climate change.

African women and girls are less able to confront climate change because of gender discrimination and the gendered division of labor that leaves them more vulnerable than men to the expected systemic disruptions to come. Without secure access to and control over the natural resources they labor to help cultivate, African women are less able to confront climate change on equal terms with men. African women and women of the Diaspora remain vulnerable to economic exploitation, as well as to sexual violence during the expected conflict and displacement climate change will cause. Insecurity will further complicate conditions for women. Gender discrimination has implications for Africa's ability to adapt to and mitigate the consequences of climate change.

Black women outside of Africa also confront challenges of a different order but due to the same source–discrimination.[50] In the aftermath of the emergency caused by Hurricane Katrina, African-American women and their children were disproportionately among those trapped in New Orleans by floodwaters.[51] Around the world, extreme weather events will affect men and

[47] *Id.* (citing Roberto Lenton, Albert M. Wright, & Kristen Lewis [2005]).
[48] UNDP 2009, *supra* note 34.
[49] *Id.*
[50] *See, e.g.*, Robert R. M. Verchick, *Risk, fairness, and the geography of disaster*, International Law Forum, Research Paper No. 1–07 (January 2007).
[51] UNDP 2009, *supra* note 34, at 57.

women in different ways in those areas where gender discrimination and general poverty are present. A study of disasters in 141 countries found that deaths are directly linked to gender differences and specifically to women's economic and social rights.[52] According to Neumayer and Plümper, in societies where women and men enjoy equal rights, disasters cause nearly the same number of deaths in both sexes. The numbers differ dramatically where inequalities exist. Their research confirmed that the difference in death rates was due to existing inequalities. They found boys are given preferential treatment over girls during rescue efforts.

All these facts should easily have led to the conclusion that climate policy and development programs must consider gender equality as a significant factor in creating legal frameworks. Yet an international environmental law of climate change that is truly inclusive of gender has been slow to evolve. Only recently have women's concerns been included in climate change negotiations. Although progress has been slow in policy circles, the power of African women to engage in collective action to accelerate initiatives to adapt to the changing climate is worthy of recognition. African women are increasingly influencing the global policy process. Whereas the language of legal and policy documents in the recent past omitted reference to gender difference, presently, the opportunities for combatting climate change make explicit reference to women's issues and interests essential. African women have contributed to the creation of a more inclusive international environmental law. The next section traces the evolution of selected international and regional instruments and shows a shift from omission to inclusion.

The Evolution of an Inclusive International Environmental Law

International environmental law has not been the product of a systematic plan or coherent strategy; rather, it is largely constituted by instruments crafted in response to risks or after a crisis.[53] As a result, the corpus of international law has evolved around collective efforts to address specific environmental threats. Indeed, "[n]either a universal declaration nor any generally applicable covenant currently establishes a binding set of principles or even a comprehensive framework for the field."[54] In the absence of a comprehensive framework, the development of international environmental law has been ad hoc and has not adequately addressed the environmental

52 *Id.* (Citing Neumayer and Plümper [2007]).

53 David Hunter, James Salzman, & Durwood Zaelke, INTERNATIONAL ENVIRONMENTAL LAW AND POLICY 463 (2006).

54 *Id.*

conditions of all the Earth's inhabitants in an equitable manner. Failure to appreciate the lived experience of African women has impoverished the field of international environmental law and inhibited the development of strategies to protect women against the harsh and disproportionate impact of climate change.

Although no comprehensive framework defines the field, and it has come to be composed of a range of disparate multilateral and regional instruments addressing specific risks, certain core concepts have emerged in international environmental law and are contained in several regional and international instruments that complement international human rights law and could address the unique challenges African women confront. There is a growing consensus around both the existence of a right to a healthy environment and a greater appreciation for the collective interest humanity shares in curbing activities that put the environment at risk: these are two core concepts contained in international environmental instruments that are consistent with the struggles of women in Africa and the Diaspora.

This section offers an assessment of the evolution of the international environmental legal instruments that address climate change. It then outlines the growing acceptance of the importance of a gender-based approach to crafting policies to address the challenges associated with climate change.

The Evolving International Environmental Law of Climate Change

Although some scholars note that the field of international environmental law has "neither a universal declaration nor any generally applicable covenant" that states binding principles or structures a comprehensive framework for approaching environmental problems,[55] the visionary 1972 Stockholm Declaration sets forth several concepts that inform current global climate change law and policy. The 1972 Stockholm Declaration on the Human Environment prepared the ground for a better understanding of the relationship of the preservation and enhancement of the environment to the enjoyment of basic human rights to take root. Article 1 of the Declaration proclaims that:

> Man is both creature and moulder of his environment . . . through the rapid acceleration of science and technology, man has acquired the power to transform his environment in countless ways and on an unprecedented scale. Both aspects of man's environment, the natural and the man-made,

[55] *Id.*

> are essential to his well-being and to the enjoyment of basic human rights the right to life itself.[56]

Although a soft law instrument, the 1972 Stockholm Declaration in its preamble provides a strong statement of the imperative of environmental protection. The Declaration calls attention to humanity's interdependence with the environment for "man is both creature and moulder of his environment."[57] Although humanity depends on the environment for sustenance, humanity has also developed the power to substantially alter the environment. The Declaration calls upon all "to exert common efforts for the preservation and improvement of the human environment, for the benefit of all the people and for their posterity."[58] The Stockholm Declaration was crafted to "inspire and guide the peoples of the world in the preservation and enhancement of the human environment," by providing "a common outlook and for common principles" to guide environmental protection.[59] It recognizes the right to a healthy environment, the importance of development, and the shared responsibility to preserve and protect the environment for present and future generations.[60]

Recognizing the existence of a right to a healthy environment, the Declaration proclaims the "common conviction" that:

> Man has the fundamental right to freedom, equality and adequate conditions of life, in an environment of a quality that permits a life of dignity and well-being, and he bears a solemn responsibility to protect and improve the environment for present and future generations.[61]

The Declaration declares the protection and improvement of the human environment to be the duty of all governments.[62] It further notes that environmental protection will require "the acceptance of responsibility by citizens and communities by enterprises and institutions at every level, all by sharing equitably in common efforts."[63] Although the Declaration speaks of equity and the fundamental rights possessed by man, it is telling and consistent with

56 *Id.* (emphasis added)

57 Stockholm Declaration on the Human Environment, U.N. Doc. A/Conf.48/14/Rev. 1(1973); 11 ILM 1416 1972), at 1(emphasis added), *available at* http://www.unep.org/Documents.Multilingual/Default.asp?documentid=97&articleid=1503 (last visited April 15, 2014).

58 *Id.*

59 *Id.*, Preamble, para. 1

60 *Id.*, Preamble, paras. 1, 6.

61 *Id.*, Principle 1(emphasis added).

62 *Id.*, para. 2.

63 *Id.*, para. 7.

the parlance of the time that its terms do not make explicit reference to woman. It would take decades of activism and awareness-raising on the part of African and other women before women's concerns were included in international environmental law and policy conversations. Women share responsibility for using land; therefore, it is important to educate and empower them. Women do their share and must be recognized for what they do to mitigate harmful environmental impacts and to create innovative adaptation to ecosystem changes. However, it would not be until 2012 that the international community would adopt a strong policy statement on gender equity in global environmental policy.

From this background, as early as 1972, environmental degradation was identified as a problem common to all, and there was an early acknowledgment that harms are different in different contexts. The Declaration recognizes that in developing countries most environmental harms are the result of underdevelopment, whereas in developed countries environmental harms are due to pollution associated with industrialization.[64] This difference between developing and developed nations continues to play out in policy circles today in contests over different countries establishing obligations to reduce their respective contributions to climate change. The realization that there is a common, but differentiated, responsibility to protect the natural environment notwithstanding, the developing world, particularly Africa, has been slow to evolve a strong environmental law framework. The absence of a strong regulatory framework and the presence of corruption leaves Africa's peoples to innovate solutions to problems created by weak regulatory frameworks and systems and the reckless practices of transnational corporations operating in the region that contribute to rights abuses and environmental degradation.

The Law of Climate Change

The Stockholm Declaration provided the structural and motivational template for the universalization of international environmental law. To the extent that international environmental law is made in reaction to crisis, there appears to be universal agreement that humanity is facing a major climate crisis. A few years after the Stockholm Declaration, the world's first climate conference was held in 1979.[65] Almost a decade later, the UN and the World Meteorological Organization formed the IPCC and charged it with the task of assessing and interpreting available scientific and economic data to

[64] *Id.*, Preamble, para. 4.
[65] *See* Hunter et al, *supra* note 54, at chapter 4.

"provide the world with a clear scientific view on the current state of knowledge in climate change and its potential environmental and socio-economic impacts."[66] The first report of the IPCC in 1990 informed the world of the magnitude and potential consequences of climate change and inspired the international community to act. The UN General Assembly established a negotiating committee to draft a binding legal instrument to regulate climate change.

INTERNATIONAL LEGAL INSTRUMENTS. The UN Framework Convention on Climate Change (UNFCCC), along with the UN Convention on Biological Diversity (UNCBD) and the UN Convention to Combat Desertification (UNCCD), all established and opened for signature at the 1992 Rio Earth Summit, are today the foundation for law and policy on the changing natural environment. The three conventions are interconnected, and a joint liaison organization was created in 2001 to further develop policy and programs in areas of mutual concern across all three treaties.[67] All three treaties are relevant to the lives of African women because threats to biodiversity and the risk of desertification will only increase as the climate changes.

The primary objective of the UNFCCC is to stabilize concentrations of greenhouse gases in the atmosphere and to structure measures to ease adaptation to expected changes in the climate. In pertinent part, the stated purpose of the UNFCCC is to ensure "stabilization of greenhouse gas concentrations in the atmosphere at a level that would prevent dangerous anthropogenic interference with the climate system ... within a time-frame sufficient to allow ecosystems to adapt naturally to climate change, to ensure that food production is not threatened and to enable economic development to proceed in a sustainable manner."

Provisions of the international climate change framework instruments could, if implemented in a manner that appreciated gender difference and that attempted to eradicate unfair gender discrimination, provide helpful support for African women working to sustain their livelihoods and families as they adapt to climate change. For instance, all states parties to UNFCCC committed to "[p]romote and cooperate in education, training and public awareness related to climate change and encourage the widest participation in

[66] Intergovernmental Panel on Climate Change homepage, *available at* http://www.ipcc.ch/organization/organization.shtml#.UjHygRZvAy8 (last visited April 15, 2014).

[67] United Nations Framework Convention on Climate Change, *Essential background, available at* http://unfccc.int/essential_background/convention/items/6036.php (last visited April 15, 2014).

this process, including that of non-governmental organizations."[68] Women and girls face discrimination in access to education. States parties agreed to "[p]romote and cooperate in the full, open and prompt exchange of relevant scientific, technological, technical, socio-economic and legal information related to the climate system and climate change, and to the economic and social consequences of various response strategies."[69] There is strong evidence that women are less likely to be included in information exchange.

In 1995, the international community came to the realization that targets set in the UNFCCC would not be sufficient to stop a rapidly accelerating rate of climate change and called for another series of negotiations. The subsequent Kyoto Protocol was adopted to facilitate compliance with the Convention's more ambitious emission reduction objectives spanning the period from 2005 to 2012. Going further, all states parties to the Kyoto Protocol assumed obligations to "[c]ooperate in and promote at the international level, and, where appropriate, using existing bodies, the development and implementation of education and training programmes, including the strengthening of national capacity building, in particular human and institutional capacities and the exchange or secondment of personnel to train experts in this field, in particular for developing countries, and facilitate at the national level public awareness of, and public access to information on, climate change."[70] Presumably, the call for cooperation contained in the Framework Convention and the Kyoto Protocol included women, but, in practice, women are excluded or underrepresented.

The UNFCCC is gender-neutral in its terms in that it does not explicitly make reference to gender difference. Common but differentiated responsibilities of nations based on differences among nations are acknowledged, but gender difference is not accorded similar appreciation. Discrimination on the basis of gender will make achieving the goals put forward in international instruments impossible. Failure to expressly recognize the role of gender in climate change and the contribution gender equality could make in the fight against climate change was a missed opportunity in 1992.

In contrast to the UNFCCC, the subsequent UNCCD, adopted in 1994, and the UNCBD, adopted in 1992, are notable for taking notice of women. The challenges women face and the contributions women make are acknowledged in the text of these conventions. More recently, subsidiary bodies have

[68] Kyoto Protocol to the United Nations Framework Convention on Climate Change, UN Doc FCCC/CP/1997/7/Add.1, Dec. 10, 1997; 37ILM 22 (1998), Art. 4, *available at* http://unfccc.int/resource/docs/convkp/kpeng.pdf (last visited April 15, 2014).

[69] *Id.*

[70] *Id.*

been set up to mainstream gender issues and to monitor progress toward achieving treaty aims.

The UNCCD. The UNCCD addresses land degradation and the growing risk of desertification. Not only does the UNCCD recognize the role women play in rural sustenance, it also promotes equal participation of women and men in efforts to reverse and prevent land degradation in drought-affected areas. The Preamble of the Convention notes "the important role played by women in regions affected by desertification and/or drought, particularly in rural areas of developing countries, and the importance of ensuring the full participation of both men and women at all levels in programmes to combat desertification and mitigate the effects of drought."[71] Unlike the UNFCCC, the UNCCD explicitly calls on states to accord attention to women. Article 5 on the Obligations of Affected Country Parties requires states to "promote awareness and facilitate the participation of local populations, particularly women, with the support of non-governmental organizations, in efforts to combat desertification and mitigate the effects of drought."[72]

The appreciation of the importance of including women that is expressed in the UNCCD is particularly pertinent in the African context, where women are often responsible for food production and water collection. Current projections show that Africa is expected to experience even greater desertification, particularly in the Sahel. The sustainable use of land is essential to prevent further degradation. African women are well-positioned to make a difference in addressing the problem of desertification, given the roles they play in rural society and the work they do.

The UNCBD. The UNCBD recognizes the importance of ecosystem biodiversity for the flourishing not only of plants and animals, but also of humanity. Unlike the UNFCCC, the UNCBD addresses the inclusion of women explicitly. The Convention notes the importance of inclusion in efforts to protect biodiversity, recognizing "the vital roles that women play in the conservation and sustainable use of biological diversity" and emphasizing "the need for the full participation of women at all levels of policymaking and implementation."[73] Subsequent conferences of the states parties for the

[71] Preamble, United Nations Convention to Combat Desertification, 1954 UNTS 3; 33 ILM 1328 (1994), *available at* http://www.unccd.int/en/about-the-convention/Pages/Text-overview.aspx (last visited April 17, 2014).

[72] *Id.*, Art. 5 (d).

[73] Preamble, United Nations Convention on Biological Diversity, 1760 UNTS 79; 31 ILM 818 (1992), *available at* http://www.cbd.int/doc/legal/cbd-en.pdf (last visited April 17, 2014).

convention (UNCBD COP) and affiliated working groups have also included reference to the role of women. The UNCBD Secretariat designated a Gender Focal Point and developed a Gender Plan of Action in cooperation with the International Union for the Conservation of Nature (IUCN). Among other things, the Plan aims to mainstream gender issues into the implementation of the Convention and the activities of the Secretariat and to promote gender equality in achieving the objectives of the Convention.[74]

AFRICAN REGIONAL INSTRUMENTS. The unfortunate neglect of women and women's issues in the international environmental regime is replicated in African regional environmental instruments. Nevertheless, African women continue to pursue regional, national, and local strategies to offset the increasing impacts of climate change.

The African Convention on the Conservation of Nature and Natural Resources (ACCNNR) and the Protocol to the African Charter on Human and Peoples' Rights on the Rights of Women in Africa (ACRWA) are particularly pertinent to women's experience of their natural and social environments. Taken together, these instruments direct policymakers to take proactive measures to include women in policy-making processes.

The objectives of the ACCNNR are threefold: (1) "to enhance environmental protection," (2) "to foster the conservation and sustainable use of natural resources," and (3) "to harmonize and coordinate policies" to achieve "ecologically rational, economically sound and socially acceptable development policies and programs."[75] States parties to the Convention assume the duty "to ensure that developmental and environmental needs are met in a sustainable, fair and equitable manner." States parties are to be guided by "the right of all peoples to a satisfactory environment favourable to their development" when undertaking initiatives to implement the Convention.

The ACCNNR contains provisions on land use[76] as well as water resource management.[77] Whereas the land use provision lists measures for states to take to control erosion and cultivate sustainable farming, it does not say anything about women.[78] Similarly, although the water resource management

[74] United Nations Convention on Biological Diversity, *Gender plan of action*, *available at* http://www.cbd.int/gender/decisions/planofaction.shtml (last visited April 17, 2014).

[75] The African Convention on the Conservation of Nature and Natural Resources, Art. II, *available at* http://www.au.int/en/sites/default/files/AFRICAN_CONVENTION_CONSERVATION_NATURE_AND_NATURAL_RESOURCES.pdf (last visited April 17, 2014).

[76] *Id.*, art. VI.

[77] *Id.*

[78] *Id.*, art. 3 (b).

provision lists measures for states to take to guarantee a suitable water supply through integrated resource management, the study of water cycles in catchment areas, and rational water husbandry in agriculture, it does not speak to women's challenges either. In light of the role of African women in food production and water gathering, the oversight points to a missed opportunity. Women's experiences enable them to obtain information about the natural environment that could inform effective policy and programmatic interventions.

Nowhere in its text does the ACCNNR make explicit reference to gender difference or gender equality; although it does speak of the right of all peoples to enjoy a satisfactory environment, it does not speak to the social environment. The text is gender-neutral and gender-blind. State obligations are not articulated with specific reference to equality of women on terms with men; rather, the ACCNNR provides that "the Parties shall adopt and implement all measures necessary to achieve the objectives of this Convention, in particular through preventive measures and the application of the precautionary principle, and with due regard to ethical and traditional values as well as scientific knowledge in the interest of present and future generations."[79] Too often, entrenched political authorities appeal to traditional values as justification for women's exclusion and inequality. Women's activists are attacked for failure to respect culture and tradition.

The Protocol to the ACRWA expands on the Article 2 equality provision of the African Charter on Human and Peoples' Rights that prohibits discrimination on the basis of sex, among other characteristics. The Protocol gives fuller expression to the Article 18 provision of the charter that calls on states parties to "eliminate discrimination against women and to ensure the protection of the rights of women as stipulated in international declarations and conventions."[80] The Preamble to the Protocol recognizes "the crucial role of women in the preservation of African values based on the principles of equality, peace, freedom, dignity, justice, solidarity and democracy."[81] To that end, the Protocol calls for special measures to be undertaken to ensure that the human rights of African women are respected.

The Protocol calls on states parties to actively combat all forms of discrimination against women by integrating "a gender perspective in their policy decisions, legislation, development plans, programmes and activities and all

79 *Id.*, art. IV.

80 Preamble, Protocol to the African Charter on Human and Peoples' Rights on the Rights of Women in Africa.

81 *Id.*

other spheres of life."[82] Moreover, the Protocol provides that states parties should "modify the social and cultural patterns of conduct of women and men through public education, information, education and communication strategies with a view to achieving the elimination of harmful cultural and traditional practices and all other practices which are based on the idea of the inferiority or superiority of either of the sexes, or on stereotyped roles for women and men."[83]

Particularly pertinent rights relevant to addressing climate change contained in the Protocol include the following: Article 9 on the Right to Participation in the Political and Decision-Making Process provides that states parties should take "specific positive action to promote participative governance and the equal participation of women in the political life of their countries through affirmative action"[84] such that "women are equal partners with men at all levels of development and implementation of State policies and development programmes."[85] Article 15 on the Right to Food Security calls on states parties to take measures to ensure women have: "access to clean drinking water, sources of domestic fuel, land, and the means of producing nutritious food."[86] Article 18 on the Right to a Healthy and Sustainable Environment provides that states parties should take measures to not only to ensure greater participation of women in environmental preservation and management. It also calls for the facilitation of women's participation in research and for women's access to new technologies and to investment capital for research.[87] Additionally, Article 18 also calls for the protection and development of women's indigenous knowledge systems.[88] Article 19 on the Right to Sustainable Development obligates states parties not only to introduce a gender perspective into planning and to ensure women's participation, but also calls upon states parties to ensure "women's access to and control over productive resources such as land and guarantee their right to property."[89]

African women have organized to realize the promise of gender equality and promote effective responses to the challenges associated with climate change. For example, the African Women Leaders in Agriculture and the Environment (AWLAE) works to gain recognition for women's contribution

[82] *Id.*, art. 2(1)(c).
[83] *Id.*, art. 2(2).
[84] *Id.*, art. 9(1).
[85] *Id.*, art. 9(1)(c).
[86] *Id.*, art. 15 (a).
[87] *Id.*, art. 18(b).
[88] *Id.*, art. 18(c).
[89] *Id.*, art. 19(b).

in agriculture and bring that contribution to the attention of policymakers and development planning.

On the domestic level, an increasing number of African countries are incorporating environmental rights protections into their constitutions. Recent research provides evidence that the recognition of environmental rights has been beneficial, resulting in safer water supplies, stronger regulation to protect against environmental damage, and more mandated remediation when the environment is polluted.[90] Africa appears to be trailing in taking environmental issues seriously, but Africa could be out front if the lead of women was followed. Certainly, the activism of African women is moving regional and international environmental law and policy on climate change forward.

Engendering Climate Change Governance: Women's Exclusion and Women's Inclusion

Whereas most international and regional instruments addressing environmental concerns relevant to the changing climate employed conventional male-centric language, which is erroneously presumed to be gender-neutral, there is a growing appreciation today that gender consciousness will be central to meeting the challenge of climate change. Greater awareness of the activities and activism of African women struggling to confront the realities of climate change enhances the importance of engendering climate change governance

Although the Seventh Conference of Parties produced a statement on gender inclusion, it was not implemented. Indeed, as African woman and environmental activists and climate scientist Fatma Denton observed, "Women are for the most part not well represented in environmental policy formation. The climate debate is perpetuating the under-valuation and misunderstanding of women's contribution to environmental management. While a great deal of lip service have [sic] been paid to women's indigenous knowledge of environmental management and soil preservation little is being done to integrate local knowledge into mainstream policy."[91] She also observes that "policies from a gender perspective tend not only to be minimal and unenforced, but are also created in isolation from other key development sectors, and therefore offer little potential for poor rural women to optimize their skills and make significant gains."[92]

90 David R. Boyd, *The constitutional right to a healthy environment*, Environment Magazine (July–August 2012).

91 Denton, *supra* note 41, at 12.

92 *Id.*

It was not until 2012, at the eighteenth meeting of the conference of states parties to the convention on climate change in Doha, that governments indicated a commitment to including women in the decisions to determine the future of the planet. In Doha, governments adopted a decision to promote gender balance and improve the participation of women in entities established pursuant to the Convention and its Protocol. Decision 23/CP.18 or the "COP-18 Gender Decision" calls on states parties to promote gender balance by improving women's participation and representation in climate negotiations. The Decision aims to incorporate gender perspectives by including women's voices and women's rights in order to ensure that climate policies are equitable and effective at both the international and national level.[93] Since the decision in Doha, the Secretariat of the UNFCCC has been charged with the responsibility to track gender balance in all UNFCCC constituted bodies and other relevant meetings. The Secretariat issued its first "Report on Gender Composition" on October 28, 2014. It reports data on the representation of women from regional groups and other party groupings and on the gender composition of party delegations to sessions of constituted bodies and to the bureau established under the Convention and its Kyoto Protocol.

Because gender-conscious policies have been proven to be more effective, UN Women projects that, if properly implemented, the COP-18 Gender Decision could have an important impact on both participation and representation of women, as well as a positive lasting influence on decisions and decision-making processes.

A 2013 report by UN Women and the Mary Robinson Foundation for Climate Justice, *The Full View: Advancing the Goal of Gender Balance in Multilateral and Intergovernmental Processes*, offers recommendations for a holistic approach to achieving gender balance.[94] The Report outlines the existing international legal instruments that promote gender equality and offers examples of local and global initiatives to include women in political processes and to offer women access to economic opportunities to inform implementation of the COP-18 Gender Decision. The Report notes that structural issues continue to impede women's equality and block the recognition of the positive contributions women can make to combat climate

[93] *See* Nathalie Eddy, *The COP 18 gender decision: A step towards gender equality in the climate regime*, Climate Pol'y & Prac., June 4, 2013, *available at* http://climate-l.iisd.org/guest-articles/the-cop-18-gender-decision-a-step-towards-gender-equality-in-the-climate-regime/ (last visited January 28, 2014).

[94] UN Women & The Mary Robinson Foundation for Climate Justice, *The full view: Advancing the goal of gender balance in multilateral and intergovernmental processes* (2013) [hereinafter Full View].

change. Systemic changes are required to overcome structural exclusions. The Report offers recommendations on achieving gender balance, enforcing gender balance, and assessing progress toward achieving gender balance.

Affirmative action policies are recommended to achieve gender balance in the composition of Convention and Protocol entities. The Report proposes a fixed gender-balance target of not less than 40 percent or more than 60 percent of male or female representatives for all existing and any new entities established pursuant to the Convention or Protocol.

To enforce gender balance in the composition of national delegations, the Report proposes the creation of a mechanism to sanction constituencies that do not respect the principle of gender parity in nominating women delegates. To encourage gender balance in national delegations, the report proposes that the creation of a fund be considered to support the participation of women delegates in Convention negotiations; the fund could be dedicated to cultivating women to serve as delegates.

To measure the success or failure of governments to meet the pledge to include the rights and voices of women in consideration of climate change policy, the Report recommends that a "robust" monitoring and reporting process be put in place to allow for assessment. Also recommended is the maintenance of a public online database of participation by the different genders, one disaggregated by regional grouping and ranked to permit comparative assessment toward achieving gender parity.

The Decision 23/CP 18 on gender equality is rooted in the experience of African women and builds on their advocacy. If implemented, the Decision holds promise. Mxakato-Diseko has said that "this decision honours, acknowledges and addresses the collective concerns women have about climate change and it endeavors to deliver a better tomorrow for them, their communities, and the world."[95]

African Women as Agents of Engendering International Environmental Law

African women, although vulnerable, are also vital to the creation of viable solutions for the challenges associated with climate change. African women possess wisdom about the changing natural environment from their experience of laboring in unforgiving environments; that wisdom should inform policy. African women are vital stakeholders in the international laws and

[95] *Id.* at 3.

policies that will impact their cultures and communities.[96] The activism of African women has reinvigorated discussions of gender equality in climate change policy-making in recent years. For example, African women played an instrumental role at the international level in the processes that led to the recent adoption of an express policy commitment to promote gender inclusion in government efforts to combat climate change. The local grassroots activism of the women of the Green Belt Movement in Kenya attracted global attention. Before women in Nigeria led a successful movement to end the flaring of natural gas by oil companies operating in the Niger Delta, the area emitted more greenhouse gases into the atmosphere than the entire sub-Saharan region combined.[97] The work of African women to cope with the changing climate and to change those policies and practices that undermine the enjoyment of environmental rights offers an instance of international law from the "bottom up."[98]

MAITE NKOANA-MASHABANE AND THE SEVENTEENTH CONFERENCE OF THE UNFCCC: FROM DURBAN TO DOHA. In 2011, South Africa hosted the seventeenth conference of states parties to the UNFCCC (COP 17) in Durban. Maite Nkoana-Mashabane, a black South African woman, presided over the seventeenth conference of states parties in her capacity as South Africa's Minister of International Relations and Cooperation. In Durban, under her leadership, delegates from participating states parties were introduced to the African traditions of *Indaba* and *Ubuntu*. According to Nkoana-Mashabane, this approach served to "create the space for real conversations" among parties.[99] An *Indaba* is a gathering that brings the community together to confer on issues of importance, whereas *Ubuntu* recognizes and respects the interrelationships between living beings, often expressed as, "I exist because

[96] *See* Iris Berger, *Decolonizing women's activism: Africa in the transformation of international women's movements*, *available at* http://wasi.alexanderstreet.com/help/view/decolonizing_womens_activism_africa_in_the_transformation_of_international_womens_movements?printable (last visited April 14, 2014).

[97] *Women in Nigeria: Agents for change in* UNDP 2009, *supra* note at 34, at 44 (citing Turner & Brownhill [2006]; The Niger Delta Women's Organization for Justice organized political awareness workshops for women, challenged the rapes and assassinations of environmental activists in the region, and are credited with contributing to the cancellation of a corporation's license to operate in the region and a court order to end natural gas flaring in the western area of the Niger Delta).

[98] For a discussion of the role of social movements in making law, *see* Balakrishnan Rajagopal, INTERNATIONAL LAW FROM BELOW: DEVELOPMENT, SOCIAL MOVEMENTS AND THIRD WORLD RESISTANCE (2003).

[99] Opening Address by COP17/CMP7 President, Minister Maite Nkoana-Mashabane, COP18/CMP8 Opening Ceremony, Doha, Qatar, November 26, 2012.

you exist."[100] Nkoana-Mashabane and other activists brought the existence of African women and their challenges in the context of a changing climate to the attention of participating states parties.

In preparation to host the international community for COP 17, South Africa held a consultative dialog on the impact of climate change on women of the African continent. Women representing grassroots organizations from across Africa gathered together in South Africa to confer. The women gathered determined that they would demand to become equal partners at every stage of climate change policy-making. African women sounded the call for the international community to remedy its failure to mainstream gender concerns throughout the policy-making process from negotiation to implementation.

It was the black women of South Africa, with their experience and exposure to inequality and exclusion, who further sensitized policymakers to the perils of exclusion in the process of planning solutions to the challenges facing the human family from climate change. Consultations conducted by African women served to bring forward the need for gender equity issues, the consequences of climate change, and the capacity of women to meet challenges with resilience.

Ambassador Nozipho Mxakato-Diseko, a black South African woman and ambassador at large to the seventeenth gathering of states parties, wrote of her experience, "As South Africans, having been exposed to the vagaries of the apartheid regime, with its patriarchal nature, we then undertook to raise the empowerment of women in the climate change negotiations, but also to ensure that women receive wider attention and support in the process in general."[101] After her consultations with other South African women, the ambassador advocated for the conference of states parties to address the continued absence of women and their concerns in the international discussions on climate change policy. She explained: "I was struck by how women were disproportionally affected by the effects of climate change, and also by how much women themselves were doing to adapt to these effects. These women, who are mainly marginalised from the processes of negotiating a global climate change regime, called on us as women leaders to ensure that their needs were addressed as well as their contributions acknowledged and built upon."[102]

These conversations with South African women, women of Africa, and women from around the world culminated in the volume "*Thuto ya Batho*":

[100] *Id.*
[101] Full View, *supra* note 97, at 3.
[102] *Id.*

Teachings from the People: Women Adapt to Climate Change.[103] It provides testament to the innovative and ingenious strategies women on the African continent and elsewhere have devised to deal with the effects of climate change. Nkoana-Mashabane launched the publication at the eighteenth conference of parties in Doha. In her opening address to the conference, she emphasized the importance of staying true to the legacy of Durban in Doha by remembering "ordinary people, especially women who are on the frontline, who daily face the harsh realities of climate realities on the ground, while we as negotiators and political leaders discuss these issues, sometimes with questionable urgency, in isolation, and in air- conditioned rooms, global responses that could address their plight."[104] Doha did produce a groundbreaking decision on gender inclusion.

Teachings of the People presents examples of the engagement of women from around the developing world in creating adaptation initiatives. It offers examples of women in Africa and other regions using networks and transferring their knowledge to adapt to the changing environment. Women and girls are involved in climate change adaptation initiatives in their communities and are working to solve problems associated with the changing environment despite discriminatory barriers that impede innovation.

African women and girls are innovating in their communities to preserve natural resources, to develop opportunities to generate income, and to increase human security. In Senegal, women farmers have increased their productivity through the use of water retention technologies to enhance soil conservation. Women in the rural regions of the Ndiass plateau in Senegal, who are experiencing the impact of heavy rainfalls, have constructed water flow control structures, including curved canals and infiltration ditches, to capture pools of surface water and reduce soil erosion. Groundwater levels have increased and, as soils stabilize, crop yields have increased.[105] Senegalese woman are also regenerating mangroves and leading reforestation activities and land restoration efforts, increasing sustainable fuel wood supplies to their communities and creating the potential for income from timber sales. In Senegal, "conservation and rehabilitation of ecosystem services have shown relatively quick results in reducing the impacts of extreme weather and worsening environmental conditions."[106]

[103] Maite Nkoana-Mashabane, "Thuto ya Batho" Teachings from the People: Women Adapt to Climate Change (2012) [hereinafter Teachings].

[104] Nkoana-Mashaane, Opening Address COP18/CMP 8.

[105] Teachings, *supra* note 103, at 55.

[106] *Id.*

In Kenya, women have undertaken "climate-smart" agroforestry. Agroforestry is the practice of combining the planting of food crops and tree crops. As a response to variable rainfall, the agroforestry approach aims to capitalize on planting fast-growing trees with crop fields to provide shade and enhance soil carbon; this improves the ability of the soil to hold moisture and protects crops from desiccation during droughts.[107] In Liberia, women are working to overcome inadequate infrastructure and transportation systems so that they can get their perishable agricultural goods to market more quickly and reduce food spoilage. Women have become stakeholders in infrastructure development projects and have joined in road construction work.[108] In Malawi, the Women's Land Rights in Southern Africa Project is working with chiefs to ensure that landless women are allocated rights to land ownership.[109] In Uganda, women are experimenting with "zero-grazing" dairy goats in response to droughts that have diminished the quality and availability of grasslands.[110] In South Africa, girls living in informal periurban settlements have taken the lead in disaster risk reduction and response initiatives.[111]

In Mozambique, women are using portable wooden hives to attract indigenous wild bees and are harvesting honey. Personal consumption improves household nutrition for children, the honey is also used for its antibacterial properties, and proceeds from the sale of surplus honey provide additional economic benefit for families.[112]

Understanding that the challenge of climate change is not confined to international conferences and negotiations, Nkoana-Mashabane explained that her aim in publishing *Teachings of the People* was to educate policymakers on how people are negotiating the changes: "[W]hile climate negotiators struggle to agree on global policies, local communities are setting an example by working together and finding practical solutions to adapt to a changing environment."[113] Her work shows that "local environments are often the incubators of innovation."[114] It invites policymakers to draw lessons from

[107] *Id.* at 56.

[108] *Id.* at 60.

[109] *See* ActionAid Malawi *Annual report* 2010 and NiZA & ActionAid International 2009, *Women's land rights in southern Africa: Consolidated baseline findings from Malawi, Mozambique, South Africa, Zambia and Zimbabwe available at*, http://www.actionaid.gr/files/File/Downloads/Womens%20Land%20Rights%20Report%20Final.pdf (last visited April 17, 2014).

[110] TEACHINGS, supra note 106, at 43.

[111] *Id.* at 45.

[112] *Id.* at 39.

[113] *Id.* at 5.

[114] *Id.* at 17.

women's lived experiences, which are linked to their local environments because "women's home-grown innovations, by their very nature, tend to be systems-based and congruent with the cultural and ecological conditions from which they have arisen ... a quality that exogenous innovations, however sophisticated, seldom achieve."[115]

Teachings also emphasizes the importance of removing the constraints on women's capacity to innovate, constraints created by unfair gender discrimination, in order to avoid the risk that coping strategies may become "maladaptive" and destabilizing. Women are well-positioned to lead local, incremental approaches that are more likely to be sustainable when they are congruent with existing local knowledge systems. Accordingly, it is important to ensure that women are included as active participants in decision-making processes. Finally, *Teachings* cautions that development strategies that prioritize technology transfer as a comprehensive solution to risk but that fail to be context-appropriate and gender-sensitive will fail: "inappropriate technologies end up discarded like old tractors rusting underneath the trees."[116] The international community would do well to learn the important lessons contained in these teachings from some of the most vulnerable people on the planet.

WANGARI MAATHAI AND THE GREEN BELT MOVEMENT. In many ways, it is possible to see the COP 18 statement as an extension of the lessons of the life work of Wangari Maathai. The legacy of the late Nobel Laureate Wangari Maathai, who founded the Green Belt Movement in 1986, exemplifies a holistic approach to addressing environmental challenges that informs more recent developments in international law and policy-making. In her native Kenya, the rapid disappearance of the forests was compromising the lives and livelihood of people living in rural communities. Maathai chose to confront the challenges associated with environmental degradation through creating opportunities for women, opportunities that helped to promote both sustainable development and gender equality. She devoted her life to fighting deforestation. Her work was not without detractors. Frequently, her devotion meant placing her life at risk. She rejected policies created through undemocratic and corrupt processes that compromised Kenya's natural environment and the well-being of women and girls.

In 2004, Maathai became the first environmentalist and the first African woman to be awarded the Nobel Peace Prize. Although her life began

[115] *Id.*
[116] *Id.* at 20.

humbly, she achieved many firsts for a Black woman. Born in rural Kenya, Maathai was the first African woman from the East and Central Africa region to earn a doctorate. After studies in the United States and Europe, she became the first woman to chair an academic department at the University of Nairobi.

She was recognized by the Nobel Committee for her innovative work against the odds to promote democracy, protect human rights, and preserve the natural environment. In awarding the prize to an African woman, the Nobel Committee provided a platform for Maathai to expose a global audience to the challenges Black women face and the ways women have faced those challenges and forced changes to ensure a more sustainable future. She thanked the Nobel Committee, explaining that in awarding her the prize, the Committee "placed the critical issue of environment and its linkage to democracy and peace before the world. ... Recognizing that sustainable development, democracy and peace are indivisible is an idea whose time has come."[117] Maathai used her platform as prizewinner to place the interrelationships among environmental conservation, sustainable development, democracy, and peace on the agenda of the international community. She began with the small seed of an idea to produce sustainable wood for fuel and to prevent soil erosion. She cultivated the idea into a campaign to mobilize women to plant more than a million trees. The Green Belt Movement she started with rural Kenyan women grew to include a range of issues related to gender equality.

Maathai's tree planting campaign was not without detractors, and she had to overcome many obstacles, including low expectations of women's abilities. Maathai recalled in an interview that "It took me a lot of days and nights to convince people that women could improve their environment without much technology or without much financial resources."[118] In her Nobel lecture, she explained: "Initially, the work was difficult because historically our people have been persuaded to believe that because they are poor, they lack not only capital, but also knowledge and skills to address their challenges. Instead they are conditioned to believe that solutions to their problems must come from 'outside.'"[119] Climate change is a problem largely created outside of the continent of Africa, but keenly felt there. Nevertheless, Maathai's work

[117] Wangari Maathai, Nobel Laureate, *Nobel Lecture in Oslo, Norway* (December 10, 2004), *available at* http://www.nobelprize.org/nobel_prizes/peace/laureates/2004/maathai-lecture-text .html (last visited September 13, 2013; hereinafter *Nobel Lecture*).

[118] BBC News, *Profile: Wangari Maathai*, February 8, 2004. Also, http://news.bbc.co.uk/2/hi/africa/ 3726084.stm (last visited April 17, 2014).

[119] Maathai, *Nobel Lecture*, *supra* note 117.

demonstrated that African women do possess the agency to adapt and to address the problems associated with a changing environment.

Other obstacles included express opposition to her work on the part of powerful men in Kenya. Her former husband was said to have remarked that she was "too educated, too strong, too successful, too stubborn and too hard to control."[120] When she became a prominent opponent of urban industrial and commercial development that would have destroyed the Kenyan capital's main green space, Uhuru Park, she was threatened. Although she ultimately succeeded in persuading the government to abandon the plans and preserve the capital's green spaces, Maathai was arrested several times. Maathai and her movement began to evolve and to challenge corrupt governance that privileged unfair economic arrangements and benefited a few at the expense of a great many Africans. She was met with violence when she mobilized Black women to challenge injustice. She was once beaten unconscious by Kenyan police. President Daniel Arap Moi's government denounced Maathai for her activism.

Maathai overcame these obstacles to become a model for similar movements across the African continent and around the world. The work done at COP 17 by Nkoana-Mashabane and Mxakato-Diseko was consistent with her legacy in its appreciation for the role of culture in creating sustainable policies and for the contributions of African women to the creation of solutions.

Maathai was uniquely and distinctly African in her approach to addressing environmental problems because she recognized and responded to the problems that Black women in rural Kenya shared. For example, Maathai explained how her work had been grounded firmly in her experiences as an African woman: "[M]y inspiration partly comes from my childhood experiences and observations of Nature in rural Kenya. . . . As I was growing up, I witnessed forests being cleared and replaced by commercial plantations, which destroyed local biodiversity and the capacity of the forests to conserve water. . . . I came to understand that when the environment is destroyed, plundered or mismanaged, we undermine our quality of life and that of future generations."[121] In her lifetime, she saw the stream from which she had fetched water dry up, forcing women to walk increasingly greater distances for water. In conversations with rural women, Maathai learned of ecosystem changes through the lived experience of rural African women. In response to concerns raised by women, she took up the challenge of creating ways to mitigate and adapt to the changing environment. She learned that the rural Kenyan women

[120] BBC News, *supra* note 122.
[121] Maathai, *Nobel Lecture*, *supra* note 121.

who were responsible for fetching water and gathering firewood for fuel were increasingly having trouble finding the resources their families needed to subsist.

Maathai mobilized poor rural women by appealing to their sense of responsibility for family and community. She drew on the ability of Black women to respond to adversity and to rely on their wisdom, despite their lack of access to resources. Women in rural Kenya knew their environment was changing. Women knew water and forest resources were diminished. Through her leadership, women's activism created a democratic space in which people could challenge the corruption in resource allocations that endangered their way of life and be effective despite resistance from powerful interests.

Collectively, poor rural women exerted their power to create change in Kenya, and they inspired other women across Africa. Under Maathai's leadership, through public participation in protest actions to attract the attention of policymakers, Black women worked to hold those in power to account for the changes that resulted in harmful environmental consequences. She led a demonstration of naked women on one occasion.

Women of the Green Belt Movement planted trees as acts of celebration. As Maathai explained in her Nobel lecture, "the tree became a symbol for the democratic struggle in Kenya. Citizens were mobilized to challenge widespread abuses of power, corruption and environmental mismanagement. In Nairobi's Uhuru Park, at Freedom Corner, and in many parts of the country, trees of peace were planted to demand the release of prisoners of conscience and a peaceful transition to democracy."[122]

Culture is often condemned in scholarly literature as an impediment to gender equality. A litany of materials attributes the abuse and rights violations visited upon African women to religion or African culture and custom. Yet Maathai consistently claimed to operate in a manner deeply rooted in her culture and tradition. She combatted cultures of corruption and greed and worked to create "culture of peace," deploying the symbolism of trees to reclaim a positive image shared across various African traditions. She explains in her Nobel lecture:

> During the ongoing rewriting of the Kenyan constitution ... trees of peace were planted in many parts of the country to promote a culture of peace. Using trees as a symbol of peace is in keeping with a widespread African tradition. For example, the elders of the Kikuyu carried a staff from the thigi

[122] *Id.*

> tree that, when placed between two disputing sides, caused them to stop fighting and seek reconciliation. Many communities in Africa have these traditions. Such practices are part of an extensive cultural heritage, which contributes both to the conservation of habitats and to cultures of peace.[123]

Maathai reminded her fellow Africans that degradation was due in part to a failure to remember respect. She maintained that the colonial period repressed cultures, forcing many Africans on the continent and elsewhere to reject their traditional cultures for a promise of modernity and progress. In the process, Africans lost the positive and protective aspects of their cultures. As a result, according to Maathai: "[w]ith the destruction of these cultures and the introduction of new values, local biodiversity is no longer valued or protected and as a result, it is quickly degraded and disappears."[124] Therefore, Maathai called for a "cultural biodiversity" that would, at root, rely on and respect the knowledge and experience of Black women who work to cultivate indigenous seeds and medicinal plants.

At the same time, Maathai rejected those aspects of culture that would constrain her or relegate her to submission as a woman and a wife. Indeed, she was well aware that her vision of environmental justice would require an evolution in human consciousness. Her vision of justice also required cooperation and collective action.

In her Nobel lecture, Maathai emphasized the importance of collective action to confront the challenges of ecosystem change, the interrelationship of respect for human rights and for the environment, and the contributions of women to creating change. Although she won the prize, she credited it to "the work of countless individuals and groups across the globe. They work quietly and often without recognition to protect the environment, promote democracy, defend human rights and ensure equality between men and women. By so doing, they plant the seeds of peace."[125]

Conclusion: From Environmental Law to a Law of Environmental Rights

The early omission of women in climate change law and policy-making was a missed opportunity. Because climate change responses tended to reflect the priorities of powerful developed nations, policymakers did not pay sufficient attention to women in poverty. Most international and regional instruments

[123] *Id.*
[124] *Id.*
[125] *Id.*

addressing environmental concerns relevant to the changing climate were gender-neutral. There is a growing appreciation today that gender consciousness will be central to meeting the challenge of climate change. The problem of continued gender blindness will result in deadly bias with respect to the evolution of environmental rights. Unfair distribution of access to resources and opportunities continues to plague women and limit possibilities for participation. Greater awareness of the activities and activism of African women struggling to confront the realities of climate change shows the importance of engendering climate change governance. Perhaps more than any other group, African women are honoring the core tenets of the Stockholm Declaration. The COP-18 Gender Decision is a promising development. The leadership and advocacy of African women has made a difference in current developments.

Combating climate change will require collective action. African women's leadership on issues associated with the changing environment has been characterized by communication and cooperation. African women leaders at the national and international level have sought to challenge patriarchy by promoting inclusion and appealing to those more egalitarian impulses in African culture that emphasize community welfare and well-being. Acting in their local contexts to meet the challenges of a changing environment, African women are experimenting with innovative ways to adapt to changing environmental conditions.

This chapter has shown that African women are resourceful in using the limited resources they have. This chapter has presented examples of the ways in which Black women have resisted discrimination and demonstrated resilience in the face of poverty, environmental degradation, and discrimination. Despite these barriers, African women continue to work to protect the natural environment and to dismantle those discriminatory laws, policies, and practices that place their security at greater risk in the context of a changing climate.

More must be done to remove the discriminatory barriers Black women in Africa and in the Diaspora confront, barriers that compromise their security and ability to enjoy human rights. Barriers to control over resources, barriers to education in farming and food production, and barriers to effective participation in policy-making and planning for disaster preparedness remain and must be removed.

Inequality instructs us that a rights framework is warranted in crafting climate change policy. The right to a healthy environment was not included in the documents that form the foundation of contemporary human rights law. Neither the Universal Declaration of Human Rights, the International

Covenant on Civil and Political Rights, nor the International Covenant on Economic, Social, and Cultural Rights makes explicit reference to the right to a healthy environment. However, the Vienna Declaration invites appreciation of the interdependent, indivisible, and interrelated way in which the enjoyment of rights are placed at risk. Increasingly, there is a greater appreciation of the interrelationships among sustainability, human rights, and gender equality. Connecting the environment to a rights analysis has been unconventional, but, although not commonplace, it is gaining currency as the right to a healthy environment is increasingly recognized in the constitutions of countries around the world. The approach of African women to the challenge of climate change values interconnection and interdependence. Policies crafted to integrate respect for human rights would be most consistent with the spirit of the Stockholm Declaration's recognition of a right to a healthy environment as central to the basic right to life itself. Insight into what would be required to protect, respect, and fulfill rights is offered in the ways African women are responding to the challenge of climate change and working to inform a more inclusive body of international environmental law and policy.

ACKNOWLEDGMENTS

Thanks to Jess Morrison, Shruti Bhutani, and Felicity Murphy for research assistance.

PART III

FEMININE SOVEREIGNTY

11

Black Women and the Development of International Reproductive Health Norms

Judith A. M. Scully

In the past several decades, nongovernmental organizations (NGOs)[1] have used their consultative status[2] with the United Nations to lobby the UN General Assembly and other organizations affiliated with the UN to pass resolutions, develop treaties, and place new issues on the UN agenda. In their consultative status, NGOs bring important public concerns to the attention of governments, monitor government accountability on various issues, and encourage participation of stakeholders on the community level. They also produce reports with policy recommendations and provide direct assistance to communities.

In September 1994, the UN coordinated an International Conference on Population and Development (ICPD) in Cairo, Egypt. More than 20,000 delegates from various governments, UN agencies, NGOs, and the media gathered for a discussion of a variety of population issues, including immigration, infant mortality, abortion, birth control, family planning, and the education of women. The conference received considerable media attention due to

[1] A nongovernmental organization (NGO) is a not-for-profit organization that is independent from government and is organized on a local, national, or international level to address issues that support the public good. NGOs have been partners in the UN process since 1947. Article 71 of the UN Charter expressly acknowledges the role of NGOs in international law and development: "The Economic and Social Council [hereafter referred to as ECOSOC] may make suitable arrangements for consultation with nongovernmental organizations, which are concerned with matters within its competence."

[2] Through Article 71, the role of NGOs in the UN is limited to one of consultation with governments. Although it is often argued that NGOs are the voice of the people, representing grassroots democracy, many people argue that NGOs often reinforce existing power structures. However, due to the close ties that most NGOs have to the on-the-ground realities of people and the fact that they are required to exclude government officials from their membership, NGOs normally represent the voice of people in a landscape of money and power. To be recognized as an NGO with consultative status with the UN, an NGO must have a democratic decision-making process.

disputes regarding a woman's right to access abortion services.[3] Despite the widely publicized controversy, conference delegates managed to achieve consensus on a variety of issues including (a) universal primary education in all countries by 2015, (b) reduction of infant and child mortality by one-third by 2000, (c) reduction of maternal mortality by 50 percent by 2015, and (d) the need for access to reproductive and sexual health services, including family planning, for all women.[4]

The 1994 ICPD was a milestone in the history of population and development, as well as in the history of women's rights. The Programme of Action[5] that was developed at the ICPD was the first UN document to prioritize reproductive and sexual health services for women.[6] This conference was followed by the 1995 Fourth UN World Conference on Women (FWCW). The NGO Forum for the FWCW[7] lasted more than three weeks and included approximately 30,000 women (and several dozen men) who discussed and

[3] The abortion issue received great media attention primarily because the Vatican sent a representative to the conference to ensure that no consensus regarding a universal right to abortion would ever be accepted. News headlines indicated that the Vatican had "hijacked" the ICPD Cairo conference. *See* Kim Murphy, *Abortion accord unravels at talks: Population: There are charges that the Vatican has "hijacked" Cairo conference. A new compromise is sought as some Latin nations oppose consensus*, September 8, 1994, Los Angeles Times, *available at* http://articles.latimes.com/1994-9-08/news/mn-36010_1.cairo-conference. *Also see* Meredith Marshall, *United Nations Conference on Population and Development: The road to a new reality for reproductive health*, 10 Emory Int'l. L. Rev. 443, 451 (1996). The pope also directly entered the spotlight by sending a written letter to the secretary general of the ICPD. In his letter, the pope condemned abortion as "deliberate and direct killing." The letter denounced murder and genocide and singled out abortion, declaring that "[a]mong all the crimes which can be committed against life, procured abortion has characteristics making it particularly serious and deplorable." The pope went on to assert that protecting the woman's health or ensuring a decent standard of living for other members of the family "can never justify" abortion. *See Letter of His Holiness John Paul II to the Secretary General of the International Conference on Population and Development, available at* http://www.vatican.va/holy_father/hoh_paul_ii/letters/1999/documents/hf-jp-il-let-19031994_population_develop_en.html/; and Jyoti Shankar Gingh, Creating a New Consensus on Population: The International Conference on Population and Development (1998).

[4] Report of the ICPD (94/10/18), *available at* http://www.un.org/popin/icpd/offering/ poa.html.

[5] The ICPD Programme of Action (1995) is also referred to as the Cairo Consensus. It is available at www.unfpa.org/public/site/global/publications/picd/1973.

[6] Rebecca Cook, Bernard Dickens, & Mahmoud Fathalla, Reproductive Health & Human Rights: Integrating Medicine, Ethics, and Law 4, 148–49 (2003).

[7] The NGO Forum on Women was held in Hairou, China, at the same time that the official delegates to the FWCW were meeting in Beijing (approximately forty-five miles away). The NGO Forum brought together more than 20,000 women from 170 countries to discuss progress toward the goals of equality, development, and peace. Throughout this article, we refer to the NGO Forum as the FWCW. Participants at the NGO Forum included grassroots activists, educators, students, policymakers, and prominent leaders from all over the world who shared a concern about the human rights of women. Plenary sessions featured speakers from around the world, including Nobel Prize winners and other women who have been active in the

debated human rights issues affecting women and girls around the world.[8] The Beijing Declaration and Platform for Action, approved in September 1995 at the FWCW, is a global commitment to achieving equality, development, and peace for women worldwide. It covers a variety of issues and, with the Programme of Action developed at the ICPD, it is the most important document governing the progress of women's reproductive health worldwide.

Black women from the United States, the Caribbean, and Africa were well represented at the FWCW NGO forum.[9] It was a historic moment for the 45,000 global sisters who gathered for three weeks of open workshops, protests, and symposiums.[10] Not only was the FWCW historic because it was one of the largest UN conferences of its kind, it was also one of the first UN conferences at which African and African-American women were consistently key players on the international front and held the captive attention of their global peers around issues related to reproductive health. Consequently, this chapter examines the impact of Black women on the international reproductive health movement, particularly the infusion of reproductive health principles into the international human rights regime.

BLACK WOMEN AND THE INTERNATIONAL REPRODUCTIVE HEALTH MOVEMENT

Three of the forty-five official U.S. delegates to the FWCW were Black women, including Atlanta businesswoman J. Veronica Biggins, who served as vice chair of the American delegation. Of the more than 8,000 Americans attending the NGO Forum, an estimated 1,000 delegates were Black.[11] The largest grouping of Black American women came out of the joint delegation of the Lawyers' Committee for Civil Rights under Law and the National Council

international feminist movement for several decades. The UN Conference brought together heads of state and government officials to debate and draft a Platform for Action to address women's needs and human rights across the globe. Although the Platform for Action is not a binding document, governments are expected to commit resources to enact the policies it outlines on the national level after the conference. Thus, the document is designed to serve as a guide for national legislation and to help shape international priorities in the future. Communication between the NGO Forum participants and the government officials at the UN Conference was constant.

8 *See* http://www.un.org/geninfo/bp/women.html.

9 *See Voices of African American women in the United States of America: The unkept promises of the Platform for Action compiled by Lawyers' Committee for Civil Rights Under Law,* Barbara Armwine, Executive Director, Adjoa Aiyetoro, Editor (May 2000); and *Black women and the World Conference*, Ebony (December 1995), *available at* findarticles.com/plarticles/mi_mt077/is_n2_v51/al_17934730/?tag=content;col1.

10 *Id.* (refers to Ebony article at 43–44).

11 *Id. at* 44.

of Negro Women, which had a combined total of 110 delegates.[12] Hundreds of Black women from Africa and the Caribbean were also instrumental in bringing issues of significance to Black women worldwide to the forefront of discussions at the conference.[13]

It was women of African descent and women from developing countries who lobbied and educated participants at the NGO forums about the ways race and economics impacted reproductive health and overall well-being. Their life stories challenged more privileged women (i.e., White women and women with economic resources) to expand their understandings of what was needed to improve the reproductive lives of all women. It is no coincidence therefore that the definition of reproductive health that came out of the Cairo and Beijing conferences was comprehensive. The definition reads:

> Reproductive health is a state of complete physical, mental and social well-being and not merely the absence of disease or infirmity, in all matters relating to the reproductive system and to its functions and processes. Reproductive health therefore implies that people are able to have a satisfying and safe sex life and that they have the capability to reproduce and the freedom to decide if, when and how often to do so. Implicit in this last condition are the right of men and women to be informed and to have access to safe, effective, affordable and acceptable methods of family planning of their choice, as well as other methods of their choice for regulation of fertility which are not against the law, and the right of access to appropriate health-care services that will enable women to go safely through pregnancy and childbirth and provide couples with the best chance of having a healthy infant.[14]

Furthermore, Chapter 7 of the Cairo Programme of Action includes the right to make decisions concerning reproduction free of discrimination, coercion, and violence, as expressed in human rights documents. In addition, Paragraph 96 of the Platform of Action that was adopted at the FWCW reaffirms the Cairo Programme by stating that "[t]he human rights of women include their right to have control over and decide freely and responsibly on matters related

[12] *Id.* at 44.

[13] *Id.* at 47–48.

[14] UN Population and Development, Programme of Action adopted at the International Conference on Population and Development, Cairo, September 5–13, 1994 (New York: United Nations, Department for Economic and Social Information and Policy Analysis, ST/ESA/SER.A/149, 1994) [hereinafter Cairo Programme], para. 7.2.; UN Department of Public Information, Platform for Action and Beijing Declaration, Fourth World Conference on Women, Beijing, China, September 4–15, 1995 (New York: UN 1995) para. 94.

to their sexuality, including sexual and reproductive health, free of coercion, discrimination and violence."

Prior to this comprehensive definition of reproductive health, discourse about international reproductive health focused primarily on access to family planning services without adequately considering the safety, affordability, and acceptability of the methods of family planning that were used. Similarly, reproductive health conversations often failed to recognize the fact that many women were more interested in having healthy babies than they were in limiting their reproductive health options to contraception and abortion. These issues were brought into focus at the ICPD and FWCW Conferences primarily by Black women and other women of color from around the globe who offered critiques of the dominant framework of "reproductive choice," and hence of feminism, in family planning.

In essence, the "reproductive choice" framework emphasized a consumer-oriented approach to family planning. Whereas economically privileged women were primarily concerned with the quantity of "choices" made available to them through their purchasing power (abortion, the pill, the IUD, diaphragms, etc.), less privileged women expressed the fact that the only choices that were made available to them were dangerous ones that resulted in permanent sterilization as a result of unconsented surgery or temporary sterilization as a result of Norplant and Depo-Provera use. Black women argued that the limited options that they were offered were a direct result of their race and/or socioeconomic status, and, by introducing this intersectionality approach, they shifted the focus of the conversation from the quantity of choices to the quality of choices.

As previously noted, this chapter will unearth the variegated contributions that Black women have made toward evolving international reproductive health concerns into international human rights issues through dialogue, advocacy, and technical assistance. It will highlight specifically how such efforts have normatively shaped international human rights standards that focus on the rights to safe birth control, to be informed about the side effects of birth control, to have children (not just to terminate pregnancy), and not to have race and economic status dictate the outcome of reproductive health. Specifically, this chapter concentrates on the way in which Black women's experience with Depo-Provera, Norplant, and sterilization abuse have impacted the international conversation about reproductive health and how these dialogues contributed to the comprehensive definition of reproductive health used in the Cairo Programme of Action and the Beijing Platform. Special attention is focused on Depo-Provera and Norplant because these contraceptives were used in ethically questionable ways on Black women all throughout the Diaspora. During the FWCW NGO Forum, a protest demonstration against Norplant and Depo-Provera was staged primarily by women of color from several different countries, including the United States, South Africa, Ghana, Mozambique, Brazil, and Egypt.[15] This chapter focuses on the experiences of Black women in Zimbabwe, South Africa, and the United States because these experiences have been documented by NGOs in those countries and were therefore most accessible in terms of research. Black women in all three of these countries have the common legacy of surviving apartheid, resisting reproductive oppression, and organizing against either Norplant or Depo-Provera in a way that captured international attention.

WHAT IS DEPO-PROVERA?

Depo-Provera is an injection of a synthetic version of the hormone progesterone that prevents pregnancy for up to three months by inhibiting ovulation and making cervical mucus uninhabitable for sperm.[16] It is commonly referred to as "the shot."[17] It is associated with osteoporosis; loss of sex drive; sterility; an increased risk of breast, cervical, and uterine cancer; and severe depression.[18] Depo-Provera use is associated with decreased condom use, which raises women's susceptibility to sexually transmitted infections (STIs) and HIV infection. Some studies also indicate that Depo-Provera may be an independent risk factor for contracting HIV and other STIs. In September 2004, *The Journal of the American Sexually Transmitted Disease Association* reported that Depo-Provera also causes a threefold increase in the risk of acquiring chlamydia and gonorrhea.[19] This association with STIs and STDs is of great concern to Black women because of the disproportionate number of them who are already at risk.

In 1967, Depo-Provera was denied approval by the U.S. Federal Drug Administration (FDA) because of its link to cancer in laboratory animals.[20]

[15] Bandana Shiva, *Beijing Conference: Gender justice and global apartheid*, *available at* http://www.twnside.org.sg/title/just-cn.htm.

[16] Dr. C. Sathyamala, An Epidemiological Review of the Injectable Contraceptive Depo-Provera (2000).

[17] *Id.*

[18] *"Is Depo-Provera really safe?,"* Ms. Magazine, January/February 1993; at 72–73.

[19] *Hormonal contraceptive USC, cervical ectopy and the acquisition of cervical infections*, 31 (9) J. Am. Sexually Transmitted Dis. Assoc. 561–67 (September 2004), *available at* http://www.stdjournal.com; *also see* Family Health International, *Depo-Provera appears to increase risk for chlamydia and gonoccocal infections*, available at http://www.nih.gov/news/pr/aug2004/nichd-23.htm (last accessed on April 10, 2012). This study was funded by the U.S. Agency for International Development (USAID) and the National Institute of Child Health and Development.

[20] Encyclopedia of Birth Control 145 (Verna L. Bullough ed., 2001).

Despite this lack of FDA approval, Depo-Provera was used on 14,000 women at the Grady Clinic in Atlanta, Georgia, between 1967 and 1978.[21] Fifty percent of the women who served as subjects in this experiment were low-income Black women.[22] Many of the women who served as test subjects in the Depo-Provera experiment did so without their knowledge or consent,[23] and most were not told that there were side effects associated with Depo-Provera.[24] Several of the women were later diagnosed with cancer, and a few women died during the trials.[25] However, reports submitted to the FDA did not include information about these deaths.[26]

In 1978, the FDA denied approval of Depo-Provera a second time because (1) animal studies done on dogs confirmed an elevated rate of breast cancer, (2) an increased risk of birth defects was noted in human fetuses exposed to the drug, and (3) there was no pressing need shown for use of the drug as a contraceptive.[27] In 1983, Depo-Provera was denied approval by the FDA yet again. However, in 1987, the FDA changed its regulations to require cancer testing in rats and mice instead of dogs. Because Depo-Provera did not cause cancer in these animals, the path for approval of Depo-Provera was paved.[28] In 1992, Depo-Provera was approved by the FDA for distribution in the United States.[29] It took Pharmacia and Upjohn Pharmaceuticals, the company that produces Depo-Provera, twenty-five years to obtain FDA approval as a "safe" drug.[30] This approval occurred over the vigilant opposition of major health organizations representing women of color, including the National Women's Health Network, the Native American Women's Health Education Resource Center, the National Latina Health Organization, and the National Black Women's Health Project. These organizations opposed the approval of Depo-Provera not only because of safety concerns, but also because women

[21] Amy Goodman, *The case against Depo-Provera*, 6 (2) MULTINATIONAL MONITOR (February/March, 1985); Dorothy Roberts, KILLING THE BLACK BODY 145 (1998).

[22] *Id. See also Depo-Provera fact sheet*, Committee on Women, Population and the Environment, published January 6, 2007; *available at* www.cwpe.org/node/185.

[23] *Id.*

[24] *Id. See also* Warren E. Leary., "*U.S. approves injectable drug as birth control,*" NEW YORK TIMES, October 30, 1992, *available at* www.nytimes.com/1992/10/30/us/us-approves-injectable-drug-as-birth-control.html.

[25] *Id. See also* Sathyamala, *supra* note 16, at 125.

[26] *Id.* at 124.

[27] *Fact Sheet on Depo-Provera by the Committee on Women, Population and the Environment* (published January 6, 2007), *available at* http://www.cwpe.org/node/185 (last visited April 11, 2012).

[28] *Id.*

[29] *Id. Also see* Leary, *supra* note 24.

[30] *See* Fact Sheet, *supra* note 27.
Id.

of color were being coerced and targeted by medical providers to use the drug, signaling to many that it was being utilized as a tool of population control rather than a freely chosen method of birth control.[31]

Although millions of women today have used Depo-Provera, many of them complain that it has had a negative impact on their physical and emotional health.[32] The side effects include hair loss, extreme weight gain (15–30 pounds), severe acne, near-suicidal depression, nervousness, dizziness, heavy menstrual flow, and irregular periods or no periods at all.[33] There is no antidote available for a woman experiencing any or all of these side effects, which could last anywhere from six to ten months after the initial injection.[34] Although the literature produced by Pharmacia and Upjohn claims that within a year of cessation of the injections ovulation should be normal again, many women have reported prolonged periods of sterility. From 1994–2000, USAID provided 41,967,200 units of Depo-Provera into the developing world, at a cost of more than $40 million. USAID sends more units of Depo-Provera into African countries, including Mozambique, Tanzania, and Nigeria, than to any other part of the world.[35] In the United States, it is

[31] Birth control and population control are two different concepts. Birth control allows individual women to have control over whether and when they will have children. Population control, on the other hand, is a philosophy that states the belief that, for the good of society and in light of overpopulation, certain groups (usually the least powerful and the poor) should reduce their birth rates. Coercion is often implemented in population control programs. Sterilization is viewed as only one tool of population control – immigration restriction and denial of services are other methods utilized by population control advocates. *The inherent racism of population control*, published by LifeSiteNews.com, is available at www.lifesitenews.com/waronfamily/Population_Control/Inherentracism.html. Sterilization, however, is a permanent solution to the challenges and consequences of unwanted population growth. In the United States, by the 1970s, so many women, particularly Black and Puerto Rican women, have been involuntarily sterilized by doctors that several organizations against sterilization formed, including the National Conference on Sterilization Abuse and the Committee to End Sterilization Abuse. The movement eventually resulted in the passing of federal legislation that set guidelines for sterilizations performed in municipal hospitals. *See generally* Thomas Shapiro, Population Control Politics: Women, Sterilization, and Reproductive Choice (1985).

[32] Marie Cassidy, *Depo-Provera and sterilization abuse overview*, *in* Birth Control and Controlling Birth: Women-Centered Perspectives (Helen B. Holmes, Betty B. Hoskins, & Michael Gross eds., 1980) 97–105; Glenda Chui, *Depo-Provera: Safe, effective, private birth control? Groups say drug carries risks, could be misused*, Salt Lake Tribune, November 8, sec. A (1992); Gena Corea, *The Depo-Provera weapon*, *in* Birth Control and Controlling Birth, 107–116; Gena Corea *Depo-Provera and the politics of knowledge*, *in* Reconstructing Babylon 161–84 (H. Patricia Hynes ed., 1991).

[33] Boston Women's Health Collective, The New Our Bodies, Ourselves: A Book by and for Women (1992). *See also supra* note 31.

[34] Ms. Editors, *supra*, note 18, at 73.

[35] *See Fact Sheet*, *supra* note 27.

reported that 33 percent of Depo-Provera users were under the age of 19; 84 percent were Black women; and 74 percent were low income.[36]

The experience of Black women in Zimbabwe, South Africa, and the United States are of particular importance.

The Zimbabwe Experience

In 1981, Minister of Health Herbert Ushewokunze banned the use of Depo-Provera in Zimbabwe.[37] Although the underlying impetus to ban the drug was its harmful side effects, Minister Ushewokunze stated, "[t]he application of Depo-Provera is racist because in Zimbabwe, only Black women are advised to try it. White women do not use it. It is all part of a plot by our former oppressors. It is racism."[38] The "former oppressors" that the Minister of Health was referring to were the White minority Rhodesian Front, the governing party that ruled Zimbabwe from 1962 through 1978. According to the Minister of Health, the Rhodesian Front used Depo-Provera to keep the African population under control.

Depo-Provera was introduced into Zimbabwe in 1969 through the support of the Family Planning Association of Rhodesia (FPAR), and, by 1974, it became the "most popular" form of birth control. During the 1970s, it was alleged that Depo-Provera was a weapon of the White regime to control the majority Black population by effectively eliminating future generations. Depo-Provera was seen as "a symbol of the intrusion of Western imperialism and racism" into the bodies of Third World women.[39]

By the 1980s, FPAR was spending up to $1 million dollars a year on Depo-Provera.[40] It was only after Zimbabwe gained independence from the United Kingdom in 1980 that the new government brought the issue of Depo-Provera and its use on Black women to the forefront. It was alleged that, by 1980, between 90,000 and 100,000 Zimbabwean women were using Depo-Provera.[41]

Some people argued, however, that Zimbabwean women welcomed the use of this drug as a powerful tool to control their own fertility, in that they could secretly practice birth control without the consent or knowledge of their

36 *Id.*

37 Amy Kaler, *A threat to the nation and a threat to the men: The banning of Depo-Provera in Zimbabwe*, 1981. 24 (2) J. SOUTH AFRICAN STUD. 347–76, 354 (1998).

38 *Id.* at 354.

39 *Id.* at 347.

40 *Zimbabwe bans contraceptive Depo-Provera: A victory for women's group*, GLOBAL NEWSWATCH, vol. 2, no. 9 (September 1981), *available at* www.multinationalmonitor.org/hyper/issues/1981/09/zimbabwe.html.

41 Kaler, *supra* note 37, at 350.

husbands.[42] This argument, however, was undermined by allegations that the drug was routinely administered to Black women without obtaining their fully informed consent and without advising them of the harmful effects of the drug.

Zimbabwean women reported that they were being coerced to take Depo-Provera under threat of losing their employment on White-run commercial farms; that Depo-Provera had been administered to their bodies without informed consent; and that when they took their children to medical clinics, they were threatened that if they did not accept the Depo-Provera injection, their children would not receive medical treatment.[43] The decision to ban Depo-Provera in Zimbabwe was prompted by African women's complaints about the administration of the drug, as well as by the fact that Depo-Provera did not receive the safety stamp of approval by the U.S. FDA and was therefore considered by many to be unsafe. In addition, the fact that Depo-Provera was being used as a political tool by the South African apartheid regime to control the Black population[44] raised suspicion that it was, in many ways, indicative of the global sentiment that Depo-Provera was a tool of colonial power used to control the bodies of African women."[45]

As a result of the lack of respect for the autonomy and human rights of Black women in Zimbabwe, Depo-Provera developed a nefarious reputation for being a form of population control rather than birth control.[46] Consequently, the decision of the new government to ban the use of Depo-Provera in 1981 was seen as a move in the right direction.[47]

The South African Experience

The history of the use of Depo-Provera against Black South African women was eerily similar to the stories of Black Zimbabwean women. Allegations of coercion, deception, lack of consent, and threats associated with the Depo-Provera injection, as well as stories of threats made by employers against Black women who refused to use Depo-Provera, abounded. Like Zimbabwean

[42] Because Depo-Provera is an injection, there is no interruption during sexual intercourse to insert contraception, and it is therefore easy for the male partner to be unaware that his female partner has decided to prevent pregnancy by using contraception.

[43] Kaler, *supra* note 37, at 347–56.

[44] *Id.* at 354.

[45] *Id.* at 351. *See also* Paula C. Johnson, *Danger in the Diaspora: Law, culture and violence against women of African descent in the United States and South Africa*, 1 J. GENDER RACE & JUST. 471, 488 (1998).

[46] *Id.* at 488.

[47] *Id.*

women, South African women were forced to use Depo-Provera to keep their jobs in White-owned factories. Just like the women who worked on the White-run farms in Zimbabwe, Black women in South African factories were threatened with the possibility of losing their employment if they refused the Depo-Provera injection.[48] Many women also received a compulsory injection after giving birth.[49] The apartheid government targeted almost exclusively Black and mixed-race women for Depo-Provera use in an "effort to reduce the growth rate of the Black African population (and concurrently increase the number of whites)."[50] In many instances Depo-Provera was the main, and often the only contraceptive offered to Black women.[51]

The ideology that permeated South Africa during the apartheid era was very similar to the racist thinking in colonial Rhodesia. These governments feared that the unchecked growth of the Black population posed a direct threat to the White power structure, as well as a threat to the safety and profits of White society. Although the South African government family planning program instituted in 1974 appeared on its face to be nondiscriminatory, it was evident from the use of intensive advertising campaigns in urban South Africa that Black women were the targeted group for Depo-Provera use.[52] This led many to assume that the implicit goal of the apartheid government was population control and not family planning.[53] These terms were artfully defined by author Monica Bahati Kuumba when she wrote, "Population control is markedly different from the concepts of family planning, access to birth control or reproductive rights. While these latter concepts rest on the notion of equality and informed decisions in the midst of multiple options, population control philosophically is an ideology rooted in inequality, racism and patriarchy."[54]

It was not until the apartheid regime ended that Black women in South Africa began to raise concerns about the impact of Depo-Provera. The timing of the end of legal apartheid in South Africa coincided with the international conversations about reproductive health at Cairo and Beijing, and so the complaints about Depo-Provera use in the Black community in South Africa received an international stage. Unfortunately, South Africa did

48 *Id.*

49 Betsy Hartmann, *Depo-Provera: Keeping an eye on the needle*, in Reproductive Rights & Wrongs: The Global Politics of Population Control, 200, 206 (1995).

50 *Id.*

51 *Id.*

52 Barbara Brown, *Facing the "black peril": The politics of population control in South Africa*, 13 (3) J. Southern African Stud. 256, 268 (1987), *available at* http://reproductiverights.org/ sites/ default/files/documents/SRSouthAfrica98en.pdf.

53 *Id.*

54 Monica Bahati Kuumba, *Perpetuating neo-colonialism through population control: South Africa and the United States*, 40 (3) Africa Today 79.

not closely examine its family planning policies as they pertained to Depo-Provera until 2009.[55]

The only way the world became aware of the failings of the new government was through the work performed by key human rights organizations. Specifically, it was a collaborative effort between the Center for Reproductive Law & Policy (CRLP) and the Women's Health Project of South Africa. These organizations jointly prepared a Shadow Report for the Nineteenth Session of the Committee on the Elimination of All Forms of Discrimination against Women. The goal of this report was to challenge South Africa's assertions that the government was committed to protecting the reproductive rights of all women in South Africa. Based on the diligent efforts of NGOs in South Africa, these assertions were challenged, calling into question South Africa's commitment to reproductive rights as "inadequate and inequitable." These NGOs, through their critical research, alleged that there were great discrepancies between the treatment of Black women and White women in South Africa. The NGOs alleged that there was a lack of quality treatment for women of color and that a lack of access to a wide range of contraceptives for Black women essentially forced them to use injectable contraceptives like Depo-Provera. The NGOs also alleged that there was a lack of information on alternative forms of contraception, such as barrier methods. In another similarity to Zimbabwe, a study of eighty-six South African women from various class and racial backgrounds, conducted by the Women's Health Project, found that 81 percent had used contraceptives without proper knowledge about what they were taking. Without the critical research and work done by these NGOs, the reproductive oppression of Black women would not have been addressed as swiftly as it was. By publishing their shadow report and publicizing the stories of these women, these organizations brought the facts to the forefront and forced the state to come into alignment with the normative standards of international human rights laws.

BLACK WOMEN IN THE UNITED STATES

Black women in the United States, like their counterparts in Zimbabwe and South Africa, have also experienced reproductive oppression. To provide a better understanding of this shared history, it is imperative to first understand

[55] *See generally*, *Women's reproductive rights in South Africa: A shadow report*, June 1998, prepared by The Center for Reproductive Law & Policy (CRLP) and Women's Health Project, *available at* http://reproductiverights.org/sites/default/files/documents/SRSouthAfrica98en.pdf.

the effect of the eugenics movement. *Eugenics* is the study of and belief in the possibility of producing a highly gifted race of people by encouraging people with superior genes to breed while discouraging "undesirable" and "defective" individuals from having children.[56] In essence, American eugenicists aimed to eliminate all "defective" people from the population. Included among those who were deemed "defective" were Black people, immigrants from Southern and Eastern Europe, the poor, the homeless, the physically disabled, and the mentally ill.[57] The methods of eugenic elimination included marginalization, institutionalization, and incarceration, as well as restrictions on immigration and miscegenation and laws permitting forced sterilization.[58]

Beginning in the early 1900s, movies, magazines, and journals romanticized the philosophy of eugenics.[59] Major philanthropic foundations such as the Carnegie Institution and the Rockefeller Foundation financed eugenics research. By 1928, there were 376 separate eugenics courses in some of the United States' leading universities, enrolling more than 20,000 students.[60] By 1910, there was a large and dynamic network of scientists, reformers, and professionals engaged in national eugenics projects. These projects produced eugenic legislation that supported forced sterilization and prohibited marriages between the "fit" and "unfit." State legislatures all across the country sponsored this legislation.[61] Through a series of laws and practices, the United States engaged in one of the most pernicious population-control endeavors in history.[62]

Several early feminist organizations also promoted eugenic philosophy. One of the most prominent feminists to champion the eugenic agenda was

56 Edwin Black, War against the Weak: Eugenics and America's Campaign to Create a Master Race (2003); Paul A. Lombardo, *Eugenics sterilization laws, available at* www.Eugenicsarchive.org/html/eugenics/essay8text.html.

57 K. Garver & B. Garver, *Eugenics past, present, and the future*, 49 (5) Am. J. Hum. Genet. 1109 (1991).

58 It is noteworthy that much of the inspiration for the Nazi programs of sterilization, euthanasia, and genocide of the Jewish population was derived from the U.S. eugenics movement. Paul Lombardo, *The American breed: Nazi eugenics and the origins of the pioneer fund*, 65 Albany L. Rev. 743 (2002). *See also* A Century of Eugenics in America: From Indiana Experiment to the Human Genome Era (Paul Lombardo ed., 2011); Edwin Black, *Eugenics and the Nazis – the California connection*, San Francisco Chronicle, November 9, 2003, *available at* www.sfgate.com/cgi-bin/article.cgi?f=/c/a/2003/11/09/ing9c2Qsk81.dtl.

59 Judith Scully, *Eugenics, women of color and reproductive health: The saga continues*, 1 (1) Africalogical Perspectives 167, 168 (January/February 2004).

60 Lombardo, *Breed, supra* note 59, at 743; *see also* Century of Eugenics, *supra* note 59; Steven Selden, *Transforming better babies into fitter families: Archival resources & the history of the American eugenics movement* 1908–1930, 149 (2) Am. Philosophical Soc'y. 199–225.

61 Scully, *supra* note 60, at 168.

62 *Id.* at 167–69.

Margaret Sanger, the leader of the American birth control movement and founder of Planned Parenthood.[63] Sanger saw birth control as a means to prevent unwanted children from being born into a disadvantaged life, and she incorporated eugenics rhetoric into the birth control movement.[64] Like traditional eugenicists, Sanger believed "defective" people would pass on mental disease or serious physical defects to their children.[65] Through the persistent lobbying of a committed group of individuals including Sanger, sterilization laws proliferated throughout the United States in the early 1900s. Since feminist organizations advocated both birth control and eugenics-based sterilizations, many Black people in the United States distrusted White feminist organizations and accused them of using contraceptives, abortions, and sterilizations to eliminate the Black population.[66] Consequently, in certain segments of the Black community across the United States, birth control was considered just another tool in the eugenics toolbox.

By the 1950s and '60s, the ideology of eugenics and population control was used by policymakers in the United States to justify disseminating birth control internationally.[67] They claimed that controlling the fertility of poor women, especially in the "developing" world, was necessary to avert poverty, prevent the spread of communism, and increase the ability of the United States to govern world affairs.[68]

It has been estimated that, in 1974, between 100,000 and 150,000 poor American women had been surgically sterilized under federally funded programs either against their will or without consent.[69] Nearly half of the

[63] Darci Burrell, *The Norplant solution: Norplant and the control of African American motherhood*, 5 UCLA WOMEN'S L. J. 401, 419 (Spring 1995)

[64] *Id.* at 419–22.

[65] *Id.*

[66] *See generally* Jennifer Nelson, WOMEN OF COLOR AND THE REPRODUCTIVE RIGHTS MOVEMENT (New York Press 2003); Angela Y. Davis, WOMEN, RACE & CLASS, 1, 202–22 (1981).

[67] Hartmann, *supra* note 49, 93–112.

[68] Linda Gordon, WOMAN'S BODY, WOMAN'S RIGHT 355 (1990).

[69] In 1974, the Southern Poverty Law Center filed a class-action lawsuit in the U.S. District Court for the District of Columbia demanding a ban on the use of federal funds for sterilization. *Relf et al. vs. Weinberger et. al,*. Civil Action No. 73–1557 U.S. District Court. Washington DC, March 15, 1974. *See also* http://www.splcenter.org/get-informed/case-docket/relf-v-weinberger and Relf v. United States, 433 F. Supp. 423 (D.D.C. 1977). In this lawsuit, it was estimated that between 100,000 and 150,000 women had been sterilized using federal funds. These sterilizations were alleged to be against the will and without the consent of the women. Among the "women" sterilized during this time period were the plaintiffs in this case – fourteen-year-old Minnie Lee Relf and her twelve-year-old sister Mary Alice Relf. These young African-American girls were sterilized after nurses asked for permission to admit the girls to the hospital for injections of the long-acting experimental contraceptive Depo-Provera. Roberts, *supra* note 21, at 93.

women who were sterilized were Black.[70] Although eugenic sterilization laws impacted several segments of the population, primarily low-income people, a disproportionate number of sterilizations were performed on Black women.[71] Most of them were sterilized shortly after giving birth.[72] Many of the Black women who were sterilized were told that if they did not "consent" to sterilization they would no longer be eligible for welfare benefits.[73] In the southern part of the United States, these involuntary surgeries were so prevalent that they became known as the "Mississippi appendectomy."[74] Unfortunately, forced sterilizations were not confined to the South or to Mississippi. They were performed throughout the country.[75] For example, in 1975, the acting director of obstetrics and gynecology at New York Municipal Hospital

Mrs. Relf unable to read or write, signed the consent form. She later discovered, however, that her daughters had been surgically sterilized. This case is tragic not only because forced sterilizations had been performed, but because Depo-Provera, a drug that had not yet been approved for contraceptive use in the United States, was at the center of this controversy. As a result of their decision to pursue their legal rights, widespread sterilization abuse funded by the federal government and practiced for decades was exposed. The lawsuit also led to the requirement that doctors obtain "informed consent" before performing sterilization procedures, and it also prohibited the practice of threatening women on welfare with benefits reductions if they refused to "consent" to sterilization.

70 In May 2001, the governor of Virginia issued an official apology to individuals who had been forcibly sterilized by the state. Michael Ollove, *Lessons of Lynchburg*, BALTIMORE SUN, May 6, 2001. In January 2003, South Carolina also apologized for decades of forcibly sterilizing women – particularly Black women – from the 1930s through the 1960s. Jaymi Freiden, *South Carolina issues apology for years of sterilizations forced procedure used into the 60's*, KNIGHT RIDDER NEWS SERVICE, January 9, 2003. In March 2003, the governor of California issued a public apology for forced sterilizations performed in that state. Carl Ingram, *State issues apology for policy of sterilization*, LOS ANGELES TIMES, March 12, 2003. In North Carolina, the governor issued a similar apology to 7,450 individuals forcibly sterilized between 1924 and 1979 by their state eugenics board. Reparations to the sterilizations victims were proposed, but the North Carolina Senate rejected a plan for compensation. Gann, Carrie et al., *North Carolina senate denies funds for sterilization victims*, June 22, 2012, *available at* http://abcnews.go.com/Health/WomensHealth/north-carolina-senate-blocks-compensation-sterilization-victims-eugenics/story?id=16628515&page=2.

71 Loretta Ross, THE COLOR OF CHOICE: WHITE SUPREMACY AND REPRODUCTIVE JUSTICE (2006).

72 Roberts, *supra* note 21, at 93.

73 *Id.*

74 *Id.* Ross, *supra* note 72; the phrase was originally used by civil rights leader Fannie Lou Hamer to refer to involuntary sterilizations. *See generally* Harriet Washington, MEDICAL APARTHEID: THE DARK HISTORY OF MEDICAL EXPERIMENTATION ON BLACK AMERICANS FROM COLONIAL TIMES TO THE PRESENT 202–05 (2007).

75 Committee to End Sterilization Abuse, STERILIZATION ABUSE OF WOMEN: THE FACTS (1975). See also Roberts, supra note 21. Similarly, a study by Dr. Bernard Rosenfeld of Los Angeles County Hospital, released in 1973, confirmed that many poor Black women were being subjected to surgical sterilization without informed consent. Bernard Rosenfeld, Sydney Wolfe, & Robert E. McGarrah, A HEALTH RESEARCH GROUP STUDY ON SURGICAL STERILIZATION: PRESENT ABUSES AND PROPOSED REGULATIONS (1973) (focusing on sterilization procedures in Baltimore, Boston, and Los Angeles).

reported that in most major teaching hospitals in New York City, medical residents were encouraged to do "elective hysterectomies" on poor Black and Puerto Rican women as part of their training experience.

In the 1990s, when hormonal contraceptives causing temporary sterilization (e.g., Norplant and Depo-Provera) were approved by the FDA, eugenic philosophy once again reared its ugly head in the United States. Unlike Depo-Provera, which can be administered through an injection, Norplant must be surgically implanted.[76] Like Depo-Provera, it causes temporary sterilization, but instead of lasting three years, Norplant sterilization lasts for up to five years.[77] Almost as soon as these temporary forms of sterilization became available in the United States, several state legislatures attempted to compel women on welfare and women whose babies were exposed to drugs as a result of their mothers' prenatal drug use to use Norplant.[78] Several state legislatures and the media touted Norplant as the panacea for reducing poverty in America's Black urban areas. The media endorsed the view that Norplant was well suited for "inner city" young women, the poor, mothers on welfare, and the "less educated."[79]

In more than twenty states, legislators proposed laws that would offer financial incentives to women on welfare who "agreed" to use Norplant. Judges gave low-income women convicted of child abuse or drug use during pregnancy the "choice" of taking Norplant or serving jail time.[80] Luckily, the legislative initiatives did not receive enough support from public officials to be

76 Rachel Stephanie Arnow, *The implementation of rights: An argument for unconditionally funded Norplant removal*, 11 BERKELEY WOMEN'S L. J. 19 (1996).

77 Burrell, *supra* note 54; Charlotte Rutherford, *Reproductive freedoms and African American women*, 4 YALE J. L. & FEMINISM 255 (Spring 1992); Laurie Nsiab-Jefferson, *Reproductive laws, women of color, and low income women in* REPRODUCTIVE LAWS FOR THE 1990S, 17, 49 (Nadine Taub & Sherrill Cohen eds., 1988).

78 Meredith Black, *Welfare and coerced contraception: morality implications of state sponsored reproductive control*, 34 U. LOUISVILLE J. FAM. L. 311 (1995–1996); Melissa Burke, *The constitutionality of the use of the Norplant contraceptive device as a condition of probation*, 20 HASTINGS CONST. L. Q. 207 (1992); Rebecca Dresser, *Long-term contraceptives in the criminal justice system*, MED. HEALTH NEWS (January 1995); Barbara Bemier, *Class, race and poverty: Medical technologies and sociopolitical choices*, 11 HARV. BLACKLETTER L. J. 115 (1994).

79 Ollove, *supra*, note 71.

80 The "reproductive choice" paradigm also divides women up into good-choice makers and bad-choice makers. Bad-choice makers are deemed to be "unfit" to be mothers. And when a woman makes a bad choice and is therefore a bad mother, society is justified in punishing her, limiting her welfare eligibility, imprisoning her, and/or terminating her parental rights. Women making "bad choices" therefore become easy targets for sterilization and incarceration. Rickie Solinger, PREGNANCY & POWER: A SHORT HISTORY OF REPRODUCTIVE POLITICS IN AMERICA (2007). The concept of "reproductive choice" divides women against each other and judges women's suitability for motherhood and reproduction. It is the opposite of reproductive justice based on the fundamental human right to reproduce safely and with dignity.

enacted into law, and the judicial sentences were widely criticized.[81] However, legislation was not needed to force young African-American women living in low-income communities to use Norplant or Depo-Provera. For example, young Black women in Charleston, South Carolina and Chicago, Illinois reported that they were pressured by medical providers to use either Norplant or Depo-Provera immediately after giving birth[82] and immediately following abortion – when women were most vulnerable and least likely to make clear decisions.[83] In most of these scenarios, doctors often failed to take the personal health history of these women into consideration before they made their "choice."[84] In addition, women were not informed of the side effects or the fact that nothing was known about the long-term consequences of using these drugs. This intentional failure to fully inform women about their choices and the practice of recommending only Norplant or Depo-Provera when women are most vulnerable was and is unethical and unlawful. Whereas eugenics was clearly practiced in the United States against Black women,[85] it is equally apparent that it was used to control the reproductive capacity of Black women (as well as other women of color) throughout the Diaspora.[86]

BLACK WOMEN REJECT THE "CHOICE" PARADIGM

Black women's experiences with Depo-Provera in Zimbabwe, South Africa, and the United States demonstrate how discrimination based on race and economic status can impact women's reproductive choices. Prior to the ICPD in Cairo, population planners focused on how to keep the world's

[81] Kristyn Walker, *Judicial control of reproductive freedom*, 78 IOWA L. REV. 779 (1993); Dorothy Roberts, *The future of reproductive choice for poor women and women of color*, 12 WOMEN'S RTS. L. REP. 59 (1990) reprinted in 20th Anniversary Edition 14 WOMEN'S RTS. L. REP. 305 (1992); Roberts, *supra* note 21.

[82] Roberts, *supra* note 21, at 128–30.

[83] *Dangerous Contraceptives: Norplant and Depo-Provera, a Committee on Women, Population and the Environment* (CWPE) fact sheet, *available at* http://cwpe.org/files/norplant%20and%20depo-provera.pdf.

[84] *Id.*

[85] *See* Angela Y. Davis, WOMEN, RACE & CLASS 215–21 (1981). In North Carolina alone, from 1933 to about 1973, 7,500 women were sterilized, supposedly due to mental deficiency. About 5,000 of them were Black. *Id.* at 217. North Carolina reparations for forced sterilizations: Sheryl Huggins Salomon, *An outrage: NC black women were sterilized*, The Root.com (November 7, 2011), *available at* www.theroot.com/buzz/outrage-nc-black-women-were-sterilized (accessed on April 12, 2012); Scully, *supra* note 60.

[86] Coerced sterilizations and sterilizations performed without the consent of women have been recently reported in Namibia, Democratic Republic of Congo, Zambia, and South Africa. *See generally* David Smith, *African women with HIV coerced into sterilization*, THE GUARDIAN, June 22, 2009, *available at* www.guardian.comUK/world/2009/Jun/22/africa-hiv-positive-women-sterilization.

poorest women from having more babies.[87] The Cairo Conference, however, focused not just on population control but on development strategies. The major development strategy relevant here was one that offered a broader range of reproductive health services.[88] Unlike other international population conferences, the ICPD "did not emphasize numerical goals or targets, such as the number of contraceptives to be delivered or births to be averted."[89] Instead, the ICPD focused on the need for greater access to information and more accessibility to reproductive health services so that women could be in a better position to make informed decisions.[90] It recognized that women needed to be empowered to control their reproductive health.[91] When addressing the UN General Assembly, a representative from the Netherlands commented on the successful people-centered approach taken at the ICPD, saying "(it was) built on a formula which essentially amounted to common decency; to face the population problem not through coercion and discrimination, but by giving people the means to follow the path of their choice, freely and responsibly."[92]

Much of this change in perspective from coercion and discrimination to a respect for human rights was a result of increased participation by and attention to the needs of Black women and women of color in the reproductive rights movement. This shift in perspective was accomplished by NGO debates at Preparatory Committee (PreCom) meetings prior to the ICPD meeting in Cairo. For the first time, reproductive health organizations like NARAL, NOW, and Planned Parenthood[93] gave voice to the concerns of Black women and other women of color.[94] Prior to the PrepCom meetings, these organizations developed women of color projects, which largely focused on the reproductive oppression that women of color experienced as a result of racism and discrimination based on their economic status. Norplant, Depo-

[87] Marshall, Meredith, *United Nations Conference on population and development: The road to a new reality for reproductive health*, 10 Emory Int'l. L. Rev. 451 (1996).

[88] *See* Mahmoud F. Fathalla, *From family planning to reproductive health*, in Beyond The Numbers: A Reader on Population, Consumption, and the Environment 143, 148 (Laurie Ann Mazur ed., 1994).

[89] Marshall, *supra* note 3, at 443.

[90] *Id.* at 443.

[91] *Id.*

[92] *Id.* at 492 citing Speakers in General Assembly Hail ICPD Outcome, ICPD (International Conference on Population and Development, New York), October 1994, 4.

[93] Faye Wattleton, one of the leading advocates for women's reproductive rights and the first African-American and youngest president of Planned Parenthood, helped usher in this phase of the evolution of the reproductive rights movement. For many years, Wattleton was the face of diversity within the predominantly White mainstream abortion rights movement. *See* Faye Wattleton, Life on the Line (1996).

[94] Nelson, *supra* note 67.

Provera, and sterilization became a regular part of reproductive health care discussions. Through the PrepCom meetings, women of color helped define the themes, issues, and objectives of the Conferences, and, in doing so, broadened the agenda.[95]

Black women at the NGO caucuses from both the United States and developing countries began to push the issue of how limited their contraceptive and reproductive health care choices were. The realization that Black women in the United States had so much in common with Black women in African countries when it came to reproductive health created a transnational force to be reckoned with.[96] Questions were constantly being raised by Black women (and other women of color) in NGO forum discussions at the FWCW: How can we ever achieve "complete physical, mental and social well-being" when we must confront racism and classism in addition to sexism every day? How can we achieve this objective when health care providers do not provide the same level of care to us as they do to White patients? How can we achieve this objective when our "choices" are limited by our economic status, and we are coerced into making decisions? In many ways, these questions culminated in one burning question: Can a human rights approach emerge that will assist women facing multiple levels of oppression in their attempt to achieve reproductive freedom?

In many ways, the questions raised at the NGO forums by Black women were not new. Organizations like the National Black Women's Health Project (NBWHP)[97] had been raising these questions for quite some time. Founded in 1984 (ten years prior to the ICPD), the NBWHP, one of the oldest organizations formed to advance the sexual and reproductive rights of Black women in the United States, had adopted in their vision statement the following

[95] The first Preparatory Committee (PrepCom) met in New York in 1991. A second meeting, PrepCom II, was held in 1993; it was followed by the 49th UN General Assembly, which reviewed the proposals put forth in PrepCom II and made recommendations to strengthen the document. In April 1994, planners met for the third PrepCom session, PrepComIII, to complete the final draft of the document to be ratified at Cairo. *See Summary of the International Conference on Population and Development*, EARTH NEGOTIATIONS BULLETIN (International Institute for Sustainable Development, Winnipeg, Manitoba, Canada), September 14, 1994, at 1. *See also* Gita Sen, *Development, population and the government: A search for balance,* in POPULATION POLICIES RECONSIDERED: HEALTH, EMPOWERMENT, AND RIGHTS 63, 68 (Gita Sen, Adrienne Germain, & Lincoln Chen eds., 1994).

[96] In addition to limited choices for contraception, Black women in the United States as well as in African suffer from poor access to health care, high rates of maternal mortality, high rates of infant mortality, high rates of birthing low-birth-weight babies, and high rates of HIV infection as compared to their White counterparts.

[97] For a comprehensive history of the National Black Women's Health Project, *see Founding the National Black Women's Health Project: A new concept in health,* in UNDIVIDED RIGHTS: WOMEN OF COLOR ORGANIZE FOR REPRODUCTIVE JUSTICE 63 (Joel Silliman et al. eds., 2009).

statement of what "good health" consisted of: "Health ... is not merely the absence of illness, but the active promotion of emotional, mental, economic and physical wellness of this and future generations."[98]

This statement regarding health reflects the reality that economic wellness, as well as emotional wellness (including the absence of discrimination), is a necessary ingredient in the recipe for good health. Since its founding, the NBWHP[99] had been bringing its concerns, voices, and perspectives to national and international attention. Byllye Avery, the founder of the NBWHP, sought to understand the lives of Black women and the fact that we often live in a conspiracy of silence.[100] She brought poor Black women and middle-class women, rural and urban women into dialogue around reproductive health issues to break this silence.[101] In 1985 (just one year after opening its doors), the NBWHP participated in the UN Third World Conference for Women in Nairobi, Kenya. This experience allowed African-American voices to be heard on a broad range of women's health issues at the national and international level. Of the 20,000 women who attended the Nairobi conference, 1,100 were African-American women. Through the 1980s and 1990s, the NBWHP was intensely engaged in negotiating its place and creating space for other women of color in the women's health movement. In 1992, the NBWHP started a campaign on unsafe contraceptives that focused on educating African-American women about Norplant and Depo-Provera. In 1993, the NBWHP co-organized a coalition of women of color to work on both the 1994 ICPD in Cairo and the 1995 FWCW in Beijing.

The impact of the public education and organizing efforts of NBWHP on unsafe contraceptives helped Black women throughout the Diaspora focus many of the NGO forum dialogues on the differences between Black women's reproductive lives and the reproductive realities of White women. These differences were of global significance because the impact of racism and economic status discrimination in health care existed not only in the United States but all across the world. What made this experience so noteworthy was

[98] National Black Women's Health Project Vision Statement (1984). *See also* BODY AND SOUL: A BLACK WOMEN'S GUIDE TO HEALTH AND WELL-BEING (Linda Villarosa ed., 1994). *See also* the WHO Constitution upon which the NBWHP vision statement was apparently based. WORLD HEALTH ORGANIZATION CONSTITUTION (45th ed. Oct. 2006), *available at* www.who.int/governance/eb/who_constitution_en.pdf. The Constitution was adopted by the International Health Conference held in New York by representatives of 61 countries. It was originally entered into force in 1948.

[99] UNDIVIDED RIGHTS, *supra* note 98.

[100] Byllye Avery, *A question of survival/a conspiracy of silence: Abortion and black women's health*, in FROM ABORTION TO REPRODUCTIVE FREEDOM: TRANSFORMING A MOVEMENT 75 (Marlene Gerber Fried ed., 1990).

[101] Silliman, *supra* note 98, 63–85.

that the voices of women connected to the NBWHP in the United States were augmented by Black women's voices in NGOs from all over the world at the ICPD and the FWCW.

In several workshops at the NGO forums, Black women throughout the Diaspora told their stories of how they had been coerced, tricked, and deceived into being sterilized either permanently or temporarily through the use of Depo-Provera and Norplant. They stressed the need for the concept of reproductive health to incorporate their concerns regarding informed consent, safety, and affordability of services. They distinguished their experiences from those of White women living in first-world countries, and they established a sense of connection with each other as they realized their reproductive health narratives were eerily similar to each other despite the fact that their governments were different, their languages varied, and their homes were separated by thousands of miles and large bodies of water. It was this shared sense of experience and history that connected Black women and women of color from all over the world. And it was this powerful connection that made it possible for the women gathered at the NGO forum to collectively define reproductive health in a way that would forever change the dialogue around the concept of choice.

The spoken word is powerful. It can change minds and make people think and rethink their positions. Sometimes spoken words have to be repeated over and over again before their significance is understood. In the case of Black women and reproductive health, the reoccurring narratives of sterilization abuse, contraceptive abuse, and the lack of autonomy and dignity that Black women faced in their relationship to their health care providers was echoed globally. Black women in the United States, in African countries, in the Caribbean, and throughout the world realized that, in many ways, their experiences were the same. By insisting on having their experiences recognized by NGOs, Black women helped to change the dialogue around reproductive health.[102] Their narratives and advocacy moved the agenda from the rhetoric of "choice" into the international human rights framework that emphasized freedom from coercion and respect for informed consent, as well as a stated value for the principle of self-determination as it pertains to reproductive health.

The conversations, particularly at the FWCW NGO forums, focused on the false "choices" being offered to Black women (and women of color) all over the world. Black women's health advocates throughout the Diaspora made it clear at the FWCW that reproductive health issues cannot adequately be

[102] Nelson, *supra* note 67.

addressed through the "choice" paradigm.[103] In essence, the choice paradigm is an individualistic consumer market concept. Under this paradigm, one has only as much "choice" as she can afford. Consequently, the human dignity that should be intimately intertwined with the delivery of reproductive health services is only guaranteed to those who can afford to choose such services. Concomitantly, safety, which should be at the heart of all reproductive health decisions, is also available only to those who have adequate purchasing power. Under this "reproductive choice" approach, women do not have a right to decide whether and when to become mothers – they merely have a consumer's choice.[104] It was for these reasons that many women of color in general, and Black women in particular, joined together to critique and ultimately reject the "choice" paradigm. Nowhere was this rejection more obvious and significant than at the ICPD and the FWCW, where the definition of reproductive health was expanded as a result of the concerns expressed by Black women and women of color. The history of Black women and their struggle for reproductive freedom is now reflected in the language and goals of international human rights conferences, declarations, and plans of action that represent normative international law in the reproductive health arena.

Loretta Ross, another African-American pioneer in the women's health movement, motivated thousands of Black women and women of color to reject the "choice" paradigm and demand not just reproductive freedom but reproductive justice.[105] Formerly the Executive Director of the National Center for Human Rights Education (NCHRE), Ms. Ross has helped infuse human rights language into the women's health agenda and has helped

[103] *Id.*

[104] Rickie Solinger, *The incompatibility of neo-liberal "choice" and reproductive justice, available at* www.protectchoice.org/downloads/Reproductive%20Justice%20Briefing%20Book.pdf.

[105] Loretta Ross, et al., *The Sister Song Collective: Women of color, reproductive health and human rights*, in Health of Women of Color, special issue, 17 Am. J. Health 85 (2001). The term "reproductive justice" was coined in 1994 by the Black Women's Caucus at a national pro-choice conference sponsored by the Illinois Pro-Choice Alliance in Chicago. *See generally* Sarah London, *Reproductive justice: Developing a lawyering model*, 13 Berkeley J. Afr.-Am. L. & Pol'y. 71 (2011). The conference took place two months after the women had returned from the 1994 International Conference on Population and Development in Cairo, Egypt. The caucus was formed as an attempt to move away from the "choice" framework and to adapt the Cairo Programme of Action in the context of the United States. *Reproductive Justice Lens Toolkit, infra* note 108. Utilizing the human rights framework of the Cairo Programme of Action, the caucus created the term "reproductive justice," which was originally defined as "reproductive health integrated into social justice." Loretta Ross, *What is reproductive justice?*, Reproductive Justice Briefing Book: A Primer on Reproductive Justice & Social Change, *available at* www.protectchoice.org/downloads/Reproductive%20Justice%20Briefing%20Book.pdf. Not wanting to use the language of "choice" because they represented communities with few real choices, they integrated the concepts of reproductive rights, social justice, and human rights to launch the term reproductive "justice."*Id.*

transform the landscape of the women's health movement in the United States and internationally. It is no coincidence that she was also instrumental in providing training on the human rights framework to women attending the FWCW NGO Forum. She is currently the executive director of the Sister Song Women of Color Reproductive Health Collective (founded in 1997), which is at the forefront of the Reproductive Justice Movement in the United States.[106]

Members of the Reproductive Justice Movement argue that women cannot have full control over their reproductive lives unless issues such as racial discrimination, inequalities in wealth and power, and differential access to resources and services are addressed.[107] Consequently, reproductive justice will not be achieved until "women and girls have the economic, social and political power and resources to make healthy decisions about their bodies, sexuality and reproduction for themselves."[108] This cannot occur until the cultural and reproductive lives of Black women are inculcated into the majority-centered reproductive rights approaches. In this sense, the Reproductive Justice Movement marks another phase in the evolution of the women's health movement.

BEYOND BEIJING

It has recently been reported that Depo-Provera is being used to limit the reproductive capacity of Black Ethiopian women living in Israel. Rachel Mangoli, an advocate of the rights of Ethiopian children in Israel,[109] noticed that, in 2008, there was a significant drop in the number of children being born in the Ethiopian community.[110] Seeing this as a red flag and suspecting that a birth-reduction policy might have been instituted against Ethiopian women, she approached a local clinic and was advised by the manager that "they had been instructed to administer Depo-Provera injections to Ethiopian women of child-bearing age."[111] In 2010, a women's rights organization, Woman to Woman (Isha L'Isha), reported that Israel had an unwritten policy

[106] Zakiya Luna, *From rights to justice: Women of color changing the face of U.S. reproductive rights organizing*, 4 SOCIETIES WITHOUT BORDERS 343–65 (2009).

[107] *See Reproductive Justice Lens Toolkit, available at* forwardtogether.org/assets/docs/acrj-rj-lens-toolkit.pdf.

[108] *Id.*

[109] Jonathan Cook, *Israel's treatment of Ethiopians "racist,"* THE NATIONAL, January 6, 2010, *available at* http://www.thenational/ae/news/world/middle-east/israels-treatment-of-ethiopians-racist (accessed on April 18, 2010).

[110] *Id.*

[111] Id. at 5.

of promoting the use of Depo-Provera in Ethiopian females who immigrated to Israel.[112] The report indicated that the use of Depo-Provera had risen to 57 percent in a community that accounts for less than 2 percent of the entire population.[113] When Woman to Woman sent non-Ethiopian women to doctors asking for Depo-Provera, they were all advised that Depo-Provera is only prescribed in highly unusual cases.[114]

The Ministry of Health's official policy toward Depo-Provera is that it should only be used when other methods of birth control are not suitable and only if there is a medical need; other than under these conditions, the use of Depo-Provera is not a recommended contraceptive method.[115] In fact, the Israeli Ministry of Health, in 2008, labeled Depo-Provera as a drug of last resort, only to be used when other methods fail or where there is a medical necessity for its use.[116] Despite these attestations, it is reported that when Ethiopians living in Israeli camps are subjected to a conversion process,[117] they are lectured on various topics including family planning and the use of contraceptives.[118] Ethiopian women have reported that the only contraceptive method that was discussed during these "workshops" was Depo-Provera.[119] No other form of birth control was mentioned. They also reported that they were not advised about the potential side effects of the use of Depo-Provera.[120]

As immigrant women, Ethiopians in Israel are one of the most vulnerable groups of women in the world. Immigrant women encounter discrimination on a regular basis. Such discrimination is complex because it occurs on multiple levels that include race, education, language, poverty, and socio-cultural barriers. Immigrant women, like all women, deserve an equal opportunity to fully participate in society, the freedom to determine the course of their lives, and the right and ability to access basic reproductive health services free of discrimination, harassment, and shame. Without respect for these rights, individual rights have little meaning, particularly the fundamental rights to live a dignified existence and to have children.

[112] Hedva Eyal, et al., *Depo-Provera: A contraceptive method given via injection, a report on its prescription policy among women of the Ethiopian community in Israel* (2010), *available at* www.isha.org.

[113] *Id.* at 8–13.

[114] *Id.*

[115] *Id.* at 7.

[116] *Id.* at 7.

[117] Ethiopians were housed at makeshift camps located in the Gondar region of northern Ethiopia where they were subjected to a conversion process, were introduced to all modern conveniences, and their African surnames were changed and replaced with Hebrew names.

[118] Eyal, *supra* note 113, at 7.

[119] *Id.* at 7.

[120] *Id.*

By placing the experience of Ethiopian women in Israel in context with Black women's experiences worldwide, we have the opportunity to push the reproductive justice framework forward by incorporating the experiences of immigrant women and standing in solidarity with them. Although Black women have played a key role in the normative development of the reproductive rights regime, those rights expressed in the Cairo Programme of Action and the Beijing FWCW Platform will mean little to the well-being of women unless national, regional, and international human rights instruments are used to ensure state compliance with the Cairo and Beijing commitments. The Universal Declaration of Human Rights, the International Covenant on Economic Social and Cultural Rights, the Convention on the Elimination of Discrimination against Women (CEDAW), and the International Covenant on Civil and Political Rights (ICCPR) can all be used to effectuate these goals. This remains the challenge to the reproductive health and reproductive justice movements – movements that have been and will continue to be heavily influenced by the life experience and advocacy of Black women worldwide.

ACKNOWLEDGMENTS

I kindly thank Sarah A. Moses for her dedicated research assistance. Without her invaluable assistance and insights this article would not have been possible.

12

Guest Work as Sex Work: Some Preliminary Thoughts on Margaret Radin and Black Women Selling Sex across Borders

Eleanor Marie Lawrence Brown

INTRODUCTION

International development policymakers persistently struggle to formulate policies to aid the increasing number of poor and jobless women in developing economies.[1] These efforts are especially urgent because the global financial crisis has displaced many women from the "real" economies of developing countries.[2] Across the developing world, governments have been implementing structural reforms through austerity measures.[3] In developing countries, these measures have consistently led to rising unemployment rates associated with the closing of local firms and – as governments seek to contain their burgeoning debts – the downsizing of government workers.[4]

Unsurprisingly, in many developing countries, the poor are finding fewer employment opportunities in traditional sectors such as farming and

The author is GWIPP Fellow and Associate Professor of Law, George Washington University; former Schwartz Fellow, New America Foundation; former chairman of the Jamaica Trade Board; former Reginald Lewis Fellow, Harvard Law School; former law clerk to the Honorable Patricia Wald (ret.), U.S. Court of Appeals for the District of Columbia Circuit; former law clerk to the Honorable Keith Ellison, U.S. District Court for the Southern District of Texas. She holds a JD, Yale (1999) and an M.Phil. Politics, Oxford (1997) (Rhodes Scholar).

[1] *See* International Labour Organization, Global Employment Trends for Women 2008 15 (2009). For similar themes, see International Labour Organization, Global Employment Trends for Women 2009 at 31 (2009); International Labour Organization, Global Employment Trends for Women 2010 at 42 (2011).

[2] *See* International Labour Organization, Global Employment Trends for Women 2008 15 (2009).

[3] This point is particularly well made in the Introduction to José Antonio Ocampo & Joseph E. Stiglitz, Capital Market Liberalization and Development 1–3 (2008) ("Capital Market Liberalization"). *See also* Paul Krugman, The Return of Depression Economics and the Crisis of 2008 (2009); James K. Galbraith, Introduction to Inequality and Instability: A Study of the World Economy Just before the Great Crisis (2012).

[4] *See* 4 World Bank, Global Economic Prospects: Uncertainties and vulnerabilities (January 2012).

manufacturing.[5] Alongside rising unemployment rates, safety nets, such as government subsidies, have been reduced.[6] Notably, in many developing countries, disruptions in the hardest hit traditional employment sectors (such as manufacturing) have disproportionately impacted men.[7] Increasingly, women must fill economic roles in families that men traditionally filled. Indeed, women have become primary breadwinners throughout the developing world.[8]

Increasingly, women are participating in transnational labor markets,[9] especially in the cash-strapped, debt-ridden Afro-Caribbean countries that constitute North America's "third border."[10] Women – who now constitute the majority of the working population in many of these countries – have been displaced from the formal labor markets in large numbers and thus seek work in informal labor markets.[11] This rise in informal employment has caused consternation among international development policymakers.[12] Although informality per se is not a terrible thing,[13] women working in informal labor markets lack the protections of formal labor markets.[14] Moreover, as informal labor markets have become increasingly transnational, informality now poses new challenges. For example, women in informal labor markets are more vulnerable to recruitment by transnational criminal gangs.[15]

Although poor women from the developing world have traditionally been regarded as "low-earning and in that regard low value-added individuals . . . a burden rather than a resource,"[16] they have simultaneously become "significant sources for profit-making, especially in the shadow economy."[17] The

5 *See* CAPITAL MARKET LIBERALIZATION, *supra* note 3 at 10.

6 *Id.*

7 *See* International Labour Organization, GLOBAL EMPLOYMENT TRENDS, 2011 15 (2012).

8 *See* International Labour Organization, WOMEN IN LABOUR MARKETS: MEASURING PROGRESS AND IDENTIFYING CHALLENGES 4 (2010).

9 *See* International Labour Organization, WOMEN GENDER AND THE INFORMAL ECONOMY 23 (2008).

10 *See Fact Sheet Caribbean Third Border Initiative*, The White House: President George W. Bush (April 21, 2001), *available at* http://georgewbush-whitehouse.archives.gov/news/releases/2001/04/20010423–5.html.

11 *See* Economic Commission for Latin America and the Caribbean, REGIONAL STUDY ON WOMEN'S UNRECOGNIZED CONTRIBUTION TO THE ECONOMY 20 (2010).

12 *See* WOMEN GENDER AND THE INFORMAL ECONOMY, *supra* note 9 at 23.

13 *See* Alejandro Portes & William Haller, *The Informal Economy* in HANDBOOK OF ECONOMIC SOCIOLOGY (Niel J. Smelser and Richard Swedberg eds., 2nd ed., 2005).

14 *See* WOMEN GENDER AND THE INFORMAL ECONOMY, *supra* note 9 at 22.

15 *Id.* at 23.

16 *See* Saskia Sassen, *Countergeographies of globalization: The feminization of survival*, at 2, Address at "Gender Budgets, Financial Markets, Financing for Development" conference (February 19–20, 2002), *available at* http://www.glow-boell.de/media/de/txt_rubrik_3/Sassen.pdf.

17 *Id.*

paradigmatic shadow transnational enterprises are human trafficking and narcotics operations.[18] As these women and enterprises have become an important source of hard currency for cash-strapped developing economies many jurisdictions – including Afro-Caribbean countries – stand accused of willfully ignoring the multitude of poor women who migrate for illicit purposes.[19]

Of course, as international development policymakers have pointed out, many of these women are employed in formal (as opposed to informal) transnational labor markets.[20] They contend that, in a regime of liberalized borders, it is unrealistic to ask developing countries to screen whether their nationals are migrating for illicit employment.[21] For example, Saskia Sassen describes "alternative circuits" of survival for "women who migrate from south to north to work as nannies (or) domestics."[22] As Sassen notes, "the image of an immigrant woman serving the white middle class professional woman (in North America) has replaced that of the black female servant working for the white master in centuries past."[23] As globalization has increased the demand for highly paid professionals in "global cities," "professional households without a wife" have proliferated (metaphorically, if not literally).[24] In these households, a growing share of tasks that were formerly considered properly "domestic" have been reallocated to the market.[25]

Thus, we have witnessed a burgeoning "serving class,"[26] which is increasingly "feminized," "transnational," and disproportionately Black.[27] In Northern urban centers like Miami and Toronto, today's migrant "domestic" is likely a Black woman of Caribbean origin.[28] Many live actively transnational lives, working in North America while sending critical foreign currency remittances to cash-

[18] *Id.* at 3.
[19] *Id.* at 3.
[20] *See* International Labour Organization, WOMEN TRAFFICKING: LINKS AND RISKS IN UNREGULATED LABOUR MARKETS (2010).
[21] *Id.*
[22] *See* Saskia Sassen, *Global Cities and Survival Circuits*, *in* GLOBAL WOMAN: NANNIES, MAIDS, AND SEX WORKERS IN THE NEW ECONOMY 254, 255 (Barbara Ehrenreich & Arlie Russell Hochschild eds., 2003).
[23] *Id.* at 262.
[24] *Id.* at 259.
[25] *Id.*
[26] *Id* at 255.
[27] *See* Nancy Foner, IN A NEW LAND: A COMPARATIVE VIEW OF IMMIGRATION 89 (2005); *see also* Nancy Foner, *Gender and migration: West Indians in comparative perspective*, *in* INTERNATIONAL MIGRATION 47:3–29 (2009).
[28] Foner, *Gender and Migration* at 7.

strapped families, communities, and countries of origin.[29] Many international development policymakers consider these jobs "ideal" because poor women gain access to hard currency earnings in the "formal" sector in a developed country. Moreover, these jobs have proven resilient in the face of global market fluctuations.[30] Nevertheless, access to these jobs is limited: most developed countries are protecting their labor markets and tightening their borders.[31]

Sassen also writes about another historically "domestic" function that has become increasingly commodified – sex. Although prostitution is often referred to as the world's "oldest profession," globalization has provided new opportunities for transnational prostitution.[32] Concurrently, increasing numbers of sex workers are migrating from developing countries to developed countries where highly paid clients abound.[33] These migrant sex workers are earning hard currency and remitting to support their families, communities,

[29] *See* Peggy Levitt, *Salsa and ketchup: Transnational migrants straddle two worlds, in* THE CONTEXTS READER, AMERICAN SOCIOLOGICAL ASSOCIATION (Jeff Goodwin and James Jasper eds., 2008).

[30] *See* WOMEN GENDER AND THE INFORMAL ECONOMY, *supra* note 9 at 21.

[31] *Id.* at 25.

[32] One prominent sociologist defines sex work as "an activity in which the persons providing the sexual labor do so with multiple partners, while publicly acknowledging their participation in this exchange." Kamala Kempadoo, EXOTIC COLONIES: CARIBBEAN WOMEN IN THE DUTCH SEX TRADE 28 (1994) (unpublished Ph.D. dissertation, University of Colorado) (on file with the author) ("Kempadoo, Exotic Colonies"). When sex work is addressed in legal scholarship, the focus is usually on the domestic sex worker. By a domestic sex worker, I mean a sex worker within the United States. Typically, neither the patron nor the client has crossed a border. This point is made by Radin in the Introduction to Margaret Radin, CONTESTED COMMODITIES (1997). There are notable exceptions to the historical tendency to treat the perspectives of sex workers with short shrift, at least with respect to domestic prostitution. *See* Sibyl Sewarzenbach, *Contractarians and feminists debate prostitution*, N. Y. U. REV. L. & SOC. CHANGE 103 (1990); Martha C. Nussbaum, *Whether from reason or prejudice: Taking money for bodily services*, 27 J. LEGAL STUD. 693, 710–12 (1995); David A. J. Richards, *Commercial sex and the rights of the person: A moral argument for the decriminalization of prostitution*, 127 U. PA. L. REV. 1195, 1215–16 (1979); Margaret A. Baldwin, *Strategies of connection: Prostitution and feminist politics*, 1 MICH. J. GENDER & L. 65 (1993); Naomi Cahn, *Policing women: Moral arguments and the dilemmas of criminalization*, 49 DEPAUL L. REV. 817 (2000); Ann M. Lucas, *Race, class, gender, and deviancy: The criminalization of prostitution*, 10 BERKELEY WOMEN'S L. J. 47, 48 (1995); Charles Rosenbleet & Barbara J. Pariente, *The prostitution of the criminal law*, 11 AM. CRIM. L. REV. 373 (1973); M. Anne Jennings, *The victim as criminal: A consideration of California's prostitution law*, 64 CAL. L. REV. 1235 (1976); David A. J. Richards, *Sexual autonomy and the constitutional right to privacy: A case study in human rights and the unwritten Constitution*, 30 HASTINGS L. J. 957 (1979); Lars Ericsson, *Charges against prostitution: An attempt at a philosophical assessment*, 90 ETHICS 335 (1980); Carol Pateman, THE SEXUAL CONTRACT (1988); Martha Nussbaum, SEX AND SOCIAL JUSTICE (1998); Viviana A. Zelizer, *The purchase of intimacy*, 25 LAW & SOC. INQUIRY 817, 826–33 (2000); Viviana A. Zelizer, THE PURCHASE OF INTIMACY (2005); Catharine MacKinnon, SEX EQUALITY (2001).

[33] *See* Kempadoo, Exotic Colonies, supra note 32.

and countries of origin, especially if they are employed in the formal sector as "escorts."[34]

Sassen does not write about another group of female sex workers earning hard currency in illicit economies – those who would have migrated had they the opportunity. Unable to travel themselves, North American and European clients travel to these women for sex.[35] When the legal scholarship addresses "transnational transactional sex," it almost exclusively focuses on women who are trafficked[36] in violation of the international human rights law.[37] Nevertheless, one author contends that many women who move to sell sex are not trafficked.[38] Although no precise statistics exist, it is undeniable that a significant percentage of transnational sex workers are independent contractors who utilize sex work as an asset-building strategy.[39] Such sex

[34] *Id.*

[35] Specifically, I am concerned with transnational sex – transactions in which either the sex worker or the patron crosses a border. I focus particularly on the contractual and other implications of impediments to labor mobility for sex workers. Jane Scoular and Teela Sanders highlight the increasing number of developed country clients traveling to the developing world in *The changing social and legal context of sexual commerce: Why regulation matters*, 37 J. L. & Soc'y. 5 (2010). *See generally* Symposium, *Regulating sex work: From crime control to neo-liberalism*, 37 J. L. & Soc'y 1 (2010).

[36] *See, e.g.*, Denise Brennan, *Key issues in the resettlement of formerly trafficked persons in the United States*, 158 U. Pa. L. Rev. 1581 (2010); Dina Francesca Haynes, *Lessons from Bosnia's Arizona Market*, 158 U. Pa. L. Rev. 1779 (2010); James Gray Pope, *A free labor approach to human trafficking*, 158 U. Pa. L. Rev. 1849 (2010); Jennifer Chacon, *Tensions and trade-offs: Protecting trafficking victims in the era of immigration enforcement*, 158 U. Pa. L. Rev. 1609 (2010); Janie Chuang, *The United States as global sheriff: Using unilateral sanctions to combat human trafficking*, 27 Mich. J. Int'l L. 437 (2006).

[37] *See* Protocol to Prevent, Suppress and Punish Trafficking in Persons, Especially Women and Children, Supplementing the United Nations Convention against Transnational Organized Crime art. 3(a), G.A. Res. 25 (II), at 54, U.N. Doc. A/55/383 (November 2, 2000): "Trafficking in persons' shall mean the recruitment, transportation, transfer, harboring or receipt of persons, by means of the threat or use of force or other forms of coercion, of abduction, of fraud, of deception, of the abuse of power or of a position of vulnerability or of the giving or receiving of payments or benefits to achieve the consent of a person having control over another person, for the purpose of exploitation. Exploitation shall include, at a minimum, the exploitation of the prostitution of others or other forms of sexual exploitation, forced labour or services, slavery or practices similar to slavery, servitude or the removal of organs."

[38] Denise Brennan, an anthropologist who has conducted ethnographic work among sex workers, made this contention in an exchange with Catherine MacKinnon at the University of Pennsylvania. For subsequent assertion of a similar point, see Denise Brennan, in a summary of the Symposium, *Trafficking in sex and labor: Domestic and international responses*, U. Pa. L. Rev. (November 2009), *available at* http://www.intlawgrrls.com/2009/11/go-on-trafficking-in-sex-labor.html; *see also* D. E. Brennan, Everything Is for Sale Here: Sex Tourism in Sosúa, the Dominican Republic (1998) (Ph.D. dissertation, Yale University) (on file with the author).

[39] *See* Brennan, Everything for Sale, at 15.

workers seek to voluntarily migrate to a different country where they voluntarily negotiate a contract for sex work.[40] Typically, they are able to negotiate more favorable rates abroad than they could back home.

I turn to an unconventional narrative for an academic paper. A few years ago, I had a chance meeting on a Caribbean Airlines flight with "Janet,"[41] a fellow Jamaican national who described herself as a "tourism worker" en route to market her services in Antigua in the Eastern Caribbean.[42] Although her specialty was exotic dance in a club that catered primarily to tourists,[43] she admitted that, for special patrons ("Johns"),[44] she offered a wider range of

[40] Although transnational transactional sex may also include patrons crossing borders, in this chapter, I am particularly concerned with sex workers who cross borders. For an excellent background summary of the scholarship surrounding transnational transactional sex, see Introduction to April Marie Gorry, LEAVING HOME FOR ROMANCE: TOURIST WOMEN'S ADVENTURES ABROAD (1999) (unpublished Ph.D. dissertation, University of California, Santa Barbara) (on file with the author); Tanya Kateri Hernandez, *Sex in the foreign city: Commodification and the female sex tourist, in* RETHINKING COMMODIFICATION: CASES AND READINGS IN LAW AND CULTURE 222 (Martha M. Ertman & Joan C. Williams eds., 2005). Although we know from the ethnographic literature that an increasing number of men have become sex workers, they still represent a minority. *See also* Gorry, supra.

[41] The name "Janet" was undoubtedly a pseudonym. Janet explained that she entered the Eastern Caribbean as a "tourism worker," although, as a Caribbean national, she might have been able to enter without declaring her work intention (and most sex workers probably do not declare a work intention). By the Eastern Caribbean, I mean members of the Organization of Eastern Caribbean States (OECS) including Antigua, Barbuda, St. Kitts, and Grenada. Janet was permitted to work in the Eastern Caribbean because of the Caribbean Single Market and Economy (CSME), which is modeled broadly on the European Union. The CSME permits "skilled" workers (with few exceptions) to provide their services anywhere in the Caribbean Community (CARICOM), which comprises primarily (although not exclusively) formerly British-colonized Caribbean islands. Some tourism workers are considered "skilled." For a good description of the CSME, including the labor mobility provisions, see Bank of Jamaica, International Department, Research and Economic Programming Division, The Caribbean Single Market & Economy (CSME), *available at* http://www.boj.org.jm/uploads/pdf/papers_pamphlets/papers_pamphlets_the_caribbean_single_market_and_economy.pdf.

[42] The terms "Caribbean" and "West Indian" are used interchangeably. I utilize the term "West Indian" as it is generally used in the sociological literature, namely, Anglophone (formerly British-colonized) Caribbean countries, although the term can also be utilized more broadly (e.g., French West Indian). *See* Orlando Patterson, *Context and choice in ethnic allegiance: A theoretical framework and Caribbean case study, in* ETHNICITY: THEORY AND EXPERIENCE (Nathan Glazer & Daniel Patrick Moynihan eds., 1975).

[43] The sale of "exotic dance" is legal in most CARICOM jurisdictions. Gloria Patricia Diaz-Barrero provides a brief summary of the legal posture of Caribbean and Latin American jurisdictions to exotic dance. *See* Migrant Latina Exotic Dancers and the Complicity of the Canadian State, 2004. Meeting of the Latin American Studies Association, *available at* http://lasa.international.pitt.edu/members/congresspapers/lasa2004/files/DiazBarreroGloriaPatricia_xCD.pdf. Whereas exotic dance is generally understood to be a euphemism that includes sex work, authorities rarely enforce statutes against prostitution.

[44] The term "John" is a pejorative for a client. For a dated but comprehensive discussion of the term, see Harold Holzman and Sharon Pines, *Buying sex: The phenomenology of being a John,*

services that sometimes included sex.[45] As a single parent and former household worker, Janet had previously depended on state aid to support her children. By transitioning to sex work in Jamaica, she had substantially improved her income.

Janet soon realized that she was unlikely to achieve her earning potential within Jamaica because her median client was either a fellow Jamaican or a "Coca-Cola" tourist.[46] Although virtually impossible for her to obtain a visa to travel to North America or Europe,[47] she realized she could access a wealthier

4 DEVIANT BEHAV. 89 (1982). For some Johns, Janet's relationship went even further. For example, she had developed an ongoing relationship with a British national who returned to the Caribbean repeatedly to see her. She daydreamed that one day he might sponsor her for a British visa.

[45] In this paper, I utilize the term "sex work" to mean the sale of sexual intercourse, as opposed to the sale of affiliated services such as sexualized dances, which I refer to as commodified touching or exotic dance.

[46] A "Coca-Cola tourist" is a middle-income (as opposed to a high-income) visitor from North America or Europe.

[47] Janet would typically be classified as a low-skilled person with poor economic prospects in her country of origin, and, as such, she would be considered a high risk for a visa overstay. Typically, her only route to enter a developed country would be on some sort of specialized visa for low-skilled workers, such as a guest worker visa. For a summary of the difficulties low-skilled persons typically face accessing visas outside of guest worker programs, please see Eleanor Marie Lawrence Brown, *Visa as property, visa as collateral*, 64 VAND. L. REV. 1047 (2011). The economist Norman Girvan has effectively summarized the visa restrictions for low-skilled CARICOM nationals and the economic implications of these restrictions. *See* Norman Girvan, *First-class and second-class CARICOM citizens?*, THE GLEANER, February 22, 2009, *available at* http://jamaicagleaner.com/gleaner/20090222/focus/focus 6.html.

Given that the only realistic route for most low-skilled workers to enter developed countries is through guest worker programs, it bears emphasis that it is unimaginable in almost every jurisdiction that sex workers would ever qualify for guest worker visas (as a guidebook for sex workers states). *See* Global Alliance in Trafficking against Women/Ban Ying Coordination and Counseling Center against Trafficking, *Migrating to Germany: Be safe* (2007), *available at* http://www.ban-ying.de/downloads/safemigrationhandbookenglish24.5.07.pdf. Moreover, the admission of sex workers to guest work programs would augment the profound misgivings that many scholars already have about guest worker programs. For broadly skeptical discussions of guest worker programs, see Hiroshi Motomura, AMERICANS IN WAITING: THE LOST STORY OF IMMIGRATION & CITIZENSHIP IN THE UNITED STATES 15–37 (2006).

Indeed in the United States, a background in volitional sex work would likely disqualify Janet from virtually every visa category. The guest worker provisions of the Immigration and Nationality Act, the primary legislation governing immigration, are found at 8 U.S.C. § 1101 (a)(15)(H) (2006). Guest worker visas are typically issued for agricultural, landscaping, restaurant, or hotel work. A background in sex work would render a potential guest worker inadmissible. Prostitution would typically be considered a crime involving moral turpitude (CIMT). This would constitute a basis to deny a visa to any applicant, including a prospective guest worker. Typically, a CIMT involves some element of moral culpability and prostitution, if entered into voluntarily, and is typically viewed in this manner. *See* U.S. Dep't of State, Defining "Moral Turpitude," 9 Foreign Affairs Manual (FAM) 40.21(a), N2.3–1, N2.3–3 (2010);

clientele by relocating from Jamaica to a more exclusive Eastern Caribbean island.[48] For "deal flow," however, she was almost entirely dependent on a pimp, euphemistically described as a "broker."[49] He had networks in Europe and North America for cultivating, screening, and referring clients. Partly because of her inability to travel, she described these networks as inaccessible. She insisted that meeting clients online was impractical given the "high-end" clientele that she was seeking. In her absence, her broker negotiated with potential clients on her behalf. Thus, she considered the broker indispensable to her revenue stream.

see also Nat'l Lawyers Guild, Immigration Law and Crimes, Moral Turpitude–Change in Definition of Moral Turpitude § 6:3 (2010).

Leaving aside the CIMT question, as a practical matter, it is unlikely that Janet would have been able to enter the United States as a guest worker. Given the limited number of guest worker visas, a low-skilled person without ties to family in the United States to "sponsor" them has no practical mechanism of entry. There are strict numerical limits on the number of guest workers. *See* 8 U.S.C. § 1101(a)(15)(H) (2006) (guest worker provisions). For a candid acknowledgment of the fact that the numerical limits on guest workers make it virtually impossible for low-skilled persons to come, see Press Release, The White House, President Signs Homeland Security Appropriation Act for 2006 (Oct. 18, 2005), *available at* http://georgewbushwhitehouse.archives.gov/news/releases/2005/10/ 20051018-2.html.

48 Since relocating, she had further multiplied her income several-fold, allowing her to buy a home in a middle-class Jamaican suburb even though she only worked a few days a month. Typically, volitional sex workers travel from poor rural areas to richer urban centers in their own countries. They travel from poorer Caribbean and Latin American states to richer neighboring states and, more rarely, to Europe and North America. *See* Anne McClintock, Screwing the System: Sexwork, Race, and the Law (1992); C. M. Press Jr., *Reputation and respectability reconsidered: Hustling in a tourist setting*, 4 Caribbean Issues 109 (1978), C. A. Karch & G. H. S. Dann, *Close encounters of the third kind*, 34 Hum. Rel., 249 (1981); Brugal Cavalcanti & M. Cordero, Prostitucion: Esclavitud Sexual Femenina (1985); C. Imbert Brugal, Tráfico de Mujeres: Visión de una Nación Exportadora (1991); E. Díaz, et al., Turismo y Prostitución en Cuba (1996); A. L. Cabezas, *Discourses of prostitution: The case of Cuba*, *in* Global Sex Workers: Rights, Resistance, and Redefinition (Kamala Kempadoo & Jo Doezema eds., 1998); A. L. Cabezas, Pleasure and Its Pain: Sex Tourism in Sosúa, the Dominican Republic (1998) (unpublished Ph.D. dissertation, University of California, Berkeley) (on file with the author); K. De Albuquerque, *Sex, beach boys, and female tourists*, 2 Caribbean Sexuality & Culture 87 (1998); Kempadoo, Exotic Colonies, *supra* note 32; Kamala Kempadoo, Sexing the Caribbean: Gender, Race, and Sexual Labor (2004); Kamala Kempadoo, *Women of color and the global sex trade: Transnational feminist perspectives*, *in* Meridians: Feminism, Race, Transnationalism 28–51 (2001); Kamala Kempadoo, *Freelancers, temporary wives, and beach-boys: Researching sex work in the Caribbean*, 67 Feminist Rev. 39 (2001); Kamala Kempadoo, *Prostitution, marginality, and empowerment: Caribbean women in the sex trade*, 5 Beyond L. 14, 69–84 (1996); Kamala Kempadoo, *Globalizing sex workers' rights*, *in* Global Sex Workers, *supra* at 2–28; Sun, Sex and Gold: Tourism and Sex Work in the Caribbean (Kamala Kempadoo ed., 1999).

49 The term "deal flow" is mine, not Janet's, but is inspired by her clear utilization of market-based language, as epitomized by the description of her pimp as a broker.

She appeared unbothered about what she was selling: her "high-end" clientele were paying a premium for a "Caribbean" experience. Notably, she readily admitted that her appeal to her mostly North American and European clientele was inextricably intertwined with fantasies regarding "exotic" Black Caribbean women – fantasies that are deeply racialized and gendered. Although she acknowledged that her work carried some stigma and risk of abuse, she had already cultivated some clients that she believed to be long-term. Moreover, her bargaining position within her family and community had significantly improved. Indeed, because of her newfound financial independence, her threats to exit an abusive relationship were finally credible.

This chapter is about the "Janets" of the world. Her story is indicative of a broader narrative – Janet had transitioned from unstable employment and welfare dependency within Jamaica to more lucrative hard-currency generating employment overseas. And rather than remain an exotic dancer – that is, an employee – in a tourist establishment (presumably in the formal sector), she essentially became an independent contractor, cultivating long-term arrangements with a broker and clients.

Thus, even as international development practitioners formulate strategies to help poor women in formal labor markets, poor women find unconventional ways to help themselves. Janet, for example, has found a way to "formalize" her work against tremendous odds. As an independent contractor, she enters into voluntary contracts for the sale of "companionate" services, typically including sex. "Janets" generally occupy the interstices of legality and extralegality – many operate as "escorts" or "exotic dancers" within formal tourism establishments (legal work) while providing freelance sex work (extralegal work). These women may have found ways to bring a semblance of order to their working lives within conditions of informality. Thus, although their work is technically still informal, the elements of formality are striking because sex workers like Janet seek to enter long-term contractual relations to stabilize client flow. Thus, it may be that the formalization of labor markets for poor low-skilled women may already be playing out in this particular sector on the ground.

Further improvement, however, critically depends on further formalization. For example, the Janets of the world must improve their status as contracting parties. This chapter is a reflection, in part, on how they might improve their capacity to contract. Moreover, to the extent that policymakers in international development are always seeking new formal sectors to provide sustainable earnings for poor women, it would be ill-advised to overlook this newly formalizing sector. The question is particularly pressing because these women are better placed than their low-skilled peers to become asset builders.

This chapter is organized as follows: in the section "How Do States Deal with Janet?," I discuss a continuum of legal responses to prostitution, ranging from limited protection to censure. An increasing proportion of transactional sex now involves North American or European clients crossing borders to lower income countries, beyond the reach of their home-country authorities. These developing countries rarely enforce prostitution laws and for good reason. According to public choice theorists,[50] welfare-maximizing states[51] compete to attract "desirable" criminal behavior, such as prostitution.[52] Indeed, a global "insourcing race" has evolved. Janet occupies a legal gray area of de jure censure alongside de facto legitimation. For good reason, the term "sex tourism" has now entered the popular lexicon even as the sale of sex is technically prohibited in many jurisdictions.[53]

In the section "How Does the Legal Scholarship Deal with Janet?," I discuss a range of legal academic responses to Janet. There has long been a split in the academy between theorists contending that the exchange of sex may be properly viewed through market lens[54] and others contending that

[50] The landmark article in public choice theory is Charles Tiebout, *A pure theory of local expenditures*, 64 J. Pol. Econ. 416 (1956). His description of the incentive structure of public actors is summarized in Tomer Broude & Doron Teichman, *Outsourcing and insourcing crime: The political economy of organized criminal activity*, 65 Vand. L. Rev. 795, 834 (2009).

[51] A similar narrative is relayed by international relations theorists, particularly those from the neoliberal and realism schools. *See* Broude & Teichman, *supra* note 50; *see also* Peter Andreas & Martin Nadelmann, Policing the Globe: Criminalization and Crime Control in International Relations v (2006).

[52] Many policymakers appear to believe that the availability of sex for sale may attract tourists who would otherwise not visit. *See* Brennan, Everything for Sale, *supra* note 38. Other spin-off benefits include excess cash that provides social benefits in inner-city communities. Broude & Teichman, *supra* note 50, at 841.

[53] *See* Andreas & Martin, *supra* note 51.

[54] The most prominent proponent of this view is Richard Posner. Richard A. Posner, Sex and Reason (1992). Advocacy organizations that support the recognition of markets in sexual services include the Sex Worker Education and Advocacy Taskforce (SWEAT) in South Africa; Durbar Mahila Samanwaya Committee (DMSC) in India; the New Zealand Prostitutes Collective (NZPC) in New Zealand; Call Off Your Old Tired Ethics (COYOTE) in the United States; and the international Network of Sex Work Projects (NSWP), founded in 1991. The writings of scholars, advocates, and sex workers who support the recognition of markets for the sale of sexual services are included in A Vindication of the Rights of Whores (Gail Peterson ed., 1989); *see also* Sex Work: Writings by Women in the Sex Industry (Frederique Delacoste & Priscilla Alexander eds., 2d ed. 1998); Global Sex Workers: Rights, Resistance, and Redefinition (Kamala Kempadoo & Jo Doezema eds., 1998); Whores and Other Feminists (Jill Nagle ed., 1997); Sex for Sale: Prostitution, Pornography, and the Sex Industry (Ronald Weitzer ed., 2d ed. 2010); Taking the Crime Out of Sex Work: "New Zealand Sex Workers'" Fight for Decriminalisation (Gillian Abel et al. eds., 2010); Margo St. James, *The reclamation of*

this notion of sex inevitably undermines important values like dignity and equality.[55] Here, I focus on Margaret Radin's case for legalizing commodified sex. A self-described "pragmatist-feminist," Radin is troubled by both the permissiveness and inflexibility of traditional theorists. She walks a fine line, seeking to craft a framework of narrow permissibility wherein which prostitutes can sell sex without developing an organized sex trade. Although Radin's focus is primarily the domestic U.S. market (as opposed to the transnational market), in Radin's framework Janet could only sell sex on her own, without the benefit of ancillary service providers (such as pimps) or enforceable contracts.

I consider the implications of Radin's analysis for sex workers who are unable to cross borders and, as such, are disproportionately likely to depend on brokers. I suggest that a hypothetical sex worker may be placed in one of four quadrants defined by two lines that capture two pressing concerns. First, is it legally permissible to perform sex work? Second, even if she is able to sell her sexual services, will she able to relocate to a market where she can command a higher premium?

Utilizing this framework, the section on legal scholarship introduces and compares a range of options for poor women. The very lucky may pursue sex work or guest work overseas. I argue that some poor women may perceive themselves to be better off with the options offered by the sex-work-rich,

whores, *in* GOOD GIRLS/BAD GIRLS: FEMINISTS AND SEX TRADE WORKERS FACE TO FACE 81 (Laurie Bell ed., 1987); Valerie Jenness, *From sex as sin to sex as work: COYOTE and the reorganization of prostitution as a social problem*, 37 SOC. PROBS. 403 (1990); Gail Peterson, THE PROSTITUTION PRISM (1996).

55 Michael Sandel and Michael Walzer, the communitarian philosophers, are the most prominent proponents of this view. *See* Michael J. Sandel, *What money can't buy: The moral limits of markets* (1998), *reprinted in* RETHINKING COMMODIFICATION, *supra* note 40 at 122–27. Michael Walzer's highly influential brand of communitarianism is skeptical of exchanges of goods that have historically been conceptualized in nonmarket terms. *See generally* Michael Walzer, SPHERES OF JUSTICE (1983). Walzer's position is effectively summarized in Viviana A. Zelizer, *The purchase of intimacy*, 25 LAW & SOC. INQUIRY 817, 826–33 (2000). The legal scholar Catharine MacKinnon focuses on how the recognition of markets in sexual services undermines the important value of gender equality. A summary of her position is included in Catharine A. MacKinnon, *Trafficking, prostitution, and inequality*, 46 HARV. C. R. C. L. L. REV. 271, 301–04 (2011). In a voluminous literature, I include a few samples of the writings of others who have expressed a similar views. These are included in the following collections and papers: Priscilla Alexander, *Feminism, sex workers and human rights*, *in* WHORES AND OTHER FEMINISTS, *supra* note 54 at 83; Ann D. Jordan, *Commercial sex workers in Asia: A blind spot in human rights law*, *in* 2 WOMEN & INT'L HUM. RTS. L. 525 (Kelly D. Askin & Doreen M. Koenig eds., 2000); Carole Leigh, UNREPENTANT WHORE: COLLECTED WORKS OF SCARLOT HARLOT (2004); Belinda Brooks-Gordon, *Clients and commercial sex: Reflections on paying the price: A consultation paper on prostitution*, CRIM. L. REV. 425 (2005).

visa-rich legal regime (e.g., the Netherlands, which permits sex work and allocates visas to pursue such work), as opposed to the visa-rich, sex-work-poor regime (e.g. the United States, which allocates visas to pursue low-skilled guest work but not sex work, which remains largely an extralegal activity). That is, given a choice between selling sex in Amsterdam and cleaning hotel rooms in New York, many women will quite reasonably choose sex work. Indeed, it is telling that this is precisely what Ophelia, the migrant hotel worker who alleged that she had been raped by former International Monetary Fund Director Dominique Strauss Kahn was accused by the tabloids of doing – pretending to be a hotel worker, when, in fact, she was a sex worker. It bears emphasis: although the claim that she was a sex worker was deeply controversial and has been discredited, the clear implication was that, given a choice between sex work and hotel work, sex work would have been an eminently reasonable choice.[56]

In the section "The Sex-Work Rich versus Visa Rich," I observe that although Radin attempts to put poor women at the center of her analysis, she has essentially tied Janet's hands by undermining her capacity to build assets. Janet's negotiations with her pimp are characterized by persistent information asymmetries. Given his network in developed country markets, the pimp can reasonably price Janet's services and project her client base. Although Janet knows her own work ethic, she is not in a position to verify his promises of projected earnings. Janet could mitigate the aforementioned challenge of information asymmetry by traveling to North America or Europe, where she would be better able to verify his projections. Absent this option, it becomes particularly important for her to be able to negotiate contractual terms up front to minimize the impact of asymmetrical information. Moreover, it is important for her to hedge by

[56] Ophelia is the pseudonym of Dominique Strauss Kahn's accuser. The tabloids claimed that Ophelia was granted a work visa while her asylum claim was being processed based in part on her commitment to pursue "legitimate" work, when, in fact, she was pursuing the far more lucrative option of sex work. The clear implication of the commentary was that there was no other likely explanation for how a formerly poor illiterate woman from rural Guinea could make ends meet in a major American city. For a representative view, see Laura Italiano, *Maid cleaning up as a "hooker,"* New York Post, July 2, 2011, *available at* http://www.nypost.com/ p/news/local/manhattan/maid_cleaning_up_as_hooker_omMd759PLuYGYYJyAoRNbI (alleging that she took "big tips for extra 'turndown service' ... DSK's accuser wasn't just a girl working at a hotel she was a working girl ... the woman had a lot of expenses paid for by men not related to her") and Dareh Gregorian, *No way she survives cross examination*, New York Post, July 3, 2011, *available at* http://www.nypost.com/ p/news/local/no_way_she_survives_cross_examination_azn4jgMV67pqvahQ7aVg8N (detailing similar accusations and the concerns of victim advocates and feminist groups that such accusations would deter other women who had been raped from coming forward).

contracting with several pimps to stabilize her client flow. This is precisely the organized marketization that Radin fears. Moreover, in Radin's framework, courts would not enforce contracts involving the sale of sexual services, effectively depriving Janet of any contractual protections she might negotiate.[57]

Radin's concern that enforcing contracts for the sale of sexual services could put the sexual lives of poor women at risk of further commodification seems remote in light of the stories sex workers tell of themselves, as revealed by the ethnographic literature on the subject. Like Janet, many sex workers emphasize that their incomes bring increased status and bargaining power back home. Incorporating Amartya Sen's theory of intermarital bargaining,[58] it appears that sex workers' threats to exit patriarchal relationships and communities are credible precisely because they are well paid. Applying Albert Hirschman's famous conceptual ultimatum, I consider the options that confront poor women when they seek to exercise agency in their relationships.[59] Because they have assets, sex workers, unlike many other poor women, can actually make credible threats to exit undesirable relationships and communities.

The goal of this chapter is less to offer a practical proposal than to challenge the ways that we traditionally think about how poor migrant women build assets. Circumstances that may appear corrupting and coercive to a detached observer may in fact be liberating to a sex worker in the context of her other options.[60] To elucidate this point, I consider ethnographic work among transnational prostitutes from the Caribbean, where sex work has always had transnational dimensions – the Caribbean was once described by Frantz Fanon as the brothel of Europe.[61] Because sex work undoubtedly generates racialized and gendered externalities that have implications for Black women more generally and undoubtedly augments misgivings among scholars, in conclusion, I confront this issue head-on.

[57] Given the potentially transnational nature of the contracting process, there is, of course, an independent important question of where these contracts would be enforced. This issue provides fertile ground for further work.

[58] *See* Amartya K. Sen, *Gender and cooperative conflicts*, *in* PERSISTENT INEQUALITIES: WOMEN AND WORLD DEVELOPMENT 123, 148 (Irene Tinker ed., 1990).

[59] *See* Albert Hirschman, EXIT, VOICE AND LOYALTY (1970).

[60] Here, I utilize the language of Williams and Zelizer in Joan Williams and Viviana Zelizer, *To commodify or not to commodify, that is not the question*, *in* RETHINKING COMMODIFICATION, *supra* note 40 at 362.

[61] Frantz Fanon, *cited in* Kempadoo, Exotic Colonies, *supra* note 32.

How Do States Deal with Janet?

The Insourcing Race

Commodified touching (i.e., exotic dance) is legal in most Caribbean jurisdictions; commodified sex is not.[62] Traveling to buy or sell exotic dance as a tourism worker is permissible; traveling to buy or sell sex is not.[63] To the extent that Janet's services encompass exotic dance, they are permissible. If she crosses the line into sex work, she is technically breaking the law. Nonetheless, with limited exceptions, laws that criminalize prostitution are not enforced in the Caribbean.[64]

How did this system evolve?[65] Tomer Broude and Doron Teichman observe that in a globalized economy, unlawful profit-driven businesses respond just like their legal counterparts when facing variances in legal regimes.[66] In an interesting permutation of regulatory arbitrage, when a criminal enterprise in one jurisdiction faces laws that impose significant costs, it may shift to other jurisdictions that impose lower sanctions.[67] Notably, a variety of schools of international relations theory interpret this phenomenon through a similar narrative: countries formulate crime control policies to maximize their own welfare, seeking to contain crime in their own jurisdictions even if it means displacing crime elsewhere.[68] Applying game theoretic analyses, Broude and Teichman demonstrate how states come to engage in crime control "races" based on their national attitudes toward prostitution.[69]

A case in question is the "outsourcing races" that evolve as some states adopt stricter policies toward the sex trade, which shifts to other states, which in turn adopt stricter policies to repel the inflow of sex workers.[70] Mechanisms exist within federal systems, such as the United

[62] Legal Review on Trafficking in Persons in the Caribbean, Report of the Inter-American Commission of Women in the Organization of American States and the International Organization for Migration (2011) ("Report, Inter-American Commission of Women").

[63] *Id.*

[64] *Id.*

[65] *See* Broude & Teichman, *supra* note 50.

[66] *Id.* at 799.

[67] *Id.* at 807–08.

[68] According to public choice theorists, local jurisdictions aiming to maximize their own welfare compete among themselves to attract activities that improve their welfare and set policies to deter activities that undermine their welfare. Thus, states attempt to contain criminal behavior in their own state. The realism and neoliberalism schools of international relations theory relay a similar narrative. *See id.* at 801–03.

[69] *Id.* at 800.

[70] *See* Broude & Teichman, *supra* note 50, at 817.

States, to address the "outsourcing" races – such as centralizing crime control policy.[71] Nevertheless, absent a centralized international authority, developing countries that spend far less on law enforcement than developed countries will inevitably find the sex trade being outsourced to them.

Broude and Teichman also discuss how insourcing races may evolve.[72] The sex trade has significant spin-off benefits, particularly for developing countries seeking the hard currency that tourism brings. Given these spin-off benefits,[73] some states are more inclined to be lenient. As these states adopt more lenient policies, thus attracting the sex trade, other states (who also seek the spin-off benefits) similarly reduce their criminal penalties. In summary, the crime control policies adopted by individual states affect the global distribution of transnational crime.[74] In each of these races, states impose externalities upon other states in what is essentially a global collective action problem.[75]

This narrative illustrates how some developing countries, such as those in the Eastern Caribbean, have become havens for transnational sex workers. They have statutes criminalizing prostitution on the books, but deploy subterfuges that allow them to avoid prosecutions, particularly if the patrons are hard currency-laden tourists.[76] Thus, de jure censure coexists with de facto legitimation.

Censure and Protection

I begin with an overview of the strategies states typically employ to address prostitution. On one extreme, governments criminalize both the supply side (the sale of sex by workers) and the demand side (the purchase of sex by

[71] Consider an analogy from the U.S. context. For example, in the aftermath of California's "three strikes" law, criminals seeking to evade tough enforcement measures fled to neighboring states, thereby imposing costs on California's neighbors. The California "three strikes" law is codified at Cal. Penal Code §§ 667(b)-(i) (West 1999) and § 1170.12 (West Supp. 2003). The law requires that a defendant with two prior serious or violent felony convictions receive "an indeterminate term of life imprisonment" with parole to be determined. Joshua R. Pater, *Struck out looking: Continued confusion in Eighth Amendment proportionality review after Ewing v. California*, 123 S. Ct. 1179 (2003), 27 Harv. J. L. & Pub. Pol'y. 399, 400 (2003); *see also* Doron Teichman, *The market for criminal justice: Federalism, crime control, and jurisdictional competition*, 103 Mich. L. Rev. 1831, 1847–48 (2005).

[72] *See* Broude & Teichman, *supra* note 50, at 840.

[73] For example, excess cash from laundered money provides social benefits in inner city communities. *Id.* at 841.

[74] *Id.* at 847.

[75] *Id.* at 832.

[76] *See* Report, Inter-American Commission of Women, *supra* note 62.

patrons). Most U.S. states[77] and developed countries adopt this "censure model."[78]

In the middle is a "modified censure model." For example, Norway does not criminalize the supply side while simultaneously imposing[79] heavy criminal penalties on the demand side. Indeed, Norwegians are even subject to prosecution in Norway for purchasing sex outside of Norway.[80]

On the other end, Nevada and the Netherlands epitomize the "protection model."[81] They decline to criminalize the sale or purchase of sex. Instead, both pursue a regulatory strategy requiring sex workers to meet certain registration requirements and clients to purchase sex from licensed providers. In so doing, they pursue a dual strategy of legitimation and containment.[82]

The Muddled Middle/Subterfuge

Although the legal scholarship places a disproportionate focus on domestic prostitution in European and North American countries, this focus does not reflect the changing reality on the ground. An increasing proportion of transactional sex now involves North American or European clients crossing borders to low- or middle-income countries with laxer laws beyond the reach

[77] See Vicki Schultz, *Introduction* to *symposium, sex for sale: Sex and work*, 18 YALE J. L. & FEMINISM 223 (2006). For a practical, easy to read guide, see a comparative chart of prostitution statutes in *A state-by-state look at consensual crime, in* Peter McWilliams, AIN'T NOBODY'S BUSINESS IF YOU DO: THE ABSURDITY OF CONSENSUAL CRIMES IN OUR FREE COUNTRY (1996), *available at* http://prostitution.procon.org/view.resource.php?resourceID=000119.

[78] *See, e.g.*, A *Summary of Prostitution in European Union Member States* (2010), *available at* http://www.europarl.europa.eu/hearings/20040119/femm/document1_en.pdf ("Summary EU Member States"); *see also* Julie Bindel & Liz Kelly, A CRITICAL EXAMINATION OF RESPONSES TO PROSTITUTION IN FOUR COUNTRIES: VICTORIA, AUSTRALIA, IRELAND, THE NETHERLANDS, AND SWEDEN 13 (2003).

[79] Norwegian law prohibits nationals from paying for sex either domestically or abroad. *See* Law Amending the Penal Code and Criminal Procedure Act of 1902, No. 104 (2008) (Nor.), *available at* http://www.lovdata.no/cgi-wift/ldles?doc=/all/nl-20081212–104.html.

[80] *Id.*

[81] Working Group on the Legal Regulation of the Purchase of Sexual Services, PURCHASING SEXUAL SERVICES IN SWEDEN AND THE NETHERLANDS: LEGAL REGULATIONS AND EXPERIENCES 27–29 (2004); Bindel & Kelly, *supra* note 78. Germany decriminalized prostitution in 2002. Gesetz zur Regelung der Rechtsverh altnisse der Prostituierten (Prostitutionsgesetz) [Act Regulating the Legal Situation of Prostitutes] (January 1, 2002). New Zealand has taken a similar course. Prostitution Reform Act (2003), *available at* http://www.legislation.govt.nz/act/public/2003/0028/ latest/DLM197815.html. Similarly, brothels and escort agencies have been legalized in Victoria, Australia. In Nevada, as of 1971, a county license board grants licenses to individuals and businesses to maintain and work in legal brothels in unincorporated towns and cities. *See* NEV. REV. STAT. § 244.345 (2009). Unlicensed prostitution is a misdemeanor in the state. *See* NEV. REV. STAT § 201.354 (2009).

[82] For example, while permitting prostitution, Nevada seeks to restrict its expansion through zoning restrictions. The Netherlands pursues a similar approach in its red light district.

of their national authorities. Thus, there should be an increased focus on transactional sex in these countries.

Some low- and middle-income countries have focused on reducing the supply of sex workers. States like the Philippines offer incentives for sex workers to transition to mainstream employment.[83] Supply-side disincentives include onerous fines and even imprisonment for sex workers and pimps. The authorities appear less inclined to prosecute clients, although purchasing sex is also unlawful.[84]

Historically, most developing countries took a similar approach to the Philippines in regulating prostitution.[85] Recently, however, many developing countries[86] have diverged from this mode and taken the Caribbean approach, which I term the "muddled middle." Although sex work is unlawful, states typically do not enforce the relevant statutes.[87] Moreover, businesses that sell access to quasi-sexual acts, such as firms that offer commodified touching, are not only permitted but encouraged, even though they are understood as gateways to the sale of sex.[88] In most such states, Janet will find neither protection nor censure.

Why is this? Sex may have become an indispensable part of the tourism product.[89] Thus, exotic dance clubs are not unlike other onshore attractions; they are vital hard-currency earners.[90] Some proportion of tourists are "but for"

83 *See* Janice G. Raymond et al., A COMPARATIVE STUDY OF WOMEN TRAFFICKED IN THE MIGRATION PROCESS: PATTERNS, PROFILES AND HEALTH CONSEQUENCES OF SEXUAL EXPLOITATION IN FIVE COUNTRIES (INDONESIA, THE PHILIPPINES, THAILAND, VENEZUELA, AND THE UNITED STATES) 64, 171–72 (2002).

84 *Id.*

85 This was usually articulated as a mechanism of preserving public health and communal values. *See* F. Henriques, PROSTITUTION IN EUROPE AND THE AMERICAS (1965) (discussing attempts to stamp out prostitution by the British colonial authorities for public health reasons); Gerald E. Aylmer, *Navy, state, trade, and empire, in*, THE ORIGINS OF EMPIRE. BRITISH OVERSEAS ENTERPRISE TO THE CLOSE OF THE SEVENTEENTH CENTURY 467, 1 OXFORD HISTORY OF THE BRITISH EMPIRE (Nicholas P. Canny ed., 1998).

86 Please note that I classify a country as "developing" in accordance with World Bank designations. *See* World Bank, GLOBAL ECONOMIC PROSPECTS 2011 (2011).

87 Report, Inter-American Commission of Women, *supra* note 62.

88 *Id.*

89 *See* SUN, SEX AND GOLD, *supra* note 48; *see also* D. J. Pruitt, FOREIGN MIND: TOURISM, IDENTITY AND DEVELOPMENT IN JAMAICA (1993) (unpublished Ph.D. dissertation, University of California, Berkeley) (on file with the author).

90 *Id.* There is solid historical evidence of this. For example, academic studies of the pre-Castro Cuban economy of the 1950s indicated that tourism was the second largest earner of foreign currency, and sex was an integral part of the tourism product. Thus, the Cuban government supported "exotic dance" clubs as an integral element of their tourism policy at the time. E. Díaz et al., TURISMO Y PROSTITUCIÓN EN CUBA (1996). Sex tourism is now a significant contributor to the GDP of several low- and middle-income countries, by one estimate constituting as much as 3% of the Thai GDP. These figures are taken from Lorna Martin, *Paradise*

tourists, that is, *but for* the availability of commodified sex (or affiliated sectors such as commodified touching), they might not visit developing countries. And there is a further point – some proportion of these tourists become repeat visitors because of commodified sex. One need only think of the protagonist in the much-discussed film "Heading South" (Vers Le Sud), an American university professor who candidly admits that her repeated visits to Haiti are inextricably tied to her access to sexual relations with young Haitian men.[91] The film was fictional and the genders were reversed (i.e., it portrayed female North American clients and male Haitian sex workers), but the point was clear. Indeed, the film provoked considerable controversy precisely because it underlined that some proportion of tourists become repeat visitors *due to* commodified sex – that is, "but for" the availability of sex, they would not be repeat visitors.[92]

Thus, whereas the de jure system is one of censure, the de facto system appears to be one of deliberate underenforcement. In a globally competitive tourism market in which sex is now increasingly perceived to be an indispensable part of the tourism product, governments are unwilling to sabotage tourism by enforcing prostitution statutes. Thus, they become insourcing states.

These are classic cases of what Calabresi has termed "subterfuges."[93] These states recognize the potential spillover economic benefits of sex work. Simultaneously, they do not want to risk alienating important domestic constituencies, such as the church, or international constituencies, such as

revealed, TAIPEI TIMES, January 25, 2006, *available at* http://www.taipeitimes.com/News/feat/archives/2006/01/25/2003290710. A comprehensive account is included in Jeremy Seabrook, TRAVELS IN THE SKIN TRADE: TOURISM AND THE SEX INDUSTRY (1996), although the industry has clearly grown substantially in the years since its publication.

91 The NEW YORK TIMES and (British) GUARDIAN reviews of the controversial and widely discussed film can be found at http://movies.nytimes.com/2006/07/07/movies/07sout.html and http://www.theguardian.com/film/2006/jul/07/ drama.worldcinema, respectively.

92 As the logic goes, the Caribbean would potentially lose tourists if prostitution statutes were enforced because sex attracts tourists. Tourists spend money at hotels and restaurants. Poor Caribbean nationals who would otherwise likely be unemployed find work. Moreover, the money foreign "Johns" spend is usually denominated in hard currencies. Selling sex builds hard-currency reserves for Caribbean central banks. *See* Pruitt, *supra* note 89.

93 Calabresi and Bobbitt famously discuss the "subterfuges" that result from "tragic choice" frameworks, in which policy elites shield tough policy choices that compromise deeply held values from public view. Guido Calabresi & Philip Bobbitt, TRAGIC CHOICES (1978). The term "subterfuge" is from Guido Calabresi, IDEALS, BELIEFS, ATTITUDES, AND THE LAW 88 (1985). Norway, of course, is explicitly seeking to take on such "legal subterfuges." The tragic choice framework has most famously been applied to the issue of health care rationing. *See, e.g.*, Leonard Fleck, *Just health care rationing: A democratic decisionmaking approach*, 140 U. PA. L. REV. 1597, 1612 (1992).

multilateral development agencies, by publicly endorsing transactional sex. Instead, they turn a blind eye to transactional sex. Thus, Janet and her Johns operate in a gray area, lacking both legal censure and legal protection.

How Does the Legal Scholarship Deal with Janet?

Janets pose a real dilemma for legal scholars. I begin with a major caveat. I put aside those aspects of the current global sex work trade that offend our deepest intuitions about justice, including underage sex workers, trafficking, and so forth. This chapter only addresses the narrow case of adults who cross borders and enter into transactions to buy and sell sex *voluntarily*. For ease of analysis, I begin with some quick typologies to summarize the current state of the legal scholarship. Like all such typologies, these generalized classifications necessarily lack nuance.

"Nothing But" versus "Hostile Worlds"

On one end of the continuum – epitomized by adherents to Chicago-School legal economics, are those who Viviana Zelizer classifies as belonging to the "nothing but economic rationality" school of thought.[94] They contend that ostensibly noneconomic relations (including sexual relations) can quite reasonably be viewed as rational economic transactions.

Judge Posner's work epitomizes this position.[95] It is one thing to simply describe sexual relations in market terms. Posner, however, goes further by affirmatively advocating the recognition of legal markets in sexual services.[96] Although Posner has not addressed transnational transactional sex, law and economics scholars generally view immigration restrictions as impermissible tariffs that prevent persons from immigrating to countries where they would receive a higher reward for their effort.[97] Thus, Posnerians would likely support cross-border transactions involving sexual services because they are

[94] Zelizer contends that members of this school reduce the complexity of social life, including sex life, to one dimension: namely, the market. Zelizer, *supra* note 32.

[95] *See* Richard Posner, *supra* note 54.

[96] *Id.*

[97] Human capital is viewed identically to other "factors of production." As long as human capital is free to seek its highest reward, it will automatically flow to where its contribution is greatest. Thus, the developing world poor will travel to the developed world to harvest farms and clean hotels. Howard Chang, *The economic analysis of immigration law*, *in* MIGRATION THEORY: TALKING ACROSS DISCIPLINES 205 (Caroline Brettell & James Hollifield eds., 2000); Michael J. Trebilcock, *Immigration policy*, *in* THE NEW PALGRAVE DICTIONARY OF ECONOMICS AND THE LAW 259 (Peter Newman ed., 1998); Michael J. Trebilcock, *The law and economics of immigration policy*, 5 AM. LAW & ECON. REV. 271 (2003).

equivalent to domestic markets, as long as the typical mechanisms exist to protect disadvantaged market participants.[98]

At the other extreme are those Zelizer terms the "hostile worlds" theorists,[99] such as Michael Walzer and Michael Sandel. "Hostile worlds" theories, which are offered largely by communitarians, block exchanges of goods that have historically been conceptualized in nonmarket terms.[100] Although Catharine MacKinnon's work is not traditionally conceptualized in communitarian terms (at least in the sense that the term is traditionally understood),[101] there are important intersections between her work and that of Walzer and Sandel in that they all root their opposition to marketization in a defense of important independent values. She believes that gender equality is worth protecting in its own right, contending that all women will suffer from what she characterizes as the commodification of a subset of women.[102]

Radin

Others scholars occupy a middle ground between "nothing but" and "hostile worlds." Although uncomfortable with full-scale commodification of sexual services, they simultaneously recognize the remunerative potential of prostitution for poor women. As such, they support limited legalization and regulation.[103] Radin's work epitomizes the final camp.[104] As a self-described

[98] For example, *duress* in the context of contract law is a *common law* defense, and, if one is successful in proving that the contract is vitiated by duress, then the contract may be rescinded, since it is then *voidable*. *See* BLACK'S LAW DICTIONARY (8th ed. 2004) ("threat of harm made to compel a person to do something against his or her will or judgment; esp., a wrongful threat made by one person to compel a manifestation of seeming assent by another person to a transaction without real volition").

[99] *See* Zelizer, *supra* note 55.

[100] *Id.*

[101] MacKinnon's position is distinct from Sandel's, but she would probably also be classified as a "hostile worlds" theorist. She is particularly concerned about the implications of the marketization of sex for the independent value of sex equality. *See* MacKinnon, *supra* note 55. MacKinnon's view is that we cannot let voluntary market participants simply "be" because prostitution legitimates subordination. In MacKinnon's famous distillation of gender dominance, she states that "femaleness means femininity, which means attractiveness to men, which means sexual attractiveness, which means sexual availability on male terms." Catherine MacKinnon, TOWARD A FEMINIST THEORY OF THE STATE at 110 (1989).

[102] Whereas Walzer and Sandel, unlike MacKinnon, have not addressed the transnational sex trade, we would expect the same skepticism of international sex that they show toward sex in the domestic marketplace.

[103] Belying the typology, some feminist theorists (e.g., Lucas) have positions similar to those of legal economists. *See* Ann Lucas, *The currency of sex: Prostitution, law and commodification, in* RETHINKING COMMODIFICATION, *supra* note 40.

[104] *See Introduction* to Margaret Radin, CONTESTED COMMODITIES (1997).

"pragmatist-feminist,"[105] she contends that both commodification and noncommodification are suboptimal alternatives for poor women.[106]

Radin is particularly concerned with the domino effect[107] whereby commodification inevitably begets more commodification. Radin also has two further fears. First, she is deeply concerned with potential coercion. Given the limited bargaining power of many sex workers in relation to their clients, it is unclear whether these transactions are truly voluntary. Second, Radin is concerned about corruption.[108] Commodified sexuality is corrupted sexuality, not only because of a broader notion that human sexuality has moral worth, but also because of what it does to the sex worker. That is, it "detaches" from her something that is fundamental to whom she is.

Yet, given women's disproportionate poverty, Radin also recognizes that noncommodification denies poor women desperately needed income-generating opportunities. Herein lies what Radin calls "the double bind"; we are damned if we commodify, and we are damned if we don't.[109] To resolve this double bind, Radin would allow individual women to sell sex while taking steps to prevent the domino effect of an organized sex trade. She would not

[105] *Id.*

[106] *Id.*

[107] *Id.*

[108] I briefly expound further on Radin's critiques, which are grounded in concerns about coercion and corruption. Sandel succinctly captures the distinction between the coercion and the corruption critiques:

> Consider two familiar objections to prostitution. Some object to prostitution on the grounds that it is rarely, if ever, truly voluntary. According to this argument, those who sell their bodies for sex are typically coerced, whether by poverty, drug addiction or other unfortunate life circumstances. Others object that prostitution is intrinsically degrading, a corruption of the moral worth of human sexuality. The degradation objection does not depend on tainted consent. It would condemn prostitution even in a society without poverty and despair, even in cases of wealthy prostitutes who like the work and freely choose it. (Sandel, *supra* note 55 at 100)

Radin's corruption critique is more narrowly construed than Sandel's. For her, commodified sexuality is corrupted sexuality, not only because of a broader notion that human sexuality has moral worth, but because of what it does to the sex worker. That is, it "detaches" from her something that is fundamental to who she is:

> To understand [things that are fundamental to personhood, including sex] as monetizable or completely detachable from the person – to think, for example that the value of one's moral commitments is commensurable or fungible with those of another, or that the "same" person remains when her moral commitments are subtracted is to do violence to our deepest understanding of what it means to be human. (Radin, *supra* note 32 at 80)

In Radin's conception, exchanging sex in the marketplace corrupts personhood because sale constitutes detachment, and detachment means loss. Sex is deeply personal; sex necessarily implicates the self.

[109] *Id.*

criminalize the act of prostitution, but she would prohibit affiliated acts like pimping, recruitment, training, advertising, and contract enforcement.

I now turn to considering the potential decision-making matrices of a hypothetical sex worker seeking to travel to a developed country. Should she be forced to remain in a developing country, I also address her options in contracting with a pimp to augment her income. Ultimately, I address the implications of Radin's analysis for this hypothetical sex worker.

Insights from the Ethnographic Work

SEX WORK AS LIBERATION. I first turn to the experiences of the sex workers themselves, as discussed in ethnographic work. Although some scholars have shown skepticism regarding the critical utility of sex work ethnography,[110] I do not share such skepticism. As long as ethnographies are considered with a healthy dose of critical distance, they are relevant to the extent that they may illuminate these women's own perceptions of their decision-making matrices and bargaining power. Indeed, it seems critically important to integrate such ethnographic work into our theorizing.

What, then, to make of the wealth of ethnographic work in which sex workers deny that they are demeaned by the experience of selling sex? Key themes repeatedly emerge in such work: women describe sex work as signifying empowerment, entrepreneurism, independence, and autonomy. Many sex workers characterize their work as not only justifiable but even admirable – precisely because it is a mechanism of upward mobility.

It appears that while the detachment implicit in a commercial transaction may seem corrupting to an observer, it may simultaneously seem liberating to a sex worker precisely because it offers the potential to improve her opportunity set. Rather than characterize themselves as disadvantaged in their contractual negotiations with their clients, sex workers appear to see themselves as savvy bargainers, much more likely to dupe than be duped.

Take for example, the Dominican sex workers who are the subject of one ethnography. They repeatedly describe themselves as strategic actors. Their goal is clear: making good on the "dream of a ticket" (i.e., an airline ticket).[111] One particularly strategic sex worker, Carmen, notes that an airline ticket without marriage is useless because her goal is not a visa but ultimately a "green card" (permanent residency in the United States). Marriage is typically the basis for the prized green card – signifying long-term upward mobility.

[110] Although some scholars bemoan the lack of critical rigor in ethnography, ethnographic work is often the primary means of incorporating the real experiences of sex workers into academic theory.

[111] *See* Brennan, EVERYTHING FOR SALE, *supra* note 38 at 155.

As the ethnographer Denise Brennan writes, "[t]o the extent that they can, they try to take advantage of the men, who are [there] to take advantage of them.[112] … Dominican sex workers often see the men … as readily exploitable – potential dupes, walking visas, means by which the women might leave the island and poverty behind."[113] This raises doubts about whether these women see their negotiations with clients as coercive. On the contrary, sex workers describe themselves as being highly strategic in their choice of partners.[114]

Carmen succinctly summarizes the broader societal view of migration as a mechanism of social mobility: "[t]here are three kinds of people: the rich, the poor, and those who travel to New York."[115] The ultimate goal is marriage as a route to New York. As Carmen tells the story, ideally marriage should be *por amor* (for love), but, if not, marriage *por residencia* (for residence visas) will suffice.[116] Subjects provide detailed accounts of former sex workers who have moved to Europe in pursuit of a lifestyle that is inconceivable for the poorest Dominicans.[117]

In Carmen's conception of moral responsibility, her primary duty is to provide for her children. To the extent that sex work allows her to achieve this goal, she appears not only comfortable, but also confident in her moral calculus. She does not seem to find the work corrupting because it is widely understood in her community that many women pursue such work to improve the opportunity sets of themselves, their families, and their communities.[118]

[112] *Id.* at 156.

[113] *Id.*

[114] *See* Pruitt, *supra* note 89 at 152.

[115] *See* Brennan, EVERYTHING FOR SALE, *supra* note 38 at 155. For a similar discussion on migration as an advancement strategy, see Eugenia Georges, THE MAKING OF A TRANSNATIONAL COMMUNITY: MIGRATION, DEVELOPMENT AND CULTURAL CHANGE IN THE DOMINICAN REPUBLIC (1990); Eleanor Marie Lawrence Brown, *Outsourcing immigration compliance*, 77 FORDHAM L. REV. 2476 (2009); and Eleanor Marie Lawrence Brown, supra note 47 at 1085.

[116] *See* Brennan, EVERYTHING FOR SALE, *supra* note 38 at 155.

[117] *Id.*

[118] Notably, the narrative and the moral calculus need not be static. Even if sex work is considered a mechanism of upward mobility in their own communities of origin, sex workers understand that, in the context of other communities, such work may be considered degrading. Thus, as they change communities, they express a willingness to modify their narratives to accord with prevailing views.

For example, another sex worker, Nanci, is well-known as a sex worker in her community of origin and, indeed, is admired for her professional success. She ultimately married a German client and relocated to Germany. Although Nanci was well-known in her original community as a sex worker, while in Germany she concealed her history as a sex worker and seemed less sure about her previously strident defenses of her professional choices. She worried how she

Indeed, Brennan describes "sex work as advancement" as follows:

> [The] sex trade is a story not simply of women who use sex work as a survival strategy but also of women who try to use sex work as an *advancement* strategy. ...These women see ... [the] sex trade and marriage to foreign tourists as a fast track to economic success – a way not just to solve short-term economic problems but to change their lives (and their families' lives) through migration overseas, in the long term.[119]

Moreover, even in other ethnographic studies where subjects do not appear so explicitly marriage/visa-focused in their goals, they still view sex work as substantially better than their other career options.

A similar study of Guyanese, St. Lucian, Trinidadian, Haitian, and Dominican prostitutes in Barbados found that a significant number of these women described sex work as a mechanism of generating income to allow them to exit inequitable domestic situations.[120] That is, they view sex work as providing them with the leverage to sever unequal relationships.[121] This theme emerges more broadly – sex workers are able to exit not only undesirable relationships, but also undesirable jobs, neighborhoods, and so forth. In one Barbados-based study, sex-worker subjects are self-described entrepreneurs, namely "self-employed individuals who decide the location of business, the services to provide, the fees to charge, the hours of service."[122] They emphasize their high degree of autonomy, and they see themselves as independent contractors.

Essentially, sex work provides them access to resources, persons, and experiences that are typically unavailable.[123] Notably, the work often has an aspirational aspect. Sex workers speak openly about their hope that some transactions will blossom into fulsome relationships sustained for longer

would be perceived, and questions of stigma that she had previously dismissed reemerged. Would she be stigmatized in Germany? Was this a legitimate judgment of her former work? She ultimately recognized that sex work is viewed differently in her new German community than in her community of origin in the Dominican Republic.

[119] *See* Brennan, Everything for Sale, *supra* note 38.

[120] *See* A. R. Paul, "It Isn't Love, It's Business": Prostitution as Entrepreneurship and the Implications for Barbados 192 (1997) (unpublished Ph.D. dissertation, University of California, Los Angeles) (on file with the author).

[121] *Id.*

[122] *Id.*

[123] *See* D. J. Pruitt & S. LaFont, *For love and money: Romance tourism in Jamaica*, 22 Ann. Tourism Res. 422–40 (1995); *see also* Pruitt, *supra* note 89; C. Fusco, *Hustling for dollars*, Ms. Magazine, September/October 1996, at 62–70; E. Díaz, et al., *supra* note 48; Brennan, Everything for Sale, *supra* note 38; A. L. Cabezas, Pleasure and Its Pain: Sex Tourism in Sosúa, the Dominican Republic (1998) (unpublished Ph.D. dissertation, University of California, Berkeley) (on file with the author).

periods through gifts and remittances. For good reason, the term "romance tourism" is often attached to sex work.[124]

This is not to deny that these arrangements appear at times to be coercive. For example, one study of Dominican and Colombian women who travel to the Dutch Caribbean island of Aruba found that many paid "recruiters" for placement in a central state-regulated brothel.[125] The arrangement had elements that appeared to be quasi-coercive because many of these women entered into long-term contracts akin to indentured servitude in which they were bonded to their recruiters until their "fees" had been paid.

Even in ostensibly coercive circumstances such as these, many sex workers indicated that they entered these arrangements as a strategic choice. They wanted the opportunity to travel to Aruba, a higher paying jurisdiction, and had not been in a position to finance the airline ticket without a recruiter. Moreover, their net wages still exceeded what they would receive from low-paying jobs in their countries of origin. They see their work as an asset-building strategy that they undertake with their eyes wide open, ironically in part because they perceive it as undermining social structures that they had perceived to be more rigid and unyielding prior to their entry into sex work.

Herein lies a repeated theme: sex work upends traditional social structures. In the next section, using elements of Sen's theory of intermarital bargaining, I consider how this upending transpires.

HOW SEX WORK MAY UPEND TRADITIONAL SOCIAL STRUCTURES: VOICE AND EXIT. Half of West Indian households are like Janet's: "fiscally fatherless" homes headed by two types of mothers. First, there are mothers who receive no support from the fathers of their children.[126] Second, in the event that they do receive such support, their marriages, whether law-based or common-law, typically involve itinerant men who may exercise occasional decision-making authority in the home but are not consistent financial contributors.[127] These West Indian households bear striking resemblances to the famous Wilsonian households of inner city Chicago.[128]

How do these households allocate assets, and what bargaining power do women have in relation to their husbands? Consider Gary Becker's "new

[124] *See* Pruitt & LaFont, *supra* note 123.

[125] *See* SUN, SEX AND GOLD, *supra* note 48.

[126] A good summary of the typology of familial types is in the classic anthropological work, Edith Clarke, MY MOTHER WHO FATHERED ME (1954).

[127] These relationships are more likely to be informal (i.e., common law) than formal (i.e., marriage). Again, Clarke's anthropological study of West Indian families is helpful in this regard.

[128] A good summary is William Julius Wilson, THE TRULY DISADVANTAGED (1987).

household economics model," which is widely utilized to explain micro-level household behavior and which has been influential in understanding how men and women allocate assets within the family.[129] In most societies, the family is the locus of ultimate distribution for most basic goods.[130] In this model, households are utility maximizing units motivated by stable preferences but constrained by pooled economic resources. Becker's original model was premised on the notion of one altruistic household member who controls the resources and presumably acts in the best interest of the family.

The original model has been widely criticized for assuming an altruistic family head, which fails to recognize the realities of intrahousehold bargaining over assets. Moreover, the traditional model ignored the connection between microeconomic gender stratification and broader social gender stratification. Given a background context of gender stratification, how do women negotiate to achieve their own ends in the family context? Amartya Sen offered a modified cooperative conflict paradigm in which "members of the household face two different types of problems simultaneously, one involving cooperation (i.e. adding to the total resources available) and the other conflict (i.e. dividing the total resources available among members of the household)."[131]

Sen's work is heavily influenced by ethnographic work conducted among poor Indian women who fared poorly in household bargaining. His work is particularly useful because his model accounts for the impact of a woman's self-perception (and how her community perceives her) on her ability to extract value in her marriage. Sen asserts that disparities often exist between an individual's subjective and objective assessment of her personal welfare.[132] Often, whether women undervalue themselves has tangible implications for the likelihood that they will accept an unequal allocation of assets within the households.

Sen's analysis is relevant to how we think of a sex worker's capability to bargain within her family. As a strategic independent contractor, a sex worker is likely to think critically about her personal interest (as opposed to the

[129] A good summary is in the Introduction to a newer edition of Gary S. Becker, A TREATISE ON THE FAMILY (2001).

[130] For example, even if the state provides resources to subsidize food or shelter, these resources are typically not distributed directly to the individuals, but instead to the family head, who is considered to act in the best interests of the individual household members.

[131] Sen, *supra* note 58 (suggesting that women's greater involvement in the outside world may shape their expectations of household divisions).

[132] *Id.*

interest of her client); such strategic thinking is also likely to permeate her negotiations with her husband. Recall Carmen, the aforementioned strategic Dominican sex worker. She explicitly segregates a portion of her income for herself because she does not assume that her husband will act in her interests or in the interest of their children. Carmen is clearly hedging her bets – her high self-regard and clear perception of her own self-interest (as distinct from familial interest) cause her to retain assets that would otherwise be pooled.

Moreover, Carmen's status as a high earner (compared to her community) should profoundly influence her household bargaining position. As Carmen relays her narrative, she experiences minimal stigma and is instead perceived as making a valuable financial contribution to her household and community. Sen reminds us that the perception of a woman in the broader community has tangible implications for her bargaining power in her household. Her threats to exit and commitments to contribute are credible.

The point here is both economic and psychological. The broader community believes Carmen to be a high-earning contributor. Recall that sex work can upend social structures through its aspirational effect: workers gain access to clients, experiences, and cash that were previously unattainable. Her outside earnings may lead to a higher perceived contribution to the family unit's economic position. Additionally, her increased earnings and autonomy may give her a clearer perception of the value of her own well-being.

Moreover, her sex work provides a daily reminder to her husband that her human capital investment is not "firm specific." When a women works exclusively inside the home, her human capital investment is "firm specific."[133] Her investment is typically not transportable elsewhere and, as such, is not a commodity. Typically, a husband's investments are not firm specific because he is employed outside the home. Should the parties choose to divorce, women (disproportionately firm-specific workers) are usually disadvantaged compared to their husbands (whose work outside the house is a commodity).

A sex worker with several clients is a quintessential market actor making non-firm-specific human capital investments – she is hedging her bets. If one particular client disappears, she has several others. If her husband disappears, she has external income (and perhaps a "husband in waiting"). Furthermore, her earnings confirm her sexual desirability to other men, which may also improve her bargaining position with her husband.

[133] *See* Katherine B. Silbaugh, *Marriage contracts and the family economy*, 93 Nw. U. L. Rev. 65, 111–22 (1998).

Albert Hirschman famously argued that members of any human grouping (be it a nation, a business, a religious group, or a family) have two main options when they perceive that the grouping is no longer beneficial to them: namely, they may voice their concerns and lobby for change in the grouping ("voice"), or they may exit the grouping ("exit").[134] Sex worker's earnings abet both Hirschman options. The sex worker is both better able to make credible threats (e.g., exiting a marriage) and, in the event that the bargaining breaks down (e.g., divorce), she has better options outside the marriage.[135]

Notably, a similar principle applies to other groupings in which sex workers may be members, particularly if, like Carmen, she is viewed as a route to economic mobility for the broader community. Her demands for better treatment are likely to be taken more seriously because she can credibly threaten to leave the community. Thus, sex work should be taken seriously as a strategy for improving women's abilities to negotiate to achieve their own ends in their families and their communities.

In the context of these ethnographic insights, I now turn to the decision-making matrix of a hypothetical sex worker. Furthermore, given that access to a visa is typically contingent on whether a visa applicant's prospective job is properly considered "work," in the next section, I reflect on Martha Nussbaum's contention that prostitution is indeed work.

The Sex-Work Rich versus Visa Rich

Bettering the Options of Sex Workers

We should be able to place any hypothetical poor worker in one of four quadrants defined by two lines that capture two pressing concerns. First, is it legally permissible to perform sex work? If the answer is no, then the worker is deemed sex-work poor. If the answer is yes, the worker is deemed sex-work rich. Second, even if she is able to sell her sexual services, is she able to relocate to a market where she can command a higher premium? If the answer is no, she is deemed visa poor. If the answer is yes, she is deemed visa rich.

I begin with those persons who occupy the first two quadrants. First, there are those who are not able to perform sex work and are generally not

[134] *See* Hirschman, supra note 59.

[135] Even if she stays in the marriage, both the woman and her community often perceive outside earnings as contributing more to the family economic position. Divorces demonstrate this fact. Women who earn externally are likely to be better placed postdivorce, because they are able to extract better concessions from their former husbands during divorce proceedings.

able to travel. They are the sex-work poor/visa poor. A Jamaican domestic worker without access to either a visa or sex work is a paradigmatic example (Quadrant A).

In the second quadrant are those who can perform sex work but cannot travel. A quintessential member of this quadrant is a Jamaican sex worker in Jamaica. Other members of this quadrant would be the aforementioned Dominican sex workers who are generally only able to travel if they can convert a client into a husband (Quadrant B).

Then there are those who are not able to perform sex work but are able to travel. These persons would generally perform low-skilled jobs in developed countries, but not higher paying sex work. The quintessential member of this quadrant would be a hotel worker in Aspen (Quadrant C).

Finally, there are those who are able to both perform sex work and travel to developed country markets – sex-work rich and visa rich. Paradigmatic examples include the historical affluent traveling sex workers who traveled with kings as royal courtesans and who today provide a "girlfriend experience"[136] for rich bankers in Amsterdam. This is the position to which Janet aspires – the Eastern Caribbean is simply a halfway house en route to her real goal – work in Europe or North America (Quadrant D).

There are several issues to unpack here, including sex as labor, sex as labor in domestic markets, and sex as labor in global markets. In an effort to further focus, recall the hypothetical low-skilled Jamaican woman who is considering her career options, options that mirror each of the aforementioned quadrants. Her first option is to work as a domestic housekeeper and command a monthly salary of $400. Or, she can become a sex worker within her own country and command a monthly salary of $900. Alternately, she can work outside her country as a hotel or agricultural worker and command a monthly salary of $2,500.[137] And, finally, she can become a sex worker outside of her country and command a monthly salary of $3,500.[138]

This is a quintessential picture of feminized poverty. Recall that in Quadrant A, she is living well below the poverty line. In Quadrant B, she is living just at the poverty line. Only Quadrants C and D allow her

[136] The girlfriend experience is a type of service a female prostitute offers that includes acting like "a girlfriend." The best summary of the concept is perhaps the controversial movie of the same name, THE GIRLFRIEND EXPERIENCE (Harvey Weinstein Studios 2010).

[137] This is the amount that a guest worker typically nets to remit home after living expenses. The figures are taken from the Remittance Project at the University of the West Indies, Mona Campus, Kingston, Jamaica (on file with author).

[138] My informal survey indicates that this is a conservative figure.

to properly school, clothe, and feed her children, given her current skill set. Essentially, she can only support her children comfortably if she travels.

Visas for "Work" versus "Sex Work"

The key is that the visa applicant must be performing functions that are considered work; that is, services that are properly distributed in the market place. If she is willing to pick apples, care for children, or clean hotel rooms, she has a fighting chance of obtaining a guest work visa. In nearly every developed country jurisdiction, the key issue in obtaining a guest work visa is whether the services that the person will be offering are appropriately considered work.[139] Women gain temporary guest work visas to developed country jurisdictions to perform a dizzying array of services from factory work to agricultural work to tourism work to child care to performance art (indeed, exotic dancers are now admissible to several EU countries as "performance artists!").[140]

The parameters of guest work change when what constitutes work shifts. For instance, seventy years ago it would have been nearly impossible to obtain a guest work visa to perform child care in most developed countries because it was considered inappropriate to commodify care.[141] Women raised children and cared for elderly grandparents and did so without market compensation.[142] Today, care is at least partially conceived of as work that can be properly distributed in the marketplace.[143]

Similarly, immigration policy has changed. Poor women can obtain visas to take care of children in Canada and grandparents in Germany.[144] Yet, the assumption that there is something intrinsically different about sex that makes it an inappropriate service for distribution in the marketplace persists. After all, sex is not work.

[139] A good introductory background is in the Introduction to Lant Pritchett, LET THEIR PEOPLE COME: BREAKING THE GRIDLOCK ON GLOBAL LABOR MOBILITY (2006).

[140] *Id.*

[141] In the voluminous literature, a good discussion of the evolution in how care is viewed is included in both Deborah Stone, *For love nor money: The commodification of care, in* RETHINKING COMMODIFICATION, *supra* note 40 at 271 and Katharine Silbaugh, *Commodification and women's household labor, in* RETHINKING COMMODIFICATION, *supra* note 40 at 297.

[142] *Id.*

[143] *Id.*

[144] *See* Salimah Valiani, Coalition of Domestic Workers International (Immigration Law Professors' listserv) (on file with author) (comparing guest worker options for domestic workers in Canada and the European Union in analysis).

Ultimately, as feminists have long asserted, societal conceptions of what properly constitutes work have tangible implications for women's ability to accumulate and retain assets. In the care context, women can now contract to provide care services that they were historically obligated to provide *gratis*. Although the analogy is rough, it is still instructive. Whether prostitution is properly understood as work has significant implications because, if prostitution is properly understood as work, female sex workers will be more able to access favorable labor markets.

Martha Nussbaum rightly questions why sex work is not considered work.[145] She observes that "[a]ll of us, with the exception of the independently wealthy and the unemployed, take money for the use of our body."[146] She juxtaposes a prostitute with other women who take money for the use of their bodies including a factory worker and a philosophy professor. She notes that, compared to a factory worker, a prostitute is likely to make more money, face fewer health risks (assuming appropriate protection), exercise more autonomy, and have greater control over her working conditions.

Her juxtaposition of the prostitute and the philosophy professor is particularly striking. She contends that both prostitution and philosophy involve the sale of services that are so intimate that they are definitive of selfhood. She writes:

> Just as the prostitute takes money for sex, which is commonly thought of to be an intimate area of self-expression, so the professor takes money for thinking and writing about what she thinks – about morality, emotion, the nature of knowledge, whatever – all parts of a human being's intimate search for understanding of the world and self-understanding. It was precisely for this reason that the medieval thinkers ... saw such a moral problem about philosophizing for money.[147]

The analogies continue:

> It may appear at first that the intimate bodily space of the professor is not invaded – but we should ask about this. When someone's unanticipated argument goes into one's mind, is this not both intimate and bodily? (And far less consensual, often, than the penetration of prostitute by customer?) Both performances involve skill. It might plausibly be argued that the professor's involves a more developed skill, or at least more expensive training – but we should be cautious here. Our culture is all too ready to think that sex

[145] Nussbaum, *supra* note 32.
[146] *Id.*
[147] *Id.*

> involves no skill and is simply "natural," a view that is surely false and is not even seriously entertained by many cultures.[148]

Through the stark juxtaposition of prostitutes and philosophy professors, Nussbaum seeks to elucidate that many of our concerns about prostitution apply equally to other more "legitimate" careers. Moreover, she seeks to elucidate that prostitution has advantages, such as autonomy and sexual "skill," not typically characteristic of jobs available to low-skilled women.

In the spirit of Nussbaum's analysis, let us focus briefly on Quadrants C and D. The women in Quadrant C do difficult work, picking fruit in Florida or cleaning hotels in Aspen. The work is not unlike the factory work Nussbaum describes, requiring repetitive, quasi-mechanical functions, and involving minimal variety and responsiveness.

The aforementioned ethnographic studies indicate that workers in "halfway-house" states engage in quasi-strategic work in their efforts to reach Quadrant D. Not only do they have to attract and maintain clients, those seeking husbands and visas must do much more. Their work does not simply pay more, it arguably requires more skill. It is simply a question of how we traditionally conceptualize skill.

Moreover, if the aim is to provide poor women autonomy through work, we already have a model in sex workers as independent contractors. Recall that many Caribbean sex workers are not attached to brothels but find their own clients and negotiate their own terms, thus allowing them control over their working hours and conditions.

It bears emphasizing that such autonomy is not typically available in other forms of guest work, which has tangible consequences for women and their children. Guest workers typically leave home on contracts that may last longer than a year. The extended period of separation from their families has led to a generation of children who sociologists alternatively call "barrel children" or "Western Union children."[149] If, as is often the case, their fathers are absent, these children become de facto parentless when their mothers are away as guest workers.

The sex work model is different. Leaving questions of societal stigma aside (admittedly a major caveat), a primary benefit of sex work is that it is often less disruptive of family life, especially for single parents. Workers typically travel to their clients for limited periods each month and otherwise remain at

[148] *Id.*

[149] *See* Pamela Marshall, BARREL CHILDREN (2011).

home.[150] One can see why female sex workers express disbelief when their inclination to travel to sell sex is questioned. The sex-work rich, visa rich quite reasonably believe themselves to be better placed than the visa rich, sex-work poor.[151]

For these women, Nussbaum contends, the goal should be to "have the option to use their body, in their work, in what Marx would call a 'truly human' manner of functioning, ... having some choices about the work to be performed, some reasonable measure of control over its conditions and outcome."[152] The next section contains some reflections about moving toward this goal for sex workers.

How Radin's Framework Constrains Janet's Ability to Build Assets

Recall that Janet is heavily dependent on a pimp to refer clients.[153] Like many principal–agent negotiations, the contracting process is characterized by chronic information asymmetries. The pimp presumably knows the market for Janet's services in Europe and North America better than Janet does. Presumably, Janet knows her own productivity better than her pimp. Both Janet and the pimp have an incentive to lie. Both would accomplish more if they honestly shared information, but each is unlikely to do so. One may apply game theoretical analogies, in which players are conceptualized as being involved in a long-term game. A mitigating factor is that in long-term relationships, reputational factors may dominate. Thus, for Janet and her pimp, concerns regarding their reputations might undermine the incentive to lie.[154]

[150] Although a less disruptive schedule benefits any parent, it is particularly beneficial to single parents. Brennan's sex worker subjects were disproportionately likely to be single parents. *See* Brennan, *supra* note #.

[151] Indeed, in the context of domestic sex work, Deborah Rhode contended that sex work was not clearly injurious to women (in strictly economic terms) in light of evidence that sex workers earned more than similarly situated low-skilled workers. Deborah Rhode, JUSTICE AND GENDER: SEX DISCRIMINATION AND THE LAW (2009)

[152] *See* Nussbaum, *supra* note 32.

[153] It is striking that Janet remains so heavily dependent on a pimp when she could presumably recruit and negotiate with clients in the thriving online marketplace for sex. Perhaps clients are unwilling to travel overseas to meet with a sex worker without the stamp of approval of an external party. Her dependence on a broker may also speak to some structural disadvantage (e.g., illiteracy) that prevents her from accessing the online market herself. This would be unsurprising, given the low rates of functional literacy among the poor in the Caribbean. *See* Human Development Index, Human Development Report 2011, United Nations Development Program, *available at* hdr.undp.org/en/statistics/hdi/.

[154] The relationship between Janet and her pimp calls to mind a classic iterated prisoners' dilemma, in which the game is played repeatedly. In the classic form of a prisoners' dilemma, rational choice leads each of the two players to defect even though each player's individual

How do Janet and her pimp respond to such informational asymmetries? Consider Janet's negotiation with the pimp prior to entering into a contractual relationship. Presumably, given his network in the North American and European markets, he can estimate reasonably accurately how much they will make. Assuming the pimp is able to supply the clients, Janet knows how many patrons she can comfortably provide services for. She also knows that the pimp has every incentive to overstate her future earnings. Nonetheless, given her poor access to the North American and European networks, she cannot verify the pimp's claims.[155]

Consider the background of these negotiations. A difficult and primary challenge for the pimp is to convince Janet that the projected earnings are credible. Presumably, however, he has several potential Janets and can diversify his risk by contracting concurrently with several prostitutes. The pimp may also have concerns about Janet's credibility because she might contract with several pimps as a mechanism of hedging her bets and may not follow through on her commitments if she finds other more lucrative clients.

It might seem that I am overstating the risk associated with Janet's inability to verify the pimp's claims. After all, any reputational cost to prostitution has already been incurred – like most women considering selling sex abroad, Janet is already selling sex domestically. Yet, when Janet moves, she incurs significant upfront costs. Moving even temporarily to the Eastern Caribbean is a logistical challenge. She must (at least temporarily) sever her relations with her Jamaican clients, thus risking a sure income stream for an indeterminate income stream. Moreover, given that the community of sex workers is relatively small, if Janet moves and is not successful, she will presumably suffer the reputational loss associated with not having made it in the "big league."

reward would be greater if she cooperated. As in broader game theory, each player is strictly concerned with maximizing her payoff; however, one player will always maximize her payoff by defecting, irrespective of what the other player does. As such, cooperation is overwhelmed by defection, so that the resulting equilibrium for the game is for all players to defect. In contrast to a conventional prisoners' dilemma, in which defection is always more beneficial than cooperation, in an iterated prisoners' dilemma, which is played over several games, each player has an opportunity to sanction the other player for prior noncooperative behavior. Cooperation may thus arise as an equilibrium outcome because the incentive to defect may be outweighed by the threat of sanction. *See* Joel Watson, STRATEGY: AN INTRODUCTION TO GAME THEORY ch. 1 (2002) (providing a good summary for the nontechnical reader).

[155] The Internet, of course, has substantially increased possibilities for marketization of sex. One need only consider THE GIRLFRIEND EXPERIENCE, the movie on sex work for "high-end" clients in New York. Although the Internet may reduce the challenges of information asymmetry, it is unclear whether the typical sex worker in a developing country would realistically have reliable Internet access.

People might also speculate as to the reasons for her lack of success. Is she no longer attractive to prospective clients? Has she "aged out?" Given that prostitution depends critically on perception, the costs of failure in the Eastern Caribbean are potentially high – in a small country, where "word of mouth" is important, her return to the Jamaican market will undoubtedly be perceived as a failure. Thus, Janet is faced with a potentially costly decision and few mechanisms to audit the information her pimp provides.[156]

But why is Janet in this position? The sexual service creates most of the value in this transaction. Janet is primarily responsible for the creation of this value. So why is the broker capturing a significant part of the value? Indeed, why is the broker necessary at all? The utilization of sex brokers remains pervasive even in a digital age in which sex workers and clients can find each other relatively easily online. As we learned from the case of former New York Governor Eliot Spitzer, there are "high-end" clients who are unwilling to find sex workers online and who value the augmented privacy a third-party negotiator enables. (Indeed, a former sex worker wrote a column making precisely this point to the golfer Tiger Woods after he was discovered engaging in sexual relations with prostitutes he had met online.)[157]

Presumably, Janet was trying to reach the Spitzers and Woods of the world. Yet, in doing so, Janet faced the systematic undervaluation of her contribution to the service. After the broker took his commission, she retained little of the money earned. Even if such clients prefer to reach sex workers through a broker (and, as such, one could reasonably argue that the broker is adding value for which he should be compensated), the broker's value in this transaction is undoubtedly augmented by the fact that this transaction is impermissible on at least one of two axes.

First, Janet cannot legally sell sex. The presence of a broker provides her with some protection through supplying plausible deniability. Thus, in the event that the authorities seek to apprehend her, she is essentially one step removed from the transaction (at least until the sex act) due to the broker's negotiation.[158]

Moreover, even if sex work were legal in either the Caribbean or the client's home country, the broker's value is undoubtedly augmented because Janet cannot legally move to recruit the potential clients herself. If we remove either of these legal impediments, Janet would be better placed to capture the value that she essentially creates.

[156] Janet might have access to networks of other women who have previously made the move.

[157] *See* Tracy Quan, *Hands off my call girl*, THE DAILY BEAST, February 25, 2010, *available at* http://www.thedailybeast.com/articles/2010/02/25/jealous-of-a-call-girl.html.

[158] A good discussion of this literature is in R. S. Burt, BROKERAGE & CLOSURE (2005).

How would Janet fare in Radin's world of narrow commodification? Radin would prohibit brokering/pimping, and, as such, Janet would have to proceed on her own. Radin, however, also prohibits advertising and recruitment, and so it appears that Janet's ability to promote her services would also be limited. Moreover, although it is also important for Janet to be able to hedge her bets by contracting with several pimps, this is precisely the organized marketization that Radin fears.

Most importantly, Radin would prohibit contract enforcement. Theoretically, Janet could mitigate the aforementioned challenges of information asymmetries utilizing contractual mechanisms such as commissions and profit sharing. Specifically, since the pimp's assertion of high revenue streams is not immediately verifiable, Janet might pay a lower commission. She might even receive an upfront payment from the pimp as compensation for her upfront costs and potential reputational loss. The pimp's willingness to sign onto such contractual terms would render his claim of high wages more credible. That said, in Radin's framework, contracts for sexual services are unenforceable, thus effectively depriving Janet of the protections that she could derive from negotiating favorable contractual terms.

Sex is already highly commodified on a global scale; the notion that enforcing contracts for the sale of sexual services could put the sexual lives of poor women at further risk of commodification seems remote. Moreover, given the increasing recognition of the link between poverty and poor access to legal protections for economic assets,[159] it seems counterproductive to deny poor sex workers access to contractual mechanisms to protect their interests. If the commodification horse has already left the gate, what poor women need is to retain the value they create through the security of enforceable contracts negotiated with their Johns and pimps.

Paradoxically, Radin's emphasis on narrow commodification, although well intentioned, may tie Janet's hands by undermining her efforts to drive a "hard bargain" with her broker.[160] Just as a paradigm of enforced noncommodification of sex work may undermine the opportunity sets for poor women, a paradigm of commodification that is too restrictive may inadvertently deny poor women asset-building opportunities.

[159] This point is particularly well made by the United Nation's Commission on Legal Empowerment of the Poor, chaired by Madeleine Albright and Hernando de Soto. *See* UN Dispatch, Mark Leon Goldberg, Hernando de Soto and Madeleine Albright Report on Legal Empowerment of the Poor, June 3, 2008, *available at* http://www.undispatch.com/hernando-de-soto-and-madeleine-albright-report-on-legal-empowerment-of-the-poor.

[160] The term is a play on the terminology utilized by Jane Larson and Linda Hirshman. Jane Larson & Linda Hirshman, HARD BARGAINS (1998).

Conclusion

To the extent that policymakers in international development are always seeking new formal sectors that can provide sustainable earnings for poor women, it would be ill-advised to overlook the voluntary sex work sector and the preliminary evidence of formalization within it. The reality is that transnational sex work may provide asset-building opportunities for poor women who otherwise lack employment opportunities. The situation is particularly pressing because these workers are rare among poor Caribbean working women (or, indeed, poor Caribbean workers more generally): because their clients are disproportionately likely to be North American and European, they earn vitally needed hard currency and are better placed than their peers to build assets.

This is an uncomfortable subject. These women, operating in a gray area between legality and extralegality, are virtually invisible in the legal scholarship. There is something deeply discomfiting about asserting that pursuing transnational sex work as an independent contractor may be a reasonable work option for low-skilled women. This discomfort is augmented by the striking demographic patterns in the sex trade, with richer White older men from the developed world constituting most of the patrons, and poorer non-White younger women from the developing world comprising most of the sex workers.[161] Indeed, as the controversy surrounding the film "Heading South" (in which the client protagonist was an older American woman and the sex worker was a younger Haitian man) illustrated, there is discomfort even when the genders are reversed. The Dickensian implications of such power differentials seem significant.

An analogy is instructive here. Rick Banks has recently reflected on why professional African-American women, "the least married, most childless

[161] Class patterns are also significant because, at the risk of stating the obvious, patrons are typically far richer than sex workers. For a somewhat dated, but nevertheless excellent analysis of the racial demographics of transnational sex work, see Cecilia Karch & G. H. S. Dann, *Close encounters of the third world*, 34 HUM. REL. 249 (1981). Indeed, women of color and migrants appear to be disproportionately represented among sex workers in several countries. *See* Barbara Goldsmith, *Women on the edge*, THE NEW YORKER, April 26, 1993, at 64, 65 (discussing the disproportionate representation of Black, Hispanic, and migrant women among sex workers in New York); Carol Leigh, *Black women and prostitution*, I GAUNTLET 113 (1994) (same with respect to Black women in the United States and Europe); *see also* Vednita Nelson, *Prostitution: Where racism and sexism intersect*, 1 MICH. J. GENDER & L. 81, 83 (1993) (same with respect to Black and Hispanic women in the U.S.); Melissa Farley et al., *Prostitution in Vancouver: Violence and colonization of First Nations women*, 42 TRANSCULTURAL PSYCHIATRY 242, 249 (finding a disproportionate representation of indigenous women [of First Nations descent] in Vancouver, Canada).

group in America" are unlikely to have children outside of marriage.[162] Indeed, many forego child rearing, despite having the desire and financial means to do so without a spouse. Banks asserts that that many of these women forego child bearing for fear of being perceived as "ghetto."[163] The term "ghetto" is clearly deeply freighted; having children outside of wedlock creates racialized and gendered perception externalities. In a context in which childbirth outside of wedlock has historically been stigmatized, Black women are perceived to be more inclined to have children outside of wedlock. Thus, having children outside of wedlock reinforces precisely the perception that Black women are more likely to engage in this stigmatized behavior – thus creating perception externalities.

According to Banks, many professional Black women appear unwilling to perpetuate these perception externalities.[164] It bears emphasis: what matters is not the reasonableness of the perception but rather that the perception exists. If Black women as a whole are worse off when engaging in such behaviors, the argument goes, it is better not to engage in such behaviors at all.[165]

Professor Banks's point is also apt in this context. Herein lies the problems with transnational sex work: there are broader gendered and racialized perception externalities created by the commodified sex trade. In a context that has historically stigmatized sex work, Black women have historically been perceived as sexually loose and likely to engage in sex acts for transactional purposes. Thus, for Black women to engage in sex work reinforces this perception. Ironically, it is precisely because many clients from the developed world have deeply racialized perceptions of sexual attractiveness that cadres of Black Caribbean women are now able to command premiums for selling sex. The premium exists precisely because of deeply problematic, historical stereotyping of Black women as "forbidden fruit."

Thus, we are faced with two competing ideas: the potentially liberating and empowering effects of commodified transnational sex trade for the poor Black female workers from the developing world versus the racialized and gendered perception externalities for Black women more generally, which inevitably accompany such commodification. In one sense, the two ideas are incommensurate. Concerns regarding the racialized and gendered perception externalities at their core go to the broader social effects of the marketized sex trade.

[162] *See* Rick Banks, Is Marriage for White People: How the African American Marriage Decline Affects Everyone (2011).

[163] *Id.* at 99.

[164] *Id.* at 102.

[165] *Id.*

That is, at some level, if one is concerned with the social effects of marketized sex trade, it may not matter what improvement in economic opportunity sets it creates for a particular cadre of Black women. Ultimately, my point is not to weigh whether the improved opportunity sets offset the broader gender and sexuality perception externalities created by commodified sex trade because it is impossible to measure these two against each other (like measuring whether a particular line is longer than a particular rock is heavy). My aim is to have the reader grapple with the challenging but necessary question of "what would you have the sex worker do if you condemn the idea of sex work or transnational sex work?" In the high-unemployment, poorly resourced countries from which most sex workers originate, the typical sex worker is unlikely to have alternative job prospects. If she is lucky, the most that she can typically hope for is a hotel or factory job that is likely to be far less remunerative than sex work. There are real questions as to whether any of these alternatives is actually better – from an economic standpoint and even perhaps an empowerment standpoint – than transnational sex work.

ACKNOWLEDGMENTS

I have benefited from workshops and both informal and formal feedback at the New America Foundation; the George Washington University Law School; the George Washington University Immigration Workshop; the Florida A&M University Law School; the Association for Law, Property, and Society; and from Pat Williams and the Feminist Legal Theory Workshop at the Columbia Law School.

13

Black Female "Things" in International Law: A Meditation on Saartjie Baartman and Truganini

Karen E. Bravo

The gestation of this project has been a long one, and I began and proceed with my labors with great trepidation:

> *I had heard of their stories . . .*
>
> *Of a Black woman – an African woman, called the Hottentot Venus, who had travelled to and performed in England. Whose remarkable buttocks had inspired the "bustle," the whalebone-constructed frame that enhanced fashionable female figures of the day.*

An issue of National Geographic spoke of a dead people – Tasmanian Aboriginals – and of their genocide. Of a woman, Truganini, the last of her race, survivor of the infamous Black Line which had scoured the island to identify and locate the remaining Tasmanian natives. A woman whose ashes had finally been laid to rest, long after her death, in the seas of her country.

On a 2000 visit to Amsterdam, I, like most tourists, was drawn by curiosity to visit the city's infamous Red Light District. Most of the women displayed for casual perusal, use, and purchase in the spotlighted windows of the District were young, white, Eastern European women who gazed back at spectators from deadened eyes. But, in one window, steps away from the Oude Kerk, was a group of three young Black women. Dressed in uniforms of skimpy lingerie, they performed for us – they danced, sang, and laughed together in their window. (Less knowledgeable about human trafficking and modern commoditization at that particular time), as I – a Black woman – stood before their window, next to my male Caucasian spouse (a "sister" who stood with the

The author is Professor of Law and Associate Dean for Graduate Studies and International Affairs, Indiana University Robert H. McKinney School of Law. Research assistance by Mercedes Rodriguez (Indiana University Robert H. McKinney School Law JD, May 2012) provided valuable contributions to this project. Ruth Lilly Law Librarians Debra Denslaw, Ben Keele, Catherine Lemmer, and Miriam Murphy, and reference staff of the Ruth Lilly Law Library were an invaluable resource.

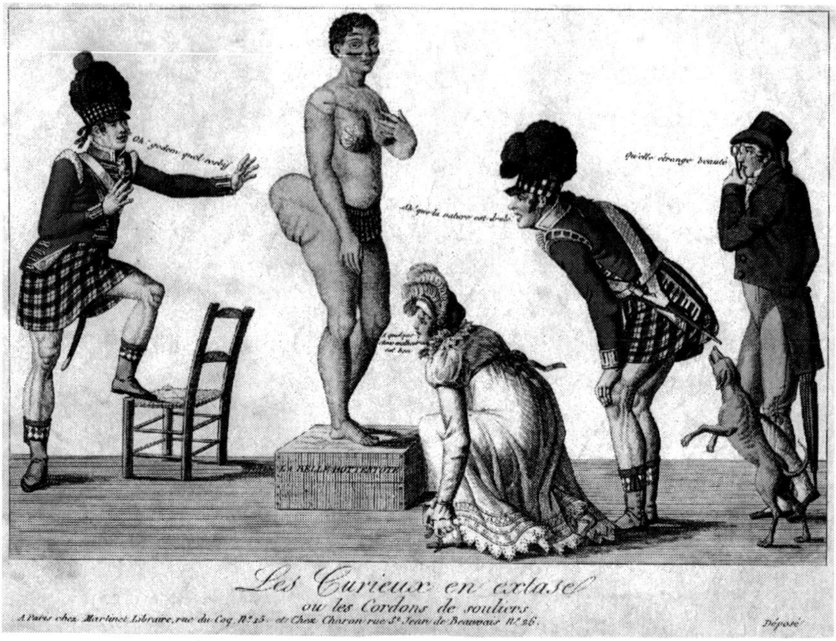

Les Curieux en extase, ou les cordons de souliers; The Trustees of the British Museum

Portrait of Truganini by Charles Alfred Woolley; National Library of Australia

enemy-customer-oppressor?), I openly displayed shock and dismay at their performance, and my perception that here were Black female commodities. Enraged at my reaction to their "choice," the women reacted in anger, shaking their fists and mouthing curses at me.

I stood before Truganini's monument on Bruny Island, Tasmania, in December 2008. The information boards accompanying the monument outlined the fates of Truganini and her people and her long-accepted status as the last Tasmanian Aboriginal. Surrounding me were the beautiful land- and seascapes of Tasmania, while across the D'Entrecasteaux Channel rose a very modern and very white Hobart. Absent from the modern beating heart were overt signs of the survival of Truganini's people.

In 2009, Dr. Jeremy Levitt of the FAMU School of Law invited me to participate in the groundbreaking 2010 symposium, *Black Women in International Law*. Now, as an academic, I had an opportunity to explore the stories of these two historic figures and the contemporary reverberations of their lives: how do the stories of the Hottentot Venus and Truganini illuminate the roles of black women in international law?

INTRODUCTION

On August 9, 2002, Saartjie Baartman,[1] a Khoisan or Khoikhoi woman known as the Hottentot Venus,[2] was laid to rest in South Africa at the culmination of nationwide celebrations.[3] One hundred eighty-seven years after leaving Cape Town,[4] after more than a century of the display of her most intimate body parts

1 "Sara," "Saartjie," "Saar-Key" are some variants on the spelling of the name of this historic black woman. *See* Rachel Holmes, African Queen: The Real Life of The Hottentot Venus xiii – xiv (2007). She referred to herself as Saartjie, meaning "Little Sara." *Id.* at xiii. The diminutive "jie" is a powerful one, expressing a range of meanings from endearment to contempt. *Id* at xiii–xiv. Her birth name (her "true-true" name) may never be known, but this chapter uses "Saartjie" (in deference to her expressed preference).

2 At the time of Baartman's birth, "Hottentot" was the name used for the Khoisan people of southern Africa – the Khoisan being the product of intermingling between nomadic hunter-gatherers, the San, and pastoralists, the Khoi. Holmes *Id.* at 9. The term "Hottentot" is a derogatory one, as, "[i]n Dutch, Hottentot meant to stammer." Clifton Crais & Pamela Scully, Sara Baartman and the Hottentot Venus: A Ghost Story and a Biography 132 (2009), reflecting the European doubt regarding whether the "Hottentots" were capable of human speech. *Id.* at 133. In the racial thinking of the nineteenth century, the economic and social differences between the San and Khoi were thought to be due to ethnic origin. The European settlers perceived the cattle-owning Khoi as potential trade partners and employees, whereas the nomadic San were seen as inassimilable. Over time, the colonizers regarded the Khoi (the so-called "Hottentots") as servile and the San as resistant;. Holmes, *supra* note 1, at 10.

3 *Id.* at 108–103.

4 *Id.* at 106.

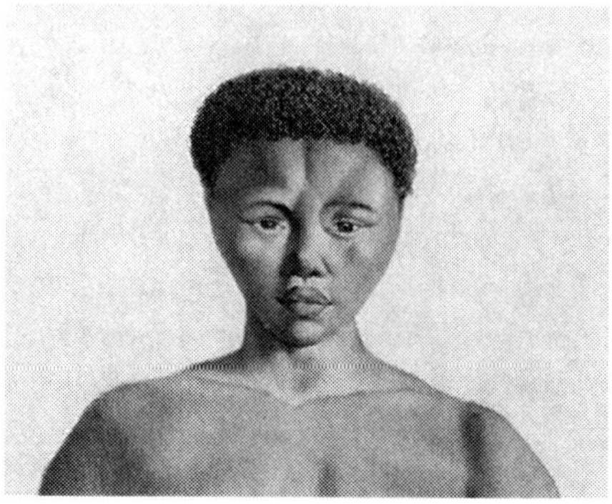

Detail from "*Femme de race bochismann*." In HISTOIRE NATURELLE DES MAMMIFÈRES, by George Cuvier, Paris, 1817

in the museums of France,[5] Saartjie Baartman had returned "home" a national symbol – a matriarch of the postapartheid South Africa.[6]

In 1976, one hundred years after her death, the ashes of Truganini,[7] the last Tasmanian Aboriginal, were scattered in the D'Entrecasteaux Channel – the sea passage between Bruny Island, her birthplace and homeland, and mainland Tasmania.[8] Her skeleton, which had alternatively hung on display in the Tasmanian Museum or had been hidden in dusty storage there, was removed by the Tasmanian government and cremated.[9] The corporeal symbol of Tasmanian Aboriginal extinction had been laid to rest amidst the emergence of ever louder claims of Tasmanian Aboriginal survival.[10]

What, if anything, do the tales of these two Black women have to do with international law or with the role of Black women in international law?[11]

5 *Id.* at 103.

6 *Id.* at 107, 114. Crais & Scully, *supra* note 2, at 3–4 ("Baartman emerged as South Africa's 'mother' and her life as the Hottentot Venus a reminder of the injustices black South Africans have endured over the past three and a half centuries.")

7 Various spellings of her name exist: Trukanini (*see* Lyndall Ryan, *The struggle for Trukanini, 1830–1997* 165 (1997 Peter Eldershaw Lecture); Trugernanna, and Truganini (Henry Reynolds, FATE OF A FREE PEOPLE 257, 2d ed. 1995); and Trucanini (*see* Nancy Cato & Vivienne Rae Ellis, TRUCANINI: QUEEN OR TRAITOR [1976]). Her preferred spelling (if indeed she had one) or pronunciation will never be determined. I use "Truganini" throughout this chapter.

8 Ryan, *supra* note 7.

9 Suvendrini Perea, *Claiming Truganini, Australia national narratives in the year of indigenous peoples*, 10 CULTURAL STUD. 393, 408 (1996).

10 Alexander Reilly, *The ghost of Truganini: Use of historical evidence as proof of native title*, 28 FED. L. REV. 453, 473–74 (2000). *See also* Ryan, *supra* note 7, at 166–67.

11 To Europeans, darker skin was synonymous with inferiority. The views of Tasmanians and other black-skinned Oceanic and Pacific natives had been tainted by the inferiority already ascribed to Black Africans. *See, e.g.*, Bronwen Douglas, "*Novus Orbis Australis*": *Oceania in the*

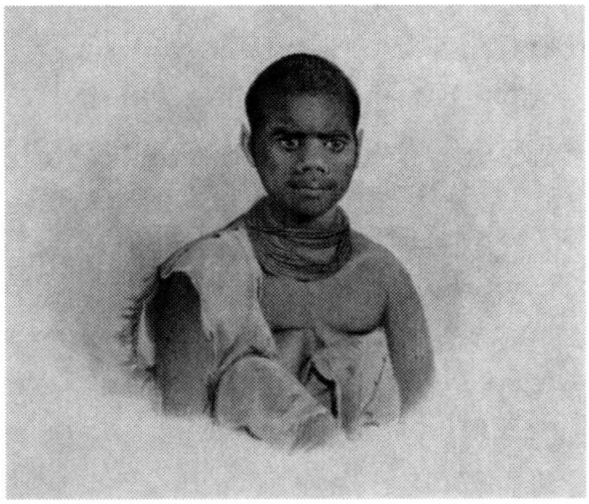

Truggernana: Native of the southern part of Van Diemen's Land, State Library of New South Wales

From a contemporary perspective, these two Black women were victims deprived of humanity and *life*. Baartman was an enslaved person, a transnational migrant, or a trafficked victim, and, ultimately, for both the scientific and popular Western audiences, a powerful and enduring symbol of African subhumanity and the virulent sexuality of the Black female.[12] Truganini had been anointed "queen"[13] of a "dead" people – an indigenous woman

science of race, 1750–1850 in FOREIGN BODIES: OCEANIA AND THE SCIENCE OF RACE 99–155 (Bronwen Douglas & Chris Ballard eds., 2010) (describing the evolving "science" of race in response to European encounters with "new" peoples in the Pacific and Australasia). Among the theories that gained foothold was one that "explained the peopling of Oceania by two 'decidedly distinct' races in terms of the supplanting of the 'most ancient tribe' of Oceanic Negroes by 'fairer' Polynesians." *Id.* at 134. Today, scientists tell us that modern humanity is descended from African origins. And Jamaican reggae great Peter Tosh sings:

> Don't care where you come from
> As long as you're a black man
> You're an African

See Peter Tosh, *Africa*, at http://www.lyricsmode.com/lyrics/p/peter_tosh/african.html.

In this chapter, I use "Black" and identify Saartjie Baartman and Truganini as "Black women" not to claim that universal human origin or to assert an essentialized African origin for all peoples with Black skin, but to acknowledge the commonality in the experiences of people *with* Black skin and of "native" status. These two attributes, Black skin and indigeneity or nativeness, together with their ascribed inferiority, gave permission to the colonial endeavors that subordinated Truganini and Saartjie's peoples. As described later in this chapter, the inferior status of people with Black skin in the universal racial hierarchy is founded in part on, among other things, the scientific inquiries based on Truganini and Saartjie.

12 Crais & Scully, *supra* note 2, at 3, 15 (the Venus Hottentot became the essence of primitiveness and then of the primitiveness of female sexuality). *See also* Deborah Willis ed., BLACK VENUS, 2010: THEY CALLED HER "HOTTENTOT" (2010).

13 For example, TRUCANINI, QUEEN OR TRAITOR, the title of the Cato and Ellis volume, *supra* note 7, uses the courtesy title "Queen" then commonly used in Australia.

dispossessed of land, people, and future, whose passing had cleared the way for total European domination of the island of Tasmania.[14]

These women and their destinies have much relevance to international law today. During their lifetimes, after their deaths, and even unto their reburials, Saartjie Baartman and Truganini were treated as "things": as both "not-quite-human" chattels and as symbols of national identity – both celebrated and regretted. Their stories raise questions about the relationship of natural law and positivist theories in the contemporary formulations of international law, the status of indigenous people in international and domestic law (including international human rights law), and the similarities between the legal status of slavery and the enslaved with those of colonization and the colonized. The potential themes and impacts of their lives span multiple disciplines – history, biology, anthropology, for example – and include the expansion of colonization, the status of native peoples in colonized lands, use of native peoples' corporeal remains to formulate and underpin the birth of scientific racism and the formation of a universal racial hierarchy, claims of ownership of indigenous remains as national patrimony (scientific "found" objects), the formation of national identity, and the contest between positivism and naturalism in international law.

This chapter explores the imposition of the subhuman status exemplified in the life stories, and the corporeal and symbolic fates, of these two Black women and their impact on the evolution and current state of international law. The chapter focuses on the legal status and consequences of the enslaved's or subordinate's choice, as well as on the choices and decisions available to and made by them. It concludes that the "choices" of these Black women add complexity to the understanding of the nature of "choice," particularly as it applies to the discussion of choice and consent in addressing contemporary trafficking in human beings. Further, in acknowledging and naming the "things" (interests) valued and pursued by Saartjie Baartman and Truganini, the study will clarify the universality of Black female "things" – concerns and issues that are shared across time, race, and gender.

BLACK FEMALE "THINGS": PARALLEL HISTORIES, PARALLEL DESTINIES, SAME MEANING?

Both Saartjie Baartman's and Truganini's stories take place against fundamental reconceptions of colonialism, empire building, and humanity. Other

[14] *See, e.g.*, Lyndall Ryan, The Aboriginal Tasmanians 2–3 (2d ed. 1996) (describing the perception of Truganini's death as marking the final extinction of Aboriginal Tasmanians).

contemporaneous forces and developments include the rise of the antislavery and anti-slave-trade movements; the expansion of European settlement and empires deep into the Antipodes; the division of Africa; encounters with and conquest of indigenous peoples;[15] and ever-broadening hierarchical categorizations of the human, animal, and plant life of the Earth.

Saartjie Baartman, the Hottentot Venus

Saartjie Baartman, an African woman of Khoisan ethnicity, was born in the 1770s or 1780s.[16] In the early 1800s, shortly after the prohibition of the British slave trade,[17] Baartman traveled to England – to London, the very heart of Empire. There and, later, in France, she was displayed as the exotic "Hottentot Venus,"[18] forever influencing European conceptions of Black females and Black female sexuality.[19] After her death in 1815, her body was dissected, a cast made for posterity, and her sexual parts were cataloged, stored, and displayed in French museums in furtherance of scientific knowledge.[20] Following the end of apartheid, the South African government convinced France to return Baartman's remains, and she was interred with great ceremony in South Africa.

Baartman was born in the Gamtoos River Valley on the eastern frontier of the Cape Colony. Her childhood took place against a backdrop of upheaval and conflict among the Dutch, the British, and the native peoples of the area

[15] The conquest of indigenous people and the imposition of enslavement was the product of struggles throughout the world. Slave rebellions occurred throughout the New World, ending most successfully in Haiti. *See, e.g.*, C. L. R. James, The Black Jacobins: Toussaint L'Ouverture and the San Domingo Revolution (1989). Tasmanian and mainland Aboriginals fought to expel the invaders from their lands. *See, e.g.*, Reynolds, *supra* note 7, at 55–68; *see also* Robert Cox, Steps to the Scaffold: The Untold Story of Tasmania's Black Bushrangers (2004).

[16] According to Holmes, Baartman was born in 1789. *See* Holmes, *supra* note 1, at xiii. In contrast, Crais and Scully claim that she was born a decade earlier – some time in the 1770s. *See* Crais & Scully, *supra* note 2, at 7. The potential decade's difference in age and experience casts in varying lights her experiences, expectations, and choices as she moved from Cape Town to London and on to Paris. For example, Crais and Scully claim that Baartman experienced the transition of her people from an independent communal life to one of service to the colonizing Dutch. *Id.* at 18–25. *See also*, *id.* at 57 (depicting Baartman as a mature woman who, by 1810, had spent a full decade in Cape Town).

[17] Britain abolished the slave trade throughout its Empire in 1807. *See* Jenny S. Martinez, The Slave Trade and the Origins of International Human Rights Law 22–23 (2012) ("As of May 1, 1807, the law completely prohibited participation in the slave trade by British subjects and the importation of slaves to British possessions").

[18] Crais & Scully, *supra* note 2, at 122–27.

[19] *See* note 12 *supra*. *See also* Crais & Scully, *supra* note 2, at 146–48.

[20] *Id.* at 139–40; 142–43.

that ended in the extermination of her people's traditional way of life.[21] Her mother died when she was less than a year old,[22] and, in 1807, her father, a cattle drover for the settlers, was killed by bandits.[23] Now an orphan "sold" by the Dutch settler for whom her family had worked, Baartman was taken into the custody of Pieter Cesars, a free Black.[24] She was to live with his brother Hendrick and sister-in-law in Cape Town, as an indentured servant – a wet nurse for a child they were adopting.[25]

When Hendrick Cesar's employer, Alexander Dunlop, a military surgeon, faced the possible loss of his livelihood, the pair hatched a plan to take Baartman to London in order to exploit her exoticism there. They would use Baartman's physique – unremarkable in an African context but exotic to Europeans – to make money by exhibiting her as a scientific curiosity to English audiences who clamored for novelty.[26] The Celadon (Hottentot) Proclamation had made it illegal to take Baartman or any Khoisan out of the colony without direct permission from the governor.[27] Baartman was therefore secreted on board a ship and set sail for England on April 1, 1810.[28]

The transatlantic slave trade had been abolished in Britain and all its colonies in 1807. However, the law allowed for existing slaves to remain the property of their owners.[29] The 1809 Celadon Proclamation (Hottentot Proclamation), issued by the colonial government, permitted Khoisan people to be legally indentured in the Cape Colony. The proclamation sought to address two issues: a labor shortage in the colony and concerns about how to quell protests by missionaries over the poor social and economic condition of the natives. Indentured servitude would ease the labor shortage and would legally guarantee the Khoi a wage and a few other basics.[30] Baartman was

[21] *See* Holmes, *supra* note 1, at 10–13; Crais & Scully, *supra* note 2, at 24.

[22] Holmes, *supra* note 1, at 8. However, Crais & Scully date her mother's death to the 1790s. Crais & Scully, *supra* note 2, at 24.

[23] Crais & Scully, *supra* note 2, at 24. Or, according to Holmes, a roving band of European commandos may have been responsible for his death. Holmes, *supra* note 1, at 13.

[24] Crais & Scully, *supra* note 2, at 24. In the Cape Town colony of that era, "Free Blacks" were "descendants of slaves from East and South Asia." Crais & Scully, *supra* note 2, at 42–43 (describing the status of the Cesars family and of Free Blacks in general).

[25] Holmes, *supra* note 1, at 15, 17–18.

[26] Holmes, *supra* note 1, at 27–29.

[27] Holmes, *supra* note 1, at 28.

[28] Holmes, *supra* note 1, at 28–32. Kidnapped, sold, indentured, transported from a "sending" to "destination" country: was Saartjie Baartman a victim of human trafficking? Or does her already indentured status in the Cape Colony mean that her coerced or seduced movement to London does not meet the definition of trafficking?

[29] Holmes, *supra* note 1, at 19.

[30] Holmes, *supra* note 1, at 25–26.

then officially registered as an indentured servant. The legal effect of the Hottentot Proclamation was to convert Khoikhoi into a common resource of the settlers. For the indigenous people present within the Cape Colony, there was no alternative to indentured servitude: natives who were not the contracted indentured servants of settlers were brought before the authorities and were entered into contract by the representatives of colonial officialdom.[31]

Upon arrival in London, Dunlop attempted to sell Baartman to Bullock's Liverpool Museum, but proprietor James Bullock "rejected his distasteful proposal."[32] Cesars and Dunlop decided to exhibit Baartman themselves.[33] She was made to dance and sing and play the ramkie, an indigenous stringed instrument. She was dressed in feathers and beads, in ways that played upon European notions of the exotic, wild peoples of Africa. The costume,

Truganini (seated, right): The last four Tasmanian Aborigines

[31] *See* Zine Magubane, *Labour laws and stereotypes: Images of the Khoikhoi in the Cape in the age of abolition*, 35 South African Hist. J. 115, 116–17 (1996).

[32] Holmes, *supra* note 1, at 36.

[33] Holmes, *supra* note 1, at 37.

skin-colored and tight fitting, also played up notions of raw sexuality. The Hottentot Venus became the talk of London.[34]

From these events sprang the litigation that came to be known as "The Case of the Hottentot Venus."[35] Zachary Macaulay, a well-known abolitionist, was a leader of the African Institution.[36] At the time of his visit to the Hottentot Venus display, he was fresh from the triumph of Britain's abolition of the slave trade. He publicly decried both the exploitation of Baartman and the vulgarity of the display. He and other members of the antislavery league believed, and were determined to show, that Baartman was being kept and displayed against her will, that she had been brought into the country illegally, and that her condition violated English law.[37] The public's interest was roused after a very public and prolonged confrontation between Dunlop and Zachary Macaulay.[38]

In an attempt to "free" or "rescue"[39] Baartman, Zachary Macaulay and the African Institution took legal action: they filed for a writ of habeas corpus for

[34] *See, e.g.*, Willis, *supra* note 12. The cover and chapters of Willis's edited volume explored the perceived continuum between the Hottentot Venus's depiction of black female sexuality and the images presented in modern hip hop music videos. *See also* Natasha Gordon–Chipembere, *Introduction: Claiming Sarah Baartman, a legacy to grasp* in REPRESENTATION AND BLACK WOMANHOOD: THE LEGACY OF SARAH BAARTMAN 10, 11 (Natasha Gordon-Chipembere ed., 2011) (also drawing the comparison between displays of the Hottentot Venus and modern hip hop representations of Black female sexuality).

[35] Holmes, *supra* note 1, at 59.

[36] Macaulay was a leading abolitionist of the period, holding the position of secretary of the African Institution; he was also a founding member, together with William Pitt and Granville Sharp among others, of the Sierra Leone Company from which the African Institution evolved. Holmes, *supra* note 1, at 51; Crais & Scully, *supra* note 2, at 82. Between 1807 and 1821, the African Institution was a key player in abolitionist activities in Britain. Crais & Scully at 86. *See also* Holmes at 52–53 (describing Macaulay's role in the British anti-slave-trade crusade).

[37] In 1762, the Lord Chancellor wrote that once anyone enters England, they are free and that "a negro may maintain an action against his master for ill usage, and may have a Habeas Corpus, if restrained from his liberty." Holmes at 60–61. A 1772 test case, the case of James Somersett, cemented the use of habeas corpus as a slavery fighting tool. Somersett, a slave, was transported from Virginia to England. He escaped but was recaptured and placed on a ship that was to sail to Jamaica. A writ of habeas corpus was issued on the ship's captain to bring him to the court. The case determined that slavery could not exist in England. Holmes, *supra* note 1, at 61. According to Holmes "Lord Chief Justice Holt in the early eighteenth century opined that 'as soon as a Negro comes into England, he becomes free." *Id.* at 60.

[38] *Id.* at 49.

[39] Modern-day adversaries of human trafficking also focus on rescuing victims from their traffickers. For example, the International Justice Mission rescues victims of human trafficking from their exploiters. *See* http://www.ijm.org/. Others have advocated a more structural approach that would address the causes of human trafficking. *See, e.g.*, Karen E. Bravo, *Free labor! Toward a labor liberalization solution for modern trafficking in humans*, 18 TRANSNAT'L. L. CONTEM. PROBS. 545 (2009). Part IV.C *infra* discusses the impact of "rescue" in the absence of structural change.

Baartman, demanding that Dunlop and Cesars provide proof of her passport from the colonial government in Cape Town, as well as the details of her travel from the Cape.[40]

The *Case of the Hottentot Venus* opened on November 24, 1810[41] before the King's Bench, at that time the highest common law court in England.[42] The court debated the question as to whether Baartman could provide her own statement to the court. Soon after the case opened, Dunlop took Baartman to have a backdated contract drawn up specifying the terms of her employment.[43] Interviewed on behalf of the court by Afrikaans speakers, she insisted that she had come to England of her own free will.[44] Dunlop's counsel painted her as "a free woman who displayed herself willingly on condition that she receive a share of the profits from her exhibition" and proposed that the African Institution set up and administer a trust for Baartman's earnings.[45]

Central to the controversy before the court was the issue of "whether Saartjie had the right to sell herself, and whether, as a subordinated subject, she was capable of giving her consent to do so."[46] Because Baartman was subject to the "Hottentot Proclamation," she could not leave the Cape Town colony without official sanction. In contrast, a free servant could depart at will.[47] The law with respect to free persons was different: "English legal precedent held that a person might enter into a contract of service for life, but not sell himself as a slave."[48] That is, a free person could not consent to become enslaved. By implication, then, in order to be legally recognized as a slave, a free person must have been *coerced* into the condition.

Lord Ellenborough wrote that Dunlop and Cesars had misled colonial authorities when they made their plans to leave Cape Town. However, *the court held that Baartman had given her labor willingly and that she was*

[40] Holmes, *supra* note 1, at 58.

[41] *Id.* at 59.

[42] Crais & Scully, *supra* note 2, at 85.

[43] Holmes, *supra* note 1, at 63.

[44] Holmes, *supra* note 1, at 64–65; Crais & Scully, *supra* note 2, at 98–101. Crais and Scully speculate that the circumstances of the deposition were such that Baartman could not speak "the truth" of her circumstances and that she would have feared retaliation by Dunlop and Cesars. Crais & Scully at 101. Holmes, too, speculates about the nature of Baartman's truth and choices. Holmes at 108–09.

[45] Holmes, *supra* note 1, at 66. That proposal, made under the assumption that Baartman could not manage her own income, was declined. The Institution would not touch earnings that originated from what they believed to be immoral entertainment. *Id.* at 66–67.

[46] *Id.* at 67.

[47] *Id.* at 68.

[48] *Id.* at 67.

deemed free.[49] That is, like other free subjects of the British Empire, she was free to contract, free to exhibit herself and to perform publicly. Although it is ultimately unclear how much *choice* Baartman had in traveling to London, the legal system did at the very least recognize that she could receive the protective attention of the courts and could access them to vindicate rights.[50]

Ironically, after the case's disposition, Dunlop and Cesars became financially dependent on exhibiting Baartman.[51] The controversy generated by the litigation had made the Hottentot Venus's show even more popular. Once the popularity had waned in London, the Hottentot Venus went on the road in provincial England.[52] Historians Clifton Crais and Pamela Scully have discovered some indications of "normalcy," of a quotidian domestic life in the period of Saartjie's subsequent "disappearance" in the English provinces: on December 1, 1811, Baartman was baptized into the Anglican Church.[53] Crais and Scully also suggest that, during the years spent in the English provinces, Baartman was married and may have given birth to a child who died.[54] In other words, the Hottentot Venus may have briefly led a

[49] *Id.* at 68. According to Holmes's interpretation of the record: "She understood that the men who had taken her managers to court offered release from exhibiting herself, and would send her home. Yet she regarded the offer with suspicion. What did these men want in return for her agreement? Macaulay and the abolitionists assumed Saartjie's desire to return to South Africa. Yet it cannot be ignored that the outcome of the case also suggests that Saartjie demanded the rights of the working immigrant to be paid for her labor and enjoy, if only temporarily, the comparative benefits of exile." *Id.* at 70. It is not possible to definitively plumb the depths of Baartman's motivations. Even in the American South, not all slaves wanted to be free, and some regretted their freedom. *See, e.g.*, BULLWHIP DAYS: THE SLAVES REMEMBER 456 (James Mellon ed., 1988): "I thought slavery wuz right. I felt that this wuz the way things had to go – the way they were fixed to go. I wuz satisfied. The white folks treated me all rights. My young missus loved me, and I loved her. She whupped me sometimes – I think, just for fun, sometimes" (quoting Joe High).

[50] However, the African Institution failed to recognize and challenge a "freedom that is dependent on and productive of slavery itself." *See* Hershini Bhana Young, *Rude performances: Theorizing agency, in* REPRESENTATION AND BLACK WOMANHOOD, *supra* note 34. That is, the limited agency available to the free person who must compete with the unfree. Such a "free" person may be forced to "choose" contractual "unfreedom."

[51] Holmes, *supra* note 1, at 71–72.

[52] *Id. See also* Crais & Scully, *supra* note 2, at 107.

[53] Holmes, *supra* note 1, at 72. *See also* Crais & Scully, *supra* note 2, at 107 ("On 1 December 1811, Saartjie Baartman entered Manchester Cathedral. She stood at the very front of the baptismal line – the individuals baptized after her were babies born the same year. [The Reverend Joshua] Brookes dipped his finger in the holy water of the font and christened Sara with the sign of the cross. Sara or Saartjie Baartman became "Sarah Bartmann." She made the papers again, this time as a Christian convert").

[54] Crais & Scully, *supra* note 2, at 108–09.

"normal" life of nineteenth-century domesticity as Sarah Baartman, her (chosen?) baptismal name.[55]

In the summer of 1812, Dunlop died of unknown causes. Following his death, Baartman disappeared from the public eye for two years, only to reappear in Paris during the summer of 1814.[56] The new show was "an ethnographic wonder,"[57] gaining startling popularity.[58] In January of 1815, Cesars went home to Cape Town after Reaux, a showman and animal trainer, offered to take over management of Baartman.[59] In the spring of 1815, Reaux

Monument to Truganini on Bruny Island, Karen E. Bravo

[55] Baartman carried her baptismal certificate with her until her death. Crais & Scully, *supra* note 2, at 107. *See, also,* Holmes, *supra* note 1, at 82–83 (reproduction of the baptismal certificate recovered from her body included among images related to Saartjie's life, death, exhibition, and burial).

[56] Holmes, *supra* note 1, at 73–74; Crais & Scully, *supra* note 2, at 113, 119.

[57] Crais & Scully, *supra* note 2, at 124.

[58] Holmes, *supra* note 1, at 79; Crais & Scully, *supra* note 2, at 126.

[59] Holmes, *supra* note 1, at 80.

arranged with the National Museum of Natural History for Baartman to pose as a life model for scientists and artists.[60] The scientists were determined to prove that differences existed in Baartman's sexual anatomy and that of other human races,[61] but were unable to confirm their theories: although the scientists pressed Baartman to pose completely nude, she refused, covering her *sexe* with a handkerchief.[62]

Following Baartman's stint as a life model, Reaux struck a deal with the museum's professorial board. Should Saartjie happen to die, the board would pay for the chance to dissect her.[63] In Paris, Baartman suffered from a recurring flu and the ill effects of excessive drinking.[64] She died on December 29, 1815, succumbing to repeated bouts of the flu, bronchitis, and excessive drinking.[65] A postmortem exam was conducted by Georges Cuvier,[66] who executed a full dissection of her body[67] and created plaster casts of her corpse (painted to mimic verisimilitude) while removing and dissecting her internal organs. Her brain and genitals were embalmed for scientific posterity in glass jars.[68] Baartman's skeleton was added to the museum's collection,[69] and her body cast, brain, skeleton, and genitals were displayed to the public until the 1970s.[70]

60 *Id.* at 82; Crais & Scully, *supra* note 2, at 134–36.

61 The physiological differences to which the scientists sought access were the alleged Hottentot Apron (extended labia) and the steatopygia (or prominent buttocks) of female Hottentots. *See* Holmes, *supra* note 1, at 86–87; Crais & Scully, *supra* note 2, at 140–41; Gordon-Chipembere, *supra* note 34, at 6.

62 Crais & Scully, *supra* note 2, at 135; Holmes, *supra* note 1, at 85–87.

63 Holmes, *supra* note 1, at 93. Under Georges Cuvier's leadership, the team included well-known scientists Henri de Blainville and Geoffrey St. Hillaire. *See* Natasha Gordon–Chipembere, *Introduction: Claiming Sarah Baartman, a Legacy to Grasp in* Representation and Black Womanhood, supra, note 34, at 10.

64 Holmes, *supra* note 2, at 79.

65 Holmes, *supra* note 1, at 93.

66 Georges Cuvier, 1769–1832, is known as the father of the field of comparative anatomy and was one of the most influential polygenists of the nineteenth century. Pursuant to polygenists, phenotypical differences in humans exist because there are different species or types. Race, Science and Medicine, 1700–1960 65 (Waltraud Ernst & Bernard Harris eds., 1999).

67 According to Crais and Scully, Cuvier sought to definitively answer his question: "Was [Baartman] of 'the last of the human species, or the negro race and the first of the apes' just above the orangutan? Cuvier thought that a key part of the answer lay in Sara's genitals." Crais & Scully, *supra* note 2, at 135. It is not possible to read Crais and Scully's description of Cuvier's dissection and rendering of Saartjie Baartman's body without feeling physically ill. Crais & Scully at 139–41.

68 Holmes, *supra* note 1, at 95–96.

69 *Id* at 99.

70 *See* Crais & Scully, *supra* note 2, at 142:

> She stood there for nearly two hundred years, lips sealed in plaster and paint, her naked body exposed to the multitudes. Thousands of people, scientists and tourists, children, families, writers and artists, stared at her while visiting the *Jardin des Plantes*, the world's

Cuvier's dissection of the corpse of Saartjie Baartman presented, for him, the basis of his later influential theories. Cuvier wrote a multivolume taxonomy and descriptions of animal life of earth, *Le Regne Animal* or *The Animal Kingdom*.[71] His classifications of humans place Caucasians, who gave rise to the most civilized nations, at the top of the hierarchy. He wrote, "Although the human species would appear to be single, since the union of any of its members produces individuals capable of propagation, there are, nevertheless, certain hereditary peculiarities of conformation observable, which constitute what are termed *races*."[72]

Cuvier compared cranial and facial features among the three groups, and he described Blacks thus: "The projecting muzzle and thick lips evidently approximate it to the Apes: the hordes of which it is composed have always continued barbarous."[73] To Cuvier, differences among populations were too great to permit a common origin for mankind.[74]

Cuvier's work and that of other polygenists deeply influenced other scientists for generations to come. At its most fundamental level, the adoption of a polygenist view of human origins, the notion that racial groups are biologically different, did not just impact academia, but the everyday treatment of people.[75] Cuvier was regarded as a great authority on racial differences,[76] and an ideological line can be drawn from Cuvier to Samuel Morton, a U.S. doctor who measured the capacity of skulls from Johann Blumenbach's five types.[77] Cuvier's influence is also apparent in the writings of Arthur de Gobineau, a French writer who developed the theory of the Aryan master race.[78]

In 1982, famed paleontologist Stephen Jay Gould accidentally rediscovered some of Baartman's remains in a museum storeroom.[79] In 1994, the new postapartheid government of South Africa initiated efforts to bring Baartman's remains home.[80] Remarkably, as in life, so in death: as had her

premier museum of natural history and the site of some of the most extraordinary scientific advances in the natural sciences. At Case Number 33, visitors viewed her brain and skeleton stitched by wire and held erect by a simple metal pole. A few beheld the excised organs that lay well preserved on a shelf in one of Cuvier's wooden cabinets.

71 Georges Cuvier, Le Regne Animal (1840).

72 *Id.* at 50.

73 *Id.*

74 *See* Ernst & Harris, *supra* note 66, at 65.

75 *Id.* at 30.

76 Michael Banton, Racial Theories, 48 (2d ed. 1998).

77 *Id.* at 50–51.

78 *Id.* at 64. Johann Blumenbach was a German anatomist who, in 1781, wrote that there were five human varieties: Caucasians, Ethiopians, Malays, Mongols, and Americans. *Id.* at 63.

79 Crais & Scully at 103.

80 *Id.*

living body, her corporeal remains became the site of contestation. Years of negotiation between the South African and French governments ensued. Baartman's remains, like the remains of thousands of anthropological specimens held by French museums, were classified as a French national patrimony and could not leave the country permanently unless allowed to do so by a specific change in the law.[81] The legislation necessary to release Baartman's remains was not adopted until 2002.

Saartjie Baartman's remains were flown to South Africa, which "greeted her with a rapturous reception."[82] Postapartheid South Africa gave her body an elaborate funeral and interment, which was attended by South African President Thabo Mbeki. In addition, Baartman became a symbol in South Africa's struggle for gender equality: "Addressing so many live issues in South Africa, Saartjie became a living ancestor. Nations, like individuals, need myths and icons to salve and heal the psychological and physical injuries inflicted by oppressive systems and internalized over centuries of marginalization. Saartjie's homecoming was a tangible act to right a historical wrong."[83]

The symbolic return home of a woman who never *did* and never *could* come home. A woman whose physical remains had been used to provide scientific bases for racial otherness and inferiority.[84] Whose subordination had been "naturalized" and expanded through positive law. What is the parallel, the commonality between Saartjie Baartman and Truganini, a Tasmanian Aboriginal woman who never left home, but who, at the end, had no "home?"

81 Crais & Scully, *supra* note 2, at 105. "Saartjie quickly became a potent symbol for political and cultural restitution. The National Khoisan Consultative Conference also pressed the French government to send back Saartjie's relics. In their view, Saartjie represented the suffering of all Khoisan people." *Id.* at 104. In 1998, the UN accorded the Khoisan first-nation status, "strengthening the call for Saartjie's return." *Id.* at 104. "The French museums proved initially resistant, anxious that Saartjie's release would create a flood of further requests from post-colonial nation-states for the return of artifacts plundered by imperial adventurers, stripping Western museums." *Id.* at 105.

82 *Id.* at 106.

83 *Id.* at 108.

84 According to Clifton Crais and Pamela Scully, "Throughout the nineteenth century and well into the twentieth century, the Hottentot Venus participated in the great debates on evolution, race, and female sexuality. Cuvier's dissection of Sara Baartman and the Hottentot Venus discussed in works such as OBSERVATIONS ON THE CADAVER OF ... *HOTENTOT VENUS* (1817) and the four-volume NATURAL HISTORY OF MAMMALS (1824–47), edited by Cuvier's brother Frederic and Etienne Saint-Hilaire, *concluded that the Khoisan were closer to the great apes than to humans*" (emphasis added). *Id.* at 144.

Truganini, "Queen" of a "Dead" People

In approximately 1812, halfway across the world and near the bottom of the globe, on the island of Tasmania, a land that had been isolated from the rest of the world – including the Australian mainland – since the last Ice Age, Truganini, said to be the last full-blood Tasmanian Aboriginal, was born.[85] Born two years after Saartjie Baartman's death and five years after the abolition of the Europeans' transatlantic slave trade in African peoples, in the period following the "discovery" of Tasmania by Europeans and their use of the island as a whaling station and penal colony, Truganini suffered the devastation visited on native peoples throughout the globe by European conquest: murders, rapine, dispersal, and diminution.[86] As a young woman, Truganini agreed to help George Arthur Robinson, the Great Conciliator, to persuade the dwindling numbers of Tasmanian Aboriginals to live together on Flinders Island, away from the European settlements, where they were promised that they would be protected and would be able to live in peace. Those promises were betrayed.

Truganini's early years were set against a background of increasing conflict between Aboriginals and White settlers. As the White population increased, the indigenous people were forced to go deeper into the bush for their hunting and gathering and to launch attacks against the invaders. Each day, the papers were filled with stories of Aboriginals murdering settlers. In turn, the Aboriginal population suffered greatly due to raids by convicts and settlers (a bounty had been placed on the capture of adult Aboriginals) and due to widespread abduction of women by whalers and sealers.[87]

The abolitionist struggles and the end of slavery in faraway London did not save the Tasmanians. Unlike Africans and other natives elsewhere in

[85] *See* Jared Diamond, *Ten thousand years of solitude: What really happens when a society is forced to go it alone?*, DISCOVER MAGAZINE, March 3, 1993.

[86] By the time Truganini was seventeen, "the invaders of her island had stabbed her mother to death, murdered her husband-to-be, shot her uncle, kidnapped her stepmother, abducted her sisters and violated her own body." Cato & Ellis, *supra* note 7, at 12–13. Although Ellis's book is more of an anti-Truganini hatchet job disguised as a work of historical fiction, rather than a work of historical research, it nevertheless remains an interesting and significant summary of Truganini's life. However, some of the speculative reveries in which Cato and Ellis indulge are downright outrageous and outlandish, betraying a deep failure to understand the collapsing world into which Truganini had been born. For example, they write: "Overall, taking into account [Truganini's] youthful exuberance and love of life, her promiscuous enjoyment of the admiration of men, both black and white, it is most likely that she simply lived for the moment. Under Robinson's dominance she simply did what she could do to help him enjoy what life offered from day to day, giving little thought to the significance of her actions." *Id.* at 75.

[87] *Id.* at 12–13. The Aboriginal women were abducted to become the sealers' sex slaves and labor force. It is from these forcible unions that the modern Tasmanian Aboriginal community is descended.

European empires, their labor was not needed by the settlers, and they had nothing to trade. Instead, they were mere obstacles in the path of European settlement. Guilt-infused colonial policies did not lead to the implementation of policies that would recognize and protect their rights to their lands, lives, and livelihoods. Colonial government policy espoused the official aim of protecting the indigenous population while turning a blind eye to or actively encouraging the settlers' mistreatment of the original population of the island.[88] In 1817, after several reported killings of Aboriginals, Lieutenant Governor Sorell issued a proclamation prohibiting ill-treatment of the Tasmanian Aboriginals.[89] Governor George Arthur, newly posted from British Honduras, where he had fought the enslavement of the indigenous people, issued proclamations aimed at protecting Tasmania's Aboriginal inhabitants. The proclamation provided, in part, that

> [t]he Natives of this island being under the protection of the same laws which protect the settlers, every violation of those laws in the persons or property of the Natives shall be visited with the same punishment as though committed on the person or property of any settler. His Honour the Lieutenant-Governor therefore declares his determination thus publicly, that if after the promulgation of this proclamation, any person or persons shall be charged with firing at, killing, or committing any act of outrage or aggression on the native people, they shall be prosecuted for the same before the Supreme Court.[90]

In 1828, responding to years of Aboriginal resistance against the settlers, Governor Arthur ordered roving parties to patrol settled areas and capture Aboriginals.[91] The coexistence model, whereby the settlers would occupy the

[88] *See* Reynolds, *supra* note 7, at 87–95. Reynolds reports that: "From the beginning of settlement in 1788, British policy towards the Aborigines was confused and contradictory." *Id.* at 87. *See also* Clive Turnbull, BLACK WAR (1948, reprinted 1965) for detailed accounts of the vagaries of colonial policy.

[89] Reynolds reports that, "Sorrell ... announc[ed] it would be the duty and determination of the government, as well as all 'just and well disposed Settlers' to bring to 'condign Punishment' anyone who was guilty of having destroyed or maltreated any of the native people." *Id.* at 90 (citing Turnbull, *supra* note 88).

[90] *Id.* at 91.

[91] The proclamation read, in part:

> 2. All practicable methods are to be employed for communicating and making known the provisions of this Proclamation to the Aborigines, and they are to be persuaded to retire beyond the prescribed limits, if that is possible.
>
> 3. On failing of the expedient last-mentioned, capture of their persons, without force, is to be attempted, and if effected, *the prisoners are to be treated with the utmost humanity and compassion*.

Id. at 105–06 (quoting from Governor Arthur's proclamation; emphasis added). Later that year, Arthur would declare martial law on the island. *Id.* at 107–12.

land and Aboriginals would do occasional labor while primarily staying out of the way in the forested areas of the island, had broken down. Armed and violent Aboriginal resistance to the loss of their homes was met with overwhelming force from both the colonial government and the settlers. Words of conciliation and care and apparent conferral of the status of British subjects[92] did not stay the guns and violence of the settlers against the original inhabitants.

In 1829, George Augustus Robinson[93] became administrator of an aboriginal settlement on Bruny Island, where he befriended Truganini. In 1830, Robinson began the Friendly Mission, his expeditions of conciliation with the Tasmanian Aboriginals.[94] That same year, the colonial government called upon male colonists to form an armed human chain known as the Black Line to flush out and force Aboriginals onto a small peninsula.[95]

For about six years, Robinson, Truganini, her husband, Woorrady, and others traveled throughout Tasmania, encountering the various tribes and attempting to bring them in peacefully.[96] The Friendly Mission was successful: it was begun on January 27, 1830, and, by 1834, all but a small family group had been removed to Wybalenna, the settlement set aside on the outlying Flinders Island.[97] We may never know the precise reason why Truganini went along with Robinson in his efforts to gather up and resettle the Tasmanians. Cato and Ellis speculate that Robinson would also have a romantic relationship with Truganini that would last for 13 years.[98]

[92] *See, e.g.*, note 90 *supra* and accompanying text.

[93] Much of Cato and Ellis's account of Truganini's life is drawn from the writings of George Arthur Robinson, the man who became known as Protector of Aboriginals and who drew up a plan to gather all the island's remaining Aboriginals through "peaceful reconciliation" to move them into protective custody on a settlement and to see that they were "instructed in the ways of civilization." Cato & Ellis, *supra* note 7, at 18.

[94] The term "Friendly Mission" encompasses the six expeditions undertaken by Robinson, accompanied (if not led) by the Mission Aboriginals (including Truganini) into the hinterlands of Tasmania. *See* Reynolds, *supra* note 7, at 136. Robinson's purpose, supported by the colonial authorities, was to peaceably remove the remaining Aboriginals from settler warfare and depredations and to settle them in a place of safety. *Id.* at 5, 133. *See* Diamond, *supra* note 85 (recounting some of the unpunished violations and abuses to which the Tasmanians were subjected by sealers and other settlers).

[95] *See* James Morris, *The Final Solution down under*, 14(1) HORIZON 60, 66 (1972).

[96] Reynolds, *supra* note 7, at 136.

[97] *Id.* at 133.

[98] Cato & Ellis, *supra* note 7, at 100. Cato and Ellis make much of the several clues of a sexual relationship between Robinson and Truganini. Their focus and certainty about this echoes the tropes of La Malinche and others, the co-opted female indigenes – consorts who betrayed their people in the throes of sexual and/or romantic fascination. *See* Suvendrini Perera, *Claiming Truganini, Australian national narratives in the Year of Indigenous Peoples*, 10 (3) CULTURAL STUD. 402–03 (1996) (discussing the discourse surrounding the figures of La Malinche, "Princess" Pocahontas, and Truganini as "two-faced signifiers in the annals of (de)

Truganini's and the other Mission Aboriginals' active participation in the Friendly Mission was crucial to its success. Without their knowledge of the land and peoples, without their diplomacy, without their physical help and rescue, Robinson would not have succeeded in persuading the remaining survivors to join him.[99] Yet, today, historians speculate about the incentives and motives of the Mission Aboriginals. To some, they were mere tools of Robinson's, fooled into betraying their fellow Aboriginals into a life of captivity, sickness, and inevitable extinction.[100] Others see evidence of agency, of choice, of a careful balancing of alternatives available to the survivors in the face of the destructive onslaught of the British colonial enterprise.[101]

Truganini's treatment at the hands of Robinson, at the hands of the scientific establishment, and at the pens of historians clearly reflected Eurocentric and ethnocentric perspectives pursuant to which she appears to have been denied a stake in her own fate because she was of a race that was too different and too primitive to allow recognition of their common humanity. Ultimately, she was, to them, a tool to be used to achieve a purpose – the success of Robinson's mission (perhaps of Robinson's biological urges as well) and the search for scientific knowledge. According to historian Henry Reynolds, "As a woman she has been seen as essentially irrational, apolitical, in thrall to her emotions: her behavior is explained by sexual attachment. . . . As an Aboriginal and a woman she has been pictured as impulsive, childlike and naturally dominated by a strong-willed European man. The idea that she had a political agenda of her own has never been considered."[102]

The gathered tribes and family groups of Tasmanian Aboriginals would eventually be placed on Flinders Island. Wybalenna, the settlement, became a place of death. During the years of its operation (1833–47), the Aboriginal death rate climbed inexorably, and the last no longer threatening survivors were allowed to return to the mainland island in 1847.[103] Historians speculate that captivity, inactivity, climate, disease, and infertility (perhaps caused by sexually transmitted diseases) caused the decline and "extinction" of the race. In the meantime, in 1833, following the rise and propagation of an extraordinary wave

colonization, available to be read as both heroine and hostage, betrayer and betrayed. . . . [and] foundational narratives . . . in a range of locations").

[99] Reynolds, supra note 7, at 136–39.

[100] *See, e.g.*, Cato & Ellis, *supra* note 7, at 1.

[101] *See* Reynolds, *supra* note 7, at 142–43.

[102] *Id.* at 141.

[103] Reynolds, *supra* note 7, at 5. Reynolds reports that, between 1832 and 1847, 132 of the more than 200 original Aboriginal inhabitants of Wybalenna died. *Id.* at 183–89. Although the mortality rate was similar to that among natives of mainland Australia, the consequences among the smaller Tasmanian population were devastating. *Id.* at 185–86. When the community was evacuated to the mainland in 1847, only 46 had survived.

Love and Beauty – Sartjee the Hottentot Venus, Trustees of the British Museum

of abolitionist (and, by extension, human rights)[104] sentiment, the British Parliament enacted an act to abolish slavery throughout the British Empire.

With the relentless march of time and death, it was Truganini, she who had been blamed by her countrymen for their dismal captivity, who was the sole survivor. Ironically, she, the betrayer, had survived them all. She became a familiar enough figure on the streets of Hobart, the harmless last holdout of a dead race.

Truganini died May 8, 1876, at the age of 73.[105] She had known of the mutilation of the body of William Lanne, the last surviving full-blooded Tasmanian aboriginal man.[106] Truganini made her wishes known – that she

[104] For example, the slogan "Am I not a Man and a Brother" accompanied the image of an enchained supplicant Black male. *See* Martinez, *supra* note 17, *passim*.

[105] Cato & Ellis, *supra* note 7, at 150.

[106] Following Lanne's death, an argument had ensued between the Royal Society and the Royal College of Surgeons over which organization should get Lanne's remains. While the corpse awaited burial, a member of the Royal College secretly skinned Lanne's head, removed his

wanted to be buried after her death and that she did not want her body to be desecrated. Immediately following her death, the Royal Society of Tasmania asked for permission from the colonial secretary to put Truganini's remains to the "best use of science." The colonial secretary considered it necessary that her body be given a decent burial, and Truganini was buried under cover of darkness in a prison yard that offered the perceived security of high walls against body thieves.[107]

Under pressure by members of the Royal Society, her remains were secretly and illegally exhumed sometime in 1877 or 1878.[108] Truganini's skeleton was placed in an apple case and taken by the curator of the Tasmanian Museum.[109] Official permission for exhumation was not given until many months afterward and was received on the condition that the skeleton not be exposed to public view.[110] Truganini's bones sat in the box until they were rediscovered by then-curator Alexander Morton in 1890. They were put on display in the museum and remained there until 1947. Appeals to bury the remains were made on religious grounds in the 1880s and 1950s, but were denied. Public sentiment was roused from periodic writing in the popular press on the fate of the Tasmanian Aboriginals.[111] In 1965, her bones were moved to a vault in the museum, and, in 1967, a memorial was built on Bruny Island, in memory of all Tasmanian Aboriginals but honoring in particular Truganini and members of her family.

Indigenous groups and members of the public demanded the burial of her remains, and a national debate began between the scientific community and Aboriginal activists.[112] It was pursuant to an act of parliament in 1975 that ownership of Truganini's remains was transferred from the museum to the Crown.[113] Once possession was secured, government officials and Aboriginal groups held conflicting views over whether to cremate or bury the bones. A group of Aboriginals who claimed to be Truganini's descendants threatened legal action. After negotiations between contending aboriginal groups in Australia, it was agreed that the bones would be cremated.

skull, and inserted a new one into his skin. *See* Cato & Ellis, *supra* note 7, at 137–40. *See also* Helen MacDonald, POSSESSING THE DEAD: THE ARTFUL SCIENCE OF ANATOMY 110–11 (2010).

[107] *Id.* at 142, 146–49.

[108] Cato & Ellis, *supra* note 7, at 155.

[109] *Id.* at 155.

[110] *Id.* at 155.

[111] *Id.* at 155.

[112] The contemporary Tasmanian Aboriginal community consists of the descendants of the often coerced relationships between Tasmanian Aboriginal women and European sealers. *See* Ryan, *supra* note 14, at 222–55 (describing the survival of the community and its "emergence" in the twentieth century).

[113] Cato & Ellis, *supra* note 7, at 159.

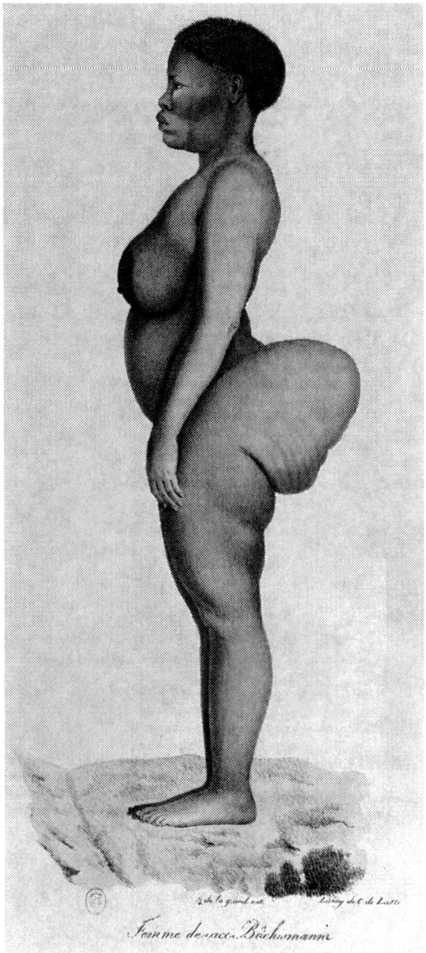

Last, Carel Christian Anthony (1808–76), *The Hottentot Venus*, Bushman woman, from L'HISTOIRE NATURELLE DES MAMMIFERES by Etienne Geoffroy Saint-Hilaire (1772–1844) and Frederic Cuvier (1773–1838), 1824.

In 1976, Truganini's ashes were scattered in the seas between her birthplace, Bruny Island, and the Tasmanian mainland – the D'Entrecasteaux Channel, close to the place of her birth at Adventure Bay.[114] However, the story of her corporeal remains does not end there: in 2002, fragments of her hair and skin were discovered at the Royal College of Surgeons in England.[115]

[114] *Id.* at 162.

[115] *See* MacDonald, *supra* note 106, at 125–51 (describing the 2002 discovery and narrating the story of the dramatis personae of scientists, officials, and grave robbers who sought access to and violated her prized corpse).

Contemporary Interpretations

The fundamental similarities in the lives and fates of these women resonate today. They were born, lived, and died in the era of multifaceted clashes of civilization; they, their people, and their homes were subjected to forcible acquisition, exploitation, and control. Chattels in both life and death – not for their bodies the sacred shroud of death, but grotesque triumphant display and post-death corporeal violation. In death, both women were exhibited as evidence of Black otherness. To the invading, alienating, and dominant outsiders, both Baartman and Truganini were subhuman, possessors of a quasi-personhood created within the interactive space of the coming together of two peoples and cultures. As indigenous females, they were displaced, dispossessed, and exploited in life. In their corporeal afterlife, they were fully "property," held hostage to the search for scientific knowledge through the dissection, exploitation, and exhibition of their bodies. In their symbolic afterlives, they are national symbols who belong to all the contemporary inhabitants of their natal domains. They, their selves, Saartjie/Sara and Trugernanner/Truganini, remain unknown.[116]

Can study and understanding of Saartjie Baartman and Truganini deepen our knowledge of the ways in which the past and present exploitation, commodification, and dehumanization of Black women shaped, were shaped by, and continue to influence international law?

The lives, destinies, and corporeal and symbolic afterlives of these two Black women give rise to still-live issues in international law. They lived their lives against the evolving predominance of positivism and positive law over natural law. Their lives and fates contributed to dominant narratives of Black female and indigenous inferiority. Yet these two Black women confront us with something infinitely more challenging. The potential themes and impacts of their lives span multiple disciplines.[117]

[116] Holmes, Crais and Scully, and Cato and Ellis, among others, have tried to inhabit or interpret Saartjie Baartman and Truganini. In either fictionalized or quasi-fictionalized historic narratives, they have named; examined; and speculated on the emotions, personalities, and motives of these two historic women. These attempts have met with sometimes severe criticism. *See, e.g.*, Desiree Lewis, *Writing Baartman's agency: History, biography, and the imbroglios of truth*, in REPRESENTATION AND BLACK WOMANHOOD, *supra* note 34, at 109–18. But they cannot be known: they left no written records of their own, and the accounts of their thought processes and psychological motivations are mediated through the perceptions of their oppressors. Natasha Gordon-Chipembere claims that "[n]o one can speak for Sarah Baartman." Gordon-Chipembere, *supra* note 34, at 14.

[117] Contemporary publications about Saartjie Baartman and Truganini include REPRESENTATION AND BLACK WOMANHOOD, *supra* note 34; Charmaine Nelson, REPRESENTING THE BLACK FEMALE SUBJECT IN WESTERN ART (2010); Willis, *supra* note 12; Crais & Scully, *supra* note

This study focuses on the ways in which Saartjie Baartman and Truganini challenge our understanding of legal and human personhood. That is, what is the capacity to be fully human, to exercise rights to choice and consent, in the face of legal and/or de facto nonrecognition and/or nonenforcement of humanity?

Historians Clifton Crais and Pamela Scully have claimed a rich legal heritage for Saartjie Baartman.[118] According to them, despite the failure to "free" Baartman, "The Case of the Hottentot Venus (along with the 1772 *Somersett* decision outlawing slavery in England) helped establish two precedents. Macaulay's intervention represented an early instance of a third-party application to intervene in order to mitigate the conditions of someone who could not otherwise speak." Crais and Scully claim that this principle is now fully entrenched in and fundamental to contemporary human rights and humanitarian law.[119] Second, Crais and Scully believe that the impact of *The Case of the Hottentot Venus* lives on in legal concepts surrounding the rights of the foreigner in domestic law, such as the scope of the right of the outsider to invoke the protections afforded to nationals under domestic law.[120] Crais and Scully overstate the impact of *The Case of the Hottentot Venus*. It has not served to extend the umbrella of human rights protection to the alien – the nonmember of the polity. Instead, in the United States, at least, its influence appears to be limited to the treatment due a member of the polity – however attenuated the nature of that membership.[121]

7; Cato & Ellis, *supra* note 7; Alexander, A.A., *Truganini (Trugernanner, Trukanini, Trucanini) (1812?–76)*, in THE COMPANION TO TASMANIAN HISTORY 370 (A. Alexander ed., 2005); Tasmania Education Department Curriculum Center, TRUGANINI: LAST OF HER TRIBE (1971); and MacDonald, *supra* note 106.

[118] Crais & Scully, *supra* note 2, at 143.

[119] *Id.* at 143 ("Today it is an unquestioned part of our moral and legal culture where the concern of strangers has helped save the lives of abused children, battered women, and the aged and infirm. It is part of our humanity, the terrain of human rights, a simple act of caring and of worrying about the fate of people we do not even know, of extending our imaginations beyond the immediacies of everyday life").

[120] *Id.* at 143–44 (noting that Justice Stevens cited to the case in his opinion in *Rasul v. Bush*, 542 U.S. 466, 479, n.11 (2004)). Note, however, that the reference is merely part of an extensive string cite discussing English and American habeas cases.

[121] In *Hamdan v. Rumsfeld*, 464 F. Supp. 2d 9 (D.D.C. 2006), the Case of the Hottentot Venus was mentioned at the tail end of a long line of decisions and years of wrangling over the fate of a Guantanamo Bay detainee who first filed a petition for habeas corpus in 2004. The district court's mention of the *Case of the Hottentot Venus* (Hamdan, 464 F. Supp. 2d at 16 in section three) helps explore the question of whether any alien is constitutionally entitled to the writ of habeas corpus in the wake of the Military Commissions Act (10 USC 948). *The Case of the Hottentot Venus* is explicitly discussed in one sentence on page 17: "In the Case of the Hottentot Venus, Saartje Baartman – a South African exhibited in a cage in Piccadilly, England – was a

Instead, Saartjie Baartman's greatest legacy may largely lie in the extralegal realm – in the impact on international law and everyday human interaction of the scientific analysis of her corporeal remains and the conclusions confirmed through their dissection. Her dissector, Georges Cuvier, confirmed his ideas about polygenism, including the inferiority and separateness of the races of humankind, based at least in part on his interactions with her and his dissection of her body. His influence extended to the scientific racists of the nineteenth century and the mid-twentieth-century genocidal horrors inflicted throughout Europe. According to Crais and Scully:

> The Hottentot Venus's greatest notoriety came with the spectacular proliferation of scientific racism in the second half of the nineteenth century. All of the most prominent writers on the supposed inferiority of non-Caucasoid races knew of the Hottentot Venus and very often explicitly discussed the Hottentot in elaborating their ideas on race and on the dangers of racial mixing. These ideas helped bequeath racial intolerance and hatred in the American South, in South Africa, and in Germany in the infamous 1935 Nuremberg Laws prohibiting marriage and intercourse between Germans and "non-Aryans." The Germans had their own history of genocidal violence against southern Africans, and the Hottentot figured in the eugenic science of European fascism and the Final Solution that destroyed Europe and condemned millions to firing squads and concentration camps. The Hottentot still figures in contemporary neo-Nazi propaganda.[122]

The confirmed scientific foundations of racial hierarchies justified and made "right" and inevitable the development and expansion of a racist international law. The certainty of the inferiority of the native meant that colonization and the subjection of the rest of the world under European

non-enemy foreigner from the British Protectorate of South Africa who could invoke the protection of the Crown by right." The court distinguishes Hamdan, stating that although he had lived (as a prisoner) within the jurisdiction of the United States for five years, "he had not become a part of the population so as to separate himself from the common law tradition generally barring non-resident enemy aliens from accessing courts in wartime." *Id.* at 17. The district court did not see Hamdan as being connected to or a resident of the United States. In 1810 London, Baartman was surely seen as something exotic and alien by the throngs of people who gathered for her stage show. However, she was perhaps more closely connected to England than was Hamdan to the United States. Her status as a colonized native of South Africa subjected her to the authority of England through the colonial government. Furthermore, the Cape Colony's Celadon (Hottentot) Proclamation put her under the so-called protection of the Cape Colony's governor. Hamdan, as an alien and enemy combatant, was ultimately not entitled to access the domestic courts.

[122] Crais & Scully, *supra* note 2, at 145.

tutelage was the right thing to do, an inevitable expression of the European's natural superiority.[123]

BLACK FEMALE "THINGS"? VICTIMS OR ACTORS? VICTIMS AS ACTORS? COUNTERNARRATIVES OF CHOICE

The stories of Truganini and Saartjie Baartman are reflective of two evolving perspectives on the very essence of what it means to be human. Pursuant to the Enlightenment's natural law principles, every person was endowed with basic, inalienable rights.[124] The drive to abolish slavery in Britain and her colonies was born of a worldview that recognized not only the brutality of the institution, but the humanity of all people. As seen in the African Institution's intervention in Saartjie Baartman's life, the legal scholars and churchmen who made up the group were willing to fight to free a human being who was possibly being enslaved – held against her will and forced to perform before gawking crowds in the heart of the Empire. They had followed in the path of the antislavery activists who had deployed the law to free the slave at the center of the *Somersett* case and had set a far-reaching legal precedent.

Moving forward into the nineteenth century, a philosophical shift would alter perceptions of indigenous people, their individual rights, and their rights to land. As described by Merete Falck Burch: "At this time traditional ideas about natural law began to be replaced by a theory that laws were simply laid down by the sovereign and should be regarded as separate from any

[123] For an in-depth analysis of the role of colonization and colonialist thought in the development of fundamental doctrines of modern international law, *see* Antony Anghie, IMPERIALISM, SOVEREIGNTY AND THE MAKING OF INTERNATIONAL LAW (2005). For example, Anghie explains "[T]he re-entry of non-European societies into the sphere of law could now take place on terms which completely subordinated and disempowered those societies. This was achieved by deploying the new, racialised scientific lexicon of positivism which, it was asserted, represented a higher and decisive truth. The language of positivism was only one part of a far larger and massively elaborate vocabulary of conquest that had been developing in many of the disciplines of the late nineteenth century. Anthropology, science, economics and philology ... participated crucially in the colonial project." Anghie at 66.

[124] *See* Merete Falck Burch, CONCILIATION – COMPULSION – CONVERSION: BRITISH ATTITUDES TOWARDS INDIGENOUS PEOPLES 1768–1814 219–20 (2004):

> By the mid-eighteenth century it was being explicitly recognized by British courts that international law formed part of the common law. Furthermore, the law of nature, seen to be the foundation of international law, enjoyed an equally strong place in English law; this meant that the 'inherent natural law concepts of equality, justice and fairness' ... were recognized as guiding principles in English law no less than in international law. These principles were also closely connected with the development of the theory of natural rights which was so influential in the eighteenth century.

considerations of morality."[125] For indigenous people, this meant that they could not have any legally defined rights because of their lack of a recognizable "sovereign" and system of laws (as perceived and judged by Europeans).[126]

In the contested space of the fluctuating influence of these two fundamental legal theories, Saartjie Baartman and Truganini were Black female "things." Like others – both male and female – who shared their races and ethnicities during that juncture of human history, in life, they were neither recognized *nor treated* as fully human. Furthermore, in death, their corporeal manifestations were used as crucial underpinnings in the formulations of gradations and subcategorizations of the attempts to taxonomically codify humanity and subhumanity and to attempt to justify the injustices of the triumph of positivism over natural law.

Despite all this, however, both women made choices – constrained choices – and took actions that furthered their interest in and commitment to the things that concerned them. Constrained and constricted in both life and death, Baartman and Truganini offer insights into the nature of choice. As do contemporary Black female "things," they chose life and survival when they are confronted institutional and individual circumstances that denied their humanity.

Their Interests

The choices made by Baartman and Truganini were founded on the universal concerns that preoccupied them. Primary among them were survival – their personal survival and the survival of their community, as well as their longing for belonging to family and community.

Bereft of family as a consequence of the effects of European settlement, witness to the dislocation, exploitation, and disregard of their communities by dominating power structures and actors, Baartman and Truganini chose different paths. Saartjie Baartman, separated from her family and tribe and acculturated into the exploitative colonial life of Cape Town, chose to escape – to a new life in a new form of exploitation elsewhere. And, if Crais

[125] *Id.* at 230.

[126] *Id.* at 230. This is evidenced by early Australian court decisions regarding land title. The decisions "came to see New South Wales as having been in a situation similar to that of uninhabited land at the arrival of first settlers." To the new settlers, the aboriginal society was too primitive to be considered independent and was thus incapable of being conquered. "Therefore the colony was seen as having been acquired through discovery and settlement." *Id.* at 224.

and Scully's research is given credence,[127] she may have achieved that new life and family, however, temporarily. She replaced her lost family with the grouping created with her former Cape Town masters and exhibitors.

Truganini chose to attempt to consolidate her people, to make a stand for Tasmanian Aboriginal survival under Robinson's and the colonial government's protection at Wybalenna. The promises of shelter and protection were more encompassing than the shelter actually provided.[128] Bereft of homes, of agency, of life opportunities, and presented with insufficient fulfillment of promises, the community at Wybalenna dwindled.[129] The survivors (including Truganini) were returned to mainland Tasmania when they were no longer perceived as threats.[130]

Their Choices

The choices of Baartman and Truganini speak to the universality of their concerns, as well as to the universality of their strategies. Saartjie Baartman's and Truganini's choices give rise to the questions of agency and consent, of whether a victim can *choose* victimization or consent to it. Is victimhood incompatible with agency? Can the victim also be an actor or is she solely acted upon? Should "consent" have legal force when the choices are constrained? Can the subhuman's choice have legal force if the subhuman is not fully a person under the law?[131]

Given the circumstances of their lives and their fundamental interests, Baartman and Truganini confronted stark options: (a) resistance or accommodation, (b) resistance and accommodation, or (c) resistance in accommodation.

[127] Crais & Scully, *supra* note 2, at 106–14. *But see* Lewis, *supra* note 116 (criticizing Crais & Scully's account of Saartjie's life).

[128] Unequal and broken treaties were an essential part of the colonization enterprise. *See, e.g.*, Karen E. Bravo, *Balancing indigenous rights to land and the demands of economic development: Lessons from the United States and Australia*, 30 COLUM. J. L.& SOC. PROBS. 529, 542–49 (1997) (describing the gradual demotion of North American tribes in the United States from co-equal sovereigns to "domestic dependent nations").

[129] Lyndall Ryan describes the dismal state of the Wybalenna community. *See* Ryan, *supra* note 14, at 196–97. According to Ryan, "In administrative terms Flinders Island had been a success. It had been cheap to run, remote from white settlement, and hidden from the public eye. It became the model for all other Australian colonies to follow when disposing of their unwanted indigenes." *Id.* at 203.

[130] *Id.* at 205–14 (describing the continued decline of the community at Oyster Cove, the new mainland location to which the survivors had been relocated).

[131] The concessions extracted from indigenous leaders, however dubious their provenance, were and are endowed with the force of law, conferring vast domains on European settlers and forming the foundational myths of nation building.

Both Saartjie Baartman and Truganini chose accommodation or resistance in accommodation to wrest life, or a semblance of life, from the alternatives available to them. In *The Case of the Hottentot Venus*, through her deposition, Baartman claimed the legal validity of "choice" to travel to London to perform. Truganini chose to accompany and lead Robinson into the interior to gather up the remnants of Tasmania's Aboriginal tribes. Their alternatives were, respectively, to stay in Cape Town in indentured servitude and to continue to exist on Bruny Island or some other permitted Aboriginal encampment. Given the conditions of their communities, armed resistance would have been futile.[132]

Saartjie Baartman's Choices

Was Saartjie Baartman a trafficking victim, an enslaved person who had been offered no choice, or whose consent, even if given, must and should be disregarded by the law? Or was Baartman a transnational migrant, a seeker of new worlds and opportunities who chose to leave behind the Cape Town exploitation, with which she was all too familiar, for another place, where she could have more control over her own exploitation?

Baartman's life as the Hottentot Venus came at a point in history when the inherent inferiority of non-Whites was taken as gospel by the public, aided by the scientific and political establishment. The court itself, in *The Case of the Hottentot Venus*, refers to the "Hottentot nation" and its "general imbecile state." Although those attitudes were challenged and perhaps legally disavowed through the abolition of slavery in Britain and her colonies, *The Case of the Hottentot Venus* established the legal significance of Baartman's own choice. By uttering the words of consent during her deposition, she removed the legal standing of Zachary Macaulay and the African Institution in the habeas proceedings. Baartman, according to the court's holding, had legal standing to demand that the law respect her choice, even if that choice appeared to others to be a poor one. Baartman was her own person in the eyes of the law.

Baartman was a person under the law, but was she ever treated as such? Society at large still saw and treated her as a curiosity to gawk at and as a thing of mystery sufficiently unknown so as to embody their projections of inferiority and subhumanity.[133] Can pro forma legal assignment of personhood triumph over social and cultural perception of subhumanity?

[132] Yet, for a time, Truganini did resist – returning to the bush and participating in guerilla actions against the settlers. *See* Cox, *supra* note 15, at 121–50.

[133] Crais and Scully quote from an 1811 letter from Lord Portchester to his wife. He notes that "her shape is enough displayed to prove her make to be very little like as human shape and more like a camel's hump in the stern." Crais & Scully, *supra* note 2, at 104.

Because of her "choice," she became the Hottentot Venus. When Baartman died, she forever became property of the world. Did she ever belong to herself? Were the years in the provinces, the baptism, the marriage and pregnancy that may have happened fulfillment of her choice to be a self-owning, self-actuated woman able to seek out and fulfill her own desires? If so, that time of self-actuation, birthed of her choice, was a brief one. After returning to public exhibition in Paris, Baartman chose not to return to Cape Town with the departing Hendrick Cesars. Did public exhibition in Paris present a better choice than did a return to indentured servitude and obscurity in Cape Town? But from this latest choice arose Saartjie Baartman's ultimate exploitation, objectification, and desecration of her corporeal remains in the cause of the advancement of science.

Truganini's Choices

Presented with the alternatives of doing nothing, of looking on as Tasmanian Aboriginals suffered mistreatment throughout more of her island home, Truganini chose to become an indigenous leader, to assist in the Friendly Mission and to rescue the remnant "wild" populations of Tasmanian Aboriginals and bring them to safe harbor at Wybalenna. When that safe harbor was betrayed, she became for a time a bushranger – part of a group that struck fear in the hearts of the colonists.[134]

Yet Truganini is not Tasmania's (or Australia's) Harriet Tubman.[135] Instead, her choice to take an active rather than passive role converted her, in the eyes of her people and of future scholars of history, into an active collaborator or betrayer when the promises that had been made to her people were not fulfilled. Her choices have opened her to questioning and ridicule. That ridicule ignored the realities of the Tasmanian colonization project. In the Tasmanian context, there was no place for Aboriginals to be free. No legal context, no physical space on their now conquered homeland belonged to a free Aboriginal who possessed the attributes of legal personhood. In Tasmania, after the Black War, an Aboriginal was to be contained, restrained, managed – on Flinders Island's Wybalenna. For an Aboriginal, Tasmania was *unfree* space.

The prevailing perception that Truganini was a promiscuous unthinking female who did the bidding of Robinson as a result of her love or sexual thralldom[136] ignores the evidence of agency, decision making, negotiation

[134] *See* Cox, *supra* note 15, at 123–50.

[135] The famed "conductor" on the Underground Railroad, Harriet Tubman guided hundreds of enslaved Blacks from the American South to Northern freedom.

[136] *See, e.g.*, Cato & Ellis, *supra* note 7, at 75.

strategy, and leadership by her and by other Aboriginal women who confronted the onslaught of settlement.[137] Historian Henry Reynolds and others question the inability of proponents of the narrative of the Tasmanian Aboriginals' childlike acquiescence in their own inevitable death to recognize the Aboriginals' co-equal humanity.[138] He attributes their blindness to an inability to "[consider] the Aboriginals to be a rational and political people"[139] – that is, the incapacity to view them as fully human beings with attributes, incentives, goals, and motivations that transcend specific cultures and races and are universal to the human species.

Baartman and Truganini demonstrated their humanity by exercising their autonomy as fully as they could within the constraints that had been built around them. For both of these women, the choices became a mirage – and yet not quite a mirage. Truganini, personally, survived as the "last" full-blooded Tasmanian Aboriginal, upon whom was bestowed the (mocking? guilty?) honorific of "Queen."[140] Baartman's exploitation in England enabled her to see more of the world, to escape her indentured servitude in Cape Town, perhaps to create a new family. However, their choices, their survival, could not overcome their status as nonhuman "things." After their deaths, both were reduced to scientific exhibits, ironically ensuring an eternal afterlife that neither woman had sought.

Yet an irony turns the litany of victimhood and exploitation on its head. From that very exploitation and victimization in the name of science and the provision of a scientific justification of exploitation and subjection is born Truganini's and Saartjie Baartman's powerful symbology. Their post-death survival and symbology provide tools to question and debunk the "scientific" bases of historical and contemporary victimization. Through the ultimate treatment of Truganini and Saartjie Baartman as Black female "things," their exploiters provided us, their present-day community, with the tools – lenses – that can be turned upon their exploiters and their philosophical heirs. Through our modern eyes, they become *subjects* as well as *objects* of international law: self-directed human individuals who exercised choice.

[137] Reynolds, *supra* note 7, at 139–49. *See also* Lyndall Ryan, *Aboriginal women and agency in the process of conquest: A review of some recent work*, 1 AUSTRALIAN FEMINIST STUD. 35 (1986).

[138] Reynolds, *supra* note 7, at 147–52.

[139] *Id.* at 147.

[140] Yet Lyndall Ryan points to at least one "full-blood" who survived Truganini as part of the sealing community on Kangaroo Island. Ryan, *supra* note 14, at 220. The demise of "Queen" Truganini, the last full-blooded Tasmanian Aboriginal put a triumphant exclamation point to European domination of the island.

Their Roles: Understanding Agency, Choice, "Rescue," and Salvation in Contemporary International Law

Contemporaneous

The roles of Saartjie Baartman and Truganini have shifted and fluxed from their time to ours. In their lifetimes, while sharing the commonality of Black female subhumanity,[141] Baartman and Truganini played constrained roles that they attempted to enlarge through the choices they made. Baartman, the Hottentot Venus, was an exemplar of otherness and inferiority, an exotic "freak" whose physical presence reinforced Europeans' notions of their own superiority. Removed from her own community, she had little active role among the Khoikhoi – to the extent that remnants of her people remained, she was a "missing one," and her role in Cape Town was of an indentured servant and wet nurse. In Europe, through her role in *The Case of the Hottentot Venus*, Saartjie Baartman also helped establish and reinforce the legal principle of the right of the outsider to intervene on behalf of a victim.[142] As the object of Georges Cuvier's dissection, her corpus, her physical remains, helped provide the foundation of the development of scientific racism.[143]

Truganini's role vis-à-vis her own contemporaries varied throughout her life: victim of settler barbarity, "leader" of the Friendly Mission Aboriginals, savior of the remnant Tasmanian Aboriginal people marooned in the interior, bushranger/guerilla fighter, betrayer, sole survivor, and "Queen." Truganini's last years of existence and her death as the last full-blooded Tasmanian Aboriginal gave permission to the European settlers to finally enjoy the fruits of their ancestors' murders: undisputed dominion over the island of Tasmania and evidence of the inevitable dominance of the European races.[144]

[141] Both the Tasmanian Aboriginal and the Khoikhoi were viewed as the very bottom of the scientifically constructed racial hierarchy. According to Marete Falck:

> [E]ven though scales of gradation had been applied earlier on, racial hierarchies established inherent differences between various "races" which shows beyond doubt that not all peoples are alike. . . . It became a common belief that Aborigines and Khoisan constituted the lowest levels of humans existence, whereas American Indians and Xhosa were more "advanced."

Falck, *supra* note 124, at 292.

[142] In her case, the African Institution and Zachary Macaulay were outsiders – concerned onlookers of her public exploitation. She, the victim, was an outsider to English society and norms and yet could be protected by the laws produced by that society.

[143] His perception of her otherness and subhumanity strengthened Cuvier's belief in and support for polygenism.

[144] *See, e.g.*, Morris, *supra* note 95: "I regret the death of the last of the Tasmanian aborigines, but I know that it is the result of the fiat that the black shall everywhere give place to the white" (quoting the recorded reaction of a European-Australian observer to the death of Truganini).

Contemporary

Saartjie Baartman and Truganini play a complex role in their contemporary communities. For both, their contemporary communities are global – their lives and afterlives have elicited the interest and regard of people worldwide. This analysis focuses on their roles in four areas: (a) symbology and role in the still-active contestation between natural law and positivism, (b) the nature of labor and its relationship to enslavement, (c) the nature and meaning of rescue, and (d) the status of human remains as quasi-property and the obligation to repatriate the remains of indigenous people.

The disassembly and reassembly of the corporeal remains of Baartman and Truganini have contemporary resonance that transcends the visceral horror evoked by the unconsented treatment of their bodies. Instead, their disassembly, reassembly, and their institution in the pantheon of symbolic "mothers" reflects the state of scientific and moral knowledge in their time and ours.

Saartjie Baartman's and Truganini's remains could be disassembled, dissected, and exhibited because, fundamentally, with the waxing influence of scientific racism, they were viewed as subhuman "things" whose bodies could be treated in ways that would not have been imposed on other nonsubordinated bodies. They, their bones, their skeletons, and/or their private parts, could be exhibited as would those of a gorilla, donkey, or chimpanzee that had benefited from the attentions of a skilled taxidermist. Their treatment also reflects the predominance of polygenism, whereby the races of mankind were believed to have stemmed from different progenitors.

Today, science tells us that human beings worldwide share common ancestry – that humankind is composed of one species, one humanity. Saartjie Baartman's and Truganini's reassembly and burial with honors reflects this new appreciation, as well as Baartman's and Truganini's reincorporation – and the reincorporation/reassembly of humankind – into a single species.[145]

What is labor? When is it free or unfree? The juxtaposition of the Celadon (Hottentot) Code of the Cape Town colony against the backdrop of abolitionist and antislavery sentiment and actions in the heart of the British Empire is startling. As natural and positivist law contest with each other with respect to the status of slavery, enslavement, natural rights, and equality, through the imposition of positive law – the Hottentot Code – the anti-slave-trade government of the United Kingdom converted the native peoples of the Cape into a

[145] *But see* Sheila Smith McKoy, *Placing and replacing "The Venus Hottentot": An archaeology of pornography, race, and power, in* REPRESENTATION AND BLACK WOMANHOOD, *supra* note 34, at 96 (asserting that "'[t]he Venus Hottentot' still exists as a dis-membered pornographic image, one that is shaped in sexual and racial fantasies that link two cultures and the two continents on which Sarah Baartman tried to live").

constrained source of unfree labor that would be accessed by European settlers through the issuance of official (positivist) paperwork. The natives could not "be" without being indentured.

The impact of the Hottentot Code – all natives were obligated to show evidence of their indenture to a settler or would be indentured involuntarily through the kind offices of officialdom – is such that it appears to be a philosophical and legal precursor to the pass system of the later apartheid regimes of the South African state. Saartjie Baartman knew of and had lived under the earliest form of the Code. Should she be viewed as a historic escapee from the early pass system that would transmogrify into the later apartheid regime?

In that light, Saartjie Baartman's choices may be viewed as an early exemplar of the choices available today to transnational migrant women who leave their homes and domestic systems of exploitation to find work, greater compensation, and greater freedom in another form of exploitation in a foreign land.[146] Is the choice that the contemporary migrant faces exile or servitude? Or, perhaps, servitude in exile? How does the fate of the modern refugee, exploited and subordinated in the state that offers sheltering exile, compare with Saartjie Baartman's?

Meditating on Saartjie Baartman and Truganini leads to questioning of the nature of "rescue." Saartjie Baartman would have been rescued by Zachary Macaulay and the African Institution if she had acquiesced to their efforts. Truganini "rescued" the marooned remnant populations of Tasmanian Aboriginals from the interior and brought them to "safety" at Wybalenna, on Flinders Island, the internal displacement camp for the terminally displaced.

But what is "rescue" without true choice, without structural change? Macaulay's rescue would have "freed" Saartjie Baartman to make her way in a new, unfamiliar, and racist London or to return to Cape Town to be again indentured under the Celadon Code. The rescue could not be genuine, could not be true or meaningful, without structural transformation of the societies that viewed and treated Baartman as subordinated, nonhuman chattel.

So, too, did Truganini's "rescue" of her people fail, and she was converted into a traitorous betrayer and collaborator. The colonial society, and independent Australia for decades more, had no fully human place for Truganini's people: pursuant to the positive law of the colony, she and the other Tasmanian Aboriginals were not capable of enforcing the fulfillment of

[146] *See, for example*, Rhacel Salazar Parrenas, SERVANTS OF GLOBALIZATION: WOMEN, MIGRATION AND DOMESTIC WORK (2001) (discussing the outmigration of Filipinas in search of work).

promises made to them.[147] Their reserve on Flinders Island could not serve as rescue absent structural legal and social change in the encircling colony.

These examples continue to reverberate in the context of modern human-to-human exploitation, including human trafficking. How to "rescue" the "victim" if the alternatives available outside their site of exploitation do not recognize the full humanity of and freedom for the rescued? Or if, indeed, the society and legal system lay the groundwork that facilitates their exploitation?[148] Instead, many "victims" choose to return to the familiarity of even extreme victimization where they have a place to belong, however subordinated they may be.

Finally, both Saartjie Baartman and Truganini, in their afterlives, played active roles in the debate about ownership of and right to the corporeal remains of indigenous peoples. Only after long debates and negotiation, negative publicity, and adoption of new national legislation did France relinquish the remains of Saartjie Baartman, which it had claimed and possessed as French national patrimony. Truganini received final restoration and return to the waters of the D'Entrecasteaux Channel only after the national government of Australia had staked legal claims to her bones (in priority over the Tasmanian Museum), and the surviving Tasmanian Aboriginal population staked moral claims to dispose of their ancestors' remains.

Similar conflicts have played out worldwide as indigenous people have demanded the return of their ancestors' corporeal remains, and domestic legislation and international treaties and arrangements have been drafted and implemented to effect the reincorporation of ancestors into their communities and of those communities into regional and global communities.

CONCLUSION

The lives of Saartjie Baartman and Truganini, Black female things, violated and exploited in the contestation of international law theories of positivism and natural law, continue to resonate with live controversies and doctrines in international and domestic law today. Beyond visceral horror, beyond symbology of revered motherhood, their lives give rise to questions fundamental to both international and domestic law.

[147] Their petitions for redress did not lead to structural redress and betterment of their status and condition. *See, e.g.*, Reynolds, *supra* note 7, at 7–9 (quoting extensively from an 1846 petition to Queen Victoria); and Ryan, *supra* note 14, at 201–02 (describing and quoting from a petition to the lieutenant governor).

[148] *See, e.g.*, Karen E. Bravo, *On making persons: Legal constructions of personhood and their nexus with human trafficking*, 31 N. Ill. L. Rev. 467 (2011).

Through their exercise of choice in constrained, fettered, and contested space, they challenge our understanding of legal and human personhood – that is, the capacity to be fully human, to choose and consent, in the face of legal and/or de facto nonrecognition and/or nonenforcement of humanity. The "choices" of these Black women adds complexity to the understanding of the nature of "choice." They reject the subhumanity assigned to them – they are not Black female "things" but human *persons*. By naming the "things" (interests) valued and pursued by Saartjie Baartman and Truganini, this study clarified the universality of Black female "things" – concerns and issues that are shared across time, race, and gender. It has also illuminated the symbiotic relationship between freedom and unfreedom.

Finally, the use of Saartjie Baartman's and Truganini's post-death corporeal manifestations as crucial foundations in formulating the taxonomic codification of humanity and subhumanity has been rejected and refuted by the reincorporation of these two Black women into the oneness of the human species.

So much has been written about them both that we might be fooled into thinking we know them. We do not – ultimately, Saartjie Baartman and Truganini continue to be "things" to whom we reach out in search of meaning. However, their selves continue to be hidden from us through the veil of history.

POSTLUDE

My work on this project was almost complete when Henrietta Lacks emerged from the clouded veils of time and neglect. Nurtured, shared, and sampled by laboratories, institutes, and scientists across space and time, the HeLa cell line of cancer cells, named for their donor and imbued with virulent life, forms the basis of a surreal disembodied corporeal eternal afterlife[149] for a woman who drew her last breath on October 4, 1951.

Henrietta Lacks was a poor African-American woman, descendant of slaves and sharecroppers, who died of cervical cancer in 1951.[150] Harvested from the sick woman without her knowledge or consent, a sample of the cervical cancer cells that would grow to kill her was cultivated and developed in medical research laboratory into the HeLa line of cells. HeLa became the "workhorse" of research on human cells and played a crucial role in innumerable

149 *See* Rebecca Skloot, The Immortal Life of Henrietta Lacks (2010). Skloot reports that the mass of the existing cells, held in laboratories worldwide, would make up 100 Empire State Buildings.

150 *Id.*

breakthroughs in modern medicine, contributing immeasurably to the advancement of scientific knowledge.

The issues raised by the death, afterlife, and symbology of Henrietta Lacks are evocative of those surrounding the lives of Saartjie Baartman and Truganini and their eternal symbolic afterlives: consent, ownership of corporeal remains, and the taking, use, and exploitation by scientists of the body parts of human beings and the fraught relationship of race and science.

Most striking to this author, in the context of this project, is the nature of Henrietta Lacks's contributions to science and human knowledge. It was work with and on her cells – the cells of a Black woman descended from an enslaved people – that led, and continues to lead, to scientific and medical breakthroughs that impact and benefit the lives of human beings of all races, nationalities, and ethnicities.

Henrietta Lacks, HeLa, and the stories uncovered about and through them disprove the nineteenth-century polygenists, as well as the twentieth- and twenty-first century racists, and point toward the indivisibility of humanity.

Index

CPSIA information can be obtained at www.ICGtesting.com
Printed in the USA
LVOW08*0532210415

435403LV00001B/5/P

9 781107 021303